Selected Writings of Randhir Singh

Introduced by
Manoranjan Mohanty

SELECTED WRITINGS OF RANDHIR SINGH

First Published 2017

ISBN 978-93-5002-348-8

Published by
AAKAR BOOKS
28 E Pocket IV, Mayur Vihar Phase I, Delhi 110 091
Phones: 011 2279 5505, 2279 5641
aakarbooks@gmail.com

Type Setting by
Arpit Printographers, Delhi-110 032

Printed at
Sapra Brothers, Delhi 110 092

To
Mohinder
Shimareet
Priyaleen

Contents

Preface

This volume of Prof. Randhir Singh's writings not only will inspire future generations of social scientists and activists but also shares with them the methodological tools and principles of Randhir Singh's incisive social analysis and explores with them application of these principles to evolve a critical and a transformative understanding of Indian social reality. My hope is that this volume will contribute in a substantial manner to build a version of India-specific Marxism which is both innovative and revolutionary.

Having inspired generations of intellectuals and students, Professor Randhir Singh requires no introduction to the fraternity of social and political thinkers. Professor Singh devoted his life to interpret reality and had no liking for any other work. He opted for Marxism and Marxist method not only to interpret reality, but also as a philosophy of life. He imbibed remarkable understanding of Marxism. To quote, 'Knowing Marx does make a difference to what sense you make of life, how you understand and live and act in the world'.

The importance of the publication of this volume is that it captures the theoretical foundation for alternate social enquiry. The first part of this reproduces his seminal work *Reason, Revolution and Political Theory: Notes on Oakeshott's Rationalism in Politics*. And, the second part of the volume contains a series of articles demonstrating the application of Marxist method to understand contemporary social reality. It examines the relevance of Marxist method to comprehend various dimensions of changing social order and reinforces the understanding that there have been alternatives in the past and there will be in the future as well. Some of the essays also critically examine the emergent issues like terrorism, democratic rights violations, and states interventions through instruments of reservations to achieve redistribution of wealth. These essays are distinct as they gloriously establish the richness of Marxist approach and generate hope that there are objective conditions available to build alternatives to existing exploitative systems.

Professor Singh's quality to interpret social reality in the language of the people has been admirable. As a positional scholar, he always prefaced his lectures with 'where he speaks from'. He believed that every speaker, inescapably, speaks from a particular philosophical-political stand point, and that was ethical to publicly state the same. In his introduction to the book *Man Against Myth* by Barrows Dunham, he elaborates that each one of us has a philosophy of our own, it is a different matter that instead of revealing contradictions it may conceal them. In his language, 'the person has a mind of ones own, but may have ideas of somebody else. There is none so poor as not to have a philosophy of ones own. One may add that there is none so rich either as to be able to do without one'. He further argues that 'to build alternatives it is pertinent to examine what philosophical preconceptions one does have'.

He opined that in Marxists' scheme of things, it is the politics which has primacy and *not* economics. He convincingly argued that to conceal contradictions of capitalism all kinds of myth-making is on and it is ensured that it is not referred to by their proper names but goes by terms like 'globalisation', 'liberalisation', 'structural adjustment', 'economic reforms', 'new economic policy', 'development' and 'progress' to blur social reality for the people. It was with this understanding that he analysed our nation's complexities after Independence. He wrote, 'We were very much globalised before 1947, but we did not like it and we labelled it as imperialism. And now globalisation has become a fad and with new phraseology, "Make in India'. "Our present day rulers, the successors of Gandhi and Patel, have forgotten that the main thrust of the freedom struggle was to reverse the structural logic of the globalisation that meant accumulation of wealth in fewer hands and poverty for the Indian people'. He elaborated that 'a Finance Minister who later became Prime Minister pushed the nation towards globalisation and told us not to be afraid of the East India Company on the "dishonest" plea that the nation has been "living" beyond its means.' His successor started trotting the globe to invite multinationals to come and harvest huge rewards under the new label 'Make in India'."

He could conceptualise the role of information and communication technologies to broaden and deepen this new nation-building project. The market-driven information and communication technologies are contributing to mass culture of consumerism to divert people from their own survival issues. He further elaborates, "Knowledge is reduced to slick, pre-digested, easy to understand capsules, inducing people to want simple answers to difficult problems . . . the inundations of consumerism and "mass culture" leave the alienated individuals of contemporary late-capitalist society eminently vulnerable to capitalism's hegemonic control. Hence, the reason for the political leadership and the media to pitch all their messages to the lowest level of mental capacity of the common people."

In the third section of this volume he argued that the subjective concerns of individual political leaders who could help, at the most helped to cover up contradictions, rather than reverse the structural logic in the absence of revolutionary politics. The new breed of politicians created the illusion of power reverting back to the people by removing red beacons from their vehicles but otherwise continue to maintain status quo. It is well-known that market-governed economic growth cannot deliver inclusive growth.

He drew a distinction between Marxism and official Marxism. He was of the opinion that official Marxism was economistic and deterministic. As a consequence, they were trapped in opposing communalism and in the process capitalism was built which further strengthened forces of communalism.

In his later years, he slowly distanced himself from the same Communist Party which he considered as his family during the pre-Independence days. On present day politics, he wondered, why is the political class working overtime to destroy itself and violating the rules of their own game.

For many of us, Professor Randhir Singh and his writings are the most valuable part of people's revolutionary reservoir and a source of hope that it is worth attempting 'the impossible' that he talks about.

Chandigarh

Pramod Kumar
Director
Institute for Development and Communication (IDC)

Introduction

Randhir Singh: Legendary Teacher, Philosopher and Revolutionary

Manoranjan Mohanty

A caravan has reached the destination,
And yet lost its way.

Randhir Singh recorded these lines in a book of poetry in Punjabi in 1950 entitled, *Rahan Di Dhoor*—the only one he wrote- which reflected his years of struggle as a participant in the communist movement in Punjab in the preceding decade. As a student in Lahore and as a full time CPI activist in the workers and peasants' movement, editing the party's theoretical monthly in Punjabi *Sada Jug*, he had spent a year in the same prison where Shaheed Bhagat Singh was jailed and hanged. When Independence came many like him felt betrayed as the new rulers who succeeded the British did not respond to the great popular struggles in Telengana and elsewhere. The Communist leadership made compromises with the new rulers. That the communist movement 'lost its way' remained a recurring concern of Randhir Singh throughout his life. As a teacher as well as an activist he devoted all his energy to study this problem, going back to classics of Marxism most minutely, studying concrete situations in depth and arguing for authentic and creative Marxist ways to pursue revolutionary politics to achieve the goal of socialism. That political experience of the formative period of the revolutionary activist remained his asset and helped him to become a legendary teacher of Politics at Delhi University, a Marxist philosopher who opened up new possibilities to interpret and transform the world around us.

The passing away of Randhir Singh on 31 January 2016 in Delhi (he was born in pre-Partition Punjab on 9 January 1922) was mourned not only by his former students and colleagues but also by a vast community of democratic and secular forces both in the academic world and in people's movements all over the country.

The publication of this volume was planned for presentation to him in his 95th year. But unfortunately he did not live to see that. Now we put it out in his memory.

Selected Works

In Marxist theory, political philosophy and democratic politics Professor Randhir Singh's contribution to the world of thought has been unique and powerful. As a legendary teacher of political theory who taught two generations of students over half a century at the University of Delhi, he shaped a thought process that had multiplier effects in the Indian intellectual arena. His writings consisting of books that presented years of research and thinking and articles, comments and lectures that were frankly polemical and challenging, always asserting the Marxist viewpoint—opened up fresh lines of enquiry on several critical issues of philosophy, social science methodology and political practice breaking out of much conventional understanding of Marxists and other political theorists and activists. This volume of selected writings of Randhir Singh makes his ideas and insightful formulations easily accessible to a wider readership.

This volume has three parts. **Part One** consists of Randhir Singh's seminal philosophical work, ***Reason, Revolution and Political Theory*** which was written not just as a response, as he claimed it was- to the British political theorist, Michael Oakeshott's book, *Rationalism in Politics and Other Essays*, but as an alternative theoretical treatise on social enquiry. The questions raised by Randhir Singh in the 1960s have acquired even more significance today as the debates on similar questions on science and philosophy, facts and values, ideology and practice unfold vigorously in the twenty first century. **Part Two** contains some of his well known essays on Marxism giving his non-determinist, dialectical materialist interpretation and how Marxist approach could be applied to concrete situations of the time. In **Part Three** we have the essays and lectures on some major aspects Indian Politics dealing with the state of democratic rights in India and other extremely serious and live issues such as terrorism and reservation. On these issues his analysis and positions stand out conspicuously as distinct from not only familiar debates in the media, but also from the formulations by the mainstream left parties.

This selection does not carry his magnum opus, the tome of thousand odd pages—*Crisis of Socialism: Notes in Defence of a Commitment* which is a detailed examination of the process of collapse of the Soviet Union and capitalist transformation of societies such as China where he presents sharp critiques of some of the policies these regimes pursued and puts out suggestions to read Marxist classics and historical developments with fresh understanding. That important work is not reproduced here mainly for reasons of space and the book in six parts is available separately also from Aakar Books. But the approach governing that analysis is very much there in this volume as well, especially in Part Two and Part Three.

Legendary Teacher

These writings bear the imprint of a teacher *par excellence* who knew how to present complex ideas in simple persuasive ways without losing the nuances of the argument. Randhir Singh was a teacher who was dedicated to studying and developing the subject of his discipline, Political Science, building the teaching community as a lively and competent body committed to values of equality, freedom and justice and a campus which promoted a climate of democracy for pursuing these goals.

At a time when universities and colleges are under severe

pressure by bureaucracy and ruling parties to conform to the neoliberal agenda of commercialisation and the teaching community is harassed with biometric attendance requirements and API scores rather than build and inspire young minds to think and learn, history will record Randhir Singh's legacy as a teacher who took the teaching profession to great heights.

After moving from Lahore to Delhi after Partition he had a short period of teaching Political Science in the Camp College of Punjab University and then joined Delhi College (later renamed Zakir Hussain College) where he taught for nearly two decades. In 1972 he was invited to occupy the chair as Professor of Political Theory in Delhi University before which he spent a brief period teaching at JNU. In 1987 he retired from DU, but continued to be active writing on his favourite themes on Marxist Philosophy and Indian Politics and lecturing all over the country in universities, colleges and democratic rights forums till about 2013 after which his health condition began to weaken. Mentally however he was alert till the very end.

As a teacher Randhir Singh was so popular that his classroom was always packed by not only students of Political Science but also from History, Philosophy, literature and even natural sciences. This was because, firstly, his teaching method addressed every student, the slow learners got clarity on the fundamental issues and were happy to feel equipped to carry on their studies, while the bright students also got insights that gave them a depth of understanding, exciting them to march ahead with many new thoughts. Secondly, he was never intimidating to the student. He explained theoretical problems giving simple examples from everyday life, showing the need to be logical and factually consistent. That was evident in all his writings including those included here. Students adored Randhir Singh because he made them feel for the people, strive for a meaningful life, live a life of dignity, beauty and ethics as equal human beings. In class and after the class, in the campus coffee house or at his home in Delhi's East Patel Nagar he was accessible and always had time and patience for the students. If we can coin a term in Hindi, he was *Chhaatra-vatsala*, literally one who had deep love for students.

In the so-called 'federal' (actually hierarchical) system of Delhi University the University's Post-graduate Department and its Head—(before K.N. Raj as Vice-Chancellor introduced the rotation of headship in 1972) exercised supreme authority in inviting college teachers to teach a specific course at the MA level. Randhir Singh was invited to teach Western Political Thought from Plato to Hegel. The Head thought that he should not teach Marx because he was a Marxist! I remember the discussion in DU campus on this allocation of courses and I was privileged to experience how the method of dialectical materialism could be applied to the study of ancient thought or for that matter in all subjects. In the Departments of History and Philosophy, however, he taught both ancient and modern political thought even while being a lecturer in Delhi College.

While in Delhi College, Randhir Singh along with Bipan Chandra, then in the History Department of Hindu College started a journal, *Enquiry* which carried major debates on critical social, economic and political issues and scholarly articles cutting across disciplines. That was perhaps the only serious, interdisciplinary journal carrying high quality research papers and expert commentaries at that time in the late 1950s and 1960s. I remember Randhir Singh carrying bundles of *Enquiry* on his Scooter going from college to college to sell and enlist subscribers. Some of the chapters of *Reason, Revolution and Political Theory* were first published in *Enquiry*. The group of scholars around *Enquiry* also formed a discussion forum which used to meet in the Hindu college quarters of Bipan Chandra. Speakers and discussants included not only some of the campus luminaries such as K.N. Raj and Amartya Sen and their critics K.A. Naqvi and S. Ganguly, but visiting scholars and activists from abroad associated with innovative ideas—I remember interacting with Betty Friedan the pioneer feminist in that forum once. Thus Randhir Singh was part of a vibrant campus life-debating critical issues of the time. That ensured a certain quality of his arguments in speaking and writing.

I am tempted to mention a little more than what he writes in his Introduction to Reason, Revolution and Political Theory which he wrote, as he says, being 'provoked by his students'. What happened was we were taught Modern Western Thought by another eminent teacher of Delhi University, Frank Thakurdas also adored by students. During 1963-64 after the publication of Oakeshott's *Rationalism in Politics* the previous year Thakurdas dwelt upon that book practically in every lecture. We would take up some of the issues raised by Oakeshott via Thakurdasand ask questions to Randhir Singh who taught us Ancient Thought. Randhir Singh would show how Oakeshott's assumptions such as separation of facts from values or the significance of tradition in political behaviour or the centrality of human experience rather than reason were questionable. That Oakeshott and Thakurdas had misconstrued the classical formulations of Marxism was spelt out in great detail by Randhir Singh. We found Randhir Singh's philosophical formulations and interpretations of Marxism very convincing. We urged him to write up what he was saying. I think his colleagues in the Enquiry Group also played some role in persuading him to write them up.

Writing *Reason, Revolution and Political Theory* provided Randhir an opportunity to set out his understanding of fundamental issues of philosophy. He was modest to say that they were 'Notes' and a response to Oakeshott.

Randhir Singh's role in the teachers movement in Delhi University is always recalled by the veterans of the Delhi University Teachers Association (DUTA). Together with a group of democratic-minded teachers from colleges he took the initiative to demand that the DUTA leadership be elected rather than nominated by the Vice-Chancellor. This was supported by progressive academics like K.N. Raj and Sukhamoy Chakrabarty of Delhi School of Economics in the mid 1960s. Thereafter, thc DUTA grew into a major force in the University impacting on national policies relating to teachers' salaries and working conditions benefiting teachers all over India. In 1983 and thereafter on occasions when DUTA went on long strikes demanding better pay and promotion. Randhir Singh, while supporting the movement, used to warn the DUTA leadership not to be so pre-occupied with economic demands as to forget political issues confronting the people and formulation of national educational policies.

That the university campus should be a place for free discussion on socio-political issues facing the country and the world where teachers, students and staff should take part as equal participants was a part of the faith of the teacher that Randhir Singh was. When teachers groups floated their partisan organisations a few teachers led by Randhir Singh launched the Delhi University Socialist Group which emerged as a broad forum of secular, socialist, democratic forum for discussion and mobilisation on important questions such as communalism, authoritarianism, commercialisation of education. The decades of the 1970s to 1990s saw cataclysmic changes in the socialist world and many new issues relating to changes in the Soviet Union leading to its collapse demanded serious examination. Randhir Singh and a few others organised such discussions under another forum called the Marx Club where various Marxist formulations were debated in depth.

Transforming the discipline of Political Science

After Randhir Singh joined the Delhi University Department of Political Science—incidentally he was also offered a professorship in JNU but he chose to join DU which he thought was a greater challenge—the discipline of Political Science started experiencing a new stirring with enormous consequences. In Delhi University as in India as a whole, Political Science until then was a legal-institutional field of study under the direct influence of British institutionalists and slowly encountering the wave of behavioural studies from the US. Randhir Singh together with a group of teachers from colleges and other Departments initiated serious debates on the state of the discipline and how to make it meaningful to students and relevant to Indian conditions. That gave birth to a biannual journal called *Teaching Politics* in 1973 which fast became an all India forum for discussion on Political Science as a discipline and strengths and weaknesses of social sciences in the country in general.

Curriculum change was one of the principal tasks undertaken by Randhir Singh to give the discipline a new face. The revision of the undergraduate syllabus through a series of general body meetings with college teachers set the tone and orientation for the process. The big transition was from the exclusive legal framework then dominating the discipline to the study of the state and social movements. Now every student could try to comprehend the debates on 'the nature of the Indian state' and socio-economic dimensions of politics. Study of problems such as poverty, caste and class inequality, social deprivation, gender injustice, communalism, peasant and workers movements was brought to the core of the study of politics. As against political behaviour political economy was suggested as the guiding framework with focus on intersectionality of class relations for analysis of problems. That there was a political dimension to every social problem in family, society, country and the world relating to the issue of power relations and pursuit of freedom was the theme of the new discipline of Political Science in India. For once students of politics felt a sense of pride in being a part of this discipline which was otherwise a drab, backward field not among the first three choices of aspiring Honours students. The essays in this volume on Marxism, communalism, Indian politics were some of the famous lectures formulated by Randhir Singh at that time and developed more fully later.

Randhir Singh had to withstand waves of opposition to such changes, some saying that DU students would be handicapped in civil service exminations as the new courseswith too much of sociology and economics were different from the UPSC curriculum. But these changes got the intellectual backing of the vast majority of teachers and later the UPSC changed the syllabus reflecting the new orientation of political Science in Delhi and at the all India level.

Challenging Behaviouralism

Randhir Singh's intellectual leadership in political theory equipped a new generation of social scientists in Delhi

University and beyond to grapple with the challenges of two tidal waves of the 1960s to 1980s, the behavioural movement that swept social sciences under the well-funded stewardship of American social science establishment and a brand of Marxism that emerged under the Soviet patronage and propagated by its supporters all over the world. In retrospect, I and many others feel so privileged to have been taught political theory and Marxism by a scholar and a teacher like Randhir Singh who opened up new ways of thinking about reality, history and revolution with which we withstood the powerful onslaught of behaviouralism and deterministic Marxism in academic and political work. Therefore, even though ICSSR and western funding agencies supported many behavioural studies including election surveys, Indian social science in general and political science in particular remained varied and a strong stream of political economy and creative theory continued to flourish in India. The writings contained in this volume bear testimony to this.

Randhir Singh showed how the fact—value dichotomy was a false assumption and the element of value entered the presentation, representation and articulation of facts directly or indirectly. Therefore, the method of observation of reality on the ground must be carefully understood and survey research despite much preparation was always inadequate. Thus we had to combine quantitative with qualitative methods and other elements which could not be reduced to either of the two. This is what he developed systematically in his masterpiece work, *Reason, Revolution and Political Theory* (1967). This book, then dominating political theory discourses, spelt out how conservative politics like that of Oakeshott promoted traditionalism on the one hand and empiricism on the other. It was empiricism—seeing the parts and missing the whole- that was essentially practiced by behaviouralism. Election studies, which dominated American academia in that era with numerous followers in India, were also faulted as empiricist exercises failing to explain deeper forces in operation in society. As an alternative to such empiricism, Marxism, its method of dialectical and historical materialism sought to understand parts as well as the whole in their dynamic process and in historical perspective. He, however never under-emphasised the need to go to the field for observation and participation. But without a useful approach to exploring the nature of reality one could miss the wood for the trees, as he explained in many of the writings. Understand the logic of structure, he stressed, but find the specificity and the changes taking place. This theory was rooted in history and contemporary practice. He demystified philosophy by relating principles to practice. That was because he never ceased to be a social activist even after becoming a teacher in a university. His essays in Part Two and Three in this volume abundantly illustrate the intellectual argumentation together with his politics as a Marxist revolutionary.

The Marxism of Randhir Singh

After leaving the CPI around 1950 Randhir Singh remained outside a party framework until the CPI (M) was formed in 1964. He spent some time in the new party but got dissociated from that as well. But he never made a virtue of being an 'independent Marxist' thus giving high value to the membership of a Communist Party. From the 1970s onwards he interacted with all streams of the Indian Communist movement and in turn all the communist formations of India had tremendous respect for him. Internationally too he had closely interacted with *Monthly Review* editors Paul Sweezy and Harry Magdoff who were his great admirers. During the 1990s and till his poor health forbade him to travel he gave an enormous amount of time to democratic rights groups in different parts of the country. He often visited Andhra Pradesh on the invitation of APCLC and Punjab on the invitation of AFDR and other democratic rights groups. Aurangabad, especially until Moin Shakir was alive—and later to give memorial lectures—was a favourite place of his. (He had presented his famous thesis on *Crisis of Socialism* first in the Moin Shakir Memorial lectures in 1992.)

As the present volume shows, the analysis of Indian political situation from a Marxist viewpoint was his favourite theme on may occasions and he applied dialectical and historical materialism to interpret concrete problems facing Indian people. He demonstrated the need to practice dialectics and see historical patterns while capturing specificity of prevailing situations. Class politics to fight capitalism can only succeed if onesaw the linkage of class with other social categories such as caste, gender, ethnicity and religion. The agenda of socialism was to end alienation caused by capitalist system and establishment of conditions of freedom. In a celebrated essay, *Marxism and Aesthetics* he showed how socialist revolution was as much about equality and liberation as about beauty and love. For Randhir Singh there were no finished answers derived from communist practice of the past. Every practitioner had to comprehend the prevailing situation and creatively apply Marxism to pursue the revolutionary agenda.

For Randhir Singh, the process of revolutionary struggle for socialism as well as after coming to power practice of democracy by a communist party was fundamental. Soviet Union collapsed, among other things, due to the lack of democratic practice, which alienated common people including ethnic minorities from the Soviet state. After the class struggle perspective was abandoned by the CPSU and economism dominated the ideology of Soviet Communists the socialist vision had gone to the background in the USSR. This had great lessons for the communists all over the world. Randhir Singh believed that socialism had a promising future because capitalism caused multidimensional alienation and new forms of oppression of humans and destroyed nature and environment in an irretrievable manner. This was the theme that he argued in great detail in his magnum opus, *Crisis of Socialism: Notes in Defense of a Commitment* (2006).

In his lectures and essays on Indian politics, he emphasised the need to understand the many old and new ways capitalism operated in India and how a deterministic analysis could be misleading. These important essays appeared in collections such as *Marxism, Socialism, Indian Politics* and *Indian Politics Today—*

An Argument for a Socialist-oriented Path of Development which are included in this volume.

The legendary teacher who set new standards, the Marxist who demystified philosophy and advanced creative theory to make it rooted in history and practice, the revolutionary who put politics of people's emancipation on the forefront of all activity will continue to inspire generations to come. Hopefully this volume will help in carrying that intellectual tradition forward.

(The author was a student and colleague of Randhir Singh at the Department of Political Science in University of Delhi. A former Editor of *Teaching Politics* and former Head of the Department of Political Science at DU, he is currently with the Council for Social Development, New Delhi, Institute of Chinese Studies, Delhi and Development Research Institute, Bhubaneswar. E-mail: mmohantydu@gmail.com)

PART I

Reason, Revolution and Political Theory: Notes on Michael Oakeshott's *Rationalism in Politics*

One must from time to time repeat what one believes in, proclaim what one agrees with and what one condemns.

GOETHE

It is the great advantage of the new movement that we do not seek to anticipate the new world dogmatically, but rather to discover it in the criticism of the old.... It is not our task to build up the future in advance and to settle all problems for all time; our task is ruthless criticism of everything that exists, ruthless in the sense that the criticism will not shrink either from its own conclusions or from conflict with the powers that be.

KARL MARX

The thinker's function, to contribute our share to the description of reality, to improve (so far as we may) the modes of getting things chosen and done. This is everybody's guarantee of honor in other people's thoughts. It is the sole true objectivity, namely, a bias in favor of mankind.

BARROWS DUNHAM

Preface

This essay does not lay claim to much originality or scholarship. Its claim is primarily one of meaningful relevance to the situation in contemporary political theory. In view particularly of the generally imitative and conformist temper of the profession in this country, its meaning and relevance lies, above all, in its critical and non-conformist approach to the more important of the recent developments in political theory in the west, more specifically in the English-speaking world. Such a critical approach, I believe, is absolutely necessary if we are to understand these developments and benefit from them in our work here, and not be simply submerged under them. Whatever the merits of my argument on general issues or on specific controversies, I hope this essay will be of some help to those in search of a more critical, and critically constructive, orientation in their study of contemporary political theory.

This essay, again, is not the fruit of any 'inner urge'; it is, in the real sense of the term, a casual exercise. It has grown out of a controversy which arose when a colleague, wanting to build a cult of Professor Michael Oakeshott (of the London School of Economics and Political Science), deemed it necessary not only to denounce Harold Laski, 'the forgotten Fabian'—whose 'more fundamental error', we are told, lay in not doing what according to Oakeshott is the proper thing for a Professor of Political Science to do; for which truly unpardonable error, we are further told, 'the English academic world—Oxbridge in particular ,'very properly 'killed' him, but 'with kindness', by their 'silence'—but also to attack Karl Marx, that unfortunately less forgotten but all the same now totally 'refuted', 'rejected' and 'dismissed' '19th century' thinker with 'pretensions to scientific philosophy'! The immediate compulsion to write, the Aristotelian 'efficient cause' as it were, was a 'provocation' from my students at Delhi University—I have already thanked them for it in the pages of *Enquiry*, where part of this essay orignially appeared—who wanted a quick critical comment, from a Marxist standpoint, on the philosophy and politics of Professor MichaeL Oakeshott. This comment I sought to provide in the form of notes on Oakeshott's recently published *Rationalism in Politics*, a collection of writings, representative of his philosophy, first elaborated in *Experience and Its Modes* (1933). That is how this essay originally came to be written.

As mentioned above, this essay, part of it to be precise, first appeared as a series of three articles in *Enquiry* (Vol. 1, Nos. 2 and 3, 1964; Vol. II, No. 1, 1965). Friends, among whom are many critics also, having thought its argument to be of interest to a wider audience, and the People's Publishing House having very kindly offered to undertake its publication in book form, it is now being so published.[1]

In putting the essay together for publication as a book, I have not considered it necessary or desirable to revise or modify the original argument. The reader may even detect marks of its first publication as a series of separate articles. I have, however, taken advantage of this new publication to make changes of another sort. I have included those parts of the essay which had to be left out of the original publication for lack of space; and I have quoted Oakeshott more fully in several places in order to make his meaning or argument clearer. I have also added a few notes and put additional material under some old ones.

This essay is not intended to be a comprehensive study of Oakeshott's philosophy, though it does come to grips, I believe, with some of its more fundamental aspects or principles. Its argument, because of the very nature of the controversy, centres around the issues concerning the validity and relevance of Oakeshott and the supposed lack of validity and relevance of Marx today. This also explains the essentially polemical and, at times, discursive nature of this argument. It has often been necessary to broaden the argument, to digress and refer to other important recent developments in contemporary political theory, in order to point out the historical and intellectual context of Oakeshott's philosophy, the ideological phenomena of which this philosophy may be said to form a part, and the socio-political significance of such ideological phenomena, etc., etc. There are, besides, digressions (especially in Chapter IV) relating to Marx and the Marxist position—of course, as I understand it—on a number of important issues. I am not apologetic about these digressions. On the contrary I believe them to be most germane to the argument of this essay as a whole. And if I have here quoted some authors more than once or at length, it is not only because they have put the argument better than I could have done but also because, in my opinion, these authors and their writings deserve to be much better known in this country than is the case at present. I have, however, put these digressions in the notes in order to concentrate in the text on Oakeshott's philosophy alone. What is more, my argument about this philosophy stands or falls independently of these digressions; those interested only in Oakeshott's philosophy and politics may, if they so like, even leave them out.

The comment on Oakeshott is, of course, polemical. One kind of critic has even complained that it is too polemical to be scholarly, that it lacks what is supposed to be the proper academic approach or expression. Now every one is entitled to his or her own understanding of what is properly 'scholarly' or 'academic'. But under the circumstances I really do not know how this comment could be any different without losing' 'its whole point. In any case, to me content of the argument, clarity of expression and explicitness of judgment have been of greater importance than the so-called scholarly approach and academic usage, or the clever, Aesopian manners of expression. The comment is also, as stated earlier, frankly Marxist, for such is my conscious, carefully arrived at philosophical position, such are my philosophical preferences. It has been suggested that it is, perhaps, a trifle too unashamedly Marxist in its emphasis and that this calls for further explanation. If so, I will offer one for what it is worth. This emphasis certainly seeks to assert the truth that so long as capitalism lasts and men live under an unjust and irrational social order, Marxism can neither be refuted nor rejected. It also aims at drawing attention to the abundance of riches, philosophical and sociological, that awaits any scholar who is willing or, perhaps bold enough to go to the classics of Marxism. But more than any thing else, this emphasis seeks to affirm the scientific character and validity of Marxism, not as a closed system or a set of 'sacred scriptures', but as a changing and developing, a living and creative theory, continuously interacting with the rest of contemporary thought, teaching it and learning from it, and growing with the growth of scientific and historical knowledge. Marxism, with its powerful analytical method, is today as relevant as ever to any attempt at understanding and, therefore, changing the world. Far from having been 'refuted', 'rejected' or 'dismissed' news given to us heaven alone knows how many times in the past hundred years and more— 'it may even be', as Macpherson has recently reminded us, 'that the utility of Marxism as a means of understanding the world is increasing over time'[2] My emphasis on Marxism is thus intended to underline its validity as social science. At the very least, one must recognise that Marxism is of central importance to any viable social science today. I know that in this age the desire to 'go beyond' is very strong in different fields of social and political inquiry. And it is a very legitimate and necessary desire too, when it is not merely an itch born of entirely un-academic or non-scholarly considerations, like the search for easy academic prestige and success, or the wish to appear more than up-to date and, perhaps, catch the eye of Ford Foundation directors by copying the very latest academic *mode* in the west, or the need to keep up in the rat race which is now on, in the universities as much as elsewhere in our society. What I want to suggest is that if, and insofar as, we 'go beyond' Marx, we go with him and not against him or away from him.

My commitment to Marxism, however, is likely to raise— it has in fact already done so—a seemingly more serious objection, particularly from those who insist on regarding Marxism entirely as 'philosophy' or 'ideology' and not at all as 'science'. This objection concerns the so-called 'bias' which any such commitment is said to involve. It in fact raises the much larger question of objectivity and impartiality, of integrity, open-mindedness or detachment in academic work, in any critical and interpretative study, like the present one, of a given system of social and political thought.

This is, no doubt, an important question in its own right. I do not think, however, that it is necessary for me to undertake a detailed discussion of it here. It is today generally recognised, at least among the knowledgeable, that in academic work, in any critical and interpretative study of a system of thought, or anywhere else for that matter, an argument must be taken seriously, at its face value, and its validity examined rationally, before other considerations become even remotely relevant, before any appeal is made, for example, to the author's real or supposed 'biases'. And this is all I ask of the critics with regard to the argument of this essay. But since the question has been raised, and quite loudly by some, and since in the mythology surrounding academic work the issue of 'biases' still occupies an important place, some reflections on the subject are necessary to make the issue, as I understand it, cear and also, if possible, to answer the charge of being 'biased', which is still regarded by many as the most damning charge that can ever be brought against anyone working in the academic field.

In making this study of Oakeshott's philosophy and politics, I certainly do not claim to have been *absolutely* objective or impartial or detached. No scholar in fact can be so in a study of this nature, though many do indeed profess or, perhaps, pretend to be. I have, however, throughout *tried* to be objective, impartial and detached in the sense that I have shown, within the limits of this essay, the utmost fidelity to the facts and sources of Oakeshott's philosophy. Before subjecting it to critical scrutiny I have, honestly and to the best of my ability, sought to know and understand this philosophy, which, incidentally, is not always an easy task as any one familiar with Oakeshott's writings would know. And I have always tried to present it as clearly and accurately as possible. All this I have done in full awareness of my so-called 'bias'. Besides, I have confessed to this 'bias'; or, as I would prefer to put it, I have frankly avowed my conscious philosophical preferences and have been quite explicit about my moral and political judgments. This, I believe, is the most that a scholar can or should be expected to do, or perhaps, even needs to do. In this connection what Sabine says of the study of history of political theory in general is in fact true of every specific study of a system of social and political thought. In a study of this nature, he writes, one 'can make no profession of impartiality beyond that fidelity to sources which is the obligation of every serious historian, or beyond that avowal of conscious preferences which should be expected of every honest man. In any other sense the claim of detachment is a superficiality or a pretense.[3]

One cannot, even if one wanted it, be entirely free from 'bias', from one's philosophical preferences or preconceptions. Or, to put it more comprehensively, one cannot be ever without one's 'philosophy'. It has been said that there is none so poor as not to have a philosophy of his own. One may add that there is none so rich either as to be able to do without one. We are all, in. a sense, philosophers, whether we know it or not; we all have our more or less open, more or less cearly or consciously formulated assumptions, opinions, beliefs, principles, attitudes towards life, on which we habitually act, by which we indeed live. These together constitute our philosophy, to which also belong our more or less general ways of looking at things and ideas, our philosophical preconceptions and preferences. The very language we use reflects and bears witness to the philosophy we have. The question is really not one of having or not having a philosophy or philosophical preconceptions but of what sort of philosophy or preconceptions one does or shall have. As A.E. Taylor says, 'we have no choice whether we shall have a philosophy or not, but only the choice whether we shall form our theories consciously and in accord with some intelligible principle, or unconsciously and at random.'[4] And scholars who profess to be free from 'bias' would do well to remember that there can be 'biases' or preconceptions, even 'principles' as Locke noticed a long time ago, 'that have been derived from no better original than the superstition of a nurse, or the authority of an old woman' and are sanctified by nothing more than 'length of time and consent of neighbours'[5] It can also be that one's philosophy or philosophical preconceptions are determined simply by one's economic or financial situation, without any conscious or intelligent thinking being involved in the matter. For there exists in our society 'a custom or even a tradition to the effect that one ought to have the sort of ideas, as one has the sort of clothes, befitting one's income.'[6]

It will not do, therefore, merely to question the 'biases' of others. (Or, is it only the other man's 'bias' which is such a nuisance?) Since we simply cannot avoid having our 'biases', and since any profession of not having or avoiding them only means smuggling them in unconsciously and uncritically, the real task lies elsewhere. It lies in becoming aware of one's own 'biases', of one's philosophical preconceptions or preferences, in correcting them to the extent they are merely biases or prejudices and, thus, putting them on a more rational and scientific basis, and, for the rest, in avowing them frankly. We must recognise and analyse our philosophical preferences or preconceptions, subject them to most careful and critical scrutiny, in order to make them, that is our philosophy as a whole, as rational and scientific as we possibly can. It can never be emphasised too much that he who is most conscious of his own 'bias' is also more capable of taking guard against it, even transcending it and, above all, of developing a more rational and scientific philosophical orientation in his academic work, an orientation which will help in achieving a more objective understanding, a more true explanation or interpretation, of a given social phenomenon, be it a segment of history or a system of social and political thought. As George Thomson once wrote:

> Our view cannot be wholly objective, and the professed impartiality of some modern scholars is an illusion; but it will be more or less objective in proportion as we recognise and analyse our own preconceptions. We must become conscious of our prejudices in order to correct them.[7]

I may add that to understand, explain or interpret a system of social and political thought without any avoidable bias, prejudice or distortion, to achieve as objective or impartial a view of it as possible, is not to abdicate the responsibility of evaluating it, of accepting or rejecting it. To choose in this way does not in any meaningful sense destroy academic impartiality so long as the choice follows from the facts of the case and does not distort them, so long as it is based on knowledge, on a true understanding of the given system of social and political thought. To know or understand is not to eschew ethics, it is not to become useless, something less than a man. To be academically impartial is not to be ethically or politically neutral. Such a neutrality is in fact not even possible. For on all really important issues, in philosophy as in real life, neutrality is an illusion. Here, everything said or done, or left unsaid or undone, assists one side or the other.

To conclude, I have sought to study Oakeshott's philosophy as objectively and impartially as possible, taking its argument seriously and in its own right, and examining its validity primarily on rational grounds. I would like my argument to be treated in the same way before any condemnatory appeal is made to my so-called 'bias'. I have sought to make my philosophical preferences or preconceptions as valid, that is, as rational and scientific, as possible so that they may be a help, and not a hindrance, towards the achievement of truth, of as true as possible an understanding or interpretation of what is under study: At least this is how I understand the nature and function of Marxist philosophical preferences in academic work. And if, or to the extent, they remain only 'biases', or at least appear to be such to others,I have frankly avowed them. Let those who would question and reject them, use this questionning and rejection to become aware of their own 'biases' and philosophical preferences, make them as rational as possible, and avow them as frankly as I have done. Let them speak of what they would insinuate and make their own moral and political judgments as explicit and acknowledged as I have made mine.

I know this will not satisfy everyone. It is not expected to. There are even those who, in talking of 'biases', believe that impartiality or objectivity consists in being at home in all currents, that integrity or detachment means never to make up one's mind, and that open-mindedness is to have a mind so open that everything falls through, or so open at one end only as to gather everything, including all the rubbish,. indigenous or foreign, that ever falls in; who not only persist in believing all this but even parade it as the proper scientific or academic attitude, an indication indeed of their supposedly superior scholarly sensibilities. It may seem unkind to say so, but they are really the wobblers of the academic world—interesting men, no doubt, but hardly worth taking seriously. It was of this type of 'scholar' that Dunham once wrote:

> Tossed like a cork upon conflicting waves, he follows the wave that is stronger, riding, as it seems to him, sagely and majestically, with the familiar sky above and the familiar flood beneath. He enjoys direct acquaintance with the waters which bear him, and he reflects with satisfaction upon his own inner constancy—the true, the pure, and unsubmersive cork.[8]

Finally a few comments are necessary to obviate possible misunderstanding of several statements made in the text—for purposes of description, explanation and interpretation, or of evaluation—about the social origins of ideas and ideologies, about their representing specific class interests, and about thinkers being the ideologists or representatives of particular classes, etc. Misunderstanding of Marxist usage here is both very common and persistent. I have occasionally tried to provide the corrective in the text itself. Even at the risk of repetition, I would like to offer two very brief clarifications on this subject.

In the first place, when Marxists speak of the derivation of ideas and ideologies from a given social environment, of these being conditioned socially or historically, their position is not to be identified with a mere 'sociology of knowledge', or with a certain sort of simple 'historical relativism', which regards all ideas and ideologies as 'merely ideology' or 'pure illusion', as so much rationalisation, or as instruments of winning and defending power and advancing particular interests only, and which, thus, implies that no question as to the truth or validity of these ideas and ideologies can or need be entertained. On the contrary Marxism holds that though they are necessarily relative and contingent, and more or less full of elements of 'false consciousness, ideas and ideologies may, and often do, contain important elements of truth also—'the rational kernel within the mystical shell' as Marx put it—and thus contribute to the growth of human knowledge. This is particularly the case with the ideology of a rising, that is, a progressive or revolutionary class, whose interests are, partly at least, the interests of the society as a whole, which can and does confront reality boldly, and whose ideology, therefore, may well partake of truth without of course expressing all of it; just as the opposite is generally the case with the ideology of a declining, that is, a conservative or reactionary class, whose interests increasingly cease to have anything in common with those of the people at large, which lacks the capacity or courage to confront reality boldly, and whose ideology, therefore, comes to be more and more taken over by anti-intellectualism, irrationalism and obscurantism. In extreme cases such an ideology may well graduate from being the half truth it once was to being a total lie.

Maurice Dobb has well-expressed the Marxist position on this question. Pointing out that for Marx and Engels 'an ideology represented the "world view" of a particular class, standing at a particular point in the historical process and viewing things from the perspective of a particular position in a prevailing system of social relations' and was, therefore, something 'inevitably relative and contingent', he writes:

> Yet ideologies were not pure illusion (as Mannheim, for example, seems to have held). Certainly there was a large, even predominating, element of 'false consciousness', especially in the ideology of an established ruling class which clung to power when already faced with a revolutionary challenge. But at the same time an ideology, especially in its revolutionary and formative phase, could contain an important 'scientific' and realistic element, which could be treated according to the objective criterion of human experience as an addition to human knowledge. Absolute truth was not a Kantian unknowable, even if it could never be reached at any finite point in the historical process: it could be approached asymptotically, and criteria existed by which one could speak about being nearer to it or more remote.[9]

It is obvious, therefore, that an inquiry into the social origins, the historically conditioned nature or the class character of an ideology or a philosophy does not dispose of the question of its truth or validity. Such an inquiry, 'the socio-analytical diagnosis' as Karl Popper calls it, is no doubt most useful in understanding or explaining the 'merely ideological', 'illusory', or non-rational elements in an ideology or a philosophy, and in establishing its larger social meaning and significance. But it has no bearing at all on the question of its truth or validity. As a matter of fact, such an inquiry itself becomes truly relevant and legitimate only *after* the validity of an ideology or a philosophy has been independently assessed. So far as this assessment is concerned it is a matter for an entirely different kind of inquiry to which the questions `of logic, evidence and truth are central and which seeks to make clear the *grounds* on which an ideology or a philosophy is to be accepted or rejected. In other words, for a Marxist the grounds for acceptance or rejection of an ideology or a philosophy lie primarily in its being true or false and not in its social origins and significance, or its socially conditioned nature or class character.

In the second place, when Marxists speak of class ideology —an ideology is seldom, if ever, all of one piece; generally it is constituted by many ideas, doctrines, systems of dogma and philosophies which seemingly compete and even contradict each other but are socially supplementary—they do not mean the ideas or doctrines or philosophies which particular members or groups of a class happen at a particular moment to hold. Nor do they in speaking of class ideologists mean to suggest that these ideologists or thinkers are themselves members of the class or even its conscious or enthusiastic admirers and defenders. (This may or may not be true as well). On the contrary, what makes an ideology or a set of ideas the ideology or philosophy of a class is the fact that it corresponds to the purposes and practices, to the actual long term needs and interests of that class, expressing not only its points of strength but its limitations, evasions and prejudices also. And what makes thinkers, no matter what their class origin or background, the ideologists of a class is the fact that in their thinking they do not transgress the limits beyond which that class will not go in real life.

What Marx hismelf said on this subject is quite explicit. Pointing out that the ideologists of a class need not be themselves members of that class—'according to their education and their individual position they may be separated from them as widely as heaven from earth' he wrote:

> What makes them representatives (of the class) is the fact that in their minds they do not get beyond the limits which the latter do not get beyond in life, that they are consequently driven, theoretically, to the same problems and solutions to which material interest and social position drive the latter practically. This is, in general, the relationship between the *political* and *literary representatives* of a class and the class that they represent.[10]

New Delhi
October 1966 **Randhir Singh**

NOTES

1. Michael Oakeshott, *Rationalism in Politics and Other Essays*, Methuen, London, 1962.
2. C.B. Macpherson, 'Post-Liberal Democracy?' *The Canadian Journal of Economics and Political Science*, Vol. 30, No. 4, November 1964.
3. George H. Sabine, *A History of Political Theory*, New York, 1949, p. viii. Sabine himself, for example, informs us that his 'own philosophical preferences' are 'in general agreement with the results of Hume's criticism of natural law'.
4. Quoted by John Lewis, *Introduction to Philosophy*, London, 1954, p. 3.
5. John Locke, *Essay Concerning Human Understanding*, Oxford, 1894, p. 87.
6. Barrows Dunham, *Giant in Chains*, Boston, 1953, p. 24.
7. George Thomson, *Aeschylus and Athens*, London, 1950, p. 2.
8. Barrows Dunham, *Man Against Myth*, London, 1949, p. 101.
9. Maurice Dobb, *On Economic Theory and Socialism*, London, 1955, p. 233.
10. Karl Marx, *The Eighteenth Brumaire of Louis Bonaparte*, Moscow, 1948, pp. 58-9.

Introduction

Reflection on politics, or on political reflection itself, can be at different levels and varied in form, but it is never a purely philosophical exercise, standing, as it were, independently on its own feet. To the thinker it may indeed often appear that since his intellectual activity is a process wherein he works with thought-material alone, he is deriving both its form and content from the realm of pure thought itself—there being no need, therefore, for him to look further for a more remote cause or process, independent of thought. This, however, is really a case, as Engels pointed out,[1] of the philosopher philosophising consciously but with 'a false consciousness', which only obscures the connection that of necessity obtains between philosophy and society, between the philosopher and the world he lives and philosophises in.

Recognition of this connection is almost universal in the field of social science today. It derives, in fact, from one of the more profound insights of Marxism, namely that 'it is not the consciousness of men that determines their existence, but, on the contrary, their social existence determines their consciousness',[2] and that 'man's ideas, views, and conceptions, in one word, man's consciousness, changes with every change in the conditions of his material existence, in his social relations and in his social life'.[3] This insight of Marx, among many others, has come to be consciously adopted, often without acknowledgment, or accepted unconsciously and used even without knowledge of it source, by almost all social scientists worthy of the name.

Recognition of the socio-historical context of a philosophy, of the social determination of a particular system of thought, does not in the least suggest that such philosophy or system of thought should not be studied in its own right or treated with utmost seriousness. Nor does this recognition in any way provide an answer to the most important; question: is a philosophy true or false? Indeed, the origins of a philosophy or theory are logically irrelevant to the question of its truth' or the validity of its conclusions. This truth or validity is a matter for rational argument and is to be treated, that is, tested and established or rejected, according to the same criteria or standards of objectivity as we apply in any other field of human knowledge.[4] If I have' nevertheless, drawn attention to the close and dialectical relationship that exists between the philosopher and his society, it is only to suggest, at the moment, two things. Firstly, there is no philosophy, including the sceptic's anti-philosophy, which is without social origins and therefore without social and political significance. Secondly, it should not be considered odd or 'inappropriate' to find that contemporary political theory or philosophy,[5] including the most abstract and esoteric, is indicative not only, positively or negatively, of the intellectual achievement of the, age, but also immediately or remotely of the great social and political conflicts of our times. The rise and decline of particular political doctrines, the supplanting of one theory, mood, or habit by another, significant shifts in the view taken of the nature and purpose, and indeed the very possibility or otherwise of political theory, changes in the methods of study and in the very tone and temper of political speculation, all *ultimately* reflect the fluctuating fortunes of political struggle, the ever changing conditions of our social and political life.

Viewed thus, Michael Oakeshott's *Rationalism in Politics* is a significant book. A collection of ten major essays, previously published together with certain new ones, and written over fifteen eventful years of the post-Second World War period, it embodies the mature reflections on diverse themes of a brilliant, highly sensitive, and genuinely philosophical mind. The book has been warmly praised and severely criticised though not always fully understood, particularly by those to whom it is supposed to bring solace and comfort or who have sought justification, encouragement, or guidance in its teachings. The faithful, whose enthusiasm would perhaps embarrass the sceptic in Oakeshott, have called upon us to find in his book a rich store-house of highly original ideas' while the critics, in equal hurry, have rediscovered in him a philosopher, original and unconventional, of modern conservatism. Others, more thoughtfully, have seen in Oakeshott 'a Tory anarchist' turning into 'a lonely nihilist',[6] or a thinker whose 'genuinely philosophical defence of traditional ways of life' involves a plea for a kind of romanticism in politics which, it is feared, may 'open the way to irrationalism and terror'.[7]

However that may be, there is no doubt that in his essays Oakeshott raises questions which are fundamental and provides answers which are far reaching and highly disturbing in their implications. In a sense, he has conceived his task in the grand manner of high political philosophy, which he himself once phrased as 'the revelation of the universal predicament in the local and transitory mischief.'[8] Oakeshott reveals 'Rationalism' as the source of 'the universal predicament' in which modern western civilisation finds itself. For deliverance he turns to the twin principles of empiricism (to expose and demolish) and traditionalism (to defend and preserve and, perhaps, build). In this, despite his studied eccentricity of manner, his 'famous' prose style and somewhat esoteric teaching, Oakeshott's philosophy remains a part, a distinctive part no doubt, of a whole trend in modern thinking which, with its distrust of reason, science and all systematic thought, its fear of change, its obsessive concern for stability and hopelessly romantic yearning for the past, its mood of doubt, disillusionment and despair, bears witness to a deep change in the general character of the times.

In the academic study of politics this trend is reflected in the significant development of an attitude of cynical indifference towards ideas and ideals, towards all ideological or theoretical considerations, an attitude of profound scepticism that questions not only the purpose but the possibility of political theory itself.

II

In 1946, Denis Brogan, in his Inaugural Address at the Cambridge University, said: "We may doubt today whether any such academic discipline as political science exists, a doubt practically unknown to earlier ages..."[9] More than a decade later... Douglas V. Verney wrote:

> Many modern writers seem to share a complacent consensus that political theory does not lead anywhere; some go so far as to make the serious suggestion that philosophizing about politics has reached a dead end... Indeed it is difficult to find a British book on political theory in the past few years which does not share the prevailing doubts and frustrations.[10]

The origins of this mood of scepticism may be traced back to the opening years of this century. It ripened with the tragedies of the period which followed—two world wars; a great depression, the rise of fascism and the rest—reaching its climax in the era that opened with the end of the Second World War. This mood is, thus, in a way, contemporaneous with what Leo Strauss has called 'the crisis of the modern Western World.'[11]

It is elementary but necessary to point out that the great tradition in western political thought, Plato onwards, is that of purposeful speculation and, not so very long ago, it was possible in the British universities to theorise about politics hopefully and without fear that this activity would be pronounced impossible or illegitimate. In a more optimistic England, for example, T.H. Green could, from Oxford, elaborate—without incurring academic disapprobation and with the approval of the Establishment—the theoretical principles which served the needs not only of Tory philanthropy but even of an actively reformist, change-seeking liberalism; though it must be added, the reforms and changes of this 'positive liberalism' always stayed safe within the limits of the established property relations of capitalism.

The twentieth century and the compulsions of a more turbulent era (with the capitalist society running into serious difficulties) inevitably permitted a limited, though significant, radicalisation of academic political theory. The names of Wallas,

Lindsay, Tawney, Cole and, above all, Laski come to one's mind. Political theory, more realistically based, often committed to socialism, and occasionally even reaching out to Marx, was regarded as a means of both understanding and changing society. This always remained a minority trend; it was, however, enormously influential because of its relevance to the basic social and political issues of the age.

The Establishment of the Right was naturally hostile to this trend; that of the Left, presided over by the right wing labour leaders, was equally suspicious and fearful; the attitude of most of their colleagues in the universities ranged from sympathetic tolerance or amused indifference to polite protest and occasional condemnation. But the practitioners of radical political theory never suffered complete loss of caste or of academic respectability.

And then the mood of scepticism, so long maturing, finally arrived. Symbolic, as it were, of the change was Oakeshott succeeding to Laski's chair at the London School of Economics and Political Science in 1951.

III

I am not here concerned with inquiring into the origins and development of this sceptical attitude or with the larger question of the much discussed 'decline of political theory'.[12] Here, only two closely interrelated points need to be noticed.

In the first place, the background to as also the ultimate determinant of these developments in the field of political theory has been the deep crisis of western capitalist civilisation—reflected in its wars, its political and economic depressions and its cultural crises as much as in the victorious revolutions and national liberation struggles against it, and in the emergence of a socialist world. In 'this terrible Twentieth Century' (as Churchill aptly phrased it from the point of view of a declining social system), man, we are told, is 'impotent... more helpless than he has been for a long time', at the mercy of 'conditions largely beyond his comprehension and still more beyond his control... a victim of tides and currents, of whirlpools and tornadoes.'[13]

The response of the political theorist, not lagging far behind the politician, is equally characteristic of such a period of history. He finds the environment no longer 'favourable' for political and social theory. The historical outcome of the 20th century has, he tells us,

> produced a revulsion, even among thinkers, against any attempt at a major reconstruction of ideas or institutions. Increasingly the temper of our times makes us willing to bear evils that we know rather than to venture to move towards dangers that we know not. As we become more and more defensive about established institutions andvalues,we tend to restrict our criticisms to relatively minor elements of the existing social and political order.[14]

This widespread fear of change, the feeling of uncertainty about the future, and the general climate of doubt and despondency; along with, of course, several other more or less important supplementary causes,[15] have had the consequence that political theory has largely ceased to exist as a subject of serious study or purposeful intellectual effort [16] Politics is declared, by an Oakeshott among others, to have nothing to do with principles and theories; and when 'political philosophy', or 'programmes and ideals' are abandoned for 'practical solutions', a Namier hails it as a token of 'greater national maturiy'.[17] The political theorist, literally shying away from the real tasks confronting him, increasingly deserts theory for 'new' and 'modern'—as also safer and more lucrative—fields like psephology. To him who stays behind all politics is suspect, all contact with real life contaminating. He seeks refuge and respectability in a new scholasticism of purely formal or analytical study. And a Plamenatz writes—and this in a study of Marxism—without any misgiving or apology: 'I have made no attempt to test Marx's hypothesis by considering the historical evidence; I have not been interested in what happens in the real world...'[18]

The second point to be noticed is that scepticism about political theory, or about human knowledge in general, easily lends itself, in one form or another, and whether its exponent is aware or desirous of it or not; to the service of political conservatism. If valid and reasonably comprehensive social or political theories are indeed not possible or available to guide us forward, to help us successfully undertake the necessary 'major reconstruction of ...institutions' there is nothing much left to do but to accept, and may be defend, 'the existing social and political order'. We may with Popper try 'piecemeal social engineering',[19] or with Oakeshott turn to 'the resources of a traditional manner of behaviour', but neither will take us very far from the status quo, which alone, if anything, survives the sceptical demolition of ideas, ideals and theories.

As a matter of fact, this scepticism has only very rarely been the product of a disinterested pursuit of philosophy, of an independent and detached consideration of the nature and possibility of political theory as such. More often it has arisen in direct opposition to radical political theory and the conservative affiliations of the sceptic have been fairly conscious and articulate. It is not without significance that the main target of the sceptical attack has been Marxism (or socialism), the theory that consistently confronts the capitalist reality with reason, exposes its essential irrationality and goes on to point the way forward to a more rational and humane social order. This theory has to be demolished, even if it involves a nihilistic demolition of reason itself, so that the world may be made safe for an outmoded social and economic system. Conservatism is, thus, very often the original impulse and the ultimate outcome of sceptical philosophy.[20]

The recent upsurge of conservative philosophy in the western world, whatever its different sources and tendencies, is a significant phenomenon, which is fully understandable only in the context of the contemporary crisis. In the United States, less sophisticated and less inhibited, political theorists and historians have been waking a strong bid to replace pragmatism with conservatism 'as the philosophy of the American business civilization'.[21] And some of them, revolting against reason but appealing to a 'higher' reason, even seek to convert political theory, in the good old medieval manner, into a branch of theology. In England, however, for reasons of historical development and current intellectual climate the contemporary effort at conservative philosophy has taken a different and somewhat more subtle and sophisticated direction. Here it becomes the elaboration not of a doctrine—for all doctrines are 'out'— but of 'a mood', 'a habit of mind', 'a style or disposition of thought'[22] Its practical consequences—and this, after all, is what matters most—would nevertheless delight the heart of the most doctrinaire conservative, dead or alive. The nature and outcome of this effort has been brilliantly summed up by Perry Anderson:

> Traditionalism and empiricism... fuse as a single legitimating system: traditionalism sanctions the present by deriving it from the past, empiricism shackles the future by riveting it to the present. A comprehensive, coagulated conservatism is the result, covering the whole of society with a thick pall of simultaneous philistinism (towards ideas) and mystagogy (towards institutions), for which England has justly won an international reputation.[23]

Such is the broad social and intellectual context of Oakeshott's essays. He has been at work, using his undoubtedly brilliant powers to attack rationalism, in politics and elsewhere, and to defend traditionalism. And in the process he has developed a view of political philosophy which would virtually drive out all purpose from the study of politics and the subject itself from the universities.

IV

In such a situation one should be grateful for small mercies and one may, therefore, pause to pay tribute to the masterly and majestic prose that makes Oakeshott's book a refreshing contrast to most academic writing on politics and its reading an experience in itself. One is indeed tempted to treat it as a work of literature, for Oakeshott conveys his message as much through apt image and vivid metaphor as through serious argument. His book is significant, not only for what it says, and what it omits to say, but also for how he says it.

This, however, is not to suggest that pleasant reading though it is, the book is also easy to understand and argue with. Quite the contrary. For one thing, undoubtedly a learned man, Oakeshott is also, in Jowett's phrase, 'a learned man, in the worst sense of the: 'term' at times it is almost impossible to understand his meaning. For another, he nowhere clearly sets forth his own philosophical outlook as a whole, the view he takes of the world and of man's place in it. We are left to infer it and at crucial points his position is often vague, occasionally even arbitrary.

Further, if it is a basic requirement of clear thinking that concepts be defined and distinctions made with sufficient precision and clarity, then Oakeshott is a great sinner. One is, indeed, struck by his amazing carelessness in this regard Rationalism, after the initial definition, which is anything but satisfactory, is more often than not simply caricatured. The enemies are many: idealism, utopianism, liberalism, Marxism, etc.; or socialism, syndicalism, planning of every conceivable sort, Labourite or any other collectivism including national socialism, etc. Distinctions simply not being considered necessary, they are lumped together and condemned on the same charge. That very important concept, Tradition, is defined and used in a vague manner which begs the question; certain words used incessantly—'intimations', 'coherence', 'incoherence', 'appropriate, 'inappropriate', etc.—have their meanings narrowed or broadened to suit the exigencies of the argument. Despite his much professed opposition to abstraction, Oakeshott's argument is frequently abstract in the bad sense of the word; concreteness and clarity are often achieved at the cost of over-simplification that hardly does justice either to Oakeshott's own case or to that of his opponents.

It is here that Oakeshott's prose style, with its studied disregard of the simple and the propositional, becomes, in fact, something of a barrier to communication of thought. Image or metaphor loaded with more meaning than it can carry and casting a veil over reality; analogy or image persistently abused as a substitute for theory or lack of it; verbal magic seeking to lull critical faculties and create the illusion of explanation; long and involved sentences, full of double-negatives and qualifications, clouding and obstructing the argument; strategically placed Chinese anecdotes and fables, very charming but ambiguous and obscure in their implications; rhetoric swamping the serious debate, dogmatic assertion offered as proof, and the attempt to make the argument true by sheer definition; and the occasional 'take it or leave it' attitude, characteristic of all philosophy in revolt against reason—this is the other side of Oakeshott's 'famous style'. There are advantages, indeed, in practising philosophy' artistically', but there are disadvantages, too. And if Oakeshott is misunderstood, he has, partly at least, himself to blame for it.

Oakeshott's 'poetic' treatment of the subject reflects, in a sense, the conservative philosopher's traditional disregard of the common man. It has even been suggested that Oakeshott does not perhaps care or hope to be understood.[24] This may or may not be true. But he is certainly never at pains to make it any the easier for his readers to understand him.

But then few philosophers have done that, anyway. Let us turn, therefore, to the book itself.

V

The basic theme of the book is presented in the opening essay, 'Rationalism in Politics', which discusses 'the character and pedigree of the most remarkable intellectual fashion of post-Renaissance Europe', namely, 'modern Rationalism', the consequent predicament of European politics— 'fixed in the vice of Rationalism'—and sees 'the hope of deliverance' in a politics based on Tradition.

This theme is further developed and consolidated, in various spheres and at different levels, in a number of essays which follow: in 'The Political Economy of Freedom' where, seeking to preserve 'liberty' and 'libertarian society' against 'the new tyrannies' threatening them both in England, Oakeshott offers a defence of private property and free capitalist enterprise against any and every form of planning or socialism; in 'The Tower of Babel' where, considering 'the *form* of the moral life, and in particular the form of the moral life of contemporary Western civilization', Oakeshott points out that 'the predicament of Western morals... is first that our moral life has come to be dominated by the pursuit of ideals, a dominance ruinous to a settled habit of behaviour; and, secondly, that we have come to think of this dominance as a benefit for which we should be grateful or an achievement of which we should be proud,' and where, disclosing or diagnosing'the corrupt consciousness, the self-deception which reconciles us to our misfortune', Oakeshott prescribes, as a remedy, the morality of habit and tradition; in 'Rational Conduct' where, seeking 'a satisfactory way of using the word *rational* in connection with conduct', Oakeshott shows such conduct to be 'an erroneous theory', and urges upon us once again to seek guidance only 'in the moral tradition' of our society; in 'On being Conservative' where, elaborating 'not a creed or a doctrine, but a disposition', Oakeshott tells us that politics is 'something which it is appropriate to be conservative about'; and, above all, in 'Political Education', the well-known Inaugural Address, where 'the adequacy of two current understandings of politics (the rationalist or ideological and the traditionalist) together with the sort of knowledge and kind of education they imply,' is examined and Oakeshott— 'a sceptic; one who would do better if only he knew how'—finally demolishes the case for 'Rationalism', and 'the so-called ideological style of politics'; leaving the only other style possible in the field, namely, the traditional.

The remaining essays, including the one on 'The Moral Life in the Writings of Thomas Hobbes', though less obviously relevant to the basic theme, go along with the rest, as Oakeshott informs us, and throw important light on his social and political philosophy as a whole.

'The Activity of being an Historian' shows Oakeshott's scepticism at work in the field of history and historiography. The so-called 'practical disposition' is attacked and dismissed with contempt and the historian's activity purged of all 'practical interest in the past'. The past, Oakeshott tells us, must never be 'viewed in relation to the present', there is to be no studying 'the past in order to explain (the) present world' or 'to make it a more habitable and a less mysterious place'. 'The "practical" attitude to the past' is indeed 'the chief undefeated enemy of "history"' and 'it is precisely the task of "the historian" to loosen the tie between the past and the "practical" present'. History represents 'an interest in past events for their own sake, or in respect of their independence of subsequent or present events'. We are further told that the proper historical 'attitude towards the past' is literally all-inclusive, 'everything that the evidence reveals or points to is recognised to have its place; nothing is excluded, nothing is regarded as "non contributory" '. 'The place of an event is not determined by its relation to subsequent events', and 'just as none is "accidental", so none is "necessary" or "inevitable" '. Here, 'there are no successes and no failures', 'nothing is approved' and 'nothing is denounced'. What is sought in history is 'neither a justification, nor a criticism , nor an explanation of subsequent or present condition of things'. The historian's past is altogether 'without the moral, the political or the social structure which the practical man transfers from *his* present to *his* past'. Therefore 'extricating general causes or necessary and sufficient conditions', 'the enterprise of distinguishing general causes in respect of past events' is something absolutely inadmissible. History simply has no such 'causes', just as it has no 'pattern or purpose', no 'meaning' or 'progress', and no lessons to offer either—though, Oakeshott concedes, rather regretfully, that even with the best of intentions a historian cannot help imparting 'to the past, and so to the world, a peculiarly tentative and intermediate kind of intelligibility'; whatever that may mean.

What Oakeshott says here is only an extreme expression of that scepticism on the subject of history and historiography which has been recently in vogue in certain academic circles in the west, especially in England. It not only reminds one of Professor Tout's statement that the ideal history would have no readers, but also makes one wander if this history would have, before long, any historians to write it either.

Oakeshott, however, is not always satisfied with this more or less conventional scepticism. He often goes beyond it. He thus draws our attention— 'briefly' and of course 'without supposing it to be the last word on this difficult subject'— to the 'many conclusions which seem to follow from (his) reading of the activity of being an historian', a reading based on the premise that ' "practice" and "history" are two logically distinct universes of discourse'. He writes: 'It would appear that the task of "the historian" cannot properly be described as that of recalling or of re-enacting the past; that, in an important sense, an "historical" event is something that never happened and an "historical" action something never performed; that an "historical" character is one that never lived.' History and historiography would indeed be hard put to survive this truly 'severe and sophisticated manner of thinking' about the past, this 'specifically "historical" attitude'!

Oakeshott does not pursue 'any of these conclusions of detail' to their logical end. He concludes his essay on a note of somewhat more conventional scepticism. He informs us that history represents 'neither an aesthetic enjoyment, nor a "scientific" recognition, nor a practical understanding'. Its world, 'the "historical" past', is a 'complicated world'. 'In it events have no over-all pattern or purpose, lead nowhere, point to no favoured condition of the world and support no practical conclusions.' It is indeed 'a world composed wholly of contingencies', where 'the historian's concern is not with causes but with occasions' and, of course, 'with past for its own sake'. The historian indeed 'adores the past', Oakeshott tells us, but 'the past he adores is dead'.[25]

And all this, we are asked for believe, constitutes 'in a general sense, a "scientific" attitude towards the past'[26]

A very interesting essay is 'The Study of "Politics" in a University' where Oakeshott considers the question: 'What study under the plausible name of "Politics" is an appropriate component of a university education?' Oakeshott makes a distinction between the three kinds or levels of education, namely, 'school, "vocational" and university education'. At school, Oakeshott would allow the teaching of 'civics' or 'current affairs' as 'an introduction to the current activities of governments and to the relevant structures and practices with some attention to the beliefs and opinions which may be held to illuminate them'. It is 'not, perhaps, a very inspiring study, and in its more dessicated passages ...holding out no evident promise of better things to come'. Nevertheless, says Oakeshott, it is capable of defence on the ground that 'with us', perhaps a trifle unfortunately; 'politics is everybody's business'. Besides, 'this sort of study is no more misleading than many other school studies (like economics and history) are bound to be'.

Then there is 'what maybe called a professional or "vocational" education in politics', an education 'designed specifically for those who are called upon or who wish to engage in political activity'—politicians, party managers, agents and their assistants, government or trade union officials, and the large numbers of those 'occasional participants' that 'the peculiar style of politics which has now imposed itself upon the world calls for and accommodates', to say nothing of 'the political commentators and entertainers'.

Oakeshott sees no reason why, for all these persons, 'one should not undertake to teach politics as one might undertake to teach plumbing, "home making", librarianship, farming or how to run a bassoon factory'. This vocational or professional teaching is, in fact, undertaken, and 'there already exists an extensive political literature ...satisfying the specification of a literature appropriate to a "vocational" education'—'a compendium of reliable information useful for those engaged in political activity'—analogous to, and 'in design and purport' indistinguishable from 'the technical literature' we have concerning, for example, 'building houses or growing tomatoes'. This is the most, according to Oakeshott, that can be said for this literature. Any other claims made for it rest 'either upon the moral prejudices of those who make them ...or upon a naive ethical naturalism'. Thus does Oakeshott dispose of the claims of the 'so-called "master science"' of politics, the vision of 'a modern "science" of government and administration' which, according to him, this vocational education has generated.

All this, however, has no place in a university, even though at the moment there is general acceptance of 'this "vocational" or participatory study as appropriate to a university education'. Oakeshott insists that 'university education is something entirely different from both school and "vocational" education', in respect of both 'what is taught' and 'how it is taught'. He deplores 'the "vocational" disposition with which "politics" has come to establish itself in a university education and which it has never succeeded in throwing off.' For this Oakeshott holds the university teachers of politics to be mainly responsible. The cause lies in 'their mistaken disposition', a disposition which, he says, is not 'commonly the result of profound reflection' but 'springs rather, from their being themselves primarily interested in politics in the vulgar sense'.[27]

Making a sharp distinction 'between a "language" (by which I mean a manner of thinking) and a "literature" or a "text" (by which I mean what has been said from time to time in a "language")', Oakeshott argues that in a university one must go 'beyond the study of "literatures" as repositors of information to the study of a "language" or a manner of thinking'. Here we are concerned only 'with the use and management of explanatory languages (or modes of thought) and not prescriptive languages'. At the university, Oakeshott tells us, 'our proper business is not with politics at all but with teaching, in connection with politics, how to manage the "languages" of history and philosophy and how to distinguish them and their different sorts of utterances'; and 'the appropriate engagement of an undergraduate student of "politics" at a university will be to be taught and to learn something about the modes of thought and manners of speaking of an historian and a philosopher, and to do this in connection with politics, while others (in other Schools) are doing it in other connections'. We must understand that 'the word "politics" at a university education signifies, not a "subject" of study, but a library of texts which, in this kind of education, is merely the occasion for learning how to handle and manage some of the "languages" of explanation: A 'text' is thus not to be understood 'as an organization of information but as the paradigm of a "language"', and the 'classics of political reflection' must not be read 'in order to discover the injunctions about political conduct they are believed to contain and in order to reflect upon the appropriateness to us of these injunctions.' When we so read them, 'when in the writings of Plato or Hobbes or Rousseau or Hegel or Mill what is being looked for is the political disposition of these writers', 'when expressions like "natural law", "general will", "freedom", "the rule of law", "justice", or "sovereignty", which, philosophically speaking, are explanatory concepts ...are turned ...into prescriptive concepts', all chance is lost 'of learning something about the philosophical mode of thought' and 'a "vocational" education in politics maybe seen to have reimposed itself'. In other words, the texts or the classics must never be used 'as books of "political theory"[28] 'that is, as 'repositories' or 'organizations of information' and 'knowledge', as having 'a political "ideal", or programme, or policy, or device to recommend' which we need 'to elicit and criticise'.[29] We must ever remember that 'a philosopher is never concerned with a condition of things but only with a manner of explanation', and that 'the only thing that matters in a philosophical argument is its coherence, its intelligibility, its power to illuminate and its fertility'. Power to illuminate, and fertility for, what? is an irrelevant question, as is any question, raised in any form; about the *truth* of 'a philosophical argument' or about 'truth' and 'philosophical argument'. We are simply not concerned with such questions, with 'what may be called "the current state of knowledge" 'or with 'doctrines and systems' or with any 'conclusions, facts, truths' and such other things.[30]

Oakeshott would, thus, purge 'the study of politics' at a university of all moral and political purpose, of all taint of truth or knowledge. Both as 'a philosophical study' and 'a historical study', it is the study only of 'concepts', 'words' and 'epithets connected with it', of their 'ambiguity and confusion'. Its purpose lies only 'in disentangling the confusion which springs from merely crooked thinking', or 'in telling the story of the ambiguity and in making sense of it without the help of those adventitious aids, the categories of truth and error." Political philosophy', Oakeshott insists, 'is not what maybe called a "progressive" science, accumulating solid results and reaching conclusions upon which further investigation may be based with confidence.' It has in fact 'nothing but a history', a history 'not of political ideas, but of the manner of our political thinking', 'a history of the incoherencies philosophers have detected in common ways of thinking and the manner of solution they have proposed rather than a history of doctrines and systems'. Political philosophy, therefore, can never be anything more than a study of relevant 'modes of thoughts', or 'manners of speaking', or ' "languages" of explanation', whereby we may learn to handle and manage some of these ourselves and, with luck, even 'acquire the connoissuership which can recognize a philosophical argument' when it sees one. If we pursue it, 'we may hope only to be less often cheated by ambiguous statement and irrelevant argument'. As 'the patient analysis of the general ideas which have come to be connected with political activity', it may help remove 'some of the crookedness from our thinking' and thus lead 'to a more economical use of concepts'. But more than this it can never do. Truth or knowledge is none of its business. And with 'a condition of things' it shall never be concerned.

Thus, with Oakeshott, political philosophy becomes an activity that divorces the ideas or words from the things they represent, the concepts from the reality they are the concepts of, the explanation from what is explained, and the language from what it expresses and from its purpose of communicating useful information about the world. It is an activity which tends, in fact, to dissolve the relationship between the thinking mind and the objective world, leaving reason to work upon itself, thought to feed upon thought. Oakeshott is right in emphasising the linguistic, analysing, and clarifying aspects of a philosophical inquiry; but beyond that his is a programme of trivialisation and impoverishment of political thought, reducing it to a mere branch of 'logical or philosophical analysis'. Henceforth, political philosophy, like a virgin consecrated to the gods, will produce no offspring—not in the universities, at any rate![31]

'The Voice of Poetry in the Conversation of Mankind' is, in an important sense, perhaps the most significant essay in the collection, revealing as it does something of Oakeshott's own positive values and philosophy. Here with rare delicacy he speaks of something which is obviously very close to his heart. It is an essay in praise of contemplation.

Oakeshott begins with the image of human activity and intercourse as a conversation', and not 'an inquiry or an argument' or an 'argumentative discourse', and distinguishes, rather rigidly, between four different kinds of human activity, or 'voices' as he calls them—'the voice of practical (political) activity', of 'history', of 'poetry' and of 'science'. The excellence of 'this conversation (as of others)', Oakeshott says, 'springs from a tension between seriousness and playfulness'. He concludes that this image 'will, perhaps, appear both frivolous and unduly sceptical', yet the model he offers is children 'who are great conversationists' and with whom 'the playfulness is serious and the seriousness in the end is only play'. Oakeshott then tells us:

> In recent centuries the conversation, both in public and within ourselves, has become boring because it has been engrossed by two voices, the voice of practical activity and the voice of 'science': to know and to contrive (to make discoveries about the world, or to contrive a better world) are our pre-eminent occupations.

But it was not always so. Oakeshott refers to 'a hierarchical order among the voices' as 'one of the most notable traditions of European thought (in which all activity was judged in relation to the *vita contemplativa*'). Though on occasion he is ostensibly not very keen to uphold this order or tradition, it is with obvious longing that Oakeshott writes:

> For many centuries in the intellectual history of Europe, contemplation, understood as a purely receptive experience of real entities, occupied the highest place in the hierarchy of human experience, scientific inquiry being recognised as, at best, preparatory to it, and practical engagements as mere distractions.

Pleading for 'some relief from the monotony of a conversation too long appropriated by politics and science', Oakeshott urges that contemplation be restored to its rightful place in the 'conversation'. What he wants, in effect, is the restoration of contemplation to the 'position of supremacy' from which it has been 'demoted' in recent times by, above all, 'a philistine concern with useful knowledge'.

Oakeshott makes his conception of contemplation clear by considering 'the voice of poetry' 'as it speaks in the conversation'. Regarding poetry as 'the activity of making images of a certain kind', as the activity of 'contemplating' or 'delighting', he informs us that 'images in contemplation are merely present; they provoke neither speculation nor inquiry about the occasion or conditions of their appearing but only delight in their having appeared. They have no antecedents or consequents; they are not recognized as causes or conditions or signs of some other image to follow, or as the products or effects of one that went before; they are not instances of a kind, nor are they means to an end; they are neither "useful" nor "useless" 'neither pleasurable nor painful'; they do not attract to themselves 'either moral approval or disapproval'; they have 'no history', they look 'neither backwards nor forwards'; they 'have the appearance of being both permanent and unique', but 'this appearance of being permanent is not to seem durable instead of transitory', etc., etc. Oakeshott points out, if it is not already clear, that the notion or conception of 'contemplating' which he is exploring and upholding has little or nothing in common with that held by Plato or by other writers in the past. Platonic conception, for example, entails 'a belief in the pre-eminence of inquiry, and of the categories of "truth" and "reality"' and such a belief Oakeshott 'would wish to avoid' at all costs.[32]

With Oakeshott contemplation is an activity of 'image-making' wherein the images are 'recognised as individuals and neither as concretions of qualities any of which might appear elsewhere... nor as signs or symbols of something else'. It is 'a non-laborious activity' as Aristotle called it, 'an activity of-making and entertaining mere images'. It is, like poetry, 'the activity of being delighted in the entertainment of its own contemplating images'. In it, as in the 'contemplative imagining' or 'contemplating and delighting' that is poetry, images are 'made, remade, observed, turned about, played with, meditated upon and delighted in'. It is thus 'that the voice of contemplation is the voice of poetry and that it has no other utterance'. But, Oakeshott insists, this utterance has nothing to do, with ' "truth" and "reality"', it expresses and conveys, represents and shares, knows and communicates nothing.[33] The poet is 'not saying anything at all about "things"' and the 'words are themselves images'. Poetry 'begins and ends as a language'. Oakeshott concludes with a phrase of characteristic beauty: 'Poetry is a sort of truancy, a dream within the dream of life, a wild flower planted among our wheat'.

But words, however beautiful, cannot hide the fact that the sceptic's fight against cognition and truth, against 'knowing', in the realm of poetry too has been carried to the point of nihilism, that the flower has been denied the right to bear fragrance.

For Oakeshott, then, poetry (or art) is neither concerned with reality, 'things', nor with any 'knowing'. It has no purpose of deepening man's feelings and understanding in order to bring him closer to truth in one way, just as science does in another.[34] Not for it the sharing of a common emotional experience that enriches the awareness of today or the dreaming of mankind's tomorrows and the need to make this dream universally intelligible. Oakeshott's is a total denial of the cognitive and the common or social aspects of poetry or art, without which it will, perhaps, cease to be.[35]

Oakeshott's theory of poetry does not merely touch upon some fringe phenomena of the contemporary world of art. Its relevance goes beyond this to a more significant development. It is of a piece with, and may even be regarded as a rationalisation of, what Morton calls 'the cryptographic character of much modern poetry and painting'— involving a sort of private artistic soliloquy or shorthand—which often means or communicates nothing except, perhaps, to a small clique of initiates. Sincere and talented work, it yet reflects the isolation of the artist in bourgeois society—simultaneously degraded by it into mere entertainer or luxury ornament and elevated into a holy fool—which compels him to seek an illusory freedom in a nihilistic protest against society and in a misplaced contempt for the people.[36]

Above and beyond his nihilism concerning poetry is Oakeshott's most important, if not indeed his only, positive commitment—to contemplation. He places contemplation at the apex of the hierarchy of human activities and persistently denigrates man's concern with 'things', 'practical activity', 'science', 'useful knowledge', 'knowing and contriving' and all that is in any sense 'vocational ('banausic' they called it in another age) in fact, everything that does not serve the pure end of contemplation. This is typical of the values of a class-divided society, values which reflect at the ethical level, and thus sanctify, its cleavage between 'head and hand', and which are as old as Plato and Aristotle.[37]

VI

For Oakeshott these essays do not .compose 'a settled doctrine', that would itself be a surrender to 'Rationalism'. They only disclose 'a consistent style or disposition of thought'. But does this distinction really make a difference? Oakeshott's aversion to doctrine, his rejection of the possibility of any social science and of all systematic theory, remain as significant a philosophical or practical position as any doctrine. His anti-theory posture itself, in fact, implies a theory and a reactionary one at that, as is also the case with not a few of his contemporaries.

Oakeshott tells us that there is 'genuinely philosophical writing about politics' whose design is 'not to recommend conduct but to explain it'. There are also 'genuine works of political vulgarization' like Locke's *Second Treatise*. Then there are the writings of a Bentham or a Marx, corrupt and corrupting progeny of political 'Rationalism' and of vulgar 'vocational' disposition. There are, according to Oakeshott, other 'manners' of thinking and writing, other 'levels' of reflection about politics too. One wonders to which category he would assign his own essays.

Oakeshott is of course emphatic that political philosophy proper 'cannot be expected to increase our ability to be successful in political activity... it has no power to guide or to direct us in the enterprise of pursuing the intimations of our tradition ...it must be understood as an explanatory, not a practical activity'. 'He is 'concerned with understanding or explaining' alone and firmly rejects the 'commonly' held notion 'that explanations are warrants for conduct'. One is reminded of Hegel's view of philosophy as retrospective speculation, as 'the thinking view of things', that seeks not to recommend and reform or 'to do' anything, but only to understand. But as with Hegel, so with Oakeshott, this activity of seemingly pure thought, despite its professed unconcern with the 'practical, gives rise to conclusions of a very practical sort, conclusions which generally serve to sanctify the status quo, to rationalise the existing evils as necessary and to provide real support to conservative, even reactionary political practice. I shall explore this aspect of Oakeshott's philosophy later. At the moment it would suffice to note that one does not have to look far to discover that Oakeshott has produced, in a real sense, a book of very practical prescriptions. 'Rationalism', for example, is explained and rejected, just as traditionalism is explained and recommended; or again, 'the jump to glory style' is disapproved of and 'a conservative disposition' pronounced appropriate in politics. Oakeshott's explanations can be seen suggesting prescriptions at every step. As a matter of fact the very use of language, of words which cannot be divorced from their connotations, would seem to forbid the sort of pure 'understanding or explanation' that is being sought. And with Oakeshott, we have the prescriptive language *par excellence*—the language of 'predicament' and 'release', of 'misfortune' and 'deliverance', of 'appropriate' and 'inapprorpriate'. The 'rationalist' contagion or the 'vocational' disposition, it appears, is inescapable.

If Oakeshott's essays are any evidence, it shows that the separation of explanation from prescription, emphasised so much by him, is impossible to realise in practice. It is doubtful if this rigid dichotomy, like the fact value dichotomy, can ever be maintained consistently in social or political philosophy.

Oakeshott's performance proves not only that explanation tends to suggest prescription, but also that it is well nigh impossible for a philosopher to keep away from being 'concerned with a condition of things' for long. Is it legitimate then to confine ourselves only to historical or philosophical analysis of words and concepts, ideas or explanations? Would it not be necessary and proper to move on from words to things, from concepts to reality, and (even though sweeping negativism of Oakeshottian philosophy forbids it) focus attention also on the *truth* of an explanation in terms of its correspondence with the objective fact ('a condition of things), as well as the *validity* of the prescription flowing from it in terms of its relevance to the needs and possibilities of the objective situation?

Be that as it may, Oakeshott's is a book of explanations and prescriptions. This is not at all surprising, for this is how it should be. In any concrete human activity, whose characteristic is *purpose*, knowing and doing are always dialectically interconnected, the prescriptions do not lag far behind the explanations. This is particularly the case in those spheres where man puts his knowledge into practice, as for example in medicine, economics, or politics. An explanation does not directly become a warrant for conduct—Oakeshott is certainly right in pointing this out. It does, however, indicate possibilities, it suggests a prescription. As diagnosis, it points to the treatment. In other words, an, explanation, if true, apart from the satisfaction it gives for its own sake, is valid knowledge, available to man in pursuit of his needs and purposes. In fact, it is always the explanation, and explanation alone, which determines, positively or negatively, the nature of the prescription. (Oakeshott's explanation of political activity, for example, yields nothing but conservative prescriptions as the most appropriate ones). Hence the need, in order to decide upon the right policy or prescription, for making our explanation not merely convenient and useful or logically coherent and self-consistent but, above all, true as true—as we can possibly make it.

I have no desire to pursue this subject further or to oversimplify the complex issues involved. I shall be content to state that no serious reflection on politics, call it political theory or political science or political philosophy, can be either 'pure explanation' or 'pure prescription'. The two are far less separable than Oakeshott thinks. They are different, no dobut, but they always involve and enter into each other. Nor is it of any real use or help to regard one or the other as more legitimate or important. In political theory it is equally legitimate and important to explain and to prescribe.[38]

Oakeshott, then, has produced a book of 'so-called "political theory" 'This according to him is 'itself a form of political activity', which requires 'to be explained, historically or philosophically'. This I shall' proceed to do.

But I shall also study it, Oakeshott's disapproval notwithstanding, from the standpoint of its 'usefulness in the pursuit of our own practical enterprises'. I shall go on, that is, not only to test the truth of his explanations in terms of their correspondence (or lack of it) to the world of political reality that is sought to be explained, but also, and in the same manner, 'to elicit and criticise' the 'programme or policy' which Oakeshott recommends. We have valid enough reasons to do so, not the least being that it is Oakeshott himself, in the first place, who has put this programme or policy there. And if this brings the Oakeshottian charge of being interested in politics 'in the vulgar sense', one may well answer with the question: is it vulgar only when radical?[39]

With this let us turn to the basic theme of the book.

NOTES AND REFERENCES

1. Letter to Mehring, 14 July, 1893, Marx and Engels, *Selected Correspondence 1846-1895*, London, 1943, p. 511.
2. Marx, *A Contribution to the Critique of Political Economy*, Calcutta, n.d., pp. l l- 2.
3. Marx and Engels, *Manifesto of the Communist Party*, Moscow, 1948, p. 68.
4. In this connection what Oskar Lange says of scientific theory in general, and of political economy in particular, applies to political theory also. He writes:

   The fact that scientific views and trends of scientific thought originate in particular historical conditions, in particular social classes or groups, does not in itself decide their truth or falsity. The truth of scientific statements depends exclusively on their agreement with objective reality and this agreement can only be verified in practice, i.e., in activity altering reality... The truth or falsity of the assertions of poetical economy is tested by a confrontation with reality, on the basis of statistical or historical verification; it is also tested by the effectiveness or ineffectiveness of the economic policy based on these assertions,... Thus the truth of scientific statements is tested in the process of the dialectic of scientific cognition. But the social conditions in which science develops and the social significance of its results may favour the attainment of scientific truth or they may hamper it and even make it impossible. (*Political Economy*, Vol. 1, London, 1963, p. 322).

5. For our purpose, it is not necessary either to enter into a discussion of 'what is political theory?' or to make distinctions, currently fashionable, between political 'theory and political 'philosophy', 'science', 'ideology, etc. On this the reader may see George H. Sabine, 'What is a Political Theory?', *The Journal of Politics*, Vol. 1, No. 1, February 1939; Arnold Brecht, *Political Theory: The Foundations of Twentieth Century Political Thought*; Princeton University Press, 1959, pp. 14-7; Andrew Hacker, *Political Theory: Philosophy Ideology, Science*, New York, 1961, Ch. 1; etc.

   Sabine points out that political theory has always and 'characteristically contained factors of... three kinds..., the factual, the causal, and the valuational'. Making a distinction between 'philosophy' as 'a disinterested search for the principles of the good state and the good society' and 'science' as 'a disinterested search for knowledge of political and social reality', with 'ideology' representing 'the rationalizations and distortions which are endemic' to the two aforementioned pursuits, Hacker writes that 'political theory is a body of philosophical and scientific knowledge which, regardless of when and where it was originally written, can increase our understanding of the world in which we live today and will live tomorrow'.

   I use the term 'political theory' in this broad sense, in the traditional sense of generalised philosophical reflection on politics, of an intellectual construction which has, in varying degrees, the elements of 'philosophy, ideology and science'. Later in these notes we shall be concerned with a specific question, namely, the *possibility* of political theory as a developing body of knowledge, of tested and accepted theory about man, society and politics, arrived at through investigation of the world in ways broadly comparable to those employed by the natural sciences and giving us an ever increasing understanding and mastery of the world in which we live.

6. Bernard Crick, 'The World of Michael Oakeshott', *Encounter*, June 1963.
7. Colin Falck, 'Romanticism in Politics', *New Left Review*, No. 18, January-February 1963.
8. M. Oakeshott, 'Introduction to Hobbes' *Leviathan*, Oxford, 1947, p. xi.
9. Quoted in G.E.G. Catlin, *Systematic Politics*, London, 1962, p. 7.
10. Douglas V. Verney, *The Analysis of Political Systems*, London, 1959, pp. 199-200.

11. Leo Strauss, 'Epilogue' to *Essays on the Scientific Study of Politics*, edited by Herbert J. Storing, New York, 1962, p. 307.

We may note that during roughly the same period another approach also came into prominence, particularly in the American universities. It has been called 'the new science of politics', or 'the scientific study of politics', or more often, 'the behavioral science of politics'. (This last name, 'the behavioral science', was perhaps thought up, C. Wright Mills once suggested, 'as a propaganda device to get money for social research from Foundations and Congressmen who confuse "social science" with "socialism" '). While achieving valuable results in limited and specialised fields, this 'new' approach, too, with its excessively piecemeal character, onesided emphasis on 'data' and a false fear of risking generalisation, has all too often not only shared in and contributed to the general climate against theory but has, thereby, also stultified its own claim to be scientific.

As a matter of fact, a very crude and shallow, and essentially unscientific, empiricism seems to be the single most important methodological weakness of what goes nowadays under the name of 'the scientific study of politics' or 'the behavioral science of politics'. William A. Glaser has spoken of 'barefoot empiricism' which is today 'common in political science' (The Types and Uses of Political Theory', *Social Research*, Vol. 1, 22, Autumn 1955). In the absence of 'a more general theory' to guide, 'facts are piled upon facts', David Easton has told us, 'until all sense of purpose is lost' ('The Decline of Modern Political Theory', *The Journal of Politics*, Vol. 13, February 1951). In so many fields, Arnold A. Rogow has written, 'the data stand mountain-high, with fresh increments arriving quarterly (when the Journals appear), alongside molehills of generalisation and theory' ('Whatever Happened to the Great Issues?', *The American Political Science Review*, Vol II, No. 3, September 1957). In a somewhat more sympathetic comment Bernard Crick has pointed out that today 'there is more accurate information to be found about contemporary American government and politics than for any other nation, and yet there is remarkably less knowledge about the causes and conditions which could reveal the coherence, the significance and the underlying tendencies of this information' (*The American Science of Politics*, London, 1959, p. 230). In short, in the so called 'scientific' or 'behavioral' study of politics, 'the immediately observable, measureable *fact*' has often been indeed 'that Moloch' as Paul Baran once put it, 'which is always seeking to devour analytic thought in contemporary social science.'

This crude and shallow empiricism is also partly responsible for that sterility, abstruse irrelevance, concern with trivialities and pretentious mediocrity, often covered up with weird, esoteric jargons and empty parroting of scientific method, which characterise much of the work produced by the new 'scientific' or 'behavioral' school.

Essays on the Scientific Study of Politics contains an extensive critique of the new school; and one must recognise, without necessarily agreeing with either the assumptions from which the criticism proceeds or the conclusions it seeks to arrive at, that much of this criticism is quite valid. I would particularly like to endorse the criticism about the general *irrelevance* of much of the work of this school, its 'sacrifice of political relevance on the alter of methodology', as Walter Berns puts it. In his '*Epilogue*', Leo Strauss points out the 'amazing disproportion between the apparent breadth of (its) goal (say, a general theory of social change) and the true pettiness of the researches undertaken to achieve that goat, and concludes, of course from his own liberal-conservative and rather backward looking Christian point of view, that 'the new political science... fiddles while Rome burns'. He adds, however, that 'it is excused by two facts: it does not know that it fiddles, and it does not know that Rome burns'.

Crick's book, *The American Science of Politics*, is an interesting critical study of the new school from an altogether different angle. He sees 'the whole school more as an expression of American political thought than of science'. Offering 'an interpretation of American political culture that seeks to show why in recent years political theory in the United States has commonly taken the form of belief in a political science', Crick speaks of redeeming 'recent American political thought from the sterility and narrowness of the idea of a science of politics'.

12. The 'decline' and occasionally even 'death' of political theory has been a subject of much recent discussion. Though covering both empirical or causal and normative or ethical theory, the focus of discussion has been more on the latter than the former. And while the gravity of the situation has been variously assessed and the diagnoses have differed, as also have the remedies suggested, there has been a wide consensus, alarmed or complacent, about the existence of a situation of real 'trouble', or 'malaise' as it has been called. See, for example, Verney, pp. XII, *op. cit.*: 'there are natural grounds for anxiety about present trends'—incidentally, Verney

holds that 'the tone of the present discontent has been set by Professor Oakeshott in his Inaugural Lecture, as Laski's successor at the London School of Economics in 1951'; David Easton, *op. cit.*: 'this poverty of political theory', and also *The Political System*, New York, 1953, Ch. 10: 'decline into 'historicism'; J. Roland Pennock, 'Political Science and Political Philosophy', *The American Political Science Review*, Vol. XLV, December 1951: 'a plea for both political philosophers and empirical political scientists to mend their ways'; Alfred Cobban, 'The Decline of Political Theory', *Political Science Quarterly*, Vol. LXVIII, September 1953: 'a general tendency to cease thinking about society in terms of political theory'; Harry Eckstein, rapporteur, 'Political Theory and the Study of Politics: A Report of a Conference', *The American Political Science Review*, Vol. L, June 1956: 'our villain, in the final analysis, and not surprisingly, was simply the "behaviorist theorist dichotomy" '; David G. Smith, 'Political Science and Political Theory', *The American Political Science Review*, Vol. LI, September 1957: 'there is a widespread conviction that political theory has entered upon a time of troubles'—the cause lies, Smith says, in its being regarded as a 'nomothetic' rather than an 'ideographic' exercise; also, in the same issue, David E. Apter, Theory and the Study of Politics', and Arnold A. Rogow, 'Comment on Smith and Apter'; Robert A. Dahl, 'Political Theory: Truth and Consequences', *World Politics*, Vol. XI, October 1958: 'In the English-speaking world... political theory is dead', a view broadly shared by Peter Laslett in his Introduction to *Philosophy, Politics and Society*, New York, 1956; Leo Strauss, *What is Political Philosophy?* The Free Press of Glencoe, Illinois, 1959, Ch. I: Today, political philosophy is in a state of decay and perhaps of putrefaction, if it has not vanished altogether'; C.B. Macpherson, 'Post Liberal Democracy?', *The Canadian Journal of Economics and Political Science*, Vol. 30, No. 4, November 1964: 'political science is now more than ever in need of rethinking its normative theory'; etc., etc.

Cobban's essay, concerned primarily with normative political theory, is noteworthy in that, while discussing, like most others, causes and conditions internal to political theory, he also draws pointed attention to the external, *social* causes or conditions, to 'the inevitable pressure of objective fact' as he calls it. 'The connection between new conditions of society and the decline of political thinking may be obscure', he says, 'but it would be dangerous to suggest that there is none.' Cobban writes that 'this is an age of revolutions', when, in the west, 'political pessimism is deeper than it has been perhaps since St. Augustine wrote the *De Civitate Dei*; and the feeling is widespread that 'ethical values have no place in the field of social dynamics and power politics'. In politics proper 'a sense of direction is lacking, a feeling of purpose'. In human affairs in general 'we' have a magnificent technical equipment for going somewhere, without anywhere to go'. Arguing for the need of recovering a sense of direction, and therefore control', for reintroducing' the idea of purpose... into political thinking', Cobban urges us to 'take up again the tradition of Western political thought', which tradition most western political theorists seem to have abandoned today.

One might add that Macpherson's essay, mentioned above, is written in the great tradition of western political thought. And the essay is particularly noteworthy because, emphasising that today 'political values have become more, not less, in need of central attention in political science', Macpherson has sought to suggest the *specific* way forward for contemporary political theory.

To keep the record straight on this subject one must mention that scholars have not been wanting who have questioned the thesis, or 'the allegation', about the 'decline' or 'death' of political theory. There is Dante Germino, for example, who has recently not only argued that 'this thesis is seriously in error', but also insisted that 'at the present moment' we are on the verge of 'a truly creative flowering', indeed, a 'renaissance of political theory in the grand manner'. 'Like the proverbial phoenix', he says, 'political theory is today rising from the ashes of its own destruction', and rather than 'schedule its funeral', 'we should instead be joyously commemorating its rebirth' ('The Revival of Political Theory', *The Journal of Politics*, Vol. 25, August 1963).

Germino's essay is a pedantic and rather confused exercise, though, one must admit, he certainly means well by political theory. The general nature and quality of his argument is clearly seen in two things. In the first place, he includes, even if a trifle hesitantly, Michael Oakeshott among the great 'restorers' of political theory, 'the scholars who are making significant contributions to the restorative effort'! In the second place, asking the question why, despite 'the present day revival of political theory' there is 'so much talk of "decline" in contemporary political theory?' Germino answers that the reason lies simply in the unwillingness or inability of both the 'funereal critics and the 'highly gifted' restorers to see and recognise what Germino so plainly sees and recognises! Or, as Germino himself puts it, there are 'two principal reasons' for it. Firstly, there is the stubborn 'majority in political science' which, though 'hardpressed', has been 'unwilling or unable to recognise the extent and importance of the resistance movement'; these men are simply 'incapable of recognising genuine political theory when they see it'. Secondly, there is 'the curious inability on the part of some of the resisters—or restorersr—themselves', as in case of Leo Strauss, for example, to recognise the same; these men too 'fail to recognise' either their own achievement, 'the extent of their influence', or 'the achievement of fellow political theorists'!

13. Churchill's speech at Boston in March 1949, quoted in R. Palme Dutt's *Problems of Contemporary History*, London, 1963, p. 35. In this speech Churchill spoke of being 'faced by perils both grave and near and by problems more dire than have ever confronted Christian civilisation'; and, for an answer to these perils and problems of the twentieth century, Churchill looked to the atom bomb!

    The twentieth century crisis and the accompanying pessimism, at once apprehensive and guilty, which colours so much of contemporary thought and practice and is the expression, partly at least, of a sense of living at the end of an epoch, has been well expressed by Ortega Y Gasset:

    > We live at a time when man believes himself fabulously capable of creation, but he does not know what to create. Lord of all things, he is not lord of himself. He feels lost amid his own abundance. With more means at its disposal, more knowledge, more technique than ever, it turns out that the world today goes the same way as the worst of worlds that have been; it simply drifts (*The Revolt of the Masses*, London, 1951, pp. 31-2).

    On the same theme, in the *Protestant Era*, Paul Tillich writes:

    > It is not an exaggeration to say that today man experiences his present situation in terms of disruption, self-destruction; mcaninglessness and despair in all realms of life. This experience is expressed in the arts and in literature, conceptualized in existential philosophy, actualized in polititał cleavages of all kinds, and analysed in the psychology of the unconscious (quoted by John Lewis, *Marxism and the Open Mind*, London, 1957, p. x).

14. Herbert A. Deane, *The Political Ideas of Harold J. Laski*, New York, 1955, pp. 342-3. Deane suggests that this sense of fear and

uncertainty among political thinkers has not only induced many of them 'to concentrate their energies on formulating *ad hoc* measures to deal with a succession of specific economic and political difficulties', but is also the major reason behind their admitted 'failure to develop a philosophy of positive liberalism in this century.

In this book Laski has been subjected to a criticism which is not always fair, despite the author's promise not to be 'guilty of malice or triviality'. And so deep is Deane's prejudice—born, perhaps, of a fear of dangerous 'un-American' thoughts—that he completely fails to see that, in a real sense, Laski's life-work, despite its failings, is precisely a search for 'a philosophy of positive liberalism *in this century*' (emphasis added). If Deane thinks that such a philosophy can, in this age, completely bypass Marxism in theory and socialism in practice, or be grounded on anti-communism, he is surely looking for disappointment.

This apart, it seems to me that the view Deane in general takes of the human situation is incapable of generating or sustaining positive philosophy of any sort whatsoever. Deane questions *Laski's socialist* faith in man, in social justice and historical progress. He not only denigrates, as 'utopian' and 'unduly optimistic', Laski's life-long fight against the tragedy and suffering of our time but also provides defence and justification for this historically specific tragedy and suffering by pronouncing 'tragedy and suffering (to be) inherent in the human situation'. It is not at all surprising therefore that 'unsparingly critical' of Laski for his failure though he is, Deane has yet preferred to concentrate his own energies on Augustinian exegesis and such other things, rather than on developing 'a philosophy of positive liberalism in this century'!

15. See notes 11 and 12 above. As noted and emphasised by various writers, some of these causes, both within and without the discipline, are: 'the historical approach', 'a form of historical analysis' or 'historical interpretation' which 'has managed to crush the life out of value theory' and has resulted not only in 'the decline of interest in creative values and the growth of moral relativism', but also in an 'indifference to causal theory' (Easton); political theory has 'fallen under the influence of two modes of thought which have had a fatal effect on its ethical content. These, and they have come to dominate the modern mind, are history and science' (Cobban); 'an unrelated emphasis on historicism, scholasticism, and methodology, 'the collapse in our time of

radical and liberal solutions to social problems' which has left the profession with 'a very large number of disillusioned reformers, some of them are too disillusioned to elaborate anything but forms, structures, and methods, and... others are too disillusioned to elaborate anything in particular' (Rogow); 'so many of the interesting political problems have been solved (at least superficially)', leaving political theorists to 'textual criticism and historical analysis', though 'the real difficulties of political theory' stem from 'the impossibility of satisfying scientific functions of political theory', from its inability to meet 'the rigorous criteria of truth' (Dahl); 'a marked trend towards empirical, value-free analysis', 'the concern with values, which was central in the great theoretical writing on poetics in the past, has been pushed out to the fringes of the subject as empirical work has proliferated' (Macpherson); 'Political theory has become generally disengaged from practice' (Cobban), and in specific cases it has forsaken 'actual politics for the abstract safety and certainty of pseudo-science' (Crick); 'an exhaustion of the nineteenth century ideologies', and a 'reaction to these ideologies' (Bell); 'a temporary failure of nerve on the part of some liberal democrats' (Verney); 'the triumph of the democratic social revolution in the West resulting in 'the end of ideology' (Lipset); 'the all pervading complacency and parochialism that characterized British life and thought in the 1950s' (Bryan Magee); etc., etc.

16. The amazing speed with which 'the new science of politics' has spread to fill the gap and its wide popularity in the American universities, it is tempting to suggest, is not to be explained entirely in terms of the reaction against the easy and 'wholesale' theorising characteristic of traditional 'political science', the need for reliable empirical research, and the recognition of the importance of a factual approach and specialised studies—valid enough though these and other reasons are. There is *also* the fact that its narrow focus, piecemeal approach, and distrust of generalised, explanatory theory have, *so far*, objectively helped 'the new science' avoid questions about the basic character of society and the general direction of its movement, and thus helped it evade also the problems of large-scale change. There is always the tacit assumption that the existing society, as a whole, is fundamentally healthy and sound, that its problems, being matters merely of 'disorganisation', are real only at the level of details, and that they arise not from the irrationality inherent in capitalist society, but from other abnormal, extraneous and transitory causes. That all

this has often been justified and defended in the name of 'scientific methodology' or 'objectivity' does not affect my argument. For this 'methodology' or 'objectivity', unbearably loud and pretentious at times, has more often than not led to ignoring the implicit assumptions about the permanence of the existing social and political system and, consequently, to an unquestioning acceptance of the mythology that has grown up in the process of defending and guaranteeing this permanence. It has truly inhibited social and political inquiry and, in effect, restricted it largely to the study only of minor problems, of relatively unrelated and insignificant areas of social and political life. The 'new science' may speak, with Dahl, of 'the rapid development of the social sciences, with their rigor and empiricism', and even of 'the intellectual revolution brought about by the development of logico-experimental reasoning, yet it has been admittedly 'concerned often with a meticulous observation of the trivial' only (*loc. cit.*, pp. 89, 97-8). More specifically, as Dwight Waldo has very rightly asserted, 'American political scientists have tended to accept the "political order"' and 'distinctive American "political theory" has tended to be concerned with means and methodology' (*Political Science in the United States: A Trend Report*, Paris, 1956, p. 17). American political scientists have tended, as Rogow has pointed out, 'to oppose "political" and "science".', and 'to assume, implicitly or explicitly, that the *more* science, the *less* politics' (*loc. cit.*, p. 772). And the entire development has provoked Cobban to comment: 'Mostly, what is called political science, seems to me a device, invented by University teachers, for avoiding that dangerous subject politics, without achieving science' (*loc. cit.*, p. 335).

There is thus no doubt that 'the new science', showing either remarkable self-restraint born perhaps of 'scientific' or 'methodological' inhibitions, or an equally remarkable timidity induced perhaps by the pressure of socio-historical' fact, or both, with one reinforcing the other, has generally refrained from questioning the basic assumptions of the system. It has also preferred to work within the limits set by 'established institutions and values' and concerned itself only with 'relatively minor elements of the existing social and political order', exactly as the much-maligned contemporary political theory has done. It too has remained on the whole a 'safe' enterprise—safe, that is, from the point of view of established property relations—and, despite the important qualifications that must be made, it generally fits into the broad patterns of development mentioned above. No wonder that whatever else it may have lacked 'the new science' has never lacked funds!

17. I, Namier, *Personalities and Powers,* London, 1955, p. 7.
   Arguing that 'the less... man clogs the free play of his mind with political doctrine and dogma, the better for his thinking', Namier wrote:

   > Some political philosophers complain of 'a tired lull' and the absence at present of argument on general politics in this country: practical solutions are sought for concrete problems, while programmes and ideals are forgotten by both parties. But to me this attitude seems to betoken a greater national maturity, and I can only wish that it may long continue undisturbed by the workings of political philosophy.

18. John Plamenatz, *German Marxism and Russian Communism,* Longmans, 1961, p. 33. It should be clear from my argument that this flight from 'the real world', and the other developments mentioned above, arc not to be viewed, as is sometimes done, simply 'as the consequence of certain intellectual trends' (Deane, *op. cit.,* p. 343), particularly of the philosophical trend called 'logical positivism or empiricism'— known in its more recent development as 'logical or philosophical analysis' or simply as linguistic philosophy— which has dominated the western academic scene, especially in Britain, for the last thirty years. The philosophers belonging to this and allied philosophical trends have, in the name of rejecting 'metaphysics', indeed questioned all serious thought and discussion about the nature of reality, the significance of human life or the basic problems of social existence; they have in fact questioned the very possibility of philosophy *as a rational sizing up of the human situation as regards both knowledge and valuation*' as Roy Wood Sellers once defined it. They have insisted that philosophy is only about *language,* about the analysis and clarification of *concepts,* and about the elucidation of *meaning,* that the function of philosophy is only to clarify thought and not to express truths or to serve, in any way, as a guide to human action—philosophy is only 'the critique of language' and 'it leaves everything as it is' (Wittgenstein). It is certainly no business of philosophy, they tell us, to seek an understanding of the world—'the desire to understand the world is, they think, an outdated folly' (Bertand Russell). Philosophy as a 'second-order study' simply cannot have anything to say about 'first-order' issues, that is, about the world, or about fundamental issues of life connected

with man's division of himself and the world, or about any substantive questions of moral or political nature that daily confront man—these philosophers 'would wish to say that philosophy has nothing to do with questions of *that* kind' (G.J. Warnock, *English Philosophy since* 1900, London, 1958, p. 167). As regards the responsibility of offering man a philosophy of life to guide him, some coherent world view that may help him in finding relatively *wise* answers to the problems of human existence, this is generally dismissed as a question of ' "cosmic" variety', and here, Warnock tells us, 'the contemporary philosopher's eye is characteristically cold and his pen, perhaps, apt to be employed as an instrument of deflation' (*op. cit.*, p. 173).

There is, thus, no doubt that logical positivism, together with the allied philosophical trends, has contributed powerfully to the development of the sceptical climate. But then ail these trends are themselves more a symptom than a cause of the disease, a product of circumstances which in turn they serve to perpetuate. Representing as they indeed do—their positive achievements notwithstanding— a retreat from philosophy, these trends are a *consequence* of the general retreat from reality, which is so significants phenomenon of our troubled times, and one manifest throughout the ideological superstructure of contemporary bourgeois society where, as, for example, Plumb has recently informed us, the arts increasingly 'get lost in jargon or recondite iconography'; where history 'has lost all faith in itself as a guide to the actions of men: no longer do historians investigate the past in the hope that it may enable their fellow men to control the future'; where philosophy 'seems to have withdrawn into an arid desert of linguistic conundrums, as remote from life as the absurder forms of scholasticism'; where social science has often 'taken refuge in a pompous jargon at once sententious and obscure'; and where the humanities in general are tending to 'retreat into social triviality' sect their practitioners, 'uncertain of their social function' and alt confidence 'in their capacity to lead or to instruct' gone, 'have taken refuge in two desperate courses—both suicidal. Either they blindly cling to their traditional attitudes and pretend that their function is what it was and that all will be well so long as change is repelled, or they retreat into their own private professional world and deny any social function to their subject', etc., etc. (Introduction to *Crisis in the Humanities*, edited by J.H. Plumb, Pelican, 1964, pp. 7-10).

19. See, for example, Karl Popper, *The Open Society and its Enemies*,

Vol. I, London, 1957, pp. 157-68, and *The Poverty of Historicism*, London, 1957, pp. 64-74. Popper tells us that 'piecemeal social engineering' allows only 'small scale' social experiments, which should be undertaken only 'one at a time' and which, presumably, must never go beyond 'health and unemployed insurance, for instance, or arbitration courts, or anti-depression budgeting, or educational reform', etc.

20. While Marxism is the main enemy, the sceptic as well as the conservative attack, with an occasional exception, takes in its sweep all liberal and radical political ideas, in fact any theory that takes such 'old fashioned' things as 'reason', 'science', or 'progress' seriously and holds that it is possible for man to use his knowledge to make this world a better home for mankind.
21. Irving Louis Horowitz, 'The New Conservatism', *Science and Society*, Vol. XX, No. I, Winter 1956.
22. Conservatism, we are told, disavows 'doctrine' or 'ideology' and is distinguished by 'a habit of mind, a mode of feeling, a way of living', etc. (Introduction to *The Conservative Tradition*, edited by Reginald J. White, London, 1950, p. l).
23. Perry Anderson, 'Origins of the Present Crisis', *New Left Review*, No. 23, January-February 1964, p. 40.
24. Bernard Crick writes: 'He is so sure that he will be misunderstood that he often seems to welcome it: so that he can always find more fools to mock (particularly would-be disciples)' (*loc. cit.*, p. 66).
25. In a characteristic piece of Oakeshottian prose, we read:

    The 'historian' adores the past; but the world today has perhaps less place for those who love the past than ever before... For it wishes only to learn from the past and it constructs a 'living past' which repeats with spurious authority the utterances put into its mouth. But to the 'historian' this is a piece of obscene necromancy: the past he adores is dead. The world has neither love nor respect for what is dead, wishing only to recall it to life again. It deals with the past as with a man, expecting it to talk sense and have something to say apposite to its plebeian 'causes' and engagements. But for the 'historian', for whom the past is dead and irreproachable, the past is feminine. He loves it as a mistress of whom he never tires and whom he never expects to talk sense. Once it was religion which stood in the way of appearance of the 'historical' past; now it is politics, but always it is this practical disposition.

    Of this passage, noticing its 'nostalgic self-pity that reminds one of Rousseau in one of his most confessional moods', a critic wrote (*The Times Literary Supplement*, 28 September, 1962): 'Unless Professor Oakeshott really prefers necrophily to necromancy, this passage suggests that there are moments when Anti-Politics ceases to be a philosophy and becomes a verbal posture, so crammed with dead metaphors that it is completely devoid of intellectual content'.

26. Oakeshott also informs us, though, that if we were to speak 'more strictly, there can in fact be no "scientific" attitude towards the past' at all. Oakeshott represents—along with Fisher, Popper, Berlin and others—a current of contemporary thought on history in the British universities which, is varying forms and degrees, denies history all laws, legitimate generalisations or predictions, meaning or progress.

E.H. Carr has noted that in the nineteenth century history was regarded in his country, with scarcely an exception, as meaningful and as a demonstration of the principle of progress. This expressed the ideology of a society in a condition of remarkably rapid progress. But today cynics and sceptics abound, not only in England but elsewhere too, especially among the intellectuals of countries whose former privileged position has been undermined. We have Cam's delicious comment:

> History was full of meaning for British historians, so long as it seemed to be going our way, now that it has taken a wrong turning, belief in the meaning of history has become a heresy ....
>
> It is significant that... our sceptics who see no meaning in history and assume that progress is dead, belong to that sector of the world and to that class of society which have triumphantly played a leading and predominant part in the advance of civilization for several generations. It is no consolation to them to be told that the role which their group has played in the past will now pass to others. Clearly a history which has played so scurvy a trick on them cannot be a meaningful or rational process (*What is History*? London, 1962, pp. 37, 111).

Carr's book is a powerful and brilliant critique of the historical reaction and obscurantism represented by Oakeshott and others. In his attempt to establish the methods and perspectives of proper history, Carr insists that 'the dual function of history' is 'to enable man to understand the society of the past and to increase his mastery of the society of the present' (p. 49). He argues that history can legitimately generalise and predict and 'teach lessons', because it *can* investigate the world in a truly scientific manner. He writes: 'Scientists, social scientists and historians are all engaged in different branches of the same study: the study of man and his environment, of the effects of man on his environment and of his environment on man. The object of the study is the same: to increase man's understanding of, and mastery over, his environment' (p. 80).

Writing as an intellectual and a historian Carr affirms his 'faith in the future of society and in the future of history, a faith in historical progress, in 'the possibility of unlimited progress—or progress subject to no limits that we can or need envisage—towards goals which can be defined only as we advance towards them, and the validity of which can be verified only in a process of attaining them' (p. 113).

27. One can almost hear George Catlin protesting 'There is always a demand that the professor of the social sciences shall become a political eunuch' (*op. cit.*, p. 17).
28. As, Oakeshott tells us in a footnote, commentaries 'like Hobhouse's *Metaphysical Theory of the State* (and later Crossman on *Plato Today* and Popper on *The Open Society and its Enemies*) have encouraged us to do.
29. An altogether different, almost opposite, view on this subject—of how to study the classics—has been expressed by Andrew Hacker in his '*Capital and Carbuncles*: The Great Books 'Reappraised', *The American Political Science Review*, Vol. XL, VIII, September 1954. In this essay Hacker discusses 'the appropriate way for students of political theory to approach the "Great Books" '. Arguing that 'theory has the dual task of explaining behaviour (causal theory) and adumbrating principles on how people ought to behave (ethical theory)', he takes the view that many of the classics of political science 'contain explanations and prescriptions which have great value for us now'. Hacker in fact holds that 'the "Great Books" are timeless for both causal and ethical theory'. But in order to handle them properly, in order to use them 'as the central theme of introductory study—and advanced research—in political theory', it is necessary that political theory 'catch up with the rest of the social sciences'. And.'this will only be done', Hacker says, 'if much of the excess historical, biographical, and logical baggage which surrounds the "Great Books" is ruthlessly thrown overboard'.

    Hacker has, however, since informed us that the passage of years has had 'some mellowing effect' on his views, especially in that he now regards the carrying of a certain amount of 'historical baggage' quite permissible in the study of the classics.

30. One is reminded of what Bertrand Russell once wrote of a certain school of modern philosophy, in fact 'the most influential school of philosophy in Britian at the present day', which, interested in clarification of thought and meaning and such other things, is not at all interested in matters of substance or truth, and has thus turned philosophy into 'a trivial and uninteresting pursuit'. To illustrate how this school of philosophy works, Russell takes, as an example, a statement containing an assertion, and proceeds:

    What does it mean by this assertion? And in what sense, if any, is the assertion true' The philosophers with whom I am concerned will consider the first of these questions, but will say that the second is none of their business. I agree entirely that, in this case, a discussion as to what is meant is important and highly necessary as a preliminary to a consideration of the substantial question, but if nothing can be said on the substantial question, it seems a waste of time to discuss what it means. These philosophers remind me of the shopkeeper of whom I once asked the shortest way to Winchester. He called to a man in the back premises:
    'Gentleman wants to know the shortest way to Winchester'.
    'Winchester?' an unseen voice replied.
    'Aye'.
    'Way to Winchester?'
    'Aye'.
    'Shortest way?'
    'Aye'.
    'Dunno.'
    He wanted to get the nature of the question clear, but took no interest in answering it. This is exactly what modern philosophy does for the earnest seeker after truth. Is it surprising that young people turn to other studies?, (*Portraits from Memory and Other Essays*, London, 1956, p. 157).

31. As already suggested in the note above, Oakeshott seems to share in many ways the view of philosophy which, springing mainly from the later work of Wittgenstein and practices of G.E. Moore, is currently in vogue at Oxford and other British universities. Known as 'logical or philosophical analysis', or simply as 'linguisitc philosophy', this view holds that philosophy is only a conceptual, an analysing and clarifying inquiry, and not a substantive one, that as a 'second-order study' it has nothing to

say about the 'first-order' issues, that is,' about the world, and that it has no informative, normative or prescriptive functions at all. As Warnock has put it, 'philosophy is the study of the concepts that we employ, and not of the facts, phenomena, cases, or events to which those concepts might be or are applied', and, collaterally, 'political philosophy involves the study of political concepts, but says nothing of the rights or wrongs of political issues' (*op. cit.*, p. 167).

Oakeshott not only himself generally shares this view of philosophy, he also, apparently, holds, much in the manner of early Christians concerned to include the more edifying pre-Christian philosophers amongst the redeemed, that most of the traditional political philosophers too did the same, though very much before their time and, perhaps, without understanding what they were really doing!

Ernest *Gellner*, in his very sharp criticism of linguistic philosophy, *Words and Things* (London, 1963), points out that its implications for politics are 'either neutralist, or conservative, or irrationalist (p. 233). He argues that linguistic philosophy 'demolishes reason in philosophy by depriving sustained reasoning not merely of any ontological, but also of all informative, critical and evaluative functions' (p. 220), that it has 'an inverted vision which treats genuine thought as disease, and dead thought as the paradigm of health' (p. 198). 'Me general public', Gellner says, 'often, supposes that Lingusitic Philosophy is an attack on *metaphysics*. But metaphysics is a red herring. In reality, it is simply an attack on thought' (p. 198). This apart, it is all the while indulging in what, in view of its minuteness, pedantry and lack of obvious purpose, Gellner describes in Veblenseque terms as 'conspicuous triviality', a kind of conspicuous waste of time and talent. And he writes: 'The emphasis and manifest enthusiasm with which philosophers of this school stress the impotence, the formality, the general irrelevance of their own work, is something which one must perhaps leave to the social historian to explain. Perhaps the finding of a philosophical theme rationalising the decline in power of an old ruling class may have something to do wlth it' (p. 241).

Apropos the 'philosophical' activity of this school, Bertrand Russell in his Introduction to Gellner's book, expressing his 'very close agreement' with its argument, says:

> When I was a boy, I had a clock with pendulum which could be lifted off. I found that the clock went very much faster

> without the pendulum. If the main purpose of a clock is to go, the clock was the better for losing its pendulum. True, it could no longer tell the time, but that did not matter if one could teach oneself to be indifferent to the passage of time. The linguistic philosophy, which cares only about language, and not about the world, is like the boy who preferred the clock without the pendulum because, although it no longer told the time, it went more easily than before and at a more exhilirating pace (p. 15).

The Marxist comment, while recognising its positive achievements, the logical and linguistic truths contained in it, has seen in 'philosophical analysis' or 'linguistic philosophy' 'the main trend of bourgeois philosophy in this period of capitalist disintegration', a trend which is busy 'rationalising its own refusal to think things through and diverting thought from dangerous problems under the cloak of sharpening the logical instrument' (John Lewis, 'Logic and Meaning of Life', *Marxism Today*, October, 1963). Barrows Dunham, in a brief reference takes into account the achievements of the Age of Analysis'—which 'for all its excesses, did in many ways improve on what it found .... The fires of Analysis, burning with remarkable quiet and calm, have consumed much that was erroneous, even if they did not light up all that was true. But he finds the development of western philosophy since 1909 to be significant in another way, too: 'whereas philosophers had once speculated boldly about the universe as a whole, they now preferred the safer latitudes of language. They began as seers, and they dwindled into grammarians'. Dunham speaks of the constraints of historical circumstances' which explain 'the shift in interest from cosmos to the language', and in view especially of 'the heats and the hunts' which are often on, he mischievously but very truthfully adds: 'Of all subjects, linguistics is the one over which the police are least watchful' (*Thinkers and Treasurers*, New York, 1955, pp. 24-31).

A full-length Marxist study on the subject is Maurice Cornforth's *Marxism and the Linguistic Philosophy* (London, 1965) which, in a historical survey makes a positive as well as a negative estimate of linguistic philosophy, and establishes it as 'a truly classical case of class conditioned ideology'. In general, Comforth says, linguistic philosophy' is the very antithesis of any philosophy, like Marxism, which seeks to find a perspective and purpose for human life by an inquiry into the foundations of human thought and action. Linguistic philosophy makes no such inquiry, but says it cannot be made. In this way it is representative of some very pervasive features of our day and age—namely, loss of perspective, lack of confidence in mankind, and its future, scepticism as to the possibility of finding out any reasons why, disengagement from the big issues of human progress and, instead, narrow specialist concern with technical questions' (p. 9).

32. Oakeshott writes:

> Nevertheless, it is not to be supposed that some superior 'reality' or importance may properly be attributed to the images of contemplative imagining. And in this connection I must distinguish what I mean by contemplation from another, and perhaps more familiar, notion. Some writers... understand contemplation as an experience in which the self is partnered, not by a world of unique but transitory images, but by a world of permanent essences: to contemplate is to 'behold' the 'universals' of which the images of sense, emotion, and thought are mere copies. And consequently, for these writers contemplation is the enjoyment of a special and immediate access to 'reality. It seems probable that Plato held some such view as this; Spinoza appears to have attributed this character to what he calls *scientia intuitiva*; and Schopenhauer found in *Kontemplation* a union of the self with *species rerum*.

33. Oakeshott rejects what he calls 'false beliefs about poetic imagining and poetic images' represented by such expressions as a concept of "poetic truth"'; "things are seen as they really are" ', poetry being 'in some sense "true" or representation of "truth"', or as '"expressing" or "conveying" or "representing" experiences', providing ' "a more familiar insight" into the experience', having something to do with 'a special quality named "beauty" ' etc., etc. Oakeshott also tells us that the 'words commonly used in this connection have each a different *nuance*, but they are all alike unsatisfactory, convey, communicate, represent, exhibit, display, embody, perpetuate, describe, find an objective correlative for, incarnate, make immortal, etc.' And if the word 'escape' has any meaning in this connection, poetry is an 'escape' only from one point of view it is 'an "escape"... from the considerabilities of practical activity', represented by 'practical enterprise, moral endeavour or scientific inquiry'. And this is not something 'to be deplored'. On the contrary, 'these are inherently burdensome activities from which we may properly seek release'.

34. Christopher Caudwell once wrote:

    Art is the expression of man's freedom in the world of feeling, just as science is the expression of man's freedom in the world of sensory perception, because both are conscious of the necessities of their worlds and can change them art the world of feeling or inner reality, science the world of phenomena or outer reality *(Illusions and Reality*, London, 1937, p. 156).

35. The necessity for art or poetry to understand and comprehend reality, to see, define and communicate it, *in its own way*, which alone esablishes the necessity of art for man, has been well argued by Ernst Fischer in his *The Necessity of Art*, Pelican, 1963.
36. A.L. Morton, 'The Arts and the People' in *The Challenge of Marxism*, edited by Brian Simon, London, 1963, pp. 132-42.
37. Oakeshott's commitment to contemplation, his insistence on 'the poetic character of all human activity', which makes not only poetry but all life, including perhaps essay writing itself, a matter for 'contemplation and delight', his rejection of what he calls 'argumentative discourse' or the voice of "science" ' for 'conversation', the 'unrehearsed intellectual adventure', in which we 'are not engaged in an inquiry or a debate', in which there is no "truth" to be discovered, no proposition to be proved, no conclusion sought', and in which we are' not concerned to inform, to persuade, or to refuse'—all this may well make one doubt if Oakeshott wants or deserves to be taken seriously.
38. Andrew Hacker writes:

    Every political theorist worthy of the name plays a double role. He is part scientist and part philosopher .... What is important to bear in mind is that no theorist can make a lasting contribution to human knowledge unless he works in the realms of both science and philosophy. The scientific parts of a theory can only achieve coherence and significance if the writer has a preconceived idea of the goals of political life. There can be no such things as 'pure' description or an 'objective' political science... There can be no such things... as 'pure' prescription or an 'objective' political philosophy (*op. cit.*, pp. 2-3).

    In a discussion of this subject, especially of the 'fact-value' problem, of the so-called 'dichotomy between value and fact', W.G. Runciman points out that the sociology and philosophy of politics are inextricably linked'. He concludes that 'it is equally important not only to continue to ask about how societies do behave, but also about how they ought to' (*Social Science and Political Theory*, Cambridge University Press, 1963, Ch. VIII).

39. There is no reason why at a university too—even if what Oakeshott recommends were possible and I have my doubts about that—we should not combine different kinds of study. In other words we may very legitimately study a 'text' or a classic from the point of view of history, philosophy and social science.

    Incidentally, Oakeshott has raised a very important problem in a study of this sort, namely that of a teacher's philosophical predilections, the 'problem of "bias" in teaching "politics" in a university'. But because of his false explanation prescription dichotomy and the inability to resist the temptation of finding an easy scapegoat in the teacher and his so-called 'mistaken disposition', he has not succeeded even in posing the problem correctly. The answer naturally evades him.

1

Of Rationalism

The basis of rationalism lies, Oakeshott tells us, in 'a doctrine about human knowledge'. Pointing out that this 'doctrine' is not 'properly speaking a philosophical theory of knowledge', Oakeshott proceeds to explain it with what he calls 'agreeable informality'.

He informs us that 'every science, every art, every practical activity requiring skill of any sort, indeed every human activity whatsoeve; involves knowledge. And, universally, this knowledge is of two sorts.' Though, both of these are 'always involved in any actual activity' and in fact 'do not exist separately', yet there are certain important differences between them, and, 'it is not making too much of it to call them two sorts of knowledge'. The first sort of knowledge Oakeshott calls 'technical knowledge or knowledge of technique'. Very often 'this technical knowledge is formulated into rules'. But whether or not it is, or has been, precisely formulated, the 'chief characteristic' of this 'technical knowledge' is that 'it is susceptible of precise formulation, although special skill and insight may be required to give it that formulation.''[1]

The second sort of knowledge is 'practical knowledge', so called because 'it exists only in use'. It is 'not reflective and (unlike technique) cannot be formulated in rules'. It would not be at all misleading, Oakeshott tells us, to speak of it as 'traditional knowledge', and 'the mastery of any skill, the pursuit of any concrete activity is impossible without it'.

These two sorts of knowledge, 'distinguishable but inseparable' are, Oakeshott says, 'the twin components of the knowledge involved in every concrete human activity, be it 'cookery, or 'the fine arts', or 'painting', or 'music', or 'poetry. They are involved in 'any genuinely scientific activity as 'also in religion'. 'And what is true of cookery, of painting, of natural science and of religion, is no less true of politics: the knowledge involved in political activity is both technical and practical'.

Oakeshott emphasises the differences between these two sorts of knowledge, particularly those which manifest themselves 'in the divergent ways in which these sorts of knowledge can be expressed and in the divergent ways in which they can be learned or acquired'. 'Technical knowledge', he says, 'is susceptible of formulation in rules, principles, directions, maxims—comprehensively,' in propositions'. It is possible to write it down 'in a book'. On the other hand, 'it is a characteristic of practical knowledge that it is not susceptible of formulation of this kind. Its normal expression is in a customary or traditional way of doing things, or, simply, in practice .... It is, indeed, a knowledge that is expressed in taste or connoisseurship, lacking rigidity and ready for the impress of the mind of the learner.'

Speaking of the divergent ways in which the two can be 'learned or acquired', Oakeshott says:

> Technical knowledge can be learned from a book; it can be learned in a correspondence course. Moreover, much of it can be learned by heart, repeated by rote, and applied mechanically: the logic of the syllogism is a technique of this kind. Technical knowledge, in short, can be both taught and learned in the simplest meanings of these words. On the other hand, practical knowledge can neither be taught nor learned, but only imparted and acquired. It exists only in practice, and the only way to acquire it is by apprenticeship to a master—not because the master can teach it (he cannot), but because it can be acquired only by continuous contact with one Who is perpetually practising it.

With this Oakeshott is in a position to track the enemy down. He writes:

> Rationalism is the assertion that what I have called practical knowledge is not knowledge at all, the assertion that, properly speaking, there is no knowledge which is not technical knowledge. The Rationalist holds that the only element of *knowledge* involved

> in any human activity is technical knowledge, and that what I have called practical knowledge is really only a sort of nescience which would be negligible if it were not positively mischievous. The sovereignty of 'reason', for the Rationalist, means the sovereignty of technique.

Having thus defined 'Rationalism', Oakeshott goes on to describe, really to attack, 'the rationalist' and 'the rationalist politics'. The 'rationalist' stands for the 'independence of mind on all occasions'. He recognises no authority 'save the authority of "reason" 'This reason gives rise to a system of abstract ideas and principles, an ideology, that is supposed to govern and guide political activity. This activity itself the 'rationalist' recognises as 'the imposition of a uniform condition of perfection' upon men and their conduct. His are indeed 'the politics of perfection' and 'the politics of uniformity'. His is the promise of a 'a short cut to heaven', which is really nothing better than 'a quick escape into the bogus eternity of an ideology'. The 'assimilation of politics to engineering' is 'the myth of rationalist politics'. 'Destruction and creation' are easier for a rationalist to understand and engage in, than 'acceptance or reform'. His politics are 'the politics of the felt need, the felt need not qualified by a genuine, concrete knowledge of the permanent interests and direction of movement of a society, but interpreted by "reason" and satisfied according to the technique of an ideology: they are the politics of the book', etc., etc.

But rationalism, says Oakeshott, its pretentious claims notwithstanding, remains the error it is. 'Its philosophical error lies in the certainty it attributes to technique and in its doctrine of the sovereignty of technique; its practical error lies in its belief that nothing but benefit can come from making conduct self-conscious'. More briefly, 'the error of the Rationalist', Oakeshott tells us, 'is of a simple sort—the error of mistaking a part (technical knowledge) for the whole, of endowing a part with the qualities of the whole'.

Yet, simple though the error be, it has been pernicious enough to play havoc with the life and politics of post-Renaissance Europe, especially since the early seventeenth century when the new rationalism first showed itself unmistakably. Oakeshott tells us that 'neither religion, nor natural science, nor education, nor 'the conduct of life itself escaped the influence of the new Rationalism; no activity was immune, no society untouched'. And if we expect religion, the greatest apparent victories of Rationalism have beet in politics' and today the ordinary practical politics of European nations 'have become fixed' in a rationalist 'vice', they are sick with 'the disease of Rationalism'. Rationalism has so 'deeply infected' all contemporary politics that today 'not only are our political vices rationalistic, but so also are our political virtues'. It has so seized hold of the politics of all persuasions and so flawed our every party line that even 'those traditional elements, particularly in English politics, which might have been expected to continue some resistance to the pressure of Rationalism, have now almost completely conformed to the prevailing intellectual temper, and even represent this conformity to be a sign of their vitality, their ability to move with the times'. Rationalism in fact 'has ceased to be merely one style in politics and has become the stylistic criterion of all respectable politics'. Everywhere 'traditions of behaviour have given place to ideologies', and everywhere 'the politics of destruction and creation have been substituted for the politics of repair'. Indeed, 'the traditional resources of resistance to the tyranny of Rationalism' have themselves succumbed, and the resistance to rationalism, Oakeshott complains, 'has now itself been converted into an ideology', and—witness Hayek's *Road to Serfdom*—into 'a self-conscious ideology' at that!

Oakeshott speaks of the 'excesses of Rationalism'. 'The loss incurred' has been great, the consequences truly disastrous. What is more, always 'dangerous and expensive', rationalism 'does most damage' not when it fails but when it 'appears to be successful'. Much of the failure of European politics arises here, including recurring wars,, for; according to Oakeshott, 'war is a disease to which a rationalist society has little resistance; it springs easily from the kind of incompetence inherent in rationalist politics'. For the rationalist's knowledge, Oakeshott says, 'will never be more than half-knowledge, and consequently he will never be more than half-right'. He is, Oakeshott adds with characteristic snobbery, 'like a foreigner or a man out of his social class... bewildered by a tradition and a habit of behaviour of which he knows only the surface; a butler or an observant house-maid has the advantage of him'.

Without wanting to alarm us with 'imaginary evils', Oakeshott points out 'two characteristics, in particular, of political Rationalism', which make it 'exceptionally dangerous to a society'. First, rationalism in politics 'involves an identifiable error, a misconception with regard to the nature of human knowledge, which amounts to a corruption of the mind. And consequently, it is without the power to correct its own shortcomings'. It leads not only to specific mistakes, but 'it also dries up the mind itself', and leaves the rationalist as 'essentially ineducable'. Secondly, it involves 'an exclusively rationalist form of education, in which education is understood not as 'an initiation into the moral and intellectual habits and achievements of (a) society, an entry into the partnership between present and past, a sharing of concrete knowledge', but as 'a training in technique, a training, that is, in the half of knowledge which can be learnt from books when they are used as cribs'. And the result of it all is that 'among much else that is corrupt and unhealthy' in contemporary European politics, we have also the spectacle of 'a set of sanctimonious, rationalist politicians' opposed by 'another set of politicians', all dabbling with their favourite rationalist projects, all 'living by the book', and all of them 'like jumped up kitchen porters deputizing for an absent cook'.

The situation as portrayed so far seems to be quite hopeless. It is, in fact, worse. For Oakeshott traces the evil back to early Christianity which, he says, in the third century, bequeathed to the western world 'a Christian moral ideology' and thus corrupted the very roots of the western civilisation. In his discussion of 'the form of contemporary western European morality', in which 'the morality of the self-conscious pursuit of moral ideals is dominant', Oakeshott informs us that it has come to us from 'the distant era'. In that Greco-Roman world 'the old habits of moral behaviour' had so 'lost their vitality', 'the impetus of moral habits of behaviour' seemed to have been so 'spent', that it was, in consequence, 'an age of intense moral self-consciousness'; and it 'unavoidably' gave rise to 'a morality of the pursuit of ideals'. No doubt, in the course of following centuries, this form 'went some way towards being reconverted into a morality of habit of behaviour', the 'ideals' becoming 'familiar' and 'finding expression in customs and institutions' ceased, to some extent at least, to be 'mere ideals'. But the fact remains that 'the moral inheritance of western Europe, both from the classical culture of the ancient world and from Christianity, was not the gift of a morality of habitual behaviour, but of a moral ideology'. And the continued dominance of this 'ideology' constitutes, according to Oakeshott, 'the corrupt consciousness' at the heart of the western civilization, the real source of its moral 'misfortune', the original cause indeed of its cruel contemporary 'predicament'.

It would thus appear that the western inheritance as a whole has been corrupted, that the entire western tradition—intellectual, moral, and political—is rotten with rationalism today. Terrible indeed is the predicament of the western man! And where shall he turn for deliverance? Under the circumstances, it must need some courage even to speak of 'the hope of deliveranee', though all that Oakeshott succeeds in doing is to give a warning: 'We must not expect a speedy release from our predicament'.

And yet this predicament, and its mountain of evil, we are told, is born of 'a simple error', a mere 'misconception', which is moreover easily 'identifiable'! We may well be forgiven for feeling somewhat sceptical.

Oakeshott is really too good a sceptic himself to believe all that he tells us; but only hopelessness and despair wait at the end for all who would take him seriously.

Since rationalism, according to Oakeshott, 'now reigns almost un-opposed' in European politics, he finds it necessary to inquire into the circumstances in which politics thus 'came to surrender almost completely to the Rationalist'. He asks the question: 'What are the circumstances that have promoted this state of affairs?' The answer he gives is simplicity itself: 'the generation of rationalist politics is by political inexperience out of political opportunity.' These conditions, Oakeshott says, 'have often existed together in European societies' and they have invariably given rise to rationalism as 'a method of covering up lack of political education'.

Pointing out that 'the politics of Rationalism are the politics of the politically inexperienced', Oakeshott tells us that 'the outstanding characteristic of European politics in the last four centuries is that they have suffered the incursion of at least three types of political inexperience that of the new ruler, of the new ruling class, and of the new political society.[2] He argues that 'how appropriate rationalist politics are' to the men who, 'not brought up or educated to their exercise, find themselves 'in a position to exert political initiative and authority' requires no elucidating. The new prince of the sixteenth century', 'the first of these needy adventurers into the field of politics', neither 'educated in a tradition', nor 'heir to a long family experience', utterly 'lacking education' and therefore not knowing 'how to behave'; 'the new and politically inexperienced social classes which, during the last four centuries, have risen to the exercise of political initiative and authority', without having had time 'to acquire a political education before (they) came to power'; the new society 'called upon without much notice to exercise political initiative on its own account'—all of them needed, and very badly too, 'a crib to politics, a political training in default of a political education', 'a political doctrine, to take the place of a habit of political behaviour', 'a magic technique of politics', as it were, which will remove the handicap of their inexperience, their obvious 'lack of political education'. And, Oakeshott says, they were all duly 'provided for'. It is thus that we have the writings of Machiavelli who sought to provide 'a technique for the ruler who had no tradition'; the *Second Treatise* of Locke (who is handled somewhat less roughly by Oakeshott and even included among 'men of real political education) which contains 'the ideology which Locke had distilled from the English political tradition' and thus ranks among those 'genuine works of political vulgarization' which are 'abridgements of a tradition, rationalizations purporting to elicit the "truth" of a tradition and to exhibit it in a set of abstract principles, but from which, nevertheless, the full significance of the tradition inevitably escapes'; the American Declaration of Independence, which is 'a characteristic product of the *saeculum rationalisticum*', and 'represents the politics of the felt need interpreted with the aid of an ideology', as also the other constitutional documents of American history and the French Revolution; writers like Bentham or Godwin, who 'cover up all traces of the political habit and tradition of their society with a purely speculative idea: these belong to the strictest sect of Rationalism'; and, above all, the work of Marx and Engels. These two are, of course, the worst offenders. 'So far as authority is concerned', Oakeshott informs us, 'nothing in this field can compare with (their) work'. They are, 'beyond question', the authors of the 'greatest of all political cribs', 'the most stupendous of our political rationalisms'.

Such is Oakeshott's description and explanation of the nature, the influence and the origins of rationalism in European politics. In view of the grave and continuing damage resulting from this rationalism; one is tempted to pause and speculate on the subject of cause and responsibility, in order to draw lessons from historical experience—even though an Oakeshottian 'connoisseur in historical inquiry will at once dismiss any such exercise as 'vulgar' and 'non-historical'.

Oakeshott does not think, and very rightly too, that 'any or all of the writers' mentioned by him 'are responsible for our predicament'. They are, he says, only 'the servants of circumstances which they have helped to perpetuate (on occasion they may be observed giving another turn to the screw), but which they did not create'. Nor is Oakeshott concerned in this connection with what he calls 'genuinely philosophical writing about politics'. For in so far as this writing has 'either promoted or retarded the tendency to Rationalism in politics', 'it has always been through a misunderstanding of its design which is not to recommend conduct but to explain it'. Nor again, says Oakeshott, do we 'owe our predicament to the place which the natural sciences and the manner of thinking connected with them has come to take in our civilization'. For the scientists who think that 'the rationalist and the scientific points of view necessarily coincide' are simply 'mistaken'; 'the influence of the genuine natural scientist is not necessarily on the side Rationalism', etc., etc.

Arguing thus Oakeshott traces the evil of rationalist politics almost entirely to the recurrent appearance of 'political inexperience' in the history of western societies. One may, therefore, well ask: Who really is responsible for 'our predicament', then? Is it the old rulers and ruling classes who did not provide—in advance and well in time—for the proper political education of their successors by taking them up for 'apprenticeship' and 'continuous contact'? Or is it the new rulers and the new social classes who did not have sense enough to wait patiently for the old ones to relent, for once apprenticed and given 'the most favourable circumstances' it would have taken them no more than 'two or three generations' to acquire 'a knowledge of the political traditions' of their societies. Or is it, after all, history that defaulted, by not knowing how to happen, or by happening at all?

Oakeshott's critique of rationalism as 'the politics of the politically inexperienced' is not merely a conservative's protest against the extension of democracy in our times. It is more than anything else a protest, as indeed all conservatism ultimately is, against the general direction of social and political development of modern society. It is a complaint against history itself in which the new group ('politically in experienced' in Oakeshott's sense)—a new class, people, nation, or continent—emerges from time to time to play the leading role in the advancement of human civilisation as a whole, even as the old dominant group, generally speaking, fails increasingly to do so precisely because it has become too burdened with its outmoded 'experience', 'too deeply imbued with the traditions, interests and ideologies of the earlier period to be able to adapt itself to the demands and conditions of the next period .'[3]

It is this inexorable movement forward of history, of life itself, that the conservative fears and would like, if he can, to call a halt to. And in the hopelessness of this desire lies, too, the secret of the pessimism and despair that generally characterise conservative philosophy, including that of Oakeshott.

II

Rationalism, which Oakeshott attacks, is not a position held widely or seriously in the social sciences or political theory today, though something like it may have existed, and immodest claims in the name of reason were in fact made, during the high tide of rationalism in the 17th, 18th and 19th centuries. Oakeshott's criticism is nevertheless valid to the extent that such views are still prevalent and the 'rationalist disposition' still obtains, particularly in the more common modes of thought and action.

Oakeshott's criticism is generally valid against a narrow and dogmatic rationalism which seeks to confine all reality into abstract ideas and categories, to discover truth by pure deduction from a *priori* principles, and to find easy and ready made solutions to complex problems of life out of first principles-believed to be derived from 'pure, reason. Welcome, too, is Oakeshott's warning against an idealism, liberal or any other, of abstract and absolute principles to be applied or adhered to regardless of conditions and consequences, and against all varieties of utopianism. Oakeshott's critique is doubly welcome if we remember that 'illusions' of 'real essences; or 'absolute standards,' or 'geometrical method', as Weldon calls them,[4] have not been uncommon in social and political theory and that its language has been far too often permeated with empty moral rhetoric, even though Oakeshott meets one error by a worse error.

Oakeshott is also right in emphasising the importance of 'practical knowledge', of 'know how', of 'skill' and 'craftsmanship' in any field of human activity, and of 'the priceless treasure of great professional traditions'. And even more legitimate is Oakeshott's insistence that 'the right conduct of policy' demands 'a patient knowledge of the material', of 'the nature and 'circumstances' of a society, that it demands 'a profound knowledge of the character of the society' and 'a clear perception of its present condition', 'a genuine and concrete knowledge' indeed of its 'permanent interests and direction of movement'—even though, once again, Oakeshott's own view and account of this or any other knowledge is, to say the least, most unsatisfactory.

One may endorse, too, without much hesitation, Oakeshott's criticism of the superficial, narrowly utilitarian and eclectic approach of the average practising politician, who with scant knowledge of what was, is, or can be, meddles with everything and somehow hopes to muddle through. And I am inclined to sympathise also with his criticism of the narrow vision and petty specialisation of the average practising political scientist, who, incapable of a total, all sided response, projects his own pettiness into the life outside, remaining ignorant, like the average politician, of the intangibles which have grown up with the evolution of his society and civilisation, and who with a philistine self-confidence and conceit of certainty is ever helping to fasten a narrow 'vocationalism' on university education.[5]

There is another aspect to Oakeshott's protest which I would like to emphasise, precisely because the lable 'conservative' is likely to obscure it. He gives typical expression to contemporary disillusionment engendered by bourgeois existence even while he is defending it. He speaks of 'a want only productivist society', madly 'in love with change' and having 'an appetite only for innovation'; 'the unhappy society' that in action 'shies and plunges like a distracted animal'. He speaks of its 'lust for change', its 'fascination of what is new' and 'the yet untried'. He finds its men 'acquisitive to the point of greed', its 'pieties fleeting' and 'loyalties evanescent'. Here 'one activity vies with another in being up-to-date' and 'discarded motor cars and television sets have their counterparts in discarded moral and religious beliefs: the eye is ever on the new model'. 'In a world dizzy with moral ideals', Oakeshott complains, 'we know less about how to behave in public and in private than ever before'. And in vain do 'we exaggerate the significance of our moral ideals to fill in the hollowness of our moral life.[6] There is 'a chaos of conflicting ideals' which, according to Oakeshott, 'breeds nothing but distraction and moral instability', besides imposing a 'distracting intellectual burden'[7] And 'Rationalism' apart, there is the 'cruder and more vulgar' reason of the market place (*'Your mind and how to use it, a plan by world famous experts for developing a trained mind at a fraction of the usual cost Technique of Success, Pelmanism'*) which belittles intelligence, and puts 'all minds on the same level', 'small wits, on a level with men of genuine education', and so on.

All this is not merely the reaction of a conservative against democracy and change or the ineffectual protest of a bourgeois aesthete. It goes beyond to become part of a more profound protest made by men as diverse as Marx and Nietzche—as also Carlyle, Ruskin, William Morris and others—against modern industrial capitalism with its standardisation and mechanisation, its levelling the excellent down to the average and mediocre, its superficiality and indifference to the deeper values of life, its accentuation of quantity and exchange value as against quality and real worth, and above all, its depersonalisation and dehumanisation of man. Oakeshott shares to an extent in this protest without sharing, however, in Marx's brilliant explanation that what is being protested against springs from the very nature of modern capitalist society. With Marx, further, the explanation not only becomes a demand for changing this society, it also shows the way in which that change can be brought about. Oakeshott, on the other hand, prefers to adapt himself to this society. He accepts this society and its evils as necessary with the help of a different explanation. And yet he wants a bourgeois society without the superstructure that inevitably rises on its foundations, a market-based economy without the market based morality and culture that necessarily go with it. In short, the bourgeois conservative wants the impossible. Utopianism is not, after all, a monopoly of 'Rationalism'.

But if there is much in Oakeshott, as mentioned above, which is valid and acceptable, it is yet neither new nor enough to make his writing significant. So far as his basic theme—the critique of rationalism—is concerned, there is an entire tradition in modern western philosophy which has, in diverse manners and contexts, warned us against the pretentious philosophising of 'pure reason', and pointed out the limits, determined by possibility of experimental verification, of all valid reasoning about the world. We have, for instance, Bacon's caustic appraisal of scholasticism and its 'degenerate learning' which endowed one, in the words of Milton, only with 'a more expert ignorance'; or lode's warning against 'an opinionated self-confidence engendered by a supposed inner illumination'; or Kant's critique of a metaphysics which declining 'all teaching of experience' is left 'groping among mere concepts'.[8]

But with these thinkers, by and large, the recognition of the limits, difficulties, and contradictions of rational understanding was the point of departure for improving the methods of thinking, for fashioning human reason or intelligence into a more reliable and effective instrument for acquiring knowledge. They never doubted the reality of this knowledge nor the part that reason plays in its acquisition. Oakeshott doubts both. What is special and significant about Oakeshott is that the recognition mentioned above becomes with him the occasion and the excuse for abandoning reason itself. His is a systematic use of reason to undermine reason. He is not, of course, the only one in our times to do so. But barring the irrationalist proper, among the practitioners and teachers of political philosophy, Oakeshott has shown rare persistence in pursuing his attack on reason. He has, in fact, developed it, in the tradition of David Hume,[9] to the point of complete scepticism about the possibility of any real knowledge or rational understanding of reality, of any systematic social or political theory whatsoever.

Oakeshott's fight against rationalism is conducted from the philosophical standpoint of what is broadly known as 'empiricism or positivism', the trend dominant in one form or another in British philosophy from Locke to Russell. Trying to rescue the western man from the crippling dogma of rationalism, he has to hand, with the additional Oakeshottian frills and refinements of course, the positivist theory of knowledge, first developed in England in the eighteenth century. Incidentally, this century also saw the almost simultaneous development of the theory of laissez-faire capitalism (Adam Smith) and of a self-conscious political conservatism (Burke), which together constitute the whole of Oakeshott's positive social, economic and political thought.

I turn now to his argument against rationalism.

III

As Oakeshott understands it, 'a political ideology'—the ideas and ideals, the principles, theories and explanations that characterise rationalism or 'the ideological style of politics—'purports to be an abstract principle, or set of related abstract principles, which has been independently premeditated. It supplies in advance of the activity of attending to the arrangements of a society, a formulated end to be pursued'. He points out that 'the simplest sort of political ideology is a single abstract idea, such as Freedom, Equality, Maximum Productivity, Racial Purity, or Happiness'. And 'political activity is understood as the enterprise of seeing that the arrangements of a society conform to or reflect the chosen abstract idea'. It is usual; however, Oakeshott says, to recognise the need for a complex scheme of related ideas, the examples being 'such systems of ideas as: "the principles of 1789", "Liberalism", "Democracy", "Marxism", or the Atlantic Charter'. According to Oakeshott, 'these principles need not be considered absolute or immune from change (though they are frequently so considered), but their value lies in their having been premeditated. They compose an understanding of what is to be pursued indepenaent of *how* it is to be pursued'. A political ideology thus 'purports to supply in advance knowledge of what "Freedom" or "Democracy" or "Justice" is, and in this manner sets empiricism to work', and 'the condition upon which it can perform the service assigned to it is that it owes nothing to the activity it controls'.

Having thus defined the character as well as the function, or the functional pretentiousness as it turns out to be, of an ideology, Oakeshott points out the false 'supposition' and the logical 'error' underlying the ideological or rationalist position. He contends that the supposedly ideological or rationalist behaviour, in the political or any other field, including 'the so-called ideological *style* of politics', is 'an erroneous theory', indeed, in the ultimate analysis, 'a misdescription of human behaviour'.

Oakeshott argues that 'the systems of abstract ideas we call "ideologies" are abstracts of some kind of concrete activity', just as 'most political ideologies' are 'abstracts of the political traditions of some society'. A political ideology, he says, 'must be understood, not as an independently premeditated beginning for political activity, but as knowledge (abstract and generalised) of a concrete manner of attending to the arrangements of a society'. 'So far from being a preface', it has witness the political ideology embodied in the *Second Treatise* of Locke or in the Rights of Man during the French Revolution— 'all the marks of a postscript', just as all 'moral ideals', all so-called 'moral and political "principles"', are really 'a sediment'; not 'in the first place, the products of reflective thought', but 'of human behaviour, of human practical activity, to which reflective thought gives subsequent, partial and abstract expression in words'. An ideology thus 'merely abridges a concrete manner of behaviour'. It is, according to Oakeshott, only 'an abstract', 'a mere index', 'at most...an abbreviation', 'in fact, the dessicated relic' of 'some manner of activity or 'traditional behaviour'.

And Oakeshott repeatedly affirms that since this is the real character of an ideology, since an ideology is 'not something that can stand on its own feet', or 'exist is advance of political activity', but ice, instead, 'a mere abridgements of this activity and a 'postscript', since its 'principles are derived from the activity and not the activity from the principles', since, again, its 'rules and principles are mere abridgements of the activity itself (and) do not exist in advance of the activity', an ideology 'cannot properly be said to govern' this activity or 'to guide' it, 'cannot provide the impetus of the activity' or be its 'preface', and nor can it ever be 'given the task of generating human behaviour—a task, which, in fact, it cannot perform'.

In a passage that fully reveals the strength as also the weakness, as we shall see later, of his argument, Oakeshott writes:

> The contention we are investigating is that attending to the arrangements of a society can begin with a premeditated ideology, can begin with independently acquired knowledge of the ends to be pursued. It is supposed that a political ideology is the product of intellectual premeditation and that, because it is a body of principles not itself in debt to the activity of attending to the arrangements of a society, it is able to determine and guide the direction of that activity. If, however, we consider more closely the character of a political ideology, we find at once that this supposition is falsified. So far from a political ideology being the

> quasi-divine parent of political activity, it turns out to be its earthly step-child. Instead of an independently premeditated scheme of ends to be pursued, it is a system of ideas abstracted from the manner in which people have been accustomed to go about the business of attending to the arrangements of their societies. The pedigree of every political ideology shows it to be the creature, not of premeditation in advance of political activity, but of meditation upon a manner of politics. In short, political activity comes first and a political ideology follows after; and the understanding of politics we are investigating has the advantage of being, in the strict sense of preposterous.

Rationalism— 'the contention' that political activity 'can begin with a premeditated ideology'—is thus based on a logical mistake and 'the ideological *style* of politics' is, strictly speaking, a logical impossibility. We can never really proceed in politics from 'premeditated' general principles. All ideology, even the most radical and revolutionary, including, of course, that which Oakeshott persistently attacks, is, and cannot but be, 'an abridgement' of the traditional way of living and doing things in a society. In this sense, whether we know it or not, all of us—including the revolutionary, his mistaken belief notwithstanding are and cannot but be traditionalists. 'The ideological style of politics', Oakeshott insists, 'is a confused style. Properly speaking, it is a traditional manner of attending to the arrangements of a society which has been abridged into a doctrine', the abridgement 'being erroneously regarded as the sole guide relied upon'.

But can this 'confused style' really do harm by misguiding people? According to Oakeshott, it cannot: 'The practical danger of an erroneous theory is not that it may persuade people to act in an undesirable manner, but that it may confuse activity by putting it on a false scent'. Oakeshott concedes that there is 'perhaps, some advantage in thinking and speaking and arguing in a manner consonant with what we are really doing', but then he does 'not think (this) to be very important'. For him the most a theory can do is to 'confuse' or to 'clarify' activity. The question of its doing anything more is never allowed to become real. Oakeshott cannot concede the possibility of ideas misguiding activity, because that would immediately involve conceding the possibility of *other* ideas guiding it. An ideology cannot really misguide and therefore it cannot guide either. In the name of attacking 'Rationalism', Oakeshott attacks human thought itself and its power to influence human activity in any sense that matters.

And if there be persons, unfortunately not gifted with the capacity to overlook the obvious and, who, therefore, still choose to put their faith in reason, in the power of human thought, Oakeshott assures them that its victories are only 'apparent', its successes 'alleged' and its inevitability only 'supposed'; that its pursuit of proposed freedoms is 'fruitless', its remedies are 'pseudo-remedies' and the welfare it seeks is only 'welfare'; that the rationalist only 'appears' or 'seems' to be successful; and that the scientist who is a rationalist is 'mistaken', is a 'Rationalist in spite of his science, is, in fact, 'not the genuine scientist' at all! Everything, all evidence to the contrary, is thus explained, and neatly explained away, with facility of simple assertion and word-magic.

We have indeed come fast and far with Oakeshott's attack on rationalism. Cause of much evil, many predicaments, and most political failure, it was first found to be 'a simple error' and is finally discovered to be a logical mistake, something which is, in the strict sense, preposterous and impossible—at most a 'confusion' which, in the final analysis, is of no consequence at all. Oakeshott has sought to prove too much—and this leaves his attack on 'Rationalism, looking very much like quixotic tilting at a windmill! The suspicion lingers that there may be more to rationalism, after all, than Oakeshott is willing to concede, which yet makes it necessary for him to fight it with such desperate doggedness..

In fairness to Oakeshott it must be noted that now and then he does make a concession to 'Rationalism', to ideology. But the concession is never seriously meant and his argument proceeds as if it was never made. The ideology, we are told, is not 'the sole guide, not 'by itself a sufficient guide (therefore no guide at all), 'the written word' and 'the book' are not 'as themselves potent' (therefore they are impotent), 'the abridgement itself, never, in fact, provides the whole of the knowledge' (therefore provides no knowledge at all), moral ideals have 'their power as critics of human habits' (but the power to criticise can never be the power to suggest and to guide), ideologies 'unquestionably have their use' (but not in any sense that matters). We are even told that an ideology's 'power to guide' is 'derived from its roots in actual political experience', but there is no recognition that this concession shifts the entire argument to more solid ground where we must discuss the really important question of which, and when, ideologies guide, misguide or don't guide at all, of their being true or false, realistic or utopian, scientific or religious. The concessions by Oakeshott are merely apparent and intended, perhaps, to create an impression of being balanced or fair about the claims of reason, when such balance or fairness is really not there at all. There is no question in Oakeshott of ideas or ideologies being more or less true, more or less scientific, and therefore more or less able to guide. What he attacks is not ideas or ideologies of any particular sort, which claim to be more than what they really are. The target of his attack is any and every idea or theory which claims in any meaningful sense to be a guide to action, it is systematic thought itself. For, according to Oakeshott's reductionist *empiricism*; an idea or ideology can never be anything more than 'a mere abridgement', 'an abbreviation', 'an abstract', 'a sediment', 'a mere index' of some kind of concrete activity. Since no ideology can be of necessity 'independently premeditated', since all ideas and theories, illusory and false ones as much as the more true and scientific ones, must ultimately arise on a real basis—this necessary truth is sufficient reason for Oakeshott to deprive all ideas and theories equally of real significance. To confuse the origin of an idea with its truth or validity, to appeal to the way it arises in order to dispose of the question of its role or significance in the social and historical process, is an error common with certain non-Marxist forms of sociology of knowledge. Oakeshott offers us the positivist version of this error.

Let us examine his argument a little more closely.

IV

Oakeshott's argument against rationalism, in politics and elsewhere, centres upon the assertion that rationalism is ultimately based on a logical mistake, that it is, strictly speaking, something preposterous and impossible. His contention is that the knowledge which reason gives rise to—a theory or an ideology is not something 'independently premeditated', something that can 'stand on its own feet' or 'exist in advance of 'human practical activity'. On the contrary, it is really 'dependent' upon and 'follows after' this activity. It is, and cannot but be; 'an abridgement', or 'an abbreviation', or 'an abstract' of 'a concrete manner' of activity, and therefore, essentially incapable of 'generating' or 'governing' or 'guiding this activity—in the political or any other field.

Unfortunately, Oakeshott nowhere carefully considers the nature of what he calls 'an abridgement'. He is usually content to use the term to slight rationalism in general and all systematic theoretical knowledge in particular. But, in doing so, he has repeated recourse to an analogy, the exploration of which may help us understand better not only his concept of 'abridgement', but also the view he takes of science and scientific knowledge in genèral. He likens 'an abridgement' to 'an hypothesis' in natural science. He speaks of 'a scientific hypothesis' which plays 'a role in scientific activity in some respects similar to that of an ideology in politics'. He informs us that 'we may abridge our political experience into a doctrine which may be used, as a scientist uses hypothesis, to explore its intimations'.

This analogy or comparison appears, on the face of it, to be quite valid. But—and here is the rub—it is intended, and Oakeshott makes it abundantly clear, not to confer upon 'an ideology' or 'a doctrine the status and dignity of being scientific, but to drain the scientific hypothesis itself of any objectively valid knowledge or truth which may be claimed for it. Oakeshott is nothing if not thorough. He would deny natural science itself any valid knowledge in order to make short work of the claim of social science to it. He informs us that a scientific hypothesis is not 'a self-generated bright idea which owed nothing to scientific activity', that 'an hypothesis is not an independent invention capable of guiding scientific inquiry, but a dependent supposition which arises as an abstraction from within already existing scientific activity'. In other words, for Oakeshott, a scientific hypothesis too is 'a mere abridgement' and nothing more.

Now what Oakeshott says is, in one sense, quite true. A scientific hypothesis is indeed not 'a self-generated bright idea' or 'an independent invention'; and it is most certainly something 'dependent'. But this is only half the truth. And Oakeshott persistently obscures the other, the more important half, that a scientific hypothesis may nevertheless—as a matter of fact precisely because of this 'dependence'—embody genuine knowledge or truth. To take half a truth for a whole truth is a mistake almost as bad as taking a lie for the truth—and this seems to be the mistake of Oakeshott. As a consequence his view turns out to be a serious misrepresentation of a scientific hypothesis, as also of much else in modern science.

Hypothesis is today an integral part of the scientific method, which is a combination of empirical observation, formulation of hypothesis and the verification (as also diversification) of this hypothesis through further observation and experiment and finally in practical application. It is thus that the false hypotheses are weeded out from the true, the true hypotheses modified, revised and extended, and human knowledge advances.

It is clear, therefore, that a scientific hypothesis is indeed 'dependent' upon, is the 'product' of, scientific activity. But it is also clear that it is not 'a mere abridgement' of this activity and its attendant 'experience', merely 'an abbreviation' or 'an abstract', a summary, a feat only of 'abstract and generalised' *description*, as Oakeshott makes it out to be. As a general idea or a theory it is even more an *explanation* that goes beyond the empirical, the evidential and the experienced, to understand and explain it. It goes behind the facts to the system of truth which explains them. And to the extent this explanation is verified, it is probable and true, arid may be regarded as valid knowledge. There is no doubt that this knowledge is relative, its validity conditional. But the essential point is that this knowledge, this hypothesis, is not merely the abridged description of some manner of activity or experience, as Oakeshott contends, but an explanatory theory that takes us — and does so precisely because it is based on concrete practical activity—beyond this experience, through the experienced fact, to the objective reality which is the system of nature, even if it is only partly seep,

It is important to note that in scientific activity, through the formulation of hypotheses, we explore not merely 'our experience', nor 'a rational world of related concepts', nor again 'a timeless world of hypothetical situations', as Oakeshott suggests from time to time, but a world of objective reality. And the outcome of this activity is genuinely valid knowledge about this world. This knowledge is not something 'certain and complete', something 'perfect' or 'final'. It is necessarily partial and incomplete, and always open to revision. But it is nevertheless valid knowledge. It reveals, however partially, genuine aspects of an objectively existing world, and its truth, therefore, though relative is none the less objective truth. The continuous revision and even replacement of particular constituents of this knowledge does not mean moving from one form of ignorance to another. It only means that we now know more and better, that the frontiers of man's knowledge have been further extended, that a more comprehensive and deeper penetration of objective reality has been achieved, and that man has moved another step closer to the objective absolute truth, which is the system of nature, itself[10]—even though 'an adequate, exhaustive scientific statement' of this system, 'the formulation in thought of an exact picture of the world system in which we live, is impossible for us, and will always remain impossible'.[11] This revision, therefore, far from casting doubt on the validity of science rather enhances it. Marking as it does an advance in our knowledge, it only strengthens our faith in the scientific method as the only means we have—'the most assured technique man has yet devised'[12]—for acquiring valid knowledge; about the world.[13]

It may be further pointed out that the knowledge which science gives us—the verified hypothesis or explanatory theory, the combined construction of sense and intellect called 'a scientific law'—can and does in fact become a guide to human activity, a means indeed of governing, controlling and changing the objective reality that is our world.[14] It has this power or potentiality to give guidance and control not because, as Oakeshott alleges, it claims to be 'a self-generated bright idea' or 'an independent invention' which 'owed nothing to scientific activity', but for the exactly opposite reason. A scientific hypothesis can guide activity, can help govern or control reality, precisely because it is 'dependent' upon this activity and realit —not for its 'supposition' or 'abstraction' but for its verification, and its truth. 'The test of scientific explanation has in the last place always been empirical: does it match the facts?'[15] Only to the extent an hypothesis or a theory does this, is it true. And only to the extent that it is true, that is, a more or less correct reflection of an objective reality, does it come to possess the potentiality of being an effective instrument of governing, controlling or changing this reality. Theories independent of objective reality and owing nothing to human practice will be altogether helpless and without power to either guide this practice or affect this reality. In other words, reason's claim to guide, control or change the world rests not upon its 'independence' of the world or of human practice, but upon its 'dependence' on both of these. It rests upon man's ability to acquire valid knowledge about this world. This is the vital truth which Bacon emphasised when he wrote (in *Novum Organum*) that 'we cannot command nature except by obeying her' and which, later, Marxism embodied in Engels' classic formulation: 'Freedom is the recognition of necessity'.[16] This is precisely how scientific knowledge guides us; helps us to control and command, to win and enlarge our freedom. Only this understanding of science gives meaning to the saying 'knowledge is power', or 'truth shall make us free.[17]

Apropos Oakeshott's argument against rationalism, it is necessary to emphasise that the role of reason in scientific activity—in the formulation of hypotheses and the acquisition of scientific knowledge—is crucial. In fact, the pursuit of 'the goal of science—the achievement of a systematic interconnection of phenomena[18] would be impossible without the help of active reason. The truth depends on facts but it is discovered by our reason, by the creative and ordering activities of our mind. It is reason which takes us behind appearances—'Against appearances in which all agree, we make headway with reason' (Galileo)—and makes possible the knowledge of universal connections and relations between things, phenomena, and processes of nature. It is clear, therefore, that the scientific procedure involves a most energetic and dynamic kind of thinking— 'high grade or scientific thinking' Collingwood called it.[19] It is thus that the constructive reason of man not only analyses and clarifies thought, or refutes error, or abridges and explores human experience, but also goes on to discover scientific laws and explanations, to discover the truth about an objectively real world.

But reason does this not by virtue of some intrinsic power of its own. It discovers truth only when it works in inseparable combination with practical activity, with directed practice, only when it comes into a dynamic and creative relationship with practical knowledge. This unity of theory and practice is of fundamental importance in all search for valid knowledge. It is the very essence of the scientific procedure.[20] And it is through this procedure that human knowledge, in general, continuously advances—and advances in particular beyond the purely practical stage, beyond practical knowledge—to achieve an ever more systematic 'interconnection of phenomena'.[21] The importance of practical knowledge at every stage of this advance is unquestionable, but equally unquestionable is the fact that to emphasise it in such a manner as to oppose it to, and in the process depreciate, theoretical knowledge, as Oakeshott does, is to seek to freeze human knowledge at the lower practical level of development and thereby prevent its further growth, in particular the growth of higher, scientific knowledge.

Human knowledge and its advancement, thus, depends upon reason, not unaided reason, but reason working in conjunction with sense experience and with practice. In other words, it depends upon the use of the scientific method. Barrows Dunham writes:

> Scientific method is an organized, systematic procedure involving sensation, logic, and practice. It seems plain that we must have all three, and that theories of knowledge have very often suffered from fastening exclusively upon one of the parts. Mere rationalists cannot tell whether their deductions correspond with fact. Mere pragmatists can't know what it is their practice confirms...[22]

It is wrong, therefore, to divorce reason from experience and practice and conceive it to be absolute and all-powerful as rationalism once did, and still does in its idealist forms. It is equally wrong to convert experience or practice into an absolute and to disparage reason and the part it plays in the acquisition of knowledge, as empiricism, or pragmatism, has done in our times, and as Oakeshott does in his critique of rationalism. Both the approaches are false because they are one-sided. Science in its search for knowledge today seeks, and knows how to achieve, a dialectical synthesis of rationalism and empiricism. In this lies the secret of its validity and power. As Bronowski says: The mastery and the greatness of sccience rest in the end on this, that here the rational and the empirical are knotted together. Science is fact and thought giving strength to one another.'[23]

It is clear that Oakeshott's understanding of science—natural or social is quite different. But it is also clear that with his persistent depreciation of 'the rational,' or 'the theoretical', he can only misunderstand and misinterpret science.

V

Misunderstand and misinterpret science is indeed what Oakeshott does. The few references to his view in the discussion above are enough evidence of that and there is more of it in his various essays. His generally very extreme empiricist view, with its exclusive emphasis on what he calls 'practical knowledge', its dismissal of all theory, including the scientific, as 'mere abridgement', its rigid separation of the world of fact and 'practice' from the world of reason and 'science' together with its arbitrary transitions between these two worlds, not only obscures, but at times positively misrepresents, the nature of modern science. His account of scientific activity, hypothesis and knowledge, and of much else besides, is, to say the least, highly misleading.

Oakeshott speaks of dualism of technique and practice'. Making the distinction between technical knowledge and practical knowledge, he informs us that though the two cannot be considered either 'identical with one another or able to take the place of one another', both 'are always involved in any actual activity', and 'in fact they do not exist separately'. From this, in order to emphasise the paramount importance of 'practical knowledge', he repeatedly argues that 'the knowledge involved in every concrete activity is never solely technical knowledge'. One wonders who today seriously maintains that it is so. Besides, can it be 'solely practical knowledge' either? Is it possible to conceive of a *human* mind which is altogether devoid of theory or ideology, of ideas and principles? If the answer is in the negative, as it must be even according to Oakeshott's own argument, then he is only indulging in tautology and this by itself proves nothing about 'practical knowledge' being the knowledge that matters. And yet, this tautological labouring of the obvious is precisely what Oakeshott is doing much of the time. For the rest his argument is that technical, that is, theoretical knowledge, can never be anything more than 'mere abridgement'. And this, as explained above, is a rather poor and fundamentally incorrect description of scientific theoretical knowledge.

The real difficulty with Oakeshott's argument in fact is that his distinction between technical and practical knowledge is valid only within very narrow limits and then too only for certain minor purposes. Outside of these limits and with regard to the really important issues concerning human knowledge, it is of no help or use at all. This is particularly so because of his own exceedingly arbitrary use of this distinction. Oakeshott concedes that these two 'sorts' of knowledge are really inseparable, that both always enter together into all human activity, that both together constitute human knowledge. But having done that he quietly side-steps the real issues involved—for example, of their interrelation, interaction and reciprocity, of how each enters into and completes the other, of the limits of their validity, or of their truth in the whole that is human knowledge, etc. He simply proceeds to convert his distinction into a rigid dichotomy, to mechanically oppose one 'sort' of knowledge to the other, to depreciate 'technical knowledge', and to conclude arbitrarily that 'practical knowledge', as defined by him, is the only 'sort' that really matters, that it is virtually 'self-complete' in a sense in which, according to him, 'technical knowledge' can never hope to be.

Oakeshott informs us that 'technical knowledge' can be 'never more than the meanest part' of knowledge involved in any activity, and his argument, utterly empiricist in its assumptions, proceeds as if it were not even that. He persistently disparages the knowledge that can be theoretically formulated —'the written word' or 'the book' he sneeringly calls it. Far from being 'real knowledge,' it is only 'a shadow' of it, says Oakeshott. This would seem to make short work of the entire *corpus* of scientific knowledge, the growing body of verified and accepted theory, which has been painfully acquired through the centuries, particularly during the last 300 years, and deposited in the sciences. According to Oakeshott it is evidently of no significance or value at all.[24] Oakeshott's view also implies the refusal to recognise the real significance of the open, explicit and public character of scientific knowledge, ruling out thereby not only science as 'the activity of learning by a whole society',[25] but also that discussion and controversy among the scientists—a discussion and controversy which is utterly ruthless in its pursuit of *truth*—without which it will soon cease to be science at all.

Oakeshott seems to hold that an hypothesis as 'an abridgement' of 'our experience' explores only this experience and 'its intimations'. This view completely obscures the fact that what a scientific hypothesis explores is an objective, independently existing reality, that 'science is a language for talking not about experience but about the world'.[26] Even this 'experience', however, Oakeshott soon finds a trifle too contaminating and he proceeds to define science as a purely rational and logical activity—the transition being facilitated, perhaps, in some devious manner, by the empiricist's rigid separation of the realms of fact and reason, familiar to us since David Hume. He now informs us that 'the scientific activity' proper— 'scientific investigation' as he also calls it—is 'constructing and exploring a rational world of related concepts'. The scientist seeks only 'to make a rational world of consequentially arranged conceptual images', and these 'images are not those of the world of practice' at all. The scientist in fact deals exclusively with 'a timeless world, a world, not of actual events, but of hypothetical situations.[27] Thus the real world itself—that indispensable premise of all scientific activity—is banished from science, and with it goes not only the scientific method as the way in which we tell the true 'concepts' or 'images' from the false ones, but ultimately the very possibility of science seeking, acquiring and communicating valid knowledge about an objectively real world. No wonder, therefore, that Oakeshott rejects the belief that science advances through hard work and continuous wrestling with the seemingly intractable problems that this real world presents to man. Instead, he commends the view that 'the root conditions of success in scientific research are, first, "to have brains and good luck", and secondly, "to sit tight and wait till you get a bright idea"!

In view of the above it is not surprising that Oakeshott dismisses most contemptuously the attitude which values not 'the scientific engagement' itself, but its products—'the discoveries about the world'—and values these too 'only for what can be contrived from them'. Science, properly speaking, has nothing to do with being useful to man in pursuit of his purposes. With Oakeshott it is to be 'cultivated for its own sake unhindered by the intrusion of desire for power and prosperity'. It begins and ends as a search for 'intellectual satisfaction'. Thus does Oakeshott finally deny what C.B. Macpherson has called the one article of faith on which all science rests: that increasing rational understanding of man and nature can give man increasing control over himself and his societies, and that this is good.[28]

It is not difficult to recognise that 'the scientific engagement, or 'the activity of being a scientist', which emerges from

Oakeshott's essays, divorced as it is from the real world and from all usefulness.to man, is little better than an exercise in sterile speculation. It may well be a gentlemanly pursuit, a pleasant pastime for the leisured intellectual, a refined method, indeed, of filling in one's empty hours, when one is not busy chasing the rationalist Aunt Sallies down the sceptical alleys of contemporary philosophy, or persuading the incredulous conservatives of the logical inevitability of their class rule—but who would call it science?[29]

VI

Oakeshott's interpretation, or misinterpretation, of science apart, the roots of error in his theory of knowledge—which exalts practical knowledge and disparages all theoretical knowledge as 'mere abridgement'— lie, as suggested earlier, in his extreme empiricist or positivist philosophy. As a theory of knowledge empiricism limits itself to facts, to the experienced phenomena, to practical activity, without looking for general laws or explanatory theories. Originally, as with Locke for example, empiricism was useful as a critique of all transcendental, metaphysical speculation and of traditional prejudices and superstitions; just as, earlier, rationalism itself was justified by its criticism of the obscurantist theological philosophising characteristic of the feudal period. In the eighteenth century, empiricism emerged as the typical philosophy or theory of knowledge of what has been called the period of 'the adolescence of modern science'. Its insistance now on fact, observation and experiment, even though one-sided, was most valid, for all science begins here—and from this dependence of all knowledge on sense experience or empirical data we can never turn back. Even its reaction against theory had a historical justification. For, in the then generally undeveloped state of empirical knowledge, a more comprehensive and systematic picture of the world—a picture of the universal interconnections and relations of phenomena—was sought to be produced, much too easily, from 'philosophy' alone, from the realm of pure reason rather than of known fact. The world was sought to be explained, as it were, by something outside of it, by pure thought; and empiricism rightly rejected this. In our own time, again, empiricism has made a positive contribution to the debunking of philosophical obscurantism, of 'truths' outside of experince, of 'knowledge through faith and mystic intuition, of anti-scientific thinking in general, besides helping in the elimination of meaningless terms and unreal problems from philosophy. But as a theory of knowledge, empiricism or positivism has failed to outgrow the limitations of the earlier period, when science in fact has long outgrown them.

Modern science works entirely with theories, with explanatory hypotheses, with conceptual schemes, rational systems and laws, which lie behind the data or empirical evidence they seek to explain.[30] And 'the truth of science is not truth to fact ...but the truth of the laws which we see within the facts.'[31] Science today is a vast and very complex body of highly general and closely interconnected theory both descriptive and explanatory. But and this is important this theory does not stand above and outside the world it seeks to describe and explain. As the truth of this world, it is 'in' the world, and the world is it. [32] The scientific theories are, as Conant says, 'explanations of the universe. What science discovers, the inferred and the invisible fact behind the visible fact, the explanatory theory, the law or the universal-which science will soon go on to explain by means of still 'wider laws or theories' or universals, achieving thereby a still deeper penetration, and therefore a still better knowledge of the world— 'transcends sense experience but is none the less part of the physical world-order and determines what happens at the level of sense experience; hence the possibility of verification by prediction and experiment.[33] In other words, modern science has increasingly realised the possibility of 'explaining the world by itself (Engels). And empiricism, with its continued indifference to or depreciation of theory, has become strictly unscientific.[34]

Empiricism rightly rejects a priori and speculative theory— the 'explanations' and 'truths' of pure reason or philosophy. But it often proceeds to reject along with it all theory, all explanations and truths, including the scientific. It proceeds, as it were, to throw out the baby with the bath water and, by one route or another, comes to abandon the very attempt to formulate a *systematic general picture* of the world in which we live.[35] Empiricism rightly rejects the total explanation, the final truth, the absolute and perfect knowledge of the idealist rationalist philosophy. For speculation beyond the range of empirical verification—which range is of necessity limited—being invalid, such explanation, truth or knowledge is simply impossible, and the acquisition of knowledge is in fact a never ending process. But empiricism often seems to take over, tacitly' rather than explicitly, from the same idealist-rationalist philosophy the assumption that there is no knowledge that matters other than this absolute and perfect knowledge, that knowledge, if it is not complete or final, is entirely relative and therefore no knowledge at all. Empiricism thus comes to acquire, and occasionally even flaunt, an easy unscientific scepticism, and thereby proceeds to reject the knowledge we *do* have, which knowledge though partial and relative is none the less genuine, objective knowledge and from the standpoint of life, of human practice, of the greatest importance. It uses, so to speak, the inaccessibility of absolute truth as an excuse for abandoning *all* truth and the search for truth itself. With this all-or-nothing attitude, empiricist scepticism turns out to be only a more orthodox and erudite name for what is in fact 'a theory of no-knowledge'[36] And Oakeshott fully shares this scepticism and its consequences.[37] That is how in rejecting 'Rationalism' he comes to reject scientific theory itself; in giving up 'certain and complete knowledge' he is left with virtually no knowledge and complete uncertainty. For him there is no truth any longer. One *knows* and *discovers* nothing. One may, if one must, only 'abridge' or 'abbreviate' or 'abstract'.[38]

Scepticism, empiricist or any other, need not always, and in everything, imply an attitude of all-or-nothing. But this is the attitude that seems to pervade the entire thinking of Oakeshott. An ideology is not 'independently premeditated'; therefore, it is completely 'dependent' and 'a mere abridgement'. A 'postscript', it can never be a 'preface'. If it cannot 'stand on its own feet', it cannot stand at all. The rationalist's 'superhuman wisdom' is an illusion; therefore, he has no wisdom whatsoever.

The 'blank sheet of infinite possibility' being impossible, there is hardly any possibility worth pursuing. And, if in politics there is no 'fixed', 'preordained and inevitable end', it is pronounced a completely 'open-ended activity'—so 'open ended' as to have no ends at all. So the argument of Oakeshott goes on, endlessly.

Thus alone can we understand and explain the nihilism implicit in Oakeshott's vision of the human situation—a nihilism which provides at best only a most shaky foundation for the policy of conservatism in life and politics which he advocates. Evoking an image which is central to his social and political philosophy, Oakeshott writes:

In political activity, then, men sail a boundless and bottomless sea; there is neither harbour for shelter, nor floor for anchorage, neither starting place nor appointed destination. The enterprise is to keep afloat on an even keel....

There is no *appointed* destination; therefore, there is none at all. We are not going *somewhere*, therefore, we are going nowhere. Nor are we, for the same reason, coming from anywhere either. Oakeshott is fond of speaking of 'partnership' between the past, the present, and the future. But really there is no past for him, nor any future; there is only the floating present. And it makes no difference if we go forward or backward, navigate or drift—so long as we 'keep afloat on an even keel'!

VII

If the validity of Oakeshott's empiricist interpretation of 'hypothesis' in natural science is questionable, the same is true of his concept of 'abridgement' in social science—the concept he relies upon to deny, genuine knowledge to social or political theory, permitting it; at most, an utterly ineffectual 'half-knowledge'. I shall have more to say about his argument in this connection in the next section. Here what I want to reject most emphatically is his view that the choice for us is between some 'perfect' or 'final' knowledge—which is patently impossible of achievement—and 'mere abridgements', a choice which in effect leaves us with only what he calls 'practical knowledge'—which knowledge, in the very nature of things, no man ever is, or can be, without. For, as Oakeshott says, 'even the most needy society and the most cramped surroundings' have some practical or political knowledge to offer, 'and we take what we can get'. I have no intention to denigrate practical knowledge as such. I have, in fact, already acknowledged its importance, not only in itself but also in the emergence and advancement of higher scientific knowledge. But what we do in fact 'take' or 'get', the level of a particular 'practical knowledge', and Oakeshott's attempt to freeze all human knowledge at this 'practical' level, is quite another matter. Oakeshott's theory of knowledge, in effect, assimilates all knowledge, and therefore social science itself, for ever into what Ernest Gellner has called 'the artisanate of cognition.'[39] I submit that Oakeshott's view, on the whole, is a highly erroneous view. Against this view, I would like to insist upon the validity of the scientific method, and the knowledge it gives, in the field of social science also. There are not two kinds of thinking, one for natural science and the other for social, science. The scientific method—the method of observation, hypothesis, and verification—is, in fact, the only means we have, whatever the field, of acquiring valid knowledge. The use of this method, therefore, is necessary in social science also if we want to find out truth. And it is possible to use it though the difficulties involved in doing this should not be underestimated. Man and his society, perpetually in transition, are exceedingly complex natural and social phenomena. The difficulties of scientific study here, of formulating and verifying hypotheses, are very great, and different in kind from those we encounter in natural science. The scientific method has to be modified and adapted to its special subject and the conclusions will never be as precise as, for example, in physics or chemistry. But the aims, methods and outcome of the rational scientific procedure remain fundamentally the same in natural and social sciences. And Apropos Oakeshott's view, it is this basic point that I am interested in making here.[40]

In other words, in social science too, it is possible to acquire scientific theory, that is valid knowledge, as a product of the scientific method. This theory will not, and need not, be only a collection of 'mere abridgements', as Oakeshott insists. It will, and it can, embody genuine knowledge about our social and political world. Of course, this knowledge will not be—it need not be— 'a steady, unchanging, independent guide', a 'certain and complete' knowledge that offers 'a perfect solution' to every human problem. But it is foolish to demand everything and then, not being able to have it, despair of having anything at all.[41] The scientific approximation which is *truth*— the truth that is ours—is better than mere pragmatic intuitionism or unscientific guess work. Knowledge, because it is imperfect, is not, therefore, illusory; partial truth is yet real and dependable truth and of the greatest practical importance. In medicine, for example—and elsewhere too—we are willing to stake our lives on theories which fall far short of finality.[42]

And despite the inevitable rationalisations and distortions involved, we *do* have today a substantial body of valid social and political theory. Not 'superhuman wisdom', it is yet wisdom enough to live by. Not 'an infallible guide', it is yet guide enough. Not 'knowing anything about a final destination', it can yet help us know and attain the next destination, take the next step forward in human progress. We do possess knowledge, in other words, which can help us do more than merely keep afloat. It can teach us the art of navigation towards goals we ourselves define and continuously redefine in the very process of attaining them.[43] What is lacking—a little too conspicuously at times, it seems to me—is the courage to navigate.

It is true, no doubt, that a rationalism which acts on the basis not of what can be validly established, but of what it wants to be true, will lose sense of reality and, by persuading men to overreach themselves, will lead only to a breakdown of practice, and to defeat and disappointment. But it is equally true that an empiricism which depreciates theory and disavows ideas and ideals, will lose perspective and, by persuading men to underreach themselves, will lead equally inevitably to a breakdown of practice, to a passive acceptance of the world and its evils as they are. And it is to underreach themselves, it is well to remember, that men have been traditionally trained and conditioned in all class-divided societies. Whether Oakeshott consciously intends it or not—perhaps he does—his theory of knowledge certainly serves to perpetuate this situation.

In fact his theory does more. The lack, and sometimes even the loss, of *significance* in modern social science has been the subject of much recent comment. Reinhard Bendix, for example, attributes it to the need of obtaining 'methodological rigor',[44] and Catlin has emphasised 'that undue concentration on Methodology may prove merely sterile.[45] This is true, but only partly so. The more important causes most certainly lie elsewhere, much deeper in the social matrix itself. But even at the methodological level, a better explanation would be, perhaps, the excessive empiricistic bias of this social science, its 'barefoot empiricism' as Glaser has called[46] And what marks out Oakeshott's approach as something special is that, pushing his empiricism to the sceptical extreme, he comes to deny the very possibility of significance in social science and rules out thereby any sort of 'reaching' by men whatsoever. They can do nothing but float. And the 'practical knowledge' they have is all that they can hope to have, or, perhaps, even need to have, to keep floating—on an even keel, of course.[47]

VIII

Oakeshott's argument that theoretical knowledge is and can only be 'an abridgement' has a certain plausibility about it for the simple reason that it contains important elements of truth. He is certainly right in insisting that an ideology—with its ideas, ideals and principles, its concepts, propositions and theories—is not, in the final analysis, 'the product of intellectual premeditation', or of reflective thought' alone; it is not 'independently premeditated' and cannot 'stand on its own feet'. It is, on the contrary, something which is, in a very real sense, 'dependent' upon, or 'derived from', or 'the product of concrete activity and practice. In other words, Oakeshott rightly points to an independent basis for man's ideological activity, though it is necessary to point out that he describes this basis in a typically empiricist manner, in terms only of 'practical human activity', 'our political experience', 'a concrete manner of behaviour', etc. He consistently refuses to move from this 'activity' or 'experience' or 'behaviour' to the real world—natural, social and political—which conditions and determines all these and which is the ultimate, only really independent basis of all ideological activity of man. This refusal to take meaningful note of the objectively real world is common in empiricist philosophy. It is, in fact, central to its theory of knowledge, wherein we can only 'abridge' our experience, or a manner of activity or behaviour, but do not and cannot *know* any objective reality. This has already been briefly discussed above and there is no need for me to say anything more on it here. For the purpose of the present argument I shall readily agree with Oakeshott when he points out the secondary and derivative character of man's ideas and ideals, when he insists that these have a basis outside of them and that it is the activity of men that determines their thought and consciousness. As a broad generalisation about the dominant lines of social and ideological causation this is quite valid. But what makes one wonder is that Oakeshott should have considered this elementary and necessary truth deserving of so much laboured emphasis at this late date, after the universally recognised work of Karl Marx[48] and with decades of work on the sociology of knowledge behind us.

It may also be readily conceded that many of man's mental products or constructions are indeed no more than 'mere abridgements' or 'abbreviations', as Oakeshott designates them. But the real issue is whether this is a true or an adequate description of *all* ideas and theories, more especially those relating to man's acquisition of valid scientific knowledge of an objectively existing reality—be that nature, society or man himself? I have already argued above that it is not. But beyond these objections is the important question which now demands consideration: do we in pointing out the dependent and derivative character of an idea or a theory exhaust all its meaning, significance or truth?

Oakeshott evidently thinks we do. He holds not only that *all* ideology is 'mere abridgement', but also that its dependent and derivative character is enough to deprive it of all meaning, significance and power.

According to Oakeshott the rationalist believes that because 'a political ideology is the product of intellectual premeditation and that, because it is a body of principles not itself in debt to the activity of attending to the arrangements of a society, it is able to determine and guide the direction of that activity'; the rationalist supposedly believes that 'the condition upon which (an ideology) can perform the service assigned to it is that it owes nothing to the activity it controls.' And against this belief Oakeshott's own argument—he seems to regard it as unanswerable and final—is that because an ideology or theory is something which is 'derived from', or 'in debt to', or 'the product of, or 'dependent' upon human practical activity, it has no power to help 'govern' or 'guide it. Oakeshott's logic here leaves one somewhat amused. The genuine rationalist—not the Oakeshottian caricature—would rather argue that this 'dependence' upon or 'indebtedness' to activity, this basis in reality of an idea or a theory, is precisely what gives it its effectiveness, its power to govern and guide—in so far as it is not an 'abridgement' but a *true* idea or theory. And to the extent an idea or a theory is 'independently premeditated', is 'the product of reflective thought' alone, 'owes nothing to the activity it controls,' stands, as it were, 'on its own feet', that is, lacks truth, lacks correspondence to objective fact— utopian we sometimes call it—it is ineffective and powerless, and if relied upon as a guide will lead only to failure and frustration.

For the modern rationalist, then—Oakeshott's allegations not withstanding it is not human thought as such, 'independent' or 'premeditated', derived, as it were, from pure reason, that rules the world, but only the thought *about* the world, derived from active tackling of this world and reflecting the real causal relations of this world. In fact, the more an idea is 'dependent' upon and determined by facts and practical activity, that is, determined by what it is about, the more true and therefore the more effective it will be—and greater the freedom it will bring to man for it will have brought him valid knowledge.

'An ideology, then, is dependent upon facts and upon practical activity for its truth, for whatever truth it happens to have, and in the truth of an ideology lies the secret of its power to guide and govern human activity. For the same reason, an ideology which is false—it too arises *ultimately* on a real basis, but its mode of generation is not the issue that concerns us here—lacks the power to guide and govern human activity. But this is not to suggest that it is, therefore, altogether powerless. On the contrary, its falseness explains also its power to misguide and misgovern human activity. The important point in fact is—and this is the point which Oakeshott generally refuses to recognise—that ideas, ideals or ideologies, however arisen, true or false or anything else, products of particular historical experiences, or summaries of human hopes and aspirations—they cannot be regarded as simply reducible to that on whose basis they arise, and on which they are dependent, as 'nothing but' products of it, as only 'abbreviations' or 'a bridgements' of that from which they are derived, or as mere effects of what they are based on, and as, in all cases, without any influence whatsoever. Once arisen they become a potent factor themselves. What is an effect also becomes a cause. 'Once an historic element has been brought into the world by other elements,... it also reacts in its turn and may react on its environment and even on its own causes.'[49] In explaining the origins of ideas and ideals, therefore, we must not explain them away. In denying their 'independent', or 'premeditated' development we must not deny their reality or the role they play in social and historical process.

The fact, therefore, that needs to be recognised and emphasised, I repeat, is not the one—the only one—that Oakeshott recognises and emphasises, namely, the secondary, derivative and dependent character of all ideology. The really important issues in any discussion of ideology, far from being settled by this recognition, in fact, only arise with it and after it. And in the context of our discussion there are two issues which seem to me to be of fundamental importance, both of which Oakeshott's argument either obscures or never allows to become real. The first issue concerns the power or influence of ideology. The plain fact we have to recognise here is that ideas and ideals, however arisen, are a most potent force in the life and history of society,[50] capable both of facilitating its progress forward and of hampering it. They can guide as also misguide men. 'An erroneous theory does not merely 'confuse activity by putting it on a false scent' as Oakeshott thinks. It can also be what he holds to be impossible, that is, 'it may persuade people to act in an undesirable manner', just as a correct theory can do the opposite.

The second issue is implicit in what has been stated above; it concerns the truth, or falseness of an ideology. What has to be recognised here is not only that true ideologies are desirable, but also that such true ideologies—relatively true, no doubt, but true nevertheless—are, indeed, possible. Ideologies, that is, are not always and invariably 'mere abridgements' —all equally true or equally false, and equally ineffectual. Ideologies are indeed full of elements of illusion and 'false consciousness', of distortions and rationalisations. They are inevitably relative and contingent, limited subjectively by the bias of the perspective from which the world is seen, and objectively by the stage of historical and social development. But they may, and do in fact, contain important realistic and scientific elements, received from the past and acquired in the present, which having stood the test of verification by the objective criterion of human practice may be regarded as valid human knowledge. If it is true that 'every ideology is historically conditional', it is also 'unconditionally true that to every scientific ideology (as distinct, for instance, from religious ideology), there corresponds an objective truth, absolute nature.'[51]

The modern rationalist insists, therefore, that we can legitimately speak of ideas being more or less *true*, and of ideals being more or less *right*, that we do have criteria by which we can speak of a theory being nearer to truth or more remote, and of ideals being more relevant to the needs and possibilities of a given situation or less. And it is to the more true and more right ideologies that man must turn for guidance in life, and in politics.

It is a serious flaw of Oakeshott's theory of knowledge and ideology that it has no room for such considerations. He, indeed, recognises the truth that ideologies are something dependent and derivative, that '*what* we do, and moreover what we want to do, is the creature of how we are accustomed to conduct our affairs: But refusing to recognise anything else, he completely fails to do justice to their real nature, significance and powers.[52] He does not face the real issues even when, as occasionally happens, his own argument confronts him with these. For example, he defines ideology as 'an abridgement' of 'a traditional manner of behaviour'; according to Oakeshott it cannot be anything else. And yet traditional ideologies do break down, people do turn to new ideologies and these often come up against 'the traditional manner' in a way that the concept of 'abridgement' can hardly account for. Oakeshott knows this, and occasionally even recognises this. But all he does after that is to proceed to save his argument by describing such ideologies too as 'abridgements', only now they are the 'abridgements of the lost knowledge of how to behave'! He simply will not admit that ideas and principles, while they do arise on a real basis, while they arise and are in the end effective only concretely, may nevertheless be *new*, created by man's reason on the basis of a new situation to be coped with, that ideas and situations constantly interact, create and recreate each other. 'When people speak of ideas that revolutionize society, they do but express the fact that within the old society the elements of a new one have been created, and that the dissolution of the old ideas keeps even pace with the dissolution of the old conditions of existence.'[53] In this manner arise also the conflicts of ideas and ideals in a society, reflecting the conflicts of real life. But Oakeshott simply does not recognise these developments as real problems, created by social and historical process itself—which process, incidentally, he generally refuses to countenance and would perhaps like abolished. He can, therefore, instead of coming to grips with them and providing *real* answers, only pillory rationalism for these developments, or, alternately, keep filing logical objections against them.

The real criticism of Oakeshott's critique of rationalism as a whole is not so much that it is mistaken or false—though in important respects it is that too—but that content with its half truths; it evades almost all the real issues that demand consideration in this connection. Against this evasion we shall simply state the fact that the forces of change at the human level, the forces of social and historical development, are all ideological, that whatever men do they do on the basis of ideas and ideals. This being the case, Oakeshott's dismissal of these as 'mere abridgements', as being logically preposterous and practically ineffectual, appears to be simply irrelevant. The appropriate thing to do is to insist, firstly, that our ideas must cease to be unscientific, that they should be true, as true as we can possibly make them; and secondly, that our ideals should cease to be utopian, that they should be relative to the needs and possibilities of the actual situation. In other words, instead of depreciating and disparaging theory, we must insist that it becomes 'realized in a people' by being 'a realization of the people's needs'.[54] Once this happens, theory becomes a mighty force,[55] it becomes capable not merely of ineffectually 'abridging' human practice or retrospectively 'explaining' the world, but of guiding the one and changing the other.

IX

In his treatment of the relation between man's 'ideology, and 'activity', between 'political ideology' and 'political practice', Oalkeshott repeatedly asserts the absolute and unconditional primacy of the latter over the former. This assertion is in fact one of his more important arguments against rationalism. He tells us—I think he is wrong here—that with the rationalist 'the rule or the ideal is determined *first*' and then translated into human behaviour', that he, as it were, '*first* has a vision of a pie and *then* tries to make it' (emphasis added). Oakeshott then informs us in my opinion rightly—that strictly speaking it is impossible to act like this. And in support of his own argument, Oakeshott) insists that ideology is 'derived from the activity and not vice versa', that it 'does not exist in advance' of activity but is 'posterior' to it, that it 'follows after' the activity which 'comes first', that it is 'a postscript' and not 'a preface', that far from 'being the quasi-divine parent' of activity it is only 'its earthly step-child', that the 'principles are derived from the activity and not the activity from the principles', etc.

Now it seems to me that this question as to which, ideology or activity, comes first this repetitive argument in terms of first and after, anterior and posterior; preface and postscript, parent and child—is like the question about the hen and the egg and as meaningless both as a logical and a historical question. The two, ideology and activity, human thought and human practice, are inseparable, they always imply and involve each other, they are necessary and complementary to each other. It is an error common with philosophical idealism to believe that ideas and concepts stand over against a reality—an activity, or a situation to which they have to be 'applied', that all ideas—including the scientific ideas that truly explain the facts and are therefore 'in' facts, just as facts are 'in' them—really belong as it were, to a realm of pure thought, that they have an intrinsic power of their own and that correct policy can be directly deduced from these general ideas and concepts alone.[56] This common idealist error Oakeshott foists on all forms of rationalism including the materialist—and then, in rejecting it, he wants us to accept as valid the opposite empiricist error of his own, which attributes a similar 'self-completeness' and 'independence', in this case from ideology, to human activity or practice. Oakeshott's argument here rests upon a false mechanistic splitting up of the essential unity of ideology and activity, of knowing and doing, of theory and practice. Theory arising out of practice reacts on it to change it and thereby change reality, and theory adjusts itself to this changed reality to become more true and to make human practice more effective—indicating new possibilities and new kinds of activity. Theory thus prefigures the new practice. This is not to dispute the primacy, the *decisive* importance of practice in this interaction. 'In practice man must prove the truth, that is, the reality and power, the this-sidedness (*Diesseitigkeit*) of his thinking'[57] It is successful practice which reveals and confirms both man's knowledge of natural or social reality and his power over it. But conceding this we must still recognise that it is an interaction, that theory and practice enter into and complete each other, that if it is practice which informs theory, it is theory which gives eyes to practice. In other words, theory is in a very real sense both the child and the parent of activity; a postscript, it can be a preface also. The empiricist view of human activity as something absolute and independent of ideology is as one-sided and false as the opposite, idealistic view of human ideology as something 'self-complete' and independent of practice. The empiricist and the idealist, with their respective errors, working from opposite ends, not only seek to break up the dialectical unity of human thought and practice but also misrepresent both. In doing so they entirely fail to understand the characteristic dialectic of the human situation wherein reason and reality, mediated by practice, continuously interact and change each other—the dialectic of growth and power of human knowledge and of changing world and changing man.

In support of his critique of rationalism, Oakeshott makes much also of another argument, namely that activity cannot 'begin' in ideology, that it cannot 'spring' from 'general principles'. He stresses the inability of an ideology to 'generate' activity or to 'regulate' it or to be its 'impetus' in any meaningful sense. The 'propositions' of an ideology, says Oakeshott, the 'purposes', 'ends, rules and principles' it postulates, can be 'neither the spring of the activity' nor can they be 'in any direct sense regulative of the activity'; and this for the simple reason that all of these 'arise as abstractions,... and are never *independently* premeditated', that 'independently premeditated propositions' are impossible, that one cannot 'project a purpose for activity in advance of the activity itself.' It is in fact 'preposterous to suppose that an activity can spring from the premeditation of propositions about the activity'. According to Oakeshott, activity always springs 'from the existing traditions of behaviour themselves'. The 'spring and government' of man's activity, of all 'his projects and his achievements' lies, he says, 'in his *skill*, his knowledge of how to go about his business', in his 'practical knowledge'.

Even apart from the question whether knowing at the *human* level can possibly be so devoid and barren of general ideas and principles as Oakeshott seems to suggest, I find his argument here rather confusing. It seems to me that he is once again invoking the false idealist view, 'the illusion' as he himself calls it, 'that the activity... could spring from and be governed by an end, a purpose or by rules independent of the activity itself or that general ideas or principles can by themselves 'generate' or 'guide' or 'regulate' activity, in order to, under cover of rejecting it, pass off as valid his equally false empiricist view of generation of human activity. It is significant that Oakeshott nowhere seriously discusses *purpose* as the spring or the generator of human activity. He does examine in one place the view that 'takes *purpose* as the distinctive mark of "rationality" in conduct', but in rejecting rationality he comes to reject purpose also. In fact, the only purpose he ever seriously takes note of is the 'rationalist' purpose, which is supposed to be 'independently premeditated', or 'preconceived' or 'final', something simply impossible. What he seems to ignore altogether is that there is another sense of purpose, which is none of these, and is yet valid human purpose, born of man's needs and the requirements and possibilities of the actual situation, and that from the standpoint of life and of human activity, this is the really important sense. Oakeshott's attack on rationalism thus becomes, in a very real sense, an attack on human purpose itself. He completely obscures the great truth that it is purpose which generated human activity, that man's purposeful decision is the act which joins his knowledge (theoretical and practical) with practice, that man acts purposefully—wills and decides, chooses and prefers, values and judges, approves and condemns—because he is *man*. One may, of course, reject 'purpose' as another rationalist error and opt for the Oakeshottian alternative. In that case one would not choose or plan, nor calculate possibilities or values. One would act, in Oakeshott's words, 'as nearly as possible without reflection', 'without hesitation, doubt or difficulty', without 'weighing up of alternatives or reflection on consequences'; one's conduct would be 'nothing more than the unreflective following of a tradition'. In other words, one would just surrender to the sequence of various stimuli as they come, and simply react. This would indeed be making 'a square meal of experience', which Oakeshott recommends, and which he tells us 'the unfortunate' rationalist, particularly the Marxist sort, can never hope to enjoy. But then, I am afraid, this meal has a rather disturbing resemblance to the one enjoyed by Pavlov's dog.

Without intending any distortion of Oakeshott's philosophy, I submit that this alternative is indeed implicit in his wide and varied attack on rationalism, and in his indiscriminate praise of traditionalism. His argument, it seems to me, fails in many important respects to catch up with man at the *human* level of his development.

Man is a product of natural evolution. He is an animal, no doubt, but with a difference. He is the only animal who has a science and an ethics, as also a society, a history and a culture.[58] Once the human level is reached, evolution or progress depends upon the use of reason, development of tools and cultural and technological organisation. It depends upon human ingenuity and choice, upon human purpose and human effort. It is constantly willed and planned by man. Thus does man transcend the types of behaviour found at lower levels of existence. He builds 'above the biosphere, or world of animal life, the noosphere or world of rational life'.[59]

There is no doubt that man is, in a real sense, a traditionalist also. He has to be. He is born into a given society, into a complex natural and social environment. All his thinking and choosing, willing, planning and building, all his progress, has this as its necessary context or basis. But as man he is neither totally involved in his environment and, therefore, unconditionally subject to it, nor totally independent of it, and therefore its unconditional master. Man is not entirely 'self-made' nor 'made' entirely by his environment, his society or his traditional inheritance.[60] Man and his environment continuously make and remake each other. Man is thus neither completely determined by 'necessity' nor is he completely 'free'. Between the ideal extremes of necessity and freedom he builds his real world. And he builds it with his reason, a creatively practical and ethical reason, that adapts his environment to man as much as it adapts man to his environment. Thus does man produce whatever freedom he is in fact capable of, his knowledge being both the means and the measure of his freedom. Hence the significance for man as a rational and freedom-producing animal of the discovery of 'the scientific method', the most important achievement, perhaps, of the past three hundred years, which has been regarded as 'the acquirement of a new organ in the course of social evolution'.[61]

Man is, thus, neither rationalist, nor traditionalist alone. He is and must be both. But it is, I repeat, because he functions intellectually and ethically, and functions dynamically in both cases, that he is man, that his whole life today is totally different from that of the animals. His capacity for science, and for ethics, is not only man's chief title to pride; it is *the difference* that at last establishes his humanity. It is this difference that Chardin noted when he spoke of the 'sudden deluge of cerebralisation' that marked the final arrival of man on this earth;[62] that Collingwood recognised: 'Everything that we call specifically human is due to man's power of thinking hard';[63] that Bronowski underlines: 'All living is action, and human living, is thoughtful action'[64] that Mumford notices: 'Man's nature is a self-surpassing and a self-transcending one: his utmost achievements are always beginnings and his fullest growth must still leave him unsatisfied';[65] that Marx pointed out when he wrote that as distinct from animals 'man... also forms things in accordance with the laws of beauty';[66] and that centuries ago Socrates emphasised when he told the Athenians that 'the unexamined life is not worth living'.

It is this difference that particularly demands our attention today when, given the magnificent possibilities of our age, man's awareness of his nature and destiny has become a decisive factor for human progress [67] And yet, it is this difference precisely that Oakeshott's attack on rationalism tends to obscure. The 'abridgement' he permits to man's reason is hardly human thinking. The 'morality of habit and tradition' he lauds is hardly human morality. Oakeshott indeed disavows that he is describing or advocating something 'primitive'. But this sort of thinking, and morality, is precisely what man has left behind in his long and arduous ascent to reach *humanity*. And there is no turning back.[68] Far from recognising the whole world of possibilities that is man, Oakeshott's description and interpretation of human existence, in its various forms, tends to drain it of its specific human quality and purpose. There is *continuity* and there is *break* in the course of natural evolution, as is the case in social evolution, too. And it was a break when man, 'a new animal type', arrived on the scene. Must the philosopher of continuity refuse to recognise even this break, even this 'discontinuity in continuity'?[69] Surely, like everything else, the cult of continuity too can be carried too far!

X

One important reason why Oakeshott's critique of rationalism for the most part fails to come to grips with the real issues is that the enemy he is busy fighting is something of a strawman. The rationalism he attacks is itself a tremendous 'rationalist' abstraction. His description of 'Rationalism' and 'the general character and disposition of the rationalist' is really a gross caricature. Rationalism is, Oakeshott informs us, belief in the 'self-completeness' of ideology, in the 'independence of mind on all occasions', in 'the open, empty or free mind', in 'a mind which is wholly self-moved' and 'devoid' of 'acquired dispositions or knowledge'. It is belief in 'the unhindered human "reason"' and 'the unencumbered intellect', in ' "Reason" exercising an uncontrolled jurisdiction', in 'Reason' regarded as 'a light whose brightness is dimmed only by education, a piece of mistake-proof apparatus, an oracle whose magic word is truth'. The rationalist—'his intellectual processes', we are told, 'are insulated from all external influence and go on in the void'—thinks himself to be in possession of 'superhuman wisdom', 'certain and complete knowledge', 'an infallible guide, 'the perfect solution' itself. 'He has no sense of the cumulation of experience'. 'He does not neglect experience, but:.. insists always upon it being his own experience." In morality, as in everything else (he) aims to begin by getting rid of inherited nescience and then to fill the blank nothingness of an open mind with the items of certain knowledge which he abstracts from his personal experience, and which he believes to be approved by the common "reason" of mankind'. He naturally 'does not recognise circumstance. 'He waits upon circumstance to provide him with his problems, but rejects its aid in their solution'. 'There is no place in his scheme for a "best in the circumstances", only a place for "the best" '. 'To do anything which requires a patient knowledge of the material, he regards as a waste of time'. With 'a general presumption against all human achievement more than about a generation old', he imagines 'unrolled' before him 'the blank sheet of infinite possibility', indeed a '*tabula rasa*, and wants 'to begin everything *de novo*'. And he wants 'the imposition of uniform condition of perfection', of 'a dream' on others, he wants 'the transformation of an existing society so as to make it correspond with an abstract ideal'. His politics are 'the politics of perfection', and 'the polities of uniformity'. 'What he cannot imagine is politics which do not consist in solving problems'. 'And the "rational" solution of any problem is, in its nature, the perfect solution.' His is 'a vision of perfection', 'the pursuit of perfection as the crow flies', 'the project of finding a short cut to heaven', his is the yearning for 'a model laid up in heaven'. He has an itch not only for 'innovations designed to meet merely hypothetical situations', but also 'to sail uncharted seas' and 'to navigate the unknown'; and 'for him... there is magic in being lost, bewildered or shipwrecked.' He believes his ideology to be 'independently premeditated', his purpose 'preconceived', his end 'preordained and inevitable'. He finds 'the intricacy of the world of time and contingency so unmanageable that he is bewitched by the offer of a quick escape into the bogus eternity of an ideology.' Thus illusioned or bewitched he is ever chasing 'a dream', 'a premeditated utopia', 'a permanently impregnable society'. Living in 'a morass where every choice is equally good or equally to be deplored', he harbours a 'craving for... mistak- proof certainty'. He has 'a deep distrust of time' and 'an impatient hunger for eternity, and 'like the fool', his eyes are fixed always 'on the ends of the earth'—and so it goes on and on and on. Phrase is thus piled upon phrase to build up an illusory and impossible picture of rationalism which Oakeshott then proceeds to pronounce illusory and impossible.

Oakeshott tells that 'activity springing from and governed by an independently premeditated purpose is impossible', that ' "rational" behaviour... is not merely undesirable; it is in fact impossible'. 'Men do not behave in this way, because they cannot'. He is in fact convinced that 'there is no danger that anyone will succeed in achieving a purely "rational" politics, in this sense ....' And yet, rationalism 'in this sense' is precisely what Oakeshott is fighting most of the time. His fight, thus, is a sham fight. 'Rationalism' is something only Oakeshott himself has put up to knock down again—a poor thing and rather fanciful, no doubt, but his own.

Oakeshott would of course dispute this. He in fact hastens to assure us that this rationalism is not 'an invention of my own', not 'a fanciful view of things, held only by a few eccentrics', and that 'it is a view, a theory which has a respectable place in the history of philosophy'. Now this may be so. But one does not need to contest all this in order to insist—and this is the main point—that *today* this view or theory is, with the possible exception of a few odd idealists, no longer seriously held in natural or social or political philosophy. Oakeshott has only flogged a dead theory into some semblance of life in order to reach, under cover of attacking it, an altogether different target—namely, reason and systematic thought itself.

In the name of attacking 'Rationalism', Oakeshott attacks any and every theory or philosophy that gives more than the most marginal recognition to reason, that argues meaningfully in terms of ideas, ideals and principles, or claims to be a guide to human activity in any sense that matters. His attack thus takes in its sweep almost any theory from the reactionary to the revolutionist, from the conservative to the liberal and the socialist, from the collectivist to the anarchist, from the religious to the atheistic, and from the idealist to the materialist. The writers criticised, or at least adversely referred to, include Machiavelli and Locke, Godwin and Bentham, Popper and even Hayek, and of course Marx and Engels. To Oakeshott all these theories and all these men are so many instances of the same all embracing, universal error. Apart from this, 'Rationalism' for Oakeshott is a word of general opprobrium with which to characterise and condemn any movement of thought or action that does not accept the status quo. The term has in fact been used as a catch all for any opinion which Oakeshott dislikes and has been thus emptied of all meaning.

That is why the argument of Oakeshott, for all its literary skill and logical sophistication, remains poor philosophy. It is not that Oakeshott does not have a point to make, or that he does not have his share of truth. His polemic is a valuable corrective against doctrinairism of all kinds. And to the extent there are still in existence philosophies or theories that resemble, more or less, Oakeshott's 'Rationalism', they are rightly to be refuted. His criticism is quite valid, for example, against certain varieties of dogmatic rationalism, more particularly against the extreme idealist variety. But many of the theories or philosophies condemned by him are not 'rationalist' in the same sense at all. The lumping together of so many diverse theories, fastening upon them all the same impossible, and oddly enough also impermissible, desires—all this produces not clarity but confusion, not light, not even genuine heat, but only darkness. And the truth with Oakeshott is simply lost in this confusion and darkness.

Oakeshott himself once wrote: 'And some political philosophers may even be suspected of spreading darkness in order to make their light more acceptable'[70] Only the darkness spread by Oakeshott almost swallows up the light that is his.

This is unfortunate, for the problems which Oakeshott raises in his essays are very real and vital. The nature and function of reason and of human knowledge, the nature of human activity, particularly in morals and politics, the controversy about history and historiography, the problem of freedom and planning, and many other issues raised by Oakeshott are among the central philosophical—and not only philosophical issues of our times. The philosophical quest apart, Oakeshott also has a narrower, practical purpose—ah, that 'vulgar' yet inescapable 'vocational,' disposition again!—and this is to defend a certain negative view of freedom and state activity, to uphold the status quo, and to recommend conservatism as the right policy in politics on the one hand, and to attack all radicalism as represented by positive liberalism, popular democracy and above all socialism on the other. A concrete and careful study of these issues would have been a positive contribution to social and political theory. But with Oakeshott, the philosophical and the practical quests both generally take the form of flaying the heresy of an abstraction, 'Rationalism'.

His argument begins and remains preoccupied with this abstraction most of the time. He does not subject any of the theories he opposes and rejects to serious factual and historical analysis. He does not deem it necessary even to do what many others similarly engaged have generally done—that is, to at least twist, cut and lop these theories to fit the charge before they meet with condemnation. He simply pronounces, through a fiat of interpretation, every such theory to be a form of 'Rationalism'. And this 'Rationalism' Oakeshott demolishes, in advance as it were, by definition itself—'Rationalism' is by definition something illusory and impossible. An amazing performance, indeed, especially for one who is professedly a philosopher of 'the concrete'!

XI

How completely inadequate, even arbitrary and unfair, Oakeshott's technique of criticism is can be clearly seen in his treatment of Marxism as a form of 'Rationalism' as defined by him. He describes Marxism, as we have already noticed, as 'the most stupendous of our political Rationalisms', and therefore the most dangerous—that is, if rationalism can ever be really that.[71] But one will search in vain in Oakeshott for any evidence to support this view, which is a gross misinterpretation of Marxism, a 'mistaken vulgarisation', to borrow a phrase from Butterfield. If Oakeshott had taken the least trouble to go to the classics of Marxism—Yes, if people could only *read*, Marx used to say[72]—he would have discovered that Marxism is none of the things that rationalism as described by him is supposed to be.[73] Marxism is not dogmatic reason in search of, or claiming to be already in possession of, 'the perfect', or 'the final', or 'the infallible'. The founder of Marxism in fact proclaimed methodological scepticism as the guiding principle in his search for valid social and political theory, when he insisted that 'everything is to be doubted' [74] As a modern materialist philosophy, Marxism most categorically rejects the 'independence' or 'self-completeness' of ideas.[75] It does not believe its ideology to be 'independently premeditated' or 'preconceived'[76] It nurses no illusion of possessing 'certain and complete knowledge', or of being 'an infallible guide'.[77] It has no hunger', impatient or patient, 'for eternity', for 'a perfect solution', or for 'a permanently impregnable society'.[78] And it certainly does not aim at 'imposing a dream' or promise 'a premeditated utopia, 'the transformation of an existing society so as to make it correspond with an abstract ideal'. Marx wrote:

> We do not set ourselves up against the world in doctrinaire fashion with a new principle: Here is the truth! Here you must kneel! We develop new principles of the world out of the principles of the existing world. We do not proclaim to it: Cease from your struggles! They are silly! We will tell you what to fight for! We only show the world what it is that it *must* acquire even against its will.[79]

Marx and Engles conducted a life-long struggle against utopianism in the socialist movement, against socialism being regarded as 'the expression of absolute truth, reason and justice', which 'needs only to be discovered to conquer the world by virtue of its own power'—that is, against a socialism which was fully 'rationalist' in the Oakeshottian sense.[80] For Oakeshott Marx-Engels' powerful critique of utopian socialism, of its 'sentimental socialistic day dreams', its 'best possible plan of the best possible state of society', its 'pocket editions of the New Jerusalem', and its 'castles in the air', simply does not exist;[81] nor does Marx's brilliant critique of Proudhon, for whom 'abstractions and categories are the primordial causes', and who sought solutions to real problems from 'the evacuating motions of his own head[82] not again, Marx's sharp critique, in 1875, of his own party for indulging in empty ideal-mongering 'Right can never be higher than the economic structure and the cultural development of society conditioned by it', he had insisted[83] And Oakeshott is entirely oblivious of Marx's life-long effort to acquire precisely that which Oakeshott himself lays down as the prerequisite for 'the right conduct of policy', namely, 'a patient knowledge of the material', 'a profound knowledge of the character' and 'the permanent interests and direction of movement of a society'—which in Marx's case was the capitalist society—which knowledge alone enabled Marx to point out socialism as the next and necessary step in the forward movement of mankind.[84]

Marxism is not and has never been 'rationalist' in the Oakeshottian sense.[85] In its search for knowledge Marxism seeks to achieve, as indeed all science does, a dialectical synthesis of the rational and the empirical, without being either 'rationalistic' or 'empiricistic'. It resolves the problem of the relation of activity and ideology, practice and theory, circumstance and principle, of concrete and abstract, fact and concept, relative and absolute, and of reality and reason in general, not through minimising the importance of one, or through reducing or mechanically opposing one to the other as Oakeshott generally tends to do—but through their dialectical unity, interaction, and synthesis. And it seeks to achieve this unity, interaction, and synthesis on a materialist basis.[86]

It is this which sets Marxism apart not only from the earlier mechanistic materialism, or the rationalist utopian socialism, but also from every variety of idealist and metaphysical rationalism. Its reason is not 'unhindered' or 'uncontrolled', its principles are not 'independently acquired' or 'premeditated' and it does not seek to lift the world by a lever outside the world. On the contrary, its reason is controlled by observation and historical experience, its principles are derived from an objective study of society and reflect the real nature and development of this society. They are a guide to action because they give a more or less true account of this society, of the world we live in. Far from composing a rationalist 'crib' for the working class, Marx and Engels taught this working class, as Lenin once put it, 'to know itself, to be conscious of itself and to put science in the place of dreams'.

Marx specifically disclaimed that his philosophy in any way stood 'outside or 'above' society, that one could achieve understanding of society or history 'by the universal passport of a general historio-philosophical theory, the supreme virtue of which consists in being super-historical'[87] As a social and political theory, Marxism does not begin from general ideas or principles 'which are the products of intellectual premeditation' —or which are 'derived from universal laws alone such as the laws... of dialectical materialism', as Popper, for example, seems to suggest in his criticism of Marxism.[88] On the contrary, Marxism begins from premises which are 'real premises'. 'They are the real individuals, their activity and the material conditions under which they live, both those which they find already existing and those produced by their activity. These premises can thus be verified in a purely empirical way.'[89] In other words, it begins from a concrete and factual analysis of the existing society. Its vision is not of 'a premeditated utopia'. Its critical analysis of the capitalist society points out not only the need for socialism but—and this is of cardinal importance—its *possibility* also. As Engels wrote, 'this possibility now exists for the first time, but it does exist'.[90] The Marxist does not want 'to begin everything *de novo*', as if the world has no history. The building up of socialism for him is always and everywhere dependent upon the necessary objective conditions or possibilities, *first* created for it by capitalism itself. Socialism, therefore, is not creating something 'out of nothing', it is not 'imposing a dream' from outside and above, something that 'does not recognise circumstance'. On the contrary, it is something demanded, and made possible, by the circumstances of capitalism itself. 'These circumstances cry out: "Things cannot remain that way, they must become different and we ourselves, we human beings, must make them different":[91] Socialism is thus envisaged not as 'a preordained and inevitable end', as 'a premeditated purpose"put upon (history) from the outside', but as history's necessary, next step that men will take—and they are, in fact, taking it.[92] Its necessity or inevitability, if we must use these words, is not something absolute or unconditional as Oakeshott and many others think. Nor is it, as Popper and some others appear to believe, something which must over take men, whatever they will and whatever the conditions, because it is so decreed by the mystic 'dialectic triad'. Socialism is inevitable only'in the sense of being that which, under conditions already existing or coming into existence, sufficient men with sufficient power seem 'certain to will sufficiently to win.[93] Socialism is the necessity that men will come to recognise and acting on the basis of that recognition become free—that is, advance further on the road to freedom.[94]

Now, this Marxist, that is, modern materialist rationalism Oakeshott nowhere seriously attempts to understand, much less to refute. He simply lumps it together with every other conceivable form of rationalism, in particular with the easily vulnerable, traditional or bourgeois idealist form, and then, in vanquishing the latter, imagines he has vanquished the former also. These two forms of rationalism are, in fact, opposites. And because they are opposites, they have certain features in common, certain similarities. Oakeshott, it seems, recognises only these less important similarities and ignores altogether the far more important differences, arising from their contrasting bases in materialism and idealism. He thus treats them as if they were identical. And then by exposing the weakness of the one, by demolishing easily—and very rightly too—the idealist rationalism, he claims in so doing to have exposed and demolished the other, the Marxist materialist rationalism also.

Such is Oakeshott's slick technique of dealing with the enemy, rationalism. Let us now see how he deals with something which is his very own, namely traditionalism.

NOTES AND REFERENCES

1. Oakeshott writes:

   The technique (or part of it) of driving a motor car on English roads is to be found in the Highway Code, the technique of cookery is contained in the cookery book, and the technique of discovery in natural science or in history is in their rules of research, of observation and verification.
2. He adds: '—to say nothing of the incursion of a new sex, lately provided for by Mr. Shaw'.
3. E.H. Carr, *op. cit*, p. 110.
4. T.D. Weldon, *Vocabulary of Politics*, Pelican, 1953, pp. 30-36.
5. I would also generally agree with Oakeshott when he speaks of 'benefactors with favourite projects of their own, a persuasive and energetic body of evangelists with a patron in their pockets, a profession set upon winning the status of a university study for its *mystique*', etc., and points out that 'greed, or the desire to appear abreast of the times, have often supervened to destroy both judgment and proper inquiry' in such matters. And this, I suggest, has a relevance to the situation in this country also, where it has apparently become a *must* for persons in the universities and allied

institutions to catch up with any and every enterprise of 'research' or 'teaching' that somebody else is ready to pay for, and where the foreign-foundations-fed fraternity is today growing at a rate which seems to be a trifle too fast to be good either for the health of the academic community here, or for the self-respect, as also the long-term interests, of the people as a whole.

The spectacle in recent years of ever proliferating foreign — mostly American-aided 'academic' institutions, centres, conferences, seminars, workshops, institutes, assistance and exchange programmes, etc., I guided' or 'helped' by more or less itinerant foreign 'experts', keeping Indian scholars, including some capable ones, busy most of the time about nothing, in any case about nothing of value in relation to the real needs and aspirations of the Indian people, and accompanied all the time by free, and often frantic, travelling, to and fro, by all concerned, on all sorts of pretexts, decent and not so decent all this, whatever its usefulness otherwise (it unquestionably has a certain usefulness) and whatever the satisfaction one may, perhaps, derive from seeing this poor country's long deprived academics making the best of 'the new opportunities', is not always an edifying spectacle; at times, it indeed looks very much like a series of exercises in what for want of a better expression may be called 'academic neocolonialism'.

6. Oakeshott would, as always, indict 'Rationalism' for all this, without ever seeking to come to, grips with the circumstances—generally of a declining society torn by internal contradictions—which produce both the moral 'hollowness' and the 'ideals' to fill it with. Touching upon an aspect of this subject, Plekhanov once wrote:

> Marx said very truly that the greater the development of antagonisms between the growing forces of production and the extant social order, the more does the ideology of the ruling class become permeated with hypocrisy. In addition, the more effectively life unveils the mendacious character of this ideology, the more does the language used by the dominant class become sublime and virtuous (see *Saint Max*). (*Fundamental Problems of Marxism*, Calcutta, 1944, p. 69).

With Marx the demand to give up illusions, illusory ideas or empty moral ideals always becomes the demand to give up, that is, to change, the conditions or circumstances which need or at least generate them. With Oakeshott, however, because of his basic commitment to things as they are, criticism of such ideas and ideals (much too easily described and dismissed by him as 'the progeny of Rationalism') never becomes a criticism of the world that makes them necessary or possible.

7. Here is the familiar existentialist man 'condemned to be free' (Sartre). And like the existentialist, Oakeshott too is a case of false philosophy touching on a true complaint.
8. Bacon's *The Advancement of Learning*, Locke's Essay *Concerning Human Understanding*, Kant's *Critique of Pure Reason*, are among the classics of this tradition.
9. See, for example, Hume's *A Treatise of Human Nature* (1739–40) and *Enquiry Concerning the Human Understanding* (1748).
10. Apropos this Lenin's comment is most relevant. He writes that from the standpoint of modern materialism or science 'the *limits* of approximation of our knowledge to the objective, absolute truth are historicalty conditional, but the existence of such truth is *unconditional*, and the fact that we are approaching nearer to it is also unconditional. The contours of the picture are historically conditional, but the fact that this picture depicts an objectively existing model is unconditional .... You will say that this distinction between relative and absolute truth is indefinite. And I shall reply: yes, it is sufficiently "indefinite" to prevent science from becoming a dogma in the bad sense of the term, from becoming something dead, frozen, ossified; but it is at the same time sufficiently "definite" to enable us to dissociate ourselves in the most emphatic and irrevocable manner from fideism and agnosticism, from philosophical idealism and the sophistry of the followers of Hume and Kant' (*Materialism and Empirio Criticism*, Moscow, 1947, pp. 134-5).
11. Engels, *Anti-Duhring*, Lawrence and Wishart, London, n.d., p. 46.
12. M.R. Cohen and E. Nagel, *An Introduction to Logic and Scientific Method*, London, 1961, p. 391.
13. With every such revision in science, the scientist, in fact, pursues his scientific activity with still greater elan and confidence. But the philosopher, of a certain sort, is only filled with alarm and dismay and finds it excuse enough to go nihilistically sceptical on the subject of human knowledge. This happens for reasons which have obviously little to do with science, but a lot with the class position of the philosopher, the state of health, rather ill-health, of his society and the intellectual climate conditioned thereby.
14. J. Bronowski writes: 'A scientific law is the rule by which we guide our conduct and try to ensure that it shall lead to a known future' (*The Common Sense of Science*, Pelican, 1960, p. 110).

15. Ibid., p. 117.
16. Pointing out that 'Hegel was the first to state correctly the relation between freedom and necessity', Engels wrote:

    To him, freedom is the appreciation of necessity. 'Necessity is *blind* only *in so far as it is not understood.*' Freedom does not consist in the dream of independence of natural laws, but in the knowledge of these laws and in the possibility this gives of systematically making them work towards definite ends ....Freedom of the will therefore means nothing but the capacity to make decisions with real knowledge of the subject. Therefore the *freer* a man's judgment is in relation to a definite question, with so much the greater *necessity* is the content of this judgment determined; while the uncertainty, founded on ignorance, which seems to make an arbitrary choice among many different and conflicting possible decisions, shows by this precisely that it is not free, that it is controlled by the very object it should itself control. Freedom therefore consists in the control over ourselves and over external nature which is founded on knowledge of natural necessity; it is therefore necessarily a product of historical development (*Anti-Duhring*, pp. 128-9).
17. On this subject see J. Bronowski's excellent essay 'Science is Human' in *The Humanist Frame*, edited by Sir Julian Huxley, London, 1961. Bronowski underlines the fact that the advent of modern science and scientific thinking marked a sharp break with the predominantly magical and supernatural ways of thinking characteristic of the earlier medieval period. Against the earlier view which sought to establish control over nature by *contradicting* the laws of nature, by flouting them as it were with the help of miracles, science established the principle that control over nature is possible only for those who *obey and use* the laws of nature. As Bronowski puts it, while 'a mediaeval formula was meant to be a spell to stop nature in her tracks', the modern scientific view is that 'the power of nature is at the command of those who use her laws' (p. 87).
18. Cohen and Nagel, *op. cit.*, p. 396.
19. R.G. Collingwood, *An Essay on Metaphysics*, Oxford, 1940, p. 36.
20. The interaction between theory and practice, the continuous 'give and take between facts and principles' which is the essential characteristic of the scientific method has been thus described by Cohen and Nagel: 'We obtain evidence for principles by appealing to empirical material, to what is alleged to be "fact"; and we select,

analyse and interpret empirical material on the basis of principles' (*op. cit.*, p. 396).

21. Speaking of 'the dialectic of scientific cognition', 'the dialectic nature of cognition in which human thought is shaped through the mutual interaction of man and surrounding reality', Lange writes:

    Scientific knowledge develops from the conflicts between the results of new observations and experiments and the scientific ideas and theories already in existence. These ideas and theories influence the direction of scientific research and indicate the paths to be followed by new observations and experiments; the results of this new research in turn call for a change in scientific ideas and theories and demand an adjustment to the newly discovered facts. New scientific concepts and theories indicate the paths to be followed by further observations and experiments, which again make it necessary to adapt scientific ideas and theories, etc. (*op. cit.*, p. 278).

    Pointing out that 'systematized or well-ordered empirical inquiries are one element in the advance of science; the other element is the use of new concepts, new conceptual schemes that serve as working hypotheses on a grand scale', James B. Conant writes: 'The essential element in the advance of modern science has been the curious interplay between such theoretical notions and the experimentation of the artisan; through such an interplay scientist have built up a fabric of interconnected concepts and conceptual schemes' (*Modern Science and Modern Man*, New York, 1953, p. 26).
22. Barrows Dunham, *Giant in Chains*, Boston, 1953, p. 200.
23. J. Bronowski, *The Common Sense of Science*, p. 104.
24. A Chinese anecdote, approvingly related by Oakeshott, is quite revealing on this point. Here a wheelwright, at work, tells a Prince, who is reading a book 'that records the words of the Sages', that what he is reading' can be nothing but the lees and scum of bygone men', that-all that was worth handing on, died with them; the rest, they put in their books.'

    Interestingly enough, the wheelwright also informs the Prince that the knowledge that really matters—'the right pace' in stroke-making which he cannot 'put into words (rules)' or 'explain' or 'hand on'—'cannot get into the hands unless it comes from the heart'. With this shifting of knowledge from head to heart, the revolt against rationalism has reached, almost inevitably it seems, the verge of irrationalism itself. Whatever Oakeshott's own intentions might be, the irrationalist proper can now take over, and 'philosophers' have not been wanting in our age who have positively urged us 'to think with our blood'.

The irrationalist implications of Oakeshott's teaching apart, it is worth pointing out that the contemporary sceptical philosophy as a whole—whatever its different forms—by its nihilistic undermining of reason opens the door wide to the same sort of ignorant belief and superstition, credulity and obscurantism which, quite often, it originally set out to destroy. Coilingwood's bitter comment on this development is very apposite. Discussing the sceptical philosophy of 'the realists' at Oxford—their disavowal of reason or philosophy as a guide in life, of 'ideals to live for and principles to live by' —he wrote that the only conclusion which flowed from this scepticism was

> that for guidance in the problems of life, since one must not seek it from thinkers or from thinking, from ideals or from principles, one must look to people who were not thinkers (but fools), to processes that were not thinking (but passion), to aims that were not ideals (but caprices), and to rules that were not principles (but rules of expediency). If the realists had wanted to train up a generation of Englishmen and Englishwomen expressly as the potential dupes of every adventurer in morals or politics, commerce or religion, who should appeal to their emotions and promise them private gains which he neither could procure them nor even meant to procure them, no better way of doing it could have been discovered (*An Autobiography*, London, 1951, p. 153).

25. Bronowski, *The Common Sense of Science*, p. 120. He writes:

> What marks out science as a system of prediction and adaptation from those of the individual and of the species is at bottom this, that it is a method which is shared by the whole society consciously and at one time. This at once implies that science must be communicable and systematic...
>
> It is the explicit character of its laws which makes science a different activity; and this character derives from communication. Science is the activity of learning by a whole society, even though that society may so divide its labour that it passes the responsibility for this activity to a few men. And the laws of science are those principles of prediction and adaptation to the future which apply to the whole society, and can be teamed by all its members in explicit form. This need to meet two requirements at once, universal usefulness and

explicit statement, is precisely what makes a world pictured by science seem strange to our personal experience (pp. 118, 120).

26. *Ibid*., p. 119: '...the practice of science supposes the existence of a real and a common world ....We do not construct the world from our experiences; we are aware of the world in our experiences. Science is a language for talking not about experience but about the world'.
27. Having obscured the nature of science mainly from the empiricist end Oakeshott now, for a change, proceeds to obscure it from the opposite, rationalist end. To this we can only say, with Bronowski: 'Science is not only rational; it is also empirical. Science is experiment, that is orderly and reasoned activity. The essence of experiment and of all science is that it is active. It does not watch the world, it tackles it' (*ibid*., p. 109).

    Rigidly separating the rational from the empirical, the 'scientific' from the 'practical'—and given the built-in spectator's bias of all empiricist philosophy-Oakeshott now seeks to reduce science to a purely intellectual or philosophical, a consequentially-arranged-concepts-and-images-making activity. This would cut the very nerve of science in its active, practical contact with the real world and may well lead to the paralysis, even death of science as we have come to know it. The history of science in classical antiquity, particularly during the post-Socratic period, has quite a few lessons for us here. See, for example, Benjamin Farrington, *Greek Science*, Pelican, 1953.
28. C.B. Macpherson, 'Edmund Burke and the New Conservatism', *Science and Society*, Vol. XXII, No. 3, Summer 1958, p. 239.
29. Oakeshott's view of science may, perhaps, be regarded as his answer to the problem of two cultures' in the western society—much discussed particularly since C.P. Snow raised it explicitly in his famous Rede Lecture (1959). It is the problem of the division, and the ever widening gulf, between the worlds of humanities and sciences, born essentially, so far as at least the west is concerned, of the inability, if not the refusal, of the traditional culture to understand and accept science. Oakeshott, it seems 'accepts' science by so interpreting it as to assimilate it into the broad pattern of traditional culture, more specifically the culture of the traditional ruling class. While fully accommodating 'the genuine scientist', this interpretation leaves others as mere scientists or technologists, concerned with 'doing', with 'knowing and contriving', with putting scientific knowledge to human use—

and thus serving the traditional class-'divided society as men involved in a really inferior, 'practical' or 'vulgar' activity: This is how it was in the past, this is how the ancient prejudice born of the obsolete class structure of English society wants it and this is what Oakeshott's philosophy seems to provide for.

Once again Oakeshott has 'explained', in this case science, only to leave things as they are, in this case the rift between the 'two cultures'!

30. Defining science as a series of interconnected concepts and conceptual schemes arising from experiment and observation' and pointing out that 'the history of science demonstrates beyond a doubt that the really revolutionary and significant advances come not from empiricism but from new theories', Conant has written: 'Science is a dynamic undertaking directed to lowering the degree of empiricism involved in solving problems, or, if you prefer, science is a process of fabricating a web of interconnected concepts and conceptual schemes arising from experiments and observations and fruitful of further experiments and observations' (*op. cit.*, pp. 30, 54, 62).
31. Bronowski, *The Common Sense of Science*, p. 135.
32. Barrows Dunham writes: 'Universals stretch through change like ligaments through the body: they are the great unifiers. They are not prior to things, for then they would be empty; and they are not merely abstractions from things, for then they would be underivable. They are "in" things, and things are "in" them' ('The Love of Wisdom: A Marxist Meditation', *Science and Society*, Vol. XXIII, No. 3, Summer 1959, p. 204).

    This is as much true of the 'universals' of social science as of natural science.
33. John Lewis, *Science, Faith and Scepticism*, London, 1959, pp. 47-8.
34. On the nature of modern science see Bronowski's *The Common Sense of Science*, particularly Chs. 7 and 8. Discussing 'the narrow view' taken by contemporary empiricist or positivist philosophy Bronowski says: There are a number of grounds why logical positivism will not do; and they have this in common, that it is a piecemeal philosophy.'

    Bronowski rejects every philosophical position which would reduce science to 'a mere description of facts' or of regularities in their occurrence and behaviour. Recognising the importance of both 'knowing' and 'doing' in science, he writes: "Because we know what we are doing": this is the crux of science. We are not merely observing and predicting facts; and that is why any philosophy which builds up science only from facts is mistaken. We know, that is we find laws; and every human action uses these laws, and at the same time tests them and feels towards new laws'. And here what matter; is not the form of these laws, but 'the recognition of the law in the facts'. It is 'the law which we verify the pattern, the order, the structure of events'. Science is thus 'not the blank record of facts, but the search for order within the facts.' And 'the truth of science is not truth to fact, which can never be more than approximate, but the truth of the laws which we see within the facts.'

But if 'we cannot define truth in science until we move from fact to law', within the body of laws in turn 'what impresses us as truth is the orderly coherence of the pieces'. Each law of science 'holds together a scattered array of facts'. But the laws themselves are not the final unifying agents. 'The great unifying thoughts are knots where the laws cross one another and are held together', namely, the concepts: the concept of matter, of space, of evolution, of inheritance, etc. They are the links and the critical joints in the whole structure of our understanding. And they are not self-evident'. 'Just as the laws unite the facts, so the concepts of science unite its laws into an orderly world which hangs on those bold knots in the network.' It is this 'internal unity and coherence of science which give it truth' and which the scientists seek. They seek 'to find nature one, a coherent unity.' And, says Bronowski, it is this that gives the scientists 'their sense of mission and, let us acknowledge it, of aesthetic fulfilment: that every research carries the sense of drawing together the threads of the world into a patterned web.' Bronowski concludes: 'Science is a process of creating new concepts which unify our understanding of the world, and the process is today bolder and more far reaching, more triumphant even than at the great threshold of the Scientific Revolution.'

In this connection see also Bronowski's's Science is Human', loc.*clt.*, where in a criticism and refutation of the essentially unscientific position taken by the contemporary empiricist or logical positivist philosophy, he argues that science, transcending the limits of bare facts or experience, always seeks to find a world picture, a pattern or an order, exemplified in and explaining the empirically given facts or experience.

35. Consider, for example, the following observations by a contemporary philosopher, J.M. Cameron: 'Making up such

pictures (i.e. treating "the cautious and provisional hypotheses of the natural sciences at a given date as accounts from which we may extrapolate a grand picture of the entire cosmic process") has nothing to do with serious work in the sciences or in philosophy and theology' (quoted by Ernest Gellner, The Crisis in the Humanities and the Mainstream of Philosophy', in *Crisis in the Humanities*, edited by J.H. Plumb, Pelican, 1964, p. 79).

Gellner comments: 'One may grant the point concerning theology. But in philosophy, can there by anything more serious than the results of science? Granting that these may be "cautious and provisional", are any other putative sources of knowledge *justifiably* less so?' He adds that 'the point about a picture being "grand" is simply part of conventional current philosophic denigration of any attempt at obtaining a general picture.'

36. Barrows Dunham, *Giant in Chains*, pp. 145-6.
37. That such is Oakeshott's philosophical position is clear not only from the nihilistic nature of his attack on rationalism but also from several other scattered statements in his essays. For example, in a passing reference to J.S. Mill, Oakeshott informs us that Milt 'abandoned reference to general principle either as a reliable guide in political activity or as a satisfactory explanatory device' and 'put in its place a "theory of human progress" and what he called a "philosophy of history"'. His own view, Oakeshott says, represents 'a further stage in this intellectual pilgrimage, a stage reached when neither "principle" (on account of what it turns out to be: a mere index of concrete behaviour) nor any general theory about the character and direction of social change seem to supply an adequate reference for explanation or for practical conduct.' 'Intellectual pilgrimage' indeed!
38. On the subject of contemporary scepticism, and of the continuously changing content of human knowledge, or reason, that yet constitutes 'the expansion of our knowledge', Paul A. Baran writes:

> This absence of a pat answer to the question as to what constitutes at any particular time the specific content of reason is invoked by contemporary bourgeois thought as an excuse for its own relativism and agnosticism. This excuse, however, is no more admissible than would be the contention that all efforts to cure disease ought to wait until medicine has reached its ultimate state of perfection. What the unavailability (and ineluctable impossibility) of *absolutely* valid statements about the meaning of reason actually points to is rather the perennial

and all-important obligation of philosophical thought: the unremitting integration and re-integration, interpretation and re-interpretation of human knowledge and experience within a dynamic framework of reason. The fault of bourgeois thought today is not that it rejects the notion of eternal truth or denies the possibility of eternally valid definitions of reason. The fault, amounting to tragic failure, consists in 'throwing out the baby with the bath', in using the inaccessibility of eternally applicable definitions of reason as an apology for abandoning the search for whatever meaning and content may be attributable to reason in any *concrete* historical situation. This leads not only to the complete abdication of philosophy in favor of opportunism and pragmatism, but also to obscurantism and the betrayal of reason itself ('On the Nature of Marxism', *Monthly Review*, November 1958, pp. 260-1).

39. Discussing the contemporary 'crisis in the humanities', Ernest Gellner writes: Now, in cognition as in production, roundabout, reproducible, changing methods are replacing the sensitive, locally rooted, but static and fairly low-productive ways of the artisans. The humanists are the artisanate of cognition' (The Crisis in the Humanities and the Mainstream of Philosophy', *loc. cit.*, p. 75).

    In suggesting 'the way forward' for the humanities, particularly philosophy, Gellner emphasises that 'the real and deeper problem' in this connection 'concerns just what, if anything, it is that the humanities have to communicate'; it concerns 'their cognitive potential so to speak, and the manner in which *knowing* and *being* are related within them.' Oakeshott, it seems, is suggesting a parallel 'way backward' for science, particularly social science. For he elaborates a theory of knowledge which would merge all knowing, including the scientific, into the humanities' 'artisanate of cognition'. Significantly enough, this movement backward continues and the humanities themselves, including philosophy, tend to abandon 'congnition' altogether in Oakeshott's *weltanschauung* as a whole.

40. This is not in any way to defend or justify all that today passes under the name of 'social science. As J.D. Bernal has pointed out, 'much social science is merely the putting of the current practice of the trades and professions into learned language', or is science 'only by courtesy or for examination purposes'. Bernal very rightly insists that studies in different social fields 'can be classed as sciences only in so far as they employ the scientific methods used in the natural sciences, that is, in so far as they rest on a material

basis and their accuracy can be checked by successful prediction' and practical use' (*Science in History,* London, 1954, p. 695).

41. John Lewis, in his very lucid Marxist critique of contemporary scepticism, writes: A scientific philosophy gives us the truth, but not the whole truth, not the final truth and not the truth about the whole ....

    'We have two errors to guard against: On the one hand the danger of dogmatism, of believing that there is an all-sufficient, all-general principle, a single fundamental proposition that adequately explains everything; on the other hand, just because we cannot have complete certainty and exhaustive truth, despair of finding any truth at all (*Science, Faith and Scepticism*, p. 52).

42. Nearly ninety years ago, William Clifford, the geometer and philosopher, looking, as it were, out of his century forward into ours, wrote:

    Remember, then, that scientific thought is the guide of action; that the truth at which it arrives is not that which we can ideally contemplate without error, but that which we may act upon without fear, and you cannot fail to see that scientific thought is not an accompaniment or condition of human progress, but human progress itself (quoted in Bronowski, *The Common Sense of Science*, p. 133).

43. Pointing out the intellectual's responsibility for 'providing society with such humane orientation and such intelligent guidance as may be obtainable at every concrete junction on its historical journey', Paul Baran wrote:

    It can be readily granted that there is no possibility of arriving at a judgment on what is good or bad for human advancement which would be *absolutely* valid regardless of time and space. But such an *absolute*, universally applicable judgment is what might be called a false target, and the insistence on its indispensability is an aspect of a reactionary ideology. The truth is that what constitutes an opportunity for human progress, for improvement in the lot of men and also what is conducive or inimical to its realization, differs in the course of history from one period to the next, and from one part of the world to another. The questions with regard to which judgments are required have never been *abstract*, speculative questions concerning 'good' or 'bad' in general; they have always been *concrete* problems placed on the agenda of society by the tensions, contradictions, and changing constellations of the historical process. And at no time has there been a possibility or, for that matter, a necessity to arrive at *absolutely* valid solutions; at all times there is a challenge to use mankind's accumulated wisdom, knowledge, and experience to attain as close as possible an *approximation* to what constitutes the best solution under the prevailing conditions (The Commitment of the Intellectual', *Monthly Review*, March 1965, pp. 7-8).

44. Reinhard Bendix, *Social Science and the Distrust of Reason*, University of California Press, 1951, p. 28. Bendix writes:

    It has been observed that methodological rigor can be obtained only at the price of dealing with relatively insignificant problems, whereas the investigation of significant problems suffers from a lack of this rigor. We cats obtain agreement on social science propositions, but the content of the propositions makes us question whether this knowledge is worth obtaining. Yet, when we deal with propositions which we feel are worthwhile, we find it almost impossible to 'prove' them. Modern social science reveals a cleavage between propositions which are significant and propositions which command assent, and there is no sign as yet that this condition will be improved.

45. G.E.G. Catlin, *op. cit.*, p. 16. ' Undue concentration of Methodology'—methods, it is interesting to note, have become 'Methodology'— could in fact prove much worse. It may well reduce social science, in the words of Bentham, to 'the art of being methodically ignorant of what everybody knows'. Speaking of political science, for example, David Easton has already pointed out: 'If political science were to insist upon universal adherence to methodological rigor at the present time as the only kind of adequate research, there is little doubt that, in attending so mechanically to form, all life and wisdom would be squeezed from even the existing insights into political behaviour' ('The Decline of Modern Political Theory', *loc. cit.*, pp. 56-7).

46. See note 11 to Ch. I, above. C. Wright Mills spoke of a 'social science' which 'is more often than not a social science having little or no concern with the pivotal events and the historic acceleration characteristic of our immediate times. It is a social science, of the narrow focus, the trivial detail, the abstracted almighty unimportant fact' (*The Marxists*, Pelican, 1963, p. 12). But this does not mean opting for the alternative 'model-making' or 'conceptual frameworks' approach which, indulging in an equally elaborate and arid formalism, replaces 'the fetishism of Empiricism' with 'the fetishism of the Concept', and thus easily becomes the opposite, rationalist error in social science.

In a trenchant criticism of the two methodological errors, 'abstracted empiricism' and 'grand theory; as two different styles in social science, C. Wright Mills wrote: 'Intellctually these schools represent abdications of classic social science. The vehicle of their abdication is pretentious over-elaboration of "method" and "theory"; the main reason for it is their lack of firm connection with substantive problems'. Mills added that, as practices, 'grand theory' and 'abstracted empiricism' *may* be understood as 'insuring that we do not learn too much about man and society—the first by formal and cloudy obscurantism, the second by formal and empty ingenuity' (*The Sociological Imagination*, pp. 74-5).

In all genuine science, natural or social, there is and must be continuous interaction, or 'alternation' as Mills put it, 'between (empirical) intake and (theoretical) assimilation', that is, 'concepts and ideas ought to guide factual investigation' and 'detailed investigation ought to be used to check up on and re-shape ideas'; or, as Bronowski has put it more simply, in science 'the rational and the empirical' are, and must be, 'knotted together'.

47. Cohen and Nagel make a mild indirect reference to the more important causes of the lack or loss of significance in social science when they note that 'it is unfortunate when scientific research in the social field is largely in the hands of those not in a favourable position to oppose established or popular opinion' (*op. cit.*, p. 402).

J.D. Bernal in his *Science and History*, Chs. 12 and 13, draws pointed attention to the deeper social causes underlying the lack of significance in social science, or, speaking more generally, underlying the universally admitted backwardness of social science as compared to natural science. He suggests that the reason for this backwardness derives 'not so much from the intrinsic differences or the mere complexity of subject-matter, but from the strong social pressure of established ruling groups to prevent serious discussion of the foundations of society'.

Discussing the differences between the social sciences and the physical and biological sciences, and the various reasons, valid and not so valid, usually mentioned for the backward state of the former, Bernal writes: 'Far more potent than any of these factors is another, intrinsic to society itself, which has operated and still operates most effectively to prevent the formulation of any genuine unbiased social science in the conditions of a class society. The history of the social sciences shows clearly enough that the effective reasons which have held back their development have been strong and positive ones, imposed by those who controlled and principally benefited by the organization of society itself'. Pointing out that it has always been 'a very dangerous thing to look too closely into the workings of one's own society', for this may well bring out its arbitrary and unjustifiable features, Bernal argues that 'the backwardness and emptiness of the social sciences are due to the overriding reason that in all class societies they are inevitably *corrupt*.

The dominant fact about social science in history has been its character as 'social science in the service of established order'. Pointing this out Bernal writes: 'The existence of classes and the exploitation of the poor by the rich have been for 4,000 years the most outstanding fact of social life. Yet in the "science" of society far greater efforts have been made to pass it over or explain it away than to study it and work out the consequences of the fact itself.'

This is indeed how social science has come to be so overloaded or corrupted with all sorts of social myths, illusions and superstitions, which have grown up in the process of attempting to defend and justify the established order and which, deceiving so many in favour of so few, have helped rob mankind of its right to abundance, equality and peace.

In his brilliant analysis of some of these social myths and superstitions Barrows Dunham points out that 'generally speaking, truth has been suffered to exist in the world just to the extent that it profited the rulers of society.' He adds that 'there was a time—and not so very long ago—when these rulers could not afford the knowledge that the earth is round'. Referring to the 'hierarchy of sciences' in the learned world—'with mathematics and physics at the top and psychology and sociology at the bottom'—and to the general backwardness and lack of prestige of the social sciences, and the many reasons for it, Dunham writes: 'The real reason is that the physical sciences are fairly neutral politically; while the social sciences are full of dynamite' (*Man Against Myth*, London, 1949, p. 22).

It is only if we bear in mind the social context, both in its general as well as particular aspects, that we can hope to gain a proper understanding of some of the more significant developments in contemporary social science. In political science in the United States, for example, we have been told that there is 'the increasing tendency of the profession to engage in major research on minor or peripheral problems' and that given 'the prevailing mood', 'the general climate of conservatism, opportunism, careerism, and "togetherness",' it is' not always easy, or "safe" to confront "great issues" ' (Rogow, *loc. cit.*); that 'too much of what has been passing for political science scholarship has been little more than footnoted rationalization and huckstering of these (i.e. official) policies' (Professor Neal Houghton's speech to Western Political Science Association, 12 April, 1958, quoted in C. Wright Mills, *The Sociological Imagination*, p. 84); that 'the prime value concept' of overwhelming majority of American political scientists is 'stability, the maintenance of the ongoing system; and that showing a truly remarkable 'reverence for the present', these scientists take up only 'safe issues', regarding these alone as 'significant issues', and dismiss the rest, the really important problems of politics relating to socio-economic issues, class conflict, large-scale change, etc., as, in Lewis Feuer's phrase, so many 'unproblems'—'Problems engendered in the society and not considered by the elite are for Dahl "unproblems"—they do not exist to be considered' (James Petras, 'Ideology and United States Political Scientists', *Science and Society*, Vol. XXIX, No. 2, Spring 1965); etc., etc.

Again it is only with reference to their social context and implications that we can properly understand some of the more significant developments in the realm of 'methodology' of contemporary social science, that is, understand the full meaning of the rise and fall, the relative importance and un-importance of different doctrines, methods and methodological approaches in social science: For this is not a matter only of intellectual competition among different approaches, of scientific adequacy and fruitfulness of one approach as against the other. It is a matter also of their social relevance and function. And if, for example, certain dominant approaches today, including particularly what Mills has called 'an empiricism as cautious and rigid as abstracted empiricism', have resulted in a significant trivialisation of social science; if they have, because of their 'methodological' inhibitions, come to be concerned mostly with 'minor or peripheral problems', 'small-scale milieus', or 'safe issues'; if they allow treatment only of 'relatively insignificant problems' and cannot yield 'propositions which are significant' or knowledge that is 'worth obtaining' (Bendix); if they eliminate 'the great social problems and human issues of our time from inquiry' and even insure that 'we do not learn too much about man and society (C. Wright Mills); if they compel the protest that 'complexity of the real world... shoud not lead us to avoid it, or to follow the road of theoretical precision or methodological refinement to a palpable, if fortuitous, avoidance' (Rogow); if, in short, these methodological approaches have meant an evasion of the more important intellectual and political tasks of social analysis, an abdication indeed of classic social science which was concerned primarily with 'significant problems; with matters relating to the structure and dynamics of society, then the essentially conservative character and function of these approaches is only too obvious and must be taken into account in any meaningful explanation or assessment .of their ascendency in the social science of contemporary capitalist world.

It requires no deep philosophical or sociological insight to recognise, on the evidence already available, that much of the 'Methodology' of this social science, notwithstanding its pretentious play with catchwords like 'value free science', 'scientific objectivity' or 'impartiality', 'ethical neutrality', etc, has involved an acceptance and; endorsement of the existing framework of capitalist society. Its practice and outcome have all too often meant a justification by default of the status quo, of the basic structural arrangements of this society. And, by seeking knowledge or truth mostly 'about things that do not matter' and accepting that the pursuit and achievement of such knowledge or truth is all that is given to social science today, this social science itself has largely managed to dodge the central issues of contemporary social and political life, and, thus; served as an important ideological device in defence of the established social and political order.

No wonder that Bernal, with his profound understanding of the situation in contemporary social science, writes: 'What social science needs is less use of elaborate techniques and more courage to tackle, rather than dodge, the central issues' (*op. cit*, p. 707).

Concerning the problems besetting truth, that is *significant* truth— its discovery, acceptance, propagation and use in the social science of a class-divided society, the comment of Hobbes, characteristically clear and pungent, has lost none of its relevance for having been made more than three hundred years ago.

Referring to the conflict between 'reason' and men's 'interest', Hobbes spoke of men 'setting themselves against reason, as oft as reason is against them', and added: 'which is the cause, that the doctrine of tight and wrong, is perpetually disputed, both by the pen and the sword: whereas the doctrine of lines, and figures, is not so; because men care not, in that subject, what be truth, as a thing that crosses no man's ambition, profit or lust. For I doubt not, but if it had been a thing contrary to any man's right of dominion, or to the interest of men that have dominion, *that the three angles of a triangle should be equal to two angles of a square*, that doctrine should have been, if not disputed, yet by the burning of all books of geometry, suppressed, as far as he whom it concerned was able' (*Leviathan*, pp. 67-8).

48. As long ago as 1846, for example, Marx and Engels subjected to very severe criticism the philosophical idealist belief that consciousness 'is something other than consciousness of existing practice, that it is *really* conceiving something without conceiving something *real* (*The German Ideology*, Calcutta, n.d., p. 16).

 More than a hundred years later, Butterfield pointed out that Marxism 'offers a corrective to that older view which evaded fundamental problems by seeing history as a field for the activity of disembodied ideas—ideas that were treated as irreducible, that is to say, as being the starting point rather than the consequence of change ....' (*History and Human Relations*, London, 1951, p. 84).

 The obvious conclusion from this is that 'the ideas that move men need to be explained by examining their antecedents.' But Oakeshott is somewhat more 'original' in holding that ideas, because they have antecedents, do not and cannot move men at all.

49. Eagels' letter to Mehring, 14 July, 1893, *Selected Correspondence 1846-1895*, p. 512. In his well-known essay, 'Dialectical and Historical Materialism', J. Stalin emphasised that ideas and theories, having arisen on the basis of 'the development of material life of society, the development of social being', themselves 'react upon social being, upon the material life of society'. In a comment on Marx's statement that 'it is not the consciousness of men that determines their being, but on the contrary, their social being that determines their consciousness', Stalin wrote:

> It does not foliow from Marx's words, however, that social ideas, theories, political views and political institutions are of no significance in the life of society, that they do not reciprocally affect social being, the development of the material conditions of the life of society. We have been speaking... of the *origin* of social ideas, theories, views and political institutions, of *the way they arise*, of the fact that the spiritual life of society is a reflection of the conditions of its material life. As regards the *significance* of social ideas, theories, views and political institutions, as regards their *role* in history, historical materialism, far from denying them, stresses the role and importance of these factors in the life of society, in its history.

> There are different kinds of social ideas and theories. There are old ideas and theories which have outlived their day and which serve the interests of the moribund forces of society. Their significance lies in the fact that they hamper the development, the progress of society. Then there are new and advanced ideas and theories which serve the interests of the advanced forces of society. Their significance lies in the fact that they facilitate the development, the progress of society, and their significance is the greater the more accurately they reflect the needs of development of the material life of society (*Problems of Leninism*, Moscow, 1947, pp. 579-80).

50. 'The world is largely ruled by ideas, true and false', wrote Charles Beard (Introduction to J.B. Bury's *The Idea of Progress*, New York, 1955, p. ix).
51. Lenin, *op. cit.*, p. 135.
52. The most that an ideology can be, or do, according to Oakeshott, is clearly revealed in the following characteristic passage. Oakeshott writes:

    Now, every society which is intellectually alive is liable, from time to time, to abridge its tradition of behaviour into a scheme of abstract ideas . . . And in this there is no harm; perhaps even some positive benefit. It is possible that the distorting mirror of an ideology will reveal important hidden passages in the tradition, as a caricature reveals the potentialities of a face; and if this is so, the intellectual enterprise of seeing what a tradition looks like when it is reduced to an ideology will be a useful part of political education.
53. Marx and Engles, *Manifesto of the Communist Party*, pp. 68-9.
54. Marx, 'A Contribution to the Critique of Hegel's Philosophy of Right', in *Early Writings*, The Pelican Marx Library, p. 252.
55. Marx wrote: Theory... becomes a material force once it has gripped the masses' (*Ibid.*, p. 251).
56. Marx examines and refutes this error in a number of his writings, particularly in his criticism of Proudhon in *The Poverty of Philosophy*.
57. Marx, 'Theses on Feuerbach', in Marx and Engels, *Selected Works*, Vol. II, Moscow, 1949, p. 365. See also Mao-Tse-tung, 'On Practice', *Selected Works*, Vol. I, London, 1954; Howard Selsam, *Philosophy in Revolution*, New York, 1957, Ch.: 'Knowledge, Practice and Reality.'
58. 'Because we are reflective we are not only different but quite other' (P.T. de Chardin, *The Phenomenon of Man*, London, 1960, p. 166).

59. John Lewis, *Man and Evolution*, London, 1962, pp. 78-9.
60. Oakeshott is quite right in pointing out that man is never literally *self-made*, but depends upon a certain kind of society and upon a large unrecognized inheritance'. He is quite wrong, however, in making this dependence one-sided and absolute.
61. John Lewis, *Man and Evolution*, p. 79.
62. Charlin *op. cit.*, p. 183. He wrote: 'This sudden deluge of cerebralisation, this biological invasion of a new animal type which gradually eliminates or subject sall forms of life that are not human, this irresistible tide of fields and factories, this immense and growing edifice of matter and ideas—all these signs that we look at, day in day out—seem to proclaim that there has been a change on the earth and a change of planetary magnitude'.
63. R.G. Collingwood, *An Essay on Metaphysics*, p. 37.
64. J. Bronowski, *The Common Sense of Science*, p. 109.
65. Lewis Mumford, *The Condition of Man*, London, 1944, p. 7.
66. Marx, *Economic and Philosophic Manuscripts of 1844*, Moscow, n.d., p. 76.
67. Julian Huxley writes: 'We, mankind, contain the possibilities of the earth's immense future, and can realize more and more of them on condition that we increase our knowledge and our love' (Introduction to Chardin's *The Phenomenon of Man*, p. 28).
68. 'If we turn back', Karl Popper says, 'then we must go the whole way we must return to the beasts' (*The Open Society and its Enemies*, Vol. I, p. 201).
69. Chardin, *op. cit.*, p. 169.
70. Oakeshott, 'Introduction to Hoboes' *Leviathan*, p. x.
71. Oakeshott also vouchsafes us the precious information that Marxist rationalism 'has created so vast an intellectual proletariat, with nothing but its technique to lose'. Oakeshott's own treatment of Marxism suggests, however, that there is, if not 'intellectual' poverty, something worse in some other seemingly high quarters.
72. Engels' letter to Conrad Schmidt, 1 July, 1891, *Selected Correspondence 1846–1895*, p. 488.
73. The extensive references in this section to the writings of Marx and Engels may appear pedantic. But I do not know how this could be avoided in view of the nature of the issue involved and the widespread vulgarisation of Marxism by its opponents, and not by them alone.
74. *Reminiscences of Marx and Engels*, Moscow, n.d. p. 266. *De omnibus dubitandum* was Karl Marx's favourite motto. His favourite maxim, we are told, was *Nihil humani a me allenum Pulo* (I regard nothing

human as alien to me).

75. 'In direct contrast to German philosophy which descends from heaven to earth, here we ascend from earth to heaven .... We set out from real, active men, and on the basis of their real-life process we demonstrate the development of the ideological reflexes and echoes of this life process .... Morality, religion, metaphysics, and all the rest of ideology and their corresponding forms of consciousness, thus no longer retain the semblance of independence. They have no history, no development; but men, developing their material production and their material intercourse, alter, along with this their real existence, their thinking and the products of their thinking. Life is not determined by consciousness, but consciousness by life. In the first method of approach the start in a point is consciousness taken as the living individual; in the second it is real living individuals themselves, as they are in actual life, and consciousness is considered solely as their consciousness' (Marx and Engels, *The German Ideology*, pp. 11-2).

    Again: 'My dialectic method is not only different from the Hegelian, but is its direct opposite. To Hegel, the life process of the human brain, *i.e.*, the process of thinking, which, under the name of "the Idea", he even transforms into an independent subject, is the demiurgos of the real world, and the real world is only the external, phenomenal form of "the Idea". With me, on the contrary, the ideal is nothing else than the naterial world reflected by the human mind, and translated into forms of thought' (Marx, *Capital*, Vol. I, Preface to Second Edition, 1873, London, 1946, p. xxx).

76. The theoretical conclusions of the Communists are in no way based on ideas or principles that have been invented, or discovered, by this or that would-be universal reformer.

    'They merely express, in general terms, actual relations springing from an existing class struggle, from a historical movement going on under our very eyes' (Marx and Engels, *Manifesto of the Communist Party*, p. 60).

77. 'We are but little beyond the beginning of human history, and the generations which will put us right are likely to be far more numerous than those whose knowledge we—often enough with a considerable degree of contempt—are in a position to correct .... the stage of knowledge which we have now reached is as little final as all that have preceded it' (Engels, *Anti-Duhring* pp. 99, 104).

78. 'Just as knowledge is unable to reach a perfect termination in a

perfect, ideal condition of humanity, so is history unable to do so; a perfect society, a perfect "state", are things which can only exist in imagination ...this dialectical philosophy dissolves all conceptions of final, absolute truth, and of a final, absolute state of humanity corresponding to it. For it nothing is final, absolute, sacred' (Engels, 'Ludwig Feuerbach,' quoted from *Reader in Marxist Philosophy*, eds., Howard Selsam and Harry Martel, New York, 1963, pp. 97-8).

79. Marx's letter to Ruge, quoted in Sidney Hook, *From: Hegel to Marx*, University of Michigan Press, 1962, p. 59.
80. See Engels, *Socialism: Utopian and Scientific*.
81. See Marx and Engels, *Manifesto of the Communist Party*.
82. See Marx, *The Poverty of Philosophy*.
83. See Marx, *Critique of the Gotha Program*.
84. This is a knowledge, however, which, though it involved detailed and painstaking empirical research, far transcends the empiricist 'abridgements' of Oakeshott. It contains important scientific truth, which, moreover, came to be usefully deposited in 'the book'—in *Capital* and other writings of Marx.
85. I am not concerned here, nor is Oakeshott for that matter, with the failings, 'rationalist', or any other, of particular practitioners of Marxism.
86. In his essay 'On the Nature of Marxism' Baran has pointed out that 'contrary to widespread opinion, Marxism is not and never was intended to be a "positive science", an assortment of statements about past and present facts, or a set of predictions about the shape or timing of future events. It was always an intellectual attitude, a way of thought, a philosophical position the fundamental principle of which is continuous, systematic, and comprehensive *confrontation of reality with reason*.' Pointing out that, while this principle did not originate with them, it was left to Marx and Engels to take 'a decisive step forward' in the centuries old effort at confronting reality with reason, Baran writes: 'They translated the notions of both' reality and reason from the metaphysical abstractions and idealistic assertions—the forms in which they appear in most pre-Marxian thought—into living, concrete, categories of real, continually moving, continually changing, human existence.' And, making the implications of this 'decisive step forward' clear, Baran adds: 'Thus, while uncompromisingly committed to the principles of confronting reality with reason, while convinced that this confrontation represents the indispensable basis of all humanist thought and

the only valid guidepost for meaningful human activity, Marxism by no means implies a dogmatic finding as to what defines reason or what constitutes reality at any given time'.

Arguing that 'to Marxism the meaning of reason and the nature of reality are closely interwoven, inseparable aspects of historical development', Baran writes:

> In terms of the long *run*, of the entire historical process, the content and the injunctions of reason are relative. They change with the changing forces of production, they transform themselves with the transformation of society, they enrich themselves with the expansion of our knowledge... Yet it is crucially important to realize that this relativity of the content of reason holds only in the longest run. In the short tun, in any given historical period, what constitutes reason is *approximately* ascertainable. The determining factors are the level of social development, society's achieved fund of scientific insight, the accumulated wealth of practical human experience...
>
> What applies to reason applies also with some modifications but with no less force to our notions of reality. In the long run, the content of reality is also subject to perpetual change, partly because of continuous transformations in the real world itself, partly because of steady advances in our practical activity, in our empirical research, and in our theoretical understanding. Whether in the realm of social relations where historical development incessantly changes the structure of society or in regard to nature where scientific discoveries and human activity progressively modify what confronts us as nature'—there is no eternal 'reality'. In the short run, an the other hand, in a concrete historical constellation, reality is subject to research and analysis; its structure can be comprehended with a degree of approximation sufficiently high to admit of purposeful and rational practice (*loc. cit.*, pp. 259-61).

87. Marx's letter to the Editor of the *Otyecestvennitye Zapisky*, Selected Correspondence, 1846 1895, p. 355.
88. Karl Popper, *The Poverty of Historicism*, p. 128.
89. Marx and Engels, *The German Ideology*, p. 6.
90. Engels, *Anti-Duhring*, p. 311.

In this connection Antonio Labriola wrote: 'Communism is neither moralizer, nor preacher, nor herald nor utopian it already holds the thing itself in its hands and into the thing itself it has put its ethics and its idealism' (*Essays on the Materialistic Conception of History*, New York, 1966, p. 73).

91. Marx, quoted in Sidney Hook, *op. cit.*, p. 58.
92. In a discussion of Marx's view of ethics, Hook points out that Marx all his life took a stand against 'abstract ethical idealism'. For him 'the only thing eternal about morality is man's desire for the better. But what the "better" is, time and circumstances redetermine from situation to situation: In a specific reference to 'Marx's conception of purpose, Hook writes:

    The process of social development has no ends to realise which are not the ends willed by men. But those ends are not realised merely because they are willed by men. What is willed must be continuous with a discovered situation which is not willed but accepted. *When* it is willed must be determined by objective possibilities in the situation. Only when these conditions are fulfilled, can the ends willed by men be realised... Marx's theory of social activity sees in the presence of need the explanation of why socialism is willed at all; and in the presence of certain objective conditions why what is willed, will probably be realised (*op. cit.*, p. 58).

93. M.O. Milligan, 'Karl Poppers Positivism and the Science of Society', *The Modern Quarterly*, Vol. 4, No. 1, Winter 1948–9, p. 66.
94. Marxism is thus neither idealism (absolute freedom) nor determinism (absolute necessity). It is amazing how the critics persist in going wrong on this point. While Oakeshott has been busy fastening some sort of idealist rationalism upon Marxism, and then criticising it for the high importance it gives to man and his reason, to ideas, ideals and theories, in social and historical development, many others—Carew Hunt (*Marxism: Past and Present* 1954), Isaiah Berlin (Historical *Inevitability* 1954), and Karl Popper (*The Poverty of Historicism,* 1957) among them—have been busy fastening upon it some sort of fatalist determinism or historicism, and then criticising it for denying the importance of 'human will, consciousness, and intelligence', for regarding ideas and ideals as largely impotent or irrelevant, and for reducing man to 'a pawn', to 'a somewhat insignificant instrument in the general development of mankind'.

    In his 'Theses, on Feuerbach' Marx pointed out that 'the materialist doctrine that men are products of circumstances and upbringing, and that, therefore, changed men are products of other circumstances and changed upbringing; forgets that it is men that change circumstances and that the educator himself needs educating.' He added that 'the coincidence of the changing of circumstances and of human activity can be conceived and rationally understood only as *revolutionising practice'*. And it is here that Marx established the point of relevance of his famous declaration: The philosophers have only *interpreted* the world in various ways; the point, however, is to *change* it' (*Reader in Marxist Philosophy, op. cit.*, pp. 316-8).

The critics refuse, however, to recognise or understand this dialectic of men and circumstances, of freedom and necessity. Projecting their own one-sidedness into Marxism, they persist in misunderstanding it for opposite, and mutually exclusive reasons. An 'academic' coincidence?

2

Of Traditionalism

Barrows Dunham has written:

> It is easy to make a theory self-consistent, if the base be narrow enough. In turn, a self-consistent theory will find believers, if its implications don't jar too sharply with the data and the exigencies of the believer's daily life:.. But, of course, though a base be narrow, the universe itself is very wide. It is probable, then, that a narrow base, though it will support a theory, will not support a theory capable of explaining the universe or any considerable portion of it.[1]

I suggest that this is largely true of Oakeshott's theory of ideology as 'abridgement', which theory constitutes, as we have seen, his most important, if not the only, serious argument against rationalism. Raised on an extremely narrow reductionist empiricist base this theory is indeed remarkably self-consistent, but it fails altogether to comprehend and explain the phenomena it sets out to comprehend and explain. As a theory it remains essentially incapable of explaining 'the universe or any cosiderable portion of it', of explaining the world, or the nature and mode of acquisition of the knowledge we have of this world, or the part this knowledge plays in man's practical or political activity. The theory has been nevertheless very welcome in certain quarters; it has found even ardent believers, for its implications not only 'don't jar too sharply with the data and the exigencies of the believer's daily life', but also bring him positive comfort and consolation for they serve to provide an 'ideological' justification for a certain sort of conservation in life and politics.

What Barrows Dunham says of a theory raised on too narrow a base is, however, equally true of a theory of the opposite sort, one raised on too broad a base. A theory can be equally easily made self-consistent if the base be broad enough. But while such a theory may indeed claim by virtue of its very broad base to explain the universe itself, it may really be incapable of explaining anything at all.

In other words, a theory can be so broad-based as to provide, an explanation which accounts for everything that happens and is compatible with any and every fact, event or situation, so that there is and can be nothing which is not so determined, or which could contradict or disprove the theory. Such a theory may indeed also come to possess a high degree of coherence, systematisation and self-consistency. But necessary conditions of truth these are never by themselves sufficient grounds for it. That is to say, every self-consistent or comprehensive or systematic theory is not necessarily true and valid also. What is more important, a theory or an explanation that explains anything and everything really explains nothing, and is entirely useless from a scientific standpoint. It is clear therefore that like a too narrowly based theory, the too broadly based theory also is incapable of really explaining 'the universe (natural, social or political) or any considerable portion of it', and is consequently of no help at all in guiding men in tackling the problems of this universe successfully. Though, one must add, a theory of this sort too will find ready believers for the comfort and consolation it may otherwise bring them, for the practical and political purposes which it may otherwise serve.

Oakeshott's theory of traditionalism, I submit, is a theory of this sort.

Oakeshott's plea for traditionalism—in politics, morals and life in general—proceeds logically from his critique of rationalism. The inevitability of traditional behaviour in politics and everything else is in fact the most important conclusion, theoretical and practical, which Oakeshott draws from his argument concerning rationalism. According to his interpretation, rationalism in politics, or any other human activity, is, strictly speaking, something preposterous; it is sheer logical impossibility. 'The ideological *style* of politics', he holds, 'is, a confused style'. For 'an ideology' is, properly speaking, never anything but 'a traditional manner... abridged into a doctrine, it is only 'an abridgement', or 'an abbreviation' of a traditional manner, 'the manner in which people have been accustomed to go about the business of attending to the arrangements of their societies'. And, since 'purely empirical politics', 'politics without a policy' are also impossible and 'the *style* of politics which approximates to pure empiricism' may very rightly be dismissed as 'an approach to lunacy', this establishes *ipso facto* the logical necessity of traditional behaviour in politics. This, in fact, is Oakeshott's sole argument or 'proof' in support of his central political belief, namely, traditionalism. In Oakeshott's understanding or interpretation of human practical or political activity, we are indeed left with nothing but 'tradition' to rely upon. Tradition alone, and not 'instant desires' or 'general principles' or anything else, can, and does indeed, 'set empiricism to work' in political or any other activity. In politics, as also elsewhere, Oakeshott tells us, 'the only concrete manner of activity detectable is one in which empiricism and the ends to be pursued are recognised as dependent, alike for their existence and their operation, upon a traditional manner of behaviour.' Political activity, according to him, cannot spring 'but from the existing traditions of behaviour themselves', and 'the form it takes, because it can take no other, is the amendment of existing arrangements by exploring and pursuing what is intimated in them'. The traditional style of politics, Oakeshott thus argues, is indeed the only style possible for man.

It is Oakeshott's contention that everything in politics is of necessity traditional. Not only is every idea and ideology, even the most revolutionary, necessarily traditional, always 'an abridgement' of 'a traditional manner of attending to the arrangements of a society', but every political activity and event too, even the most violent and revolutionary— 'such as the Noraman Conquest of England, or the establishment of the Soviet *regime* in Russia'—can never be anything but traditional. Oakeshott is quite explicit on this point. Speaking of his understanding or interpretation of political activity, he writes:

> There will be some people who, though in general agreement with this understanding of political activity, will suspect that it confuses what is, perhaps, normal with what is necessary, and that important exceptions (of great contemporary relevance) have been lost in a hazy generality. It is all very well, it may be said, to observe in politics the activity of exploring and pursuing the intimations of a tradition of behaviour, but what light does this throw upon a political crisis. But if we exclude (as we must) a genuine cataclysm which for the time being made an end of politics by altogether obliterating a current tradition of behaviour (which is not what happened in Anglo-Saxon England or in Russia), there is little to support the view that even the most serious political upheaval carries us outside this understanding of politics.

A tradition, Oakeshott tells us, 'is not a fixed and inflexible manner of doing things; it is a flow of sympathy'. It may be 'temporarily disrupted by the incursion of a foreign influence', or it may 'reveal so deep-seated an incoherence that (even without foreign assistance) a crisis appears'. But howsoever caused 'political crisis... always appears within a tradition of political activity'. This is true of every 'serious political crisis', of 'even the most serious political upheaval', and 'even when it seems to be imposed upon a society by changes beyond its control'. Thus even a revolutionary crisis—'so-called "revolutionary" ' Oakeshott calls it—always appears '*within* a tradition'. And in order to meet this crisis a society has nowhere to turn to except this tradition itself. For, according to Oakeshott, no 'steady, unchanging, independent guide' exists to which a society might resort; as for the other possible guides, particularly the scientific knowledge or political theory, Oakeshott has already disposed of these, with remarkable philosophical slickness, as so much 'abridgement' or 'abbreviation', which is essentially incapable of ever being a guide to human action. Oakeshott insists therefore that even in a crisis, however serious it may be, men in a society 'have no resources outside the fragments, the vestiges, the relics of its own tradition of behaviour which the crisis has left untouched', that ' "salvation" comes from the unimpaired resources of the tradition itself .

And he adds that this is 'what none is without and all, in fact, rely upon.'[2]

There is thus an absolute inevitability about traditional Behaviour in politics. 'In politics', says Oakeshott, 'every enterprise is a consequential enterprise, the pursuit... of an intimation.' Oakeshott emphasises that his is 'a description of what political activity actually is', that his view of the matter 'is neither intended as a description of the motives of politicians nor of what they believe themselves to be doing, but of what they actually succeed in doing.' And what political activity actually is, what politicians actually succeed in doing, is never anything more than what Oakeshott calls 'the pursuit of intimations' of 'a traditional manner of behaviour'. The politician, revolutionary' or 'idealistic' or any other, who thinks otherwise is only indulging in 'self-deception'.

Oakeshott thus not only claims that every ideology and all normal political behaviour is necessarily traditional, but, by his generous definition of traditionalism, he pronounces revolution itself to be only another form of traditional political activity—unless of course it be 'a genuine cataclysm', that is, some sort of end of everything 'for the time being'. Revolution, the French or the Russian or the Chinese or any other, that historians—and occasionally lapsing into perverseness, even common people—talk about so much is only 'so-called', is not the 'genuine' thing, is not really a revolution at all. As for the customary view which contrasts revolution with tradition, Oakeshott would perhaps dismiss it as another 'erroneous belief' or 'insidious piece of misobservation', as one more example of 'misdescription' of what is really only another exercise in traditionalist politics. For according to Oakeshott, revolution is, strictly speaking, something preposterous and impossible. It simply cannot take place.

In Oakeshott's political philosophy, logic, it appears, has uses other than helping us think clearly and better. It certainly does more than merely help one avoid being 'cheated by ambiguous statement and irrelevant argument'. It enables one to explain away, to logic-off as it were, anything one wants to—from Rationalism to the Russian Revolution. This assimilation of revolution itself into tradition may be a safe enough procedure with regard to the revolutions of the past. But one wonders if Oakeshott would be quite willing to extend the legitimatising benefits of his generous definition of traditionalism to the revolutions now emergent in different parts of the world, to the revolutions of the present and the future also?

It is clear that Oakeshott's understanding and explanation of traditionalism, and with it of revolution and revolutionism, has no basis at all in political reality, past or present. And this deprives his theory of traditionalism of virtually all value, philosophical or practical. His argument in fact turns out to be quite banal. For if all politics is necessarily traditional, if even the most rationalist and revolutionary politics is yet only traditionalist politics, then it really does not matter whether you choose to be a traditionalist or not—and Oakeshott's advocacy of traditionalism in politics becomes simply meaningless. For no matter what you choose and what you do or believe yourself to be doing, the result in all cases is the same.

One cannot help concluding that in trying to say too much for traditionalism Oakeshott succeeds, in effect, in saying only too little. One will, of course, really concede Oakeshott's right to his own definitions: But the fact remains that traditionalism as defined by him is of little use in clarifying our understanding of political activity and none whatsover in guiding it. What is more, on the basis of his own theory of traditionalism Oakeshott has no right to argue against those—the reformers, radicals and revolutionaries—whose politics he despises and condemns, while on behalf of his own immediate programme—of what he calls 'slow, small changes' —he has no right to claim the support of this theory. For if everything is of necessity traditional, then, everything is, *indeed*, traditional, and thc choice between traditionalism and the supposedly anti-traditional rationalism, which Oakeshott offers, has no real basis at all to rest upon. If *all* styles of politics, no matter what their practitioners believe themselves to be doing, are necessarily traditional, then they all must be regarded equally necessarily as legitimate too. After this what precisely is Oakeshott's complaint against the rational, or ideological, style of politics? .

II

Oakeshott knows, however, that the ideological and the traditional styles of politics, as he calls them, are not the same—one is supposedly radical or revolutionary and the other equally supposedly conservative. And Oakeshott informs us in no uncertain terms that they cannot be regarded as equally legitimate or desirable. He himself most categorically rejects the former for the latter. It is not only that Oakeshott's sympathies and predilections are most of the time unambiguously conservative, he also states and defends them as such, most eloquently in his essays. He has an unqualified respect for tradition, for the established ways of life, particularly in morals and politics, and he warns against meddling with these in the name of reason, or abstract ideas and ideals, or anything else. 'There is', he says, 'a freedom and inventivenss at the heart of every traditional way of life', which we would do well to recognise and trust. He writes at length in prasie of 'being conservative', which is, he says, 'to prefer the familiar to the unknown, to prefer the tried to the untried, fact to mystery, the actual to the possible, the limited to the unbounded, the convenient to the perfect, present laughter to utopian bliss.' To be conservative is good and, in more mundane language, 'it is to be equal to one's own fortune, to live at the level of one's own means, to be content with the want of greater perfection which belongs alike to oneself and one's circumstances.' Deeply concerned about 'stability', which is any day 'more profitable than improvement', Oakeshott, naturally enough, places a very high value 'upon the complicated set of arrangements we call "the institution of private property" '. He is suspicious of both change and innovation, one 'appears always, in the first place, as deprivation', and the other always 'entails cerain loss' and only 'possible gain'. And 'there is no such thing as an unqualified improvement'. Therefore, even when a change or an innovation 'commends itself as a convincing improvement', Oakeshott would have us 'look twice at its claims before accepting them'. If change and innovation ever become necessary as they indeed do at times, if 'revolutionary change' is to be avoided, which according to Oakeshott 'is usually the product of the eventual overthrow of an aversion from change', then, obviously, 'small and slow changes' are 'more tolerable than large and sudden', 'small and limited innovations' are to be preferred 'to large and indefinite'.[3] And one should never forget the dangers of sacrificing 'a known good' to 'an unknown better'. 'Cool and critical in respect of change and innovation', one should 'value highly every appearance of continuity' and go in for only that 'reform' which is 'a response to some specific defect' or is 'designed to redress some specific disequilibrium'. Anything more, according to Oakeshott, is 'innovations designed to meet merely hypothetical situations', it is to be 'in love with what is dangerous and difficult', to betray 'the impulse to sail uncharted seas' and 'to navigate the unknown'. In other words, if change or innovation or reform does become necessary it must be carried out 'in such a manner that the society is not disrupted', it must always remain well within what Oakeshott calls the 'existing arrangements' of a society.

Oakeshott defines political activity as 'attending to arrangements' rather than as 'making arrangements' of a society, and stresses the conservative implications of this distinction. He argues that 'in any generation, even the most revolutionary, the arrangements which are enjoyed always far exceed those which are recognised to stand in need of attention, and those which are being prepared for enjoyment are few in comparison with those which receive amendment: the new is an insignificant proportion of the whole.' And he extols what according to him is man's 'propensity to use and to enjoy what is available rather than to wish for or to look for something else; to delight in what is present rather than what was or what maybe,' his propensity to 'esteem' the present merely 'on account of its familiarity'. In politics, as elsewhere, says Oakeshott, we must 'avoid the fruitless pursuit of proposed freedoms' and aim only 'to realize more fully the intimations of our society'. We should 'find freedom' in preference of those 'slow, small changes which have behind them a voluntary consensus of opinion'. Oakeshott insists that 'it is more important for a society to move together than for it to move either fast or far', and that we should be 'suspicious of those who offer us more; those who call upon us to make great sacrifices and those who want to impose upon us an heroic character'. He emphasises 'what Burke called the partnership between present and past' and holding that 'the politics of our society 'are a conversation' and 'not an argument', pleads for 'policy, precedent and prescription' in determining our political enterprise. Politics, he argues, should be properly understood only as 'the pursuit of intimations', as 'the amendment of existing arrangements by exploring and pursuing what is intimated in them'. It permits, if at all, only the most limited, the most cautious and piecemeal change in society. If others would identify this conservatism as 'timidity', Oakeshott recognises and lauds it as 'prudence', even 'rational prudence', as something 'pretty deeply rooted in what is called "human nature" '. And he ridicules the radical and the revolutionary for not recognising this, for their 'ignorance', 'conceit', and 'self-deception'. He mocks their politics as a search for 'a premeditated utopia', 'a permanently impregnable society' or 'a short cut to heaven', as an attempt at 'imposing a dream' on others, an attempt born of mistake rationalism and bound to prove disastrous. Oakeshott thus places radicalism and revolution, all large-scale change, permanently under ban in politics; he rules out the radical or revolutionary, the rational or ideological, style as entirely undesirable and impermissible in political or any other practical activity.

Now all this—and there is much more to this effect in Oakeshott's various essays—constitutes a substantial conservative position, though Oakeshott himself hesitates to call it 'a settled doctrine', and prefers instead to speak of it only in terms of 'a consistent style or disposition of thought'. 'Doctrine' or 'disposition of thought', there is no doubt, however, that Oakeshott's position is fundamentally conservative. Oakeshott is of course free to hold this or any other position he wants in politics; but, as pointed out above, this conservative position and the traditional style of politics it entails certainly do not follow as the only possible political position and style from Oakeshott's basic argument in defence of traditionalism. And I submit that Oakeshott has simply no other argument to offer in support of his conservatism. By arguing that the rational or ideological style is logically impossible and that all political activity is of necessity traditional, Oakeshott in fact deprives himself of all argument in favour of conservatism, and for that matter against revolutionism, too. On his premises, logically speaking, even the need for argument on this subject tends to disappear. It is not surprising therefore that in the final analysis Oakeshott can do no better than urge upon us 'the acceptance of the current... human circumstances', 'simply because they are current'. His conservatism ultimately represents only an *a priori* defence of the *status quo*, which reflects an equally *a priori* satisfaction with things as they are, simply because they *are*.[4]

Even a brief consideration of the matter makes it clear that such is indeed the case. Writing of 'conservative disposition' Oakeshott says that there are circumstances and occasions, kinds of human conduct, activities and relationships, when 'a disposition to be conservative will be more appropriate than any other', when it may indeed be 'the most appropriate disposition'. But he concedes that there are other circumstances and occasions, other kinds of human conduct, activities and relationships, when 'a disposition to be conservative' is not particularly appropriate', when a conservative disposition is indeed 'unmistakably at a discount'. He even concedes, rather regretfully, that 'to be conservative on all occasions and in all connections is so remote from our habit of thought as to be almost unintelligible', and that most of us find ourselves 'inclined to reject conservatism as a disposition appropriate in respect of human conduct in general'. Oakeshott then carries this argument into politics. He speaks of the ideological or radical style of politics— 'this jump to glory style of politics' he calls it—and concedes that 'it is not at all unintelligible' and even that 'there is much in our circumstances to provoke it'. He then points out that based on 'another quite different understanding of government', there is another quite different style, namely the traditional or conservative style of politics. This style, he says, 'is no less intelligible and in some respects perhaps more appropriate to our circumstances'. Now, this is quite unexceptionable. It means that both the styles of politics are in general valid, that whether one or the other is in fact appropriate or otherwise in a particular situation would depend entirely on 'our circumstances', and that all that Oakeshott is saying on behalf of his own position is that sometimes, in certain circumstances, 'in some respects perhaps', it is better, it is more appropriate, to be conservative than to be otherwise.

What Oakeshott says here is indeed very true and unexceptionable—though I doubt if even the most enthusiastic admirer will claim that it is very original or profound. It is in fact plain homespun commonsense. But it is really interesting that Oakeshott's argument as it proceeds altogether ignores these commonsense implications of his own statements. The tacit assumption is that any recognition of 'our circumstances' must result in conservative politics—an assumption which is patently false, for this recognition can as well lead, depending on the circumstances, to revolutionary politics. This assumption made, the real issues are easily obscured—the decisive, determining importance of circumstances is simply not allowed to become central to the discussion. Instead we are treated to unqualified and indiscriminate praise—in the guise, of course, of 'describing' or 'understanding or explaining'—of 'the conservative disposition' in politics. Occasionally we have a somewhat cautious, and also somewhat vacuous, observation that a conservative disposition in respect of politics 'would occupy an important place in any set of circumstances'. More often we have the substantial conservative assertion that, 'whatever the apparent appropriateness on occasion of the ideological style of politics', 'the proper attitude of government towards the current condition of human circumstances is one of acceptance', and that, therefore, politics is 'something which it is appropriate to be conservative about'.

Oakeshott, in his own way, makes it clear that no other argument, if this simple assertion may be called an argument, is really involved in his defence of conservatism. He speaks of 'writers who have considered this question', who 'commonly direct our attention to beliefs about the world in general, about human beings in general, about associations in general and even about the universe; or who say 'that the conservative in politics is so by virtue of holding certain religious beliefs; a belief, for example, in a natural law... and in a providential order reflecting a divine purpose in nature and in human history'; or who tie up the defence of conservatism with such notions as 'an "organic" theory of human society', 'a belief in the absolute value of human personality', or 'a belief in a primordial propensity of human beings to sin', etc.; or who have found it necessary in this connection to appeal to 'certain general ideas' to the effect 'that there is absolute value in the free play of human choice, that private property (the emblem of choice) is a natural right, that it is only in the enjoyment of diversity of opinion and activity that true belief and good conduct can be expected to disclose themselves', etc., etc.

Oakeshott, however, will have none of this. For him, as he says, 'something much smaller and less pretentious will do'. And this, all that is needed to defend and justify conservatism in politics, is the view Oakeshott takes of 'the activity of governing and the instruments of government': 'it is the observation of our current manner of living combined with the belief... that governing is a specific and limited activity, namely the provision and custody of general rules of conduct, which are understood, not as plans for imposing substantive activities, but as instruments enabling people to pursue the activities of their own choice with the minimum frustration'. It is, says Oakeshott, highly 'inappropriate for government' to do anything more, 'to be conspicuously "progressive" ' as he puts it. A government must rest 'upon the acceptance of the current activities and beliefs of its subjects', its activity must always be governed by 'a genuine acceptance of current beliefs simply because they are current and current activities simply because they are afoot'. 'Oakeshott's defence of conservatism thus rests upon a truly a *priori* 'acceptance of the current condition of human circumstances', an acceptance based simply on 'the observation that this condition of human circumstance is, in fact, current'. It is thus that the simple assertion is made: 'the proper attitude of government towards the current condition of human circumstance is one of acceptance'; and the equally simple conclusion drawn that politics is 'something which it is appropriate to be conservative about'.

This, one might add, is about as sound as the argument: if you agree with Oakeshott and therefore want to do nothing in politics, then a disposition to do nothing is the most appropriate one—and that is all there is to it. But what if you are unfortunately unable to share this particular form of Oakeshottian enlightenment, if you want to do something in politics, if you are a reformer, a radical or a revolutionary? Oakeshott would probably answer that this only proves you to be an 'unregenerate believer' in rationalism, a truly 'self-deceiving' rationalist, and what is worse 'essentially ineducable'—which, perhaps, also absolves Oakeshott from the obligation either to argue carefully, or to offer a more convincing or substantial defence of his conservatism.

III

That a more substantial, though not necessarily more convincing, defence of conservatism is both necessary and possible can be seen in the writings of several contemporary philosophers, historians, political thinkers and publicists, who obviously take their conservatism more seriously than does Oakeshott. This is not the place or occasion to undertake an examination of this defence.[5] But what I would like to point out here is that this defence almost invariably declines the support of reason.[6] It is in fact deeply suspicious and distrustful of human reason—'the more we cultivate reason, the more we cultivate nihilism', says Leo Strauss.[7] And this is not very surprising. For reason, by its very nature, is critical and revolutionary and generally subversive of the old and traditional socio-political systems. Contemporay conservatism; therefore, while inevitably making its fundamental appeal to tradition, is also frankly against rationalism. It bases its defence of traditionalism not on reason, nor, however, on some rather shaky and altogether negative scepticism, as Oakeshott does, but on something more 'positive'. Contemporary conservative philosophy has generally preferred to follow Burke[8] and de Maistre and to build up its defence of traditionalist conservatism with the help of the time-honoured principles of cosmic pietism, moral authoritarianism and social elitism.[9] The entire edifice of this conservatism is raised on religious foundations and well-secured with supernatural and providential sanctions. Its philosophers constantly speak of 'the eternal order of values', of 'the divine nature of law and the divine establishment of spiritual hierarchy', of 'natural distinctions' among men, and above all of 'the variety and mystery of traditional life'; they inform us that there is a supreme design' in history, that 'divine intent rules society' and that 'Providence is the proper instrument of change.'[10] Taking full advantage of the sceptic's systematic use of reason to undermine *human* reason, they appeal, often a bit too noisily, to some 'higher reason'. God himself is pressed into service, so to speak, to provide much needed support to the traditional social and political order.[11]

Though substantial in some respects, this defence of traditionalist conservatism is intellectually not very sound or respectable and many in our age may well regard its philosophical bona fides as rather poor if not altogether suspect.[12] At any rate it is clearly demod', so far as Oakeshott is concerned. He is evidently too bored, even when satisfied, with things as they are, too distrustful of moral or political enthusiasm, too sceptical about serious political commitment—he is altogether too 'modern' in fact to join in a defence of this sort. He defence or advocacy of conservatism, as he himself tells us, has 'nothing to do with a natural law or a providential order', with 'morals or religion', or with 'any high-falutin metaphysical beliefs'. But in noticing this difference one must still point out that Oakeshott's seemingly 'modern' defence ' of conservatism and its more orthodox defence by others are, even philosophically, not so far apart as might otherwise appear. A scientific doctrine which frankly trusts in 'Providence' and 'divine intent' in fact supplement and support each other, the latter really takes over the argument where the former leaves it. The 'scientific' nihilism of a philosophy like that of Oakeshott makes it only the easier for the unscientific theologically sanctioned 'truth' or 'purpose' to prevail over the minds of men—in the interests of the *status quo* and the established power. In any case so far as the practical consequences are concerned—and this is what really matters in philosophies of this sort—

both the unorthodox and the orthodox defence of conservatism in the end come to the same thing. Both denigrate human reason and human purpose, and leave man with no real criteria for judging the worth of human actions and attitudes. Both distrust scientifically grounded ethics and politics, and doubt or mock the reality of man's Promethean struggle for 'the better', for 'social justice', for 'happiness and prosperity' here on this earth. Both defend 'the irrationality of tradition against the powers of human reason' and deny 'the legitimacy of man's attempt individually to control his own fate and collectively to build his own world'.[13] For both social action, especially of a radical nature, is suspect. Both not only emphasise its futility but question in fact the very assumption of human capacity to solve problems of human existence. And both therefore, sooner or later, urge upon man to bear the evils and iniquities of this world as necessary and inescapable, to acquiesce patiently in the injustices of the existing order based on private property, privilege and minority rule.

It is thus that Oakeshott's teaching remains, despite its profound scepticism and lack of much positive political doctrine, and despite also the almost fatal logical flaw of its theory of traditionalism, an important part of contemporary conservative philosophy, and lends substantial, though largely indirect, support to the defence of the *status quo*, to the conservative cause in politics.

IV

I have pointed out earlier the serious logical weakness of Oakeshott's theory of traditionalism insofar as it seeks to justify the conservative style as the only possible and permissible style in politics. But in noticing this weakness, we do not exhaust all consideration of Oakeshott's concept of tradition. We still need to examine it further, and a little more closely too, particularly because this concept is central to whatever is positive in Oakeshott's political teaching.

Giving what he calls 'an exceedingly matter-of-fact description of the characteristics of any tradition' Oakeshott writes:

> A tradition of behaviour is a tricky thing to get to know. Indeed, it may even appear to be essentially unintelligible. It is neither fixed nor finished; it has no changeless centre to which understanding can anchor itself; there is no sovereign purpose to be perceived or invariable direction to be detected; there is no model to be copied, idea to be realized, or rule to be followed. Some parts of it may change more slowly than others. Nevertheless, though a tradition of behaviour is flimsy and elusive, it is not without identity, and what makes it a possible object of knowledge is the fact that all its parts do not change at the same time and that the changes it undergoes are potential within it. Its principle is a principle of *continuity*: authority is diffused between past, present, and future; between the old, the new, and what is to come. It is steady because, though it moves, it is never wholly in motion; and though it is tranquil, it is never wholly at rest. Nothing that ever belonged to it is completely lost; we are always swerving back to recover and make something topical out of even its remotest moments: and nothing for long remains unmodified. Everything is temporary, but nothing is arbitrary. Everything figures by comparison, not with what stands next to it, but with the whole. And since a tradition of behaviour is not susceptible of the distinction between essence and accident, knowledge of it is unavoidably knowledge of its detail: to know only the gist is to know nothing. What has to be learned is not an abstract idea, or a set of tricks, not even a ritual, but a concrete, coherent manner of living in all its intricateness.

What Oakeshott says here may be very true, but it is all too vague and amorphous. With its broad generalities and empty rhetoric, and its unmistakable Hegelian flavour, this passage, which could well be a 'description' of almost anything under the sun, is not likely to be of much help ins understanding 'a tradition'. While not denying itself the benefit of an occasional rhetorical flourish of idealist 'holism—'the whole'—it is really a typical example of 'description' in the true logical positivist style, with of course the additional Oakeshottian touch of the mystical and the mysteriously 'unintelligible'. The problem of the 'identity' of a tradition and 'its knowledge' is raised but never really resolved. It is in fact impossible of resolution on Oakeshottian premises. For 'the distinction between essence and accident' is simply, and it seems to me much too lightly, brushed aside. That there is 'no changeless centre', 'no sovereign purpose' or 'invariable direction' is taken to be sufficient reason to conclude that there is no centre or purpose or direction whatsoever to a tradition which we may meaningfully describe or discuss. The knowledge of a tradition is declared to be always and 'unavoidably' knowledge only of 'its detail' or 'its parts', of its aspects, elements or particulars. One may indeed wonder that if this is indeed the case, how is Oakeshott justified in talking about '*a tradition*' at all, or in wanting to have 'knowledge of *it*'?

I submit that Oakeshott's description and discussion of 'a tradition' evades the most fundamental question, namely the *identity* of a tradition as a whole. The point that a tradition 'is not susceptible to the distinction between essence and accident' and that 'to know only the gist (whatever that may mean) is to know nothing' are only conventional current philosophical cliches to help this evasion. For a tradition does have its identity and uniqueness even in the midst of its change and flux. It is the specific form of unity of 'its detail' and 'parts'—even if it is a relative and transitory unity, and even if 'it is neither fixed nor finished' which defines the essence of a tradition, which makes it *the* tradition and no other, and which determines its centre, purpose and direction even if these are not—they need not be—changeless, sovereign or invariable respectively. Without thus establishing the identity of a tradition, without finding out which of its innumerable details or parts, relations and characteristics are most closely bound up with its very existence as *the* tradition, a tradition can never be really understood or explained nor, one might add, its 'intimations' elicited and pursued, which is what Oakeshott wants and prescribes as the sole legitimate form of political activity. In the absence of such a notion of identity, it is literally impossible to discuss meaningfully not only the particular problems of a tradition—its emergence and becoming, its difference "from another tradition, its decay and disappearance or displacement, its continuity and discontinuity, its intimations to be pursued, etc.— but also the problems in general of continuity and change, of old and new, and of evolution and revolution.

Oakeshott's exclusively empiricistic concern with the 'flow

of sympathy' or the 'principle of continuity' which is tradition results in an evasion of the really important question of the formal structure and specific identity of *what* flows or continues. For Oakeshott there is nothing outside tradition, nothing it seems can ever be lost to it, nor anything really added. Tradition has everything—all its parts and all its detail—and everything continues. New is therefore not really new, break is not really a break, revolution is not really a revolution. Oakeshott's concept of tradition, if true, is a truism, and one utterly useless in understanding or explaining or guiding political activity.

V

The concept of tradition as defined and interpreted by Oakeshott comes very close to being precisely the sort of all-understanding and all-explaining rationalist-idealist 'principle' or 'generality', which he very rightly criticises elsewhere in his essays. And he shows an almost studied carelessness in using this concept to understand and explain political activity. As a consequence it is his own case for conservatism which suffers the most. By obliterating the distinction between tradition and revolution, he drains not only revolution but tradition itself of all meaning. By refusing to recognise that the new though based on the old is nevertheless genuinely new—and does not merely 'seem' to be new—he drains the old of all meaning. By denying the reality of the break—of the 'jerky' and the 'discontinuous' as he calls it—he drains the much proclaimed 'principle of continuity' of all meaning.

Though basic, this is not our only difficulty with Oakeshott's use of the concept of tradition to justify his conservatism. Allied with it are several other difficulties of which two may be immediately mentioned.

In the first place, Oakeshott occasionally tries to provide some real basis for his theory of traditionalism by interpreting tradition as we ordinarily understand it—without even abandoning, however, the broader interpretation we have discussed above. He generally interprets tradition rather too broadly, as something synonymous with the 'total situation' of a society, including within itself everything, that is, everything that has happened or can happen, in order to establish the inescapable necessity of traditional behaviour in politics. But he proceeds at will to interpret and use it in the usual, narrower and commonly accepted, sense also. He alters the meaning of 'acting within a tradition'—after having used it broadly to cover all political activity—in such a manner as to confine it to only the cautious and conservative political activity which he wishes to commend. Now we are all traditionalists in the first sense—this is an obvious and necessary truth. Not only is society and everything in it the product of a long historical development, something handed down from generation to generation, but everything we think and do as men has this inherited, objectively real, and highly complex natural and social situation as its necessary context and basis. All our ideology and all our activity, political and every other, must arise within this total situation—or 'tradition' if one chooses to so call it with Oakeshott. We are in a very real sense the products of this situation in whatever we think and do—even when we criticise it in our ideology or rebel against it in our political activity. In this sense, we are indeed, all of us traditionalists—though it is obvious that to *be* such is also meaningless. But all of us are not traditionalists in the other, narrower and generally conservative sense. Oakeshott's pressing of both the interpretations of traditionalism simultaneously into service or in shifting from one to the other at will to suit the convenience of his argument, is, to say the least, highly questionable. Far from helping us understand his teaching better or clarifying the issues involved, this procedure only compounds the ambiguities and confusions of Oakeshott's political philosophy.

The other difficulty I have in mind relates to certain statements which Oakeshott makes in the course of his description, explanation or defence of the traditional behaviour in morals, politics and life in general. Oakeshott's basic position, as already noticed, is one that asserts the absolute validity of the traditional behaviour. He holds such behaviour to be necessary and appropriate at all times and in all circumstances. But in explaining or elaborating his case Oakeshott makes concessions, or admits facts and developments, which are hopelessly at odds with this basic position. These concessions and admissions may have their value in giving Oakeshott's argument a veneer of much-needed realism, but they seriously undermine it, directly or indirectly, as an argument in defence of unqualified traditionalism, in defence particularly of the traditional or conservative style as the only appropriate style in politics.

Oakeshott thus admits that there are historical situations when the morality, and by implication the politics, of habit and tradition suffers 'a breakdown', when its 'vitality' is lost and its 'impetus' entirely 'spent', when it 'degenerates into superstition' and 'has little power of recovery', and when there indeed occurs a general 'loss of confidence' in the traditional direction' of moral and political life of a society. He takes note of 'the want of moral sensibility, the hollowness of moral character, which seem often to inhere in peoples whose morality is predominantly one of custom'. He writes of a 'social and political system' going 'bankrupt', and of 'ideals', 'the self-conscious morality', arising to fill 'the vacuum left by the collapse' of a 'traditional' morality or politics, and he does not even wish to suggest that this is always avoidable. He speaks of the existence, in America for example, of a *habit* of rationalism, of a tradition, as it were, of anti-traditionalism itself. 'Long before the Revolution', he tells us, 'the disposition of mind of the American colonists, the prevailing intellectual character and habit of politics, were rationalistic; 'the native political habit, the product of the circumstances of colonisation, was what may be called a kind of natural and unsophisticated rationalism'. He admits, as a 'predicament' of course, the fact that the entire western tradition, *over the centuries*, has come to be permeated, 'corrupted' and 'diseased' in Oakeshott's words, with rationalism. And above all, Oakeshott recognises that 'habits of behaviour' may be 'converted' into 'abstract ideas' or 'ideals', and that 'ideas' or 'ideals' may be 'reconverted into a habit of behaviour '—'such conversion is certainly possible', he concedes.

These facts and developments are rather difficult of explanation in terms of traditionalism as Oakeshott upholds it, particularly as a defence of conservatism. It is certainly impossible to reconcile them with his basic position that traditionalism is the only legitimate and always available guide to conduct in morals and politics.

The implications of the facts and developments admitted by Oakeshott are all destructive of his advocacy of unqualified traditionalism. The most important and obvious implication is that the rigid dichotomy between 'habits' and 'ideals', between traditionalism and rationalism, between the conservative and the radical or revolutionary styles in politics, on which the entire edifice of Oakeshott's political philosophy ultimately rests, has broken down and that it must be abandoned as both logically false and practically impossible. The admissions of Oakeshott in fact concede the necessity as well as the legitimacy of a great deal of both rationalism and radical or revolutionary change in society. For, to put it briefly, in admitting the 'breakdown' of 'the traditional direction' of life, or the 'bankruptcy' of a 'social and political system', Oakeshott really concedes the need for new ideas and ideologies to arise and for radical and revolutionary changes to take place. And in recognising, however confusedly, that this does in fact happen and cannot even be regarded as 'avoidable', Oakeshott really concedes the historical fact that men, aware of the 'breakdown' or 'bankruptcy' of the old and the traditional, not only become aware, inevitably as it were, of the need to strive consciously for the new but also proceed, sooner or later, to act on the basis of this need; they proceed, in other words, to invent and engineer in a truly radical, even revolutionary style.

In a fundamental sense men have to invent and engineer, to strive consciously, at all times. Men 'attending' to the 'existing arrangements' of a society, as Oakeshott calls them, always find it necessary, not only to 'amend' or 'unmake' some of these arrangements but also to undertake the task of making many new ones. The movement of social and political life itself constantly creates new problems and new solutions have to be found for them. And men find these solutions with the help of reason, with the help of whatever knowledge they happen to possess. Such is the process of social and historical change which goes on all the time. But this process has quantitative as well as qualitative aspects. A process 'of continuous movement and change, of continuous renewal and development', it is not 'a simple process of growth'. It is marked also by 'leaps', by 'open, fundamental changes'. Revolutions are as natural and inevitable a part of this process as are slow changes or reforms.[14] And when a revolution occurs it involves a change of such depth and magnitude that we may legitimately speak not only of the death of the old order, but also of the birth of a new one.[15]

This process of social and historical change, with its continuous conflict between the old and the new, inevitably gives rise to new ideas and theories, which arise, in Marx's words, as 'ideological forms in which men become conscious of this conflict and fight it out.[16] While some of these may well only be the ideological defence of the old order, others prepare men for the task of carrying out the changes necessary for the further progress of society. These new ideas and theories arise and come to be widely accepted, they 'take on', precisely because they are necessary to society, necessary for the further social development, because it is impossible to carry out the new tasks men have come to set themselves 'without their organizing, mobilizing and transforming action.[17]

Just as these new ideas and theories, the more significant among them at any rate, cannot be understood or treated, as Oakeshott does, merely as 'abridgements' of 'a traditional manner of attending to the arrangements of a society', so also the radical or revolutionary activity which they often enough generate and guide cannot be understood or treated, as Oakeshott again does, merely as another kind of traditional political activity. A revolution is not merely a continuation of traditional politics by other means, or in another form. It is far more truly a consequence of the 'breakdown' of this traditional politics, a product invariably of some deep-seated irrationality, or 'incoherence' as Oakeshott might call it, in the 'existing arrangements' of a society. No doubt, a revolution develops, along with the material conditions of existence of the new social order, within the old, traditional order; it matures, as it were, 'in the womb of the old society'. But as a more or less conscious act of men, it goes *outside and beyond* this society in so fundamental a manner as to transform it into something different and new. It gives rise to a *new society* —even though this new society rises 'in every respect, economically, morally and intellectually, still stamped with the birthmarks of the old society from whose womb it emerges.'[18] This new society soon comes to give men, of course at a higher level of social development, the same security as the old once did; it becomes, with all its 'arrangements' and 'ideals', traditional. But it is also destined, in its turn, to grow old and outmoded and to fade away. A correct understanding therefore must treat revolution as a real and genuine phenomenon, as an inevitable concomitant of the historical process in which 'all successive historical situations are only transitory stages in the endless course of development of human society from the lower to the higher:[19]

A correct understanding of the dialectical nature of social and political reality, of historical process, must not therefore limit itself to accommodating only the old, the traditional and the evolutionary. It must also recognise the place of the new, the rational and the revolutionary in this reality or process. In the same way a correct understanding of political activity must recognise the need and legitimacy not only of 'the traditional' style in politics, but also of 'the ideological' style as Oakeshott chooses to call it. In other words, one cannot be either wholly traditional and conservative in politics, or wholly 'rational' and radical or revolutionary. One needs to be both. Both the styles are, in general, valid and neither can be regarded, in any meaningful sense, as self-sufficient. Only objective circumstances can help us decide the precise extent of their validity or appropriateness, or their proper mutual balance in a given situation. Circumstances alone determine whether men will seek guidance more in one 'style' than in the other. There are circumstances, generally of a comfortable or pleasant sort, when 'the traditional' may indeed be the more appropriate style; though it is quite fatuous to assume that such circumstances are universal or even widespread, or even permanently available. Besides, it is always well to remember that even' in order to preserve it may be necessary not only 'to reform', as Burke fully realised, but also to invent and engineer in a manner and to a degree that the traditional style in politics, .the Oakeshottian politics of 'pursuit of intimations', will simply not permit. But there are other circumstances, far more common in contemporary societies, when men, those not so comfortably situated, may find 'the square meal of experience' they are having to be neither very appetising nor nourishing; when 'the present' does not merely 'appear' to be but is 'arid', 'a residue of inopportunities' only; when, therefore, men may feel compelled to prefer the 'new' to the 'old', 'the future' however 'unknown' to 'the present' however' familiar', when they may discover not only that they must move both 'fast' and 'far', but also that only 'to move together' means an immobility at once impossible and disastrous, and when they may even decide that not 'slow, small changes' but revolution itself has to be undertaken by them.

It is the circumstances, I repeat, the objective situation alone, which determines the appropriateness or otherwise, or the precise degree of appropriateness, of what Oakeshott calls 'the traditional' and 'the ideological' styles of politics. And Oakeshott has, therefore, no justification at all either in fact or logic for arbitrarily opposing one style to the other, for unreservedly praising one and denigrating the other—all of course in the guise of 'describing' or 'explaining' them—and for arguing, as he indeed does, that 'the traditional' or the conservative is the appropriate style in politics while 'the ideological', the radical or the revolutionary is not.

Oakeshott argues in this manner despite the fact that the events and developments admitted by him in the course of his argument point to an altogether different conclusion. Oakeshott speaks of a 'bankrupt social and political system', of 'the vacuum left by the collapse of a traditional morality', of 'a breakdown' of morality or politics of habit and tradition, of 'conversion' and 'reconversion' of 'habits' and 'ideals' into each other, etc., etc. But he refuses to see the obvious implications of such phenomena. He admits these phenomena, it seems, only to make his argument appear more plausible; and then proceeds to deny their reality and genuineness in order to save the same argument from their destructive implications. He argues, as we have seen, that no matter what happens, it must always happen '*within* a tradition' and that no matter what the 'salvation' is, it must also come only from 'the tradition', from 'the fragments, the vestiges, the relics,... the unimpaired resources of the tradition itself.

Oakeshott, of course, speaks also of 'a genuine cataclysm' which makes 'an end of politics' itself, at least 'for the time being'. Such a cataclysm may indeed—it alone, if anything, it seems, can—leave Oakeshott really resourceless and stranded, and, perhaps, at the mercy of rationalism at last! But he excludes, and very rightly so, the consideration of such a contingency, for a cataclysm of this sort is, obviously, a rare if not an altogether impossible phenomenon in *real* history. We are back therefore where we started: with Oakeshott there is simply no getting away from 'the tradition', never. Certainly, not so long as politics lasts. Only this leaves one wondering what words like 'breakdown', 'bankruptcy' or 'collapse' really mean, or what justification Oakeshott has for using them at all!

VI

The ambiguities and confusions and serious logical difficulties of his concept of tradition notwithstanding, Oakeshott makes an attempt to draw some meaning out of it in order to explain and validate his conservatism, the traditionalist politics of 'the pursuit of intimations', as he calls it, which permits only 'small and slow changes'.[20]

Oakeshott defines politics as 'the activity of attending to the general arrangements of a collection of people who, in respect of their common recognition of a manner of attending to its arrangements, compose a single community', which we call 'a state'. It has been his argument, as we have already noticed, that the understanding of this activity as one carried out 'under the guidance of an independently premeditated ideology is... no less a misunderstanding than the understanding of it as a purely empirical activity'. Both these understandings are 'inadequate', says. Oakeshott, because both of them lack 'something to set empiricism to work'. Properly speaking, neither 'a merely instant desire, nor 'a political ideology' can do so. Only 'tradition' can. Thus, according to Oakeshott,

> political activity springs neither from instant desires, nor from general principles, but from the existing traditions of behaviour themselves. And the form it takes, because it can take no other, is the amendment what is intimated in them. The arrangements which constitute a society capable of political activity... are at once, coherent and incoherent; they compose a pattern and at the same time they intimate a sympathy for what does not fully appear. Political activity is the exploration of that sympathy...[21]

Such is Oakeshott's view of the nature of political activity. It correctly emphasises 'the existing traditions' or the 'existing arrangements', that is, the given objective situation, of a society, as the necessary condition and basis of all politics. This emphasis is valid at all times and is particularly important against all dogmatically-rationalist or doctrinaire politics. Oakeshott's view also clearly suggests that in politics the ideal must always be grounded in the nature of the actual, it must be possible. This again is a valuable truth to which our attention has been drawn by many thinkers. It was stressed, for example, by Marx for whom 'ought to be' was always a temporal function of 'what is[22]. and more recently by Hobhouse who wrote that 'the ethically desirable must be sociologically possible'. But these generally valid and oft-emphasised truths apart, Oakeshott's view has, I am afraid, little to offer by way of positive guidance in the pursuit of practical politics.

Oakeshott's discussion of the subject abounds, as usual, in negatives. He tells us that 'there is no piece of mistake-proof apparatus by means of which we can elicit the intimations most worthwhile pursuing', that 'our activity of amendment is often found to lead us where we would not go', that 'the whole enterprise is liable at any moment to be perverted by the incursion of an approximation to empiricism in the pursuit of power', etc. He warns us against the great danger of making 'gross errors of judgment in this matter'. And he warns us once more against the still great danger of harbouring rationalist 'illusions'. But of concrete positive guidance we get precious little. The really important questions as to how we recognise or detect 'an incoherence' or determine 'the remedy' for it, as to what standard or criterion will help us choose between various 'intimations', between desirable and undesirable, possible and impossible political projects, as to whose assessment of the intimations to be pursued is to be accepted as authoritative and final, as to when and why in fact we should decide to do one thing rather than another—ail these questions remain simply unanswered.

There is of course the appeal, fundamental to the politics of 'pursuit of intimations', to always consult 'tradition'. But at the practical level this appeal is not of much help for it turns out to be highly ambiguous. Oakeshott's argument would be more plausible, in theory at least, if the society we live in contained an unified and homogeneous tradition or at least a mutually harmonious stable set of traditions. But this is simply not the case. There is no magic spell of a single unbroken tradition on which any modern society may be said to be steadily based. The political tradition—if one must use this abstracting phrase—of a modern society, often highly complex and class-divided, really consists of *several* traditions, each with its own memories, purposes and striving for power, each representing a different kind of 'knowledge of how to behave' as Oakeshott calls it. And these are far from being mutually harmonious, not all of them at any rate[23] Many of these may in fact be sharply in conflict with each other. In such a situation Oakeshott's recommendation to always consult tradition, to pursue the politics of traditionalism alone, far from yielding a necessarily conservative line, may in fact yield no conceivable line of conduct in politics at all. Oakeshott's identification of traditionalism and political conservatism has, thus, simply no real basis to rest upon.[24]

Not only may the several political traditions of a modern society be mutually contradictory and disharmonious, it may also not be possible to regard them all as equally valid or sacrosanct. A tradition, *qua* tradition, cannot be considered as valuable in itself, regardless of its influence upon men or their practical, political activity. Something more is needed in fact to confer sanctity or validity on a tradition and to make it acceptable than the mere fact that it exists, that it *continues to be.*

Oakeshott's argument to the contrary notwithstanding, 'familiarity' by itself 'has no worth'; a tradition has no value 'merely because it exists' or even 'because it has existed for many generations'. For it can well happen that a tradition inherited from 'all the dead generations' may weigh 'like a nightmare on the brain of the living', as Marx once put it.[25]

Oakeshott seemingly gets over the difficulty created by the obvious plurality of political traditions in a society, by talking, most of the time, about 'a tradition' or 'the tradition', or 'our tradition' or 'concrete tradition', of political behaviour. But this procedure is obviously illegitimate and only results in obscuring the real problem that given a highly complex modern society with its competing and conflicting traditions, and given also the divergence of men entrusted with the task of 'exploring' and 'eliciting' their intimations, these intimations may well compete and conflict with each other. In other words, 'a chaos' of conflicting intimations is as much of a possibility in the traditional style of politics as 'a chaos of conflicting ideals': for which rationalism is persistently ridiculed and condemned by Oakeshott in his essays. Only now, with reason put virtually under an interdict, there seems to be no possible way of choosing or deciding between them.

Under the circumstances it would have perhaps made better sense to speak of the dominant or ruling tradition, tradition of the ruling class in a society, and to interpret politics proper as a 'conversation' with this tradition only, its intimations alone being regarded worth eliciting and pursuing. This is, I think, what Oakeshott really means and intends. But for obvious reasons he cannot frankly confess to it. For this position would simply not yield the conclusions Oakeshott wants in order to buttress his argument for traditionalist conservatism. It may in fact be destructive of his entire case for conservatism in politics.[26]

VII

The theoretical and practical difficulties of Oakeshott's use of the concepts of tradition and traditionalism to buttress his case for conservatism are many and formidable. Some of these have been already discussed. In conclusion I would like to suggest one more: his interpretation of politics as 'the pursuit of intimations' is vague and broad enough to accommodate every kind of politics, from the most conservative to the most revolutionary.

There is no doubt that Oakeshott himself holds that his understanding of politics rules out radical or revolutionary attempts to 'solve problems', that the most we can do is to 'remedy incoherencies' and this permits only the most cautious reforms, the carrying out of only 'slow, small changes'. But this is not necessarily the case. The demand for farreaching radical changes can as well be framed and defended in terms of 'the pursuit of intimations' as of, what according to Oakeshott is absolutely impermissible, allegedly 'abstract' ideals. 'Solving problems' which Oakeshott condemns, and 'remedying incoherencies' by 'pursuing intimations' which Oakeshott praises, are in the final analysis only different ways of describing the same thing—and this may as well involve a large-scale as a small-scale change. In other words, the politics of 'pursuit of intimations' can be as 'problem-solving' as the so-called ideological politics. There may well be societies and circumstances in which the 'relevant political reasoning' which Oakeshott permits, if boldly conducted, may indicate the need for radical, even revolutionary changes. Even a socialist could, perhaps, frame and defend his demands in terms of Oakeshott's conceptual framework of politics as 'the pursuit of intimations' without unduly stretching it. He could not only speak of the 'deep seated incoherence' of the capitalist society or the need for radical 'amendment of existing arrangements', he could defend socialism itself as something that Oakeshott permits, that is, as 'the next step dictated or suggested by the character of the (capitalist) society.'[27] Oakeshott is certainly right in insisting that mere ideals are not enough, that the possible must be *based* on the actual. But the range of the possible is not for that reason necessarily limited or small. It rather depends, speaking in Oakeshottian terms, among other things, upon how vital and significant is the 'sympathy present but not yet followed up', how deep and fundamental is 'the incoherence' in the 'existing arrangements' of a society, and even more upon *how deep* and *how far* one is able or willing to see into the real nature of these 'arrangements', into 'the character', 'the permanent interests and direction of movement' of a society. Oakeshott may be right in insisting that politics can never be anything more than 'the pursuit of intimations'—but this does not and need not justify 'slow and small changes' alone.

In arguing for conservatism, for the traditional style in politics, what Oakeshott himself forbids is only 'proposals for change in excess of what the situation calls for', proposals which offer more than the situation will bear. But this would rule out by the same logic those other proposals also which offer less than what the situation requires. If Oakeshott's argument here means anything it is this: in a given situation the proposals of change most adequately suited to it should be adopted. This is a perfectly sound principle. It was in fact first worked out in its general form a long time ago by Aristotle himself, when he argued that every occasion has just one act which is adequately suited to it. This is the essential meaning of his theory of 'the mean'.[28]

But while the principle is right, Oakeshott is quite wrong in drawing only conservative conclusions from it. For not only will this suitable proposal change with changing situation, a particular situation may well call for proposals of radical, even revolutionary change—the only necessary condition being that these should be realistically grounded. It is thus the objective situation alone that serves not only as a standard by which all proposals for change—small-scale or large-scale—are to be tested, but it also ensures protection from wishful thinking in this matter. If Oakeshott is right in warning us against the wishful thinking of the radical or the revolutionary—'the rationalist' he calls him—he is quite wrong in refusing to recognise that we need to be equally on guard against wishful thinking of the opposite sort—that of the conservative or the traditionalist, who assumes *a priori* that deliberate radical or revolutionary changes are always and everywhere unnecessary or undesirable or even impossible, that to 'recognise circumstance' is to be necessarily conservative and in favour of only 'small and slow changes'.

Oakeshott himself, of course, has a preference for these 'small and slow changes'. Strictly speaking he regards only these to be possible and permissible. He is also convinced that the traditional style of politics permits these and these changes alone. Against this he regards the changes decreed by the rationalist style as impossible and impermissible. These are, according to him, inevitably large-scale and bound to prove costly failures. But the difficulty with his entire argument is that he gives us no really independent criteria which may help us to identify the permissible from the impermissible proposals of change, to distinguish between the changes undertaken by the so-called traditionalist and rationalist styles respectively. In the absence of such criteria it is impossible to decide whether, the 'rationalist' changes are all impossible or impermissible or bound to be costly failures, or not. It is really begging the question to condemn them simply because they are rationally recommended, or are large scale. And it is worse still to make failure itself a defining characteristic of the changes associated with the rationalist style.[29] As a matter of fact it is quite possible—Oakeshott's own argument almost concedes as much—for the traditionalist style of politics to undertake more than 'small and slow changes' in a situation, just as it is possible for the rationalist style to undertake only 'slow and small changes' in another. It is, therefore, altogether arbitrary to hold, as Oakeshott does, that the traditional style is the only appropriate style in politics and that 'small and slow changes' are the only changes possible or permissible in a society.

Oakeshott speaks of 'the projects of Rationalism' with which 'the modern history of Europe is littered'. Arguing that 'the odd generation of rationalism in politics is by sovereign power out of romanticism', he presents us with a long list of these projects. He writes:

> The most sublime of these is, perhaps, that of Robert Owen for 'a world convention to emancipate the human race from ignorance, poverty, division, sin and misery'—so sublime that even a Rationalist (but without much justification) might think it eccentric .... The notion of founding a society, whether of individuals or of States, upon a Declaration of the Rights of Man is a creature of the

> rationalist brain, so also are 'national' or racial self-determination when elevated into universal principles. The project of the so-called Re-union of the Christian Churches, of open diplomacy, of a single tax, of a civil service whose members 'have no qualifications other than their personal abilities', of a self-consciously planned society, the Beveridge Report, the Education Act of 1944, Federalism, Nationalism, Votes for Women, the Catering Wages Act, the destruction of the Austro-Hungarian Empire, the World State-of H.G. Wells or anyone else), and the revival of Gaelic as the official language of Eire, are alike the progeny of Rationalism.

The projects mentioned here are quite varied. They are all very interesting too, for the characteristically Oakeshottian choice and the form in which they are described. But one does not need to examine them very carefully in order to suggest that several of them at least can any day be understood and defended as 'the progeny' as much of traditionalism as of rationalism, and that some of them could be even better understood and explained in terms of the politics of 'pursuit of intimation' than of 'the politics of Rationalism' as Oakeshott defines it. In fact, Oakeshott himself in a later essay so understands and explains the realisation of one of these projects, namely 'the technical "enfranchisement" of women' as he calls it. Looking for 'the only cogent reason', 'the one valid argument' for this reform, Oakeshott explains it as a case of 'an incoherence in the arrangements of the society which pressed convincingly for remedy'. It would appear that almost anything from the Votes for Women to the Russian Revolution can be explained in terms of traditionalism—but only *after* it has happened. An 'intimation', it seems, is known only after it somehow gets realised. This, it is clear, hardly gives any guidance *in advance* about what can and should be done in politics, about what projects, if any, are indeed permitted, not to speak of decreed necessary, by the politics of 'pursuit of intimations'.

Even a tentative effort by Oakeshott to suggest some concrete reforms, say' for contemporary England, in terms of the politics of 'pursuit of intimations' he recommends, clearly pointing out what it does or does not permit, would have helped us to understand his political teaching better. But that, perhaps, would have been an exercise in 'vulgar' rationalism, and taboo to any traditionalist worthy of the name. The result is that while Oakeshott condemns rationalism and rejects 'the abstract' and 'the doctrinaire' in politics, he has himself nothing better to offer us in the end—despite his constant talk of the 'practical' and the 'concrete'—than an utterly abstract and doctrinaire traditionalism. We know, however, that Oakeshott himself, on other and rather arbitrary grounds, permits very little in politics: For him the best politics is that which does nothing but manage 'to keep afloat'— this is indeed what traditionalist politics means to Oakeshott.[30] Those who would live by his teaching really need to do nothing but somehow keep floating. And if anything more nevertheless gets done, they can always depend upon Oakeshott to so 'explain' it as to claim it for traditionalism—and thus confound the rationalist!

VIII

It is clear—the conclusion is in fact unavoidable—that Oakeshott's interpretation of politics as 'the pursuit of intimations' is incapable of offering us any positive guidance in pursuing political activity.[31] The real situation is, however, much worse and far more disturbing in its implications than this bare conclusion would appear to suggest:

Oakeshott insists most emphatically that political philosophy, properly understood, 'has no power to guide or to direct us in the enterprise of pursuing the intimations of our tradition', that 'it will not help us to distinguish between good and bad political projects'. This guidance or direction or help cannot come from political theory also. Oakeshott rejects all social and political theory, including the scientific, as so much 'abridgement', and in so doing rejects the only knowledge which may help us see deep and far into 'the character' or 'tradition', into 'the permanent interests and direction of movement' of a society. He offers us instead his own understanding of political activity. But the most it can do for us, in his own words, is: 'the more profound our understanding of political activity, the less we shall be at the mercy of plausible but mistaken analogy, the less we shall be tempted by a false or irrelevant model'. And, in addition, Oakeshott limits very severely, altogether arbitrarily, and in advance, as it were, the need and possibility of deliberate, consciously carried out change in a society. Under the circumstances it is not difficult to visualise that the activity of 'pursuit of intimations' will in effect be reduced to merely looking for the right 'analogy', the correct 'model' or the relevant 'precedent' in the present or past 'arrangements' of a society, and following it. Political activity will really come to mean acting on hunches, or guessing 'the moves to come' and going along with them. And its outcome will be precisely that 'obstinate refusal to budge', that 'approach to lunacy' empiricism, or 'pure pragmatism', that 'merely doing what was done "last time" 'or 'the preference for the short-cut', which Oakeshott otherwise disclaims; it will be a superficial, narrowly utilitarian and eclectic practicalism, an utterly ignorant tinkering, meddling and muddling through in politics, which Oakeshott's argument otherwise, and very rightly too, seeks to condemn.

But if carried to its logical end, and practised seriously, the politics of 'pursuit of intimations' could well mean a descent into plain irrationalism in politics. It is not only that a scepticism of the sort which Oakeshott professes and preaches, may well drive men to seek guidance from 'fools' or become 'dupes of every adventurer in politics' as Collingwood once pointed out; or that his deliberate disavowal of rational principled philosophy in politics will leave men entirely at the mercy, in Locke's words, of 'doctrines that have been derived from no better original than the superstition of a nurse, or the authority of an old woman', and grown up 'by length of time and consent of neighbours, to the dignity of *principles*,'[32] —leave them slaves, as Engels once put it, 'to the most vulgarised relics of the worst philosophies'. All this is indeed bound to happen: 'In the absence of a more or less rational theory', Cobban says, men will inevitably 'fall victim to an irrational one.[33] But it is not only indirectly that Oakeshott's philosophy makes for irrationalism in politics. His positive teaching also tends in the same direction.

Oakeshott's nihilistic attack upon reason takes in its sweep all notions, as he puts it, of 'a "reason" common to all mankind', of 'a common power of rational consideration', of 'intellectual equalitarianism', and of men judging and deciding things 'by rational argument'. Carrying this attack into politics Oakeshott questions any and every genuine exercise of reason in the conduct of political activity; he questions the validity of *rational* discussion of ends and means, denies the need for *rational* justification of choices men make in politics, and generally denigrates principles as 'abstract'—not realising that as the distillation of our experience they offer some criteria at least for judging between different purposes and projects and choosing the best there is. All this may well lead to the abandonment altogether of reason and principles and rational procedures in politics. What is more, Oakeshott's disparagement of reason in general and of rational scientific knowledge in particular, is accompanied by an exclusive emphasis on what he calls 'practical knowledge'— a knowledge which he virtually centres in 'the heart' and assimilates into the intuitive knowledge of the craftsman and the artist. This essentially untheoretical 'practical knowledge' and equally untheoretical, even romantic, concept of 'pursuit of intimations' may well make politics a matter only of craftsmanship, artistry and connoisseurship. Oakeshott indeed informs us that 'to acquire a mastery', in politics or anything else, 'is to acquire an appropriate connoisseurship'. On Oakeshott's interpretation, therefore, politics may well come to be regarded exclusively as an art, to be practised according to the inexpressible, essentially intuitive insight of an artist, a political artist that is. It may indeed be reduced to an entirely intuitive activity, essentially romantic and ultimately even irrational. Such in important respects was the fascist understanding of politics. Whatever the conscious intentions of Oakeshott himself might be, this understanding is implicit in his concept of politics as 'the pursuit of intimations.'[34]

IX

Fundamental to an understanding of Oakeshott's traditionalism are two points which I will now proceed to consider. Oakeshott assumes, in the first place, that serious problems do not and will not arise in the politics of a society; and he argues, in the second place, that there is always a privileged group of men in a society who have the answers to whatever problems may in fact arise in the politics of that society.

Underlying Oakeshott's notion of politics as 'the pursuit of intimations' is the assumption that a political community is an essentially harmonious entity—harmonious in its existence, its functioning and its development. No doubt, Oakeshott occasionally speaks of 'serious political crisis', even 'upheaval', in a society. But this is only to rope in everything, *every* sort of political activity and event within the ambit of his traditionalism in order to win the argument for the logical necessity of traditional behaviour in politics. Ordinarily and more fundamentally he speaks of 'a single community' or society whose institutions and arrangements are internally compatible and constitute a well-integrated whole. .His concept of tradition and his entire case for traditionalism in politics imply the assumed existence of unity or harmony in a society. He constantly refers in a typical Burkeian manner to a political community's 'common way of life', its 'common recognition' of 'its tradition' or 'traditions of behaviour', its 'voluntary consensus of opinion', its need and ability 'to move together', its 'rhythm and continuity' and to its 'partnership between present and past'. He insists that a political community finds 'its guide in a principle of *continuity* (which is a diffusion of power between the different legitimate interests of the present)'. And Oakeshott warns us to escape 'the illusion that politics is ever anything more than the pursuit of intimations; a conversation, not an argument'

Given this assumption of unity or harmony in society and the consequent understanding of politics as 'a conversation, not an argument', it is clear that for Oakeshott there can be no clash or conflict of a fundamental nature in a political community, it will never be 'a jerky, discontinuous affair'. There can be only minor 'incoherencies', only lesser maladjustments which require only modest reforms, only minor 'amendments' of the 'existing arrangements' of a society. The social and political development presumably free from serious tensions or conflicts will never involve rapid or revolutionary changes. Major political problems therefore will simply not arise in the political life of a society; its politics will never involve an 'argument'. As for the rest, the traditional or conservative style of politics will be quite capable of coping with the situation, of carrying on the necessary 'conversation'. One may not take even this 'conversational' politics seriously for it is obviously not of much consequence. One could be, in the final analysis, altogether indifferent to the politics of a society.

This assumption of unity, of a pre-existent harmony, in a society is a commonplace of conservative political theory and even of most liberal theory, which tends by virtue of this assumption to be conservative rather than radical towards the problems of society. It is there, for example—in varying forms and subsumed under different concepts—in Burke (Providence), Hegel (Idea or Nation), Green (Common Good), Hobhouse (Harmony), MacIver (General Will) and several other political thinkers,[35] and, of course, in most modern writing in defence of conservatism.[36] It is not surprising, therefore, to find this assumption in Oakeshott too, subsumed in this case under the concept of Tradition.

Though commonly made, this assumption is altogether gratuitous so far as the contemporary capitalist, even when formally democratic, political community is concerned. It has no basis at all in the social and political reality of a bourgeois society. It requires indeed a privileged degree of credulity to see this unity or harmony in a modern class-divided political community, whose divisions go deep into its foundations, whose members are so fundamentally divided in their interests as to turn it on important occasions into a community divided against itself, whose clashes and conflicts, born of iniquities of life, result at times in major upheavels, whose politics, far from being a continuous 'conversation', is quite often a violent 'argument', and whose history far from being an evolutionary process, proceeding from a pre-existent harmony and illustrative only of 'a principle of *continuity*' or '*consensus*', is full of bitter struggles, class conflicts, revolutions, and counter-revolutions—a history, as it were, of a continuous effort at establishing and re-establishing the 'unity' or 'harmony' of this community on better or different bases. The entire evidence of social and historical science clearly points in the opposite direction, it refutes the assumption of unity or harmony in a class-divided society. Far from being true, this assumption only helps the conservative as well as liberal political theory to gloss over some of the fundamental problems of this society, above all to evade the most important task of creating a *real* and *necessary* basis for unity or harmony in such a society by first abolishing the historically produced class-divisions themselves.[37]

X

If political activity viewed as 'a conversation' eliminates all serious problems from politics, elitism implicit in Oakeshott's political philosophy apparently takes care of the rest. Underlying Oakeshott's interpretation of politics as 'the pursuit of intimations' is the argument that the pursuit of politics is the exclusive concern of a traditional ruling class. This class possesses the requisite knowledge and would, therefore, always know what to do in the politics of a society.

According to Oakeshott's theory of knowledge, discussed earlier, the knowledge that really matters in politics, or any other practical human activity, is 'practical' or 'traditional' knowledge. This knowledge is born of 'a traditional manner of attending ' the arrangements of a society', and its 'normal expression' too is 'in a customary or traditional way of doing things'. It is essentially inexpressible and' exists only in practice', 'only in use'. 'It is, indeed, a knowledge that is expressed in taste or connoisseurship. ' This knowledge is available, therefore, only with a traditional ruling class, which has been practising politics for a long time. The pursuit of politics being, as Oakeshott repeatedly emphasises, a matter of skill and craftsmanship, of taste and connoisseurship, only this ruling class is qualified to engage in political activity, it alone knows 'where to go next in the exploration of an already existing traditional kind of society'. This class, possessing the requisite traditional knowledge, has, presumably, all the answers to the problems of politics practised as 'the pursuit of intimations'. It is for this ruling class to 'elicit the intimations most worthwhile pursuing', and to pursue them, to recognise 'the incoherencies' which are pressing 'convincingly for remedy' and to remedy them. The others, including the philosopher of conservatism himself, it seems, would do well to trust this class in the business it knows best, and to desist from asking or answering awkward meddlesome questions.

This traditional ruling class obviously must always remain the ruling class. For it appears rather difficult, if not altogether impossible, for an outsider—though living in the same society he is really 'like a foreigner, or a man out of his social class'—to gain entry into its ranks. This is so not only because, Oakeshott tells us, 'there will always remain something of a mystery about how a tradition of political behaviour is learned'—how the conservative loves to cover the ugly reality of his class-rule with same 'mystique'! but even more because the 'practical' or 'traditional' knowledge, whose possession, is a prerequisite of entrance into the class of rulers 'can neither be taught nor learned, but only imparted and acquired ...and the only way to acquire it is by apprenticeship to a master ,...by continuous contact with one who is perpetually practising it: Obviously, this knowledge is not easy to acquire. For ruling classes, if history is any guide, are not known to be particularly generous or free with 'apprenticeship '. They have generally preferred, and for understandable reasons, to pick up for 'continuous contact' only lackeys, and servants, only 'butlers or housemaids', from the other classes.

Oakeshott himself admits that the prospects of entry into the ruling class are bleak. There are no 'easy methods' and 'there is no short cut to it'. The requisite political education or knowledge will be acquired, 'more readily acquired' as Oakeshott says, only 'if we have the good fortune to be born into a rich and lively political tradition and among those who are well educated politically'. He adds, however, that 'even the most needy society and the most cramped surroundings have some political education to offer, and we take what we can get'

The conclusion is obvious: the rulers rule—and others, the overwhelming majority of mankind, must be content to 'take what we can get'. And if there be any amongst them who nevertheless harbour other ambitions, they may, if they can, use influence in proper quarters 'to be born' more appropriately next time!

Oakeshott's theory is nothing but the 'Guardians' of Plato all over again,[38] or the 'natural aristocracy' of Burke, who with a characteristically conservative turn of phrase, also called them 'the wiser, the more expert, and the more opulent', who 'conduct, and by conducting enlighten and protect, the weaker, the less knowing, and the less provided with the goods of fortune',[39] or simply the 'betters' of Bagehot. With Oakeshott, too, the rulers rule and the workers work as they have indeed done throughout the ages in all class-divided societies. In theory, the claim of the few to rule is ostensibly based on their possession of 'knowledge'—but the nature and the mode of acquisition of this knowledge have been so defined as to eliminate altogether the possibility of the mass of mankind ever coming to possess it. The right to rule is thus made to belong, almost naturally, to the classes already ruling. They are 'born' to the necessary knowledge and therefore 'born' to rule also. The entire argument is only an elaborate justification of the *status quo*. Oakeshott knows, of course, that in 'our society' there is no equality of opportunity in the acquisition of knowledge, or in anything else. But, then, equality is never a consideration with him, his political philosophy in fact disavows it completely. What is more serious, however, is the fact that there is no awareness, at all in Oakeshott that the ruling classes and the elite everywhere tend to develop their own vested interests and to identify these with the interests of the community at large, that they have an almost built-in psychological inability to admit freedom and rights other than their own. Oakeshott simply refuses to admit the elementary lesson of history—Laski used to emphasise it very much—that those who do not share in political power will not share in its benefits either, not for long at any rate.

It is doubtful if Oakeshott's elitism is an answer to any of the real problems of contemporary politics, traditionalist or any other. It is certainly an evasion—as was Plato's elitism in another age—of the problems of *democratic* politics. But then Oakeshott is not concerned with democracy at all, or for that matter with equality or public good or social justice—or even with freedom as we understand it in mid-twentieth century—that necessarily go with democracy. Oakeshott's concern, it seems, is solely with order and stability this is the problem of politics for him. Concern for stability is a characteristic conservative concern at all times. But during periods when rapid historical change poses a serious threat to the old order, it tends to become an exclusive, even obsessive concern with the dominant privileged sections of this old order and its ideologues. At such historical junctures, not only does change become entirely an object of fear for the ruling minority, but this minority increasingly comes to recognise security and stability as the sole political good. It is this sort of fear of change which Oakeshott reflects and which explains not only his obsessive concern for stability, for whatever security, 'shelter' or 'safe harbour', habit and tradition may still offer, but also his recognition and advocacy of elitism as the answer to the problem of political stability.

Elitism has indeed been one of the basic premises of ail authentic conservatism. It is the central political demand of contemporary conservative philosophy.[40] In whatever else Oakeshott may differ from this philosophy as a whole, he fully shares in its demand for elitism.[41] This elitism is always the expression of an attitude of contempt or indifference towards the masses, an attitude in whose recesses lurk fears which can transform it in a single moment of genuine confrontation into an attitude of violent, merciless hostility. This elitism means not only the fear and rejection of popular democracy, which is obvious enough. It also involves a defence and justification of the continued existence of an unjust, privilege-based, minority ruled and self-divided society. It seeks to make the present class divisions of mankind—'the schisms of humanity'—a permanent feature of social existence, which divisions are, it is well to remember, in their origins a historical product and which in the course of further historical development may well cease to be.[42]

Whatever the nature and implications of Oakeshott's elitism, one thought is irresistible: if only Oakeshott would for once shed his pose of bored philosophic indifference and do what he is ever urging the rationalist to do, that is, descend from the world of political mythology to the world of political reality, and take a good look at things as they are, and see his elite for what it really is![43]

One wonders what justification Oakeshott's elitism has, for example, in England, what relevance indeed it has to the reality of its traditional ruling class, 'the traditional pseudo-aristocratic elite' as Tom Nairn has called it, with its archaic political habits and equally archaic economic wisdom and myopic vision of the world, with its complete failure, as Sampson puts it, 'to absorb and communicate new challenges and new ideas',[44] and with its *la dolce vita* existence, Profumo affairs, succession-fixing and a hundred other scandals. The fiascoes of its policy in every sphere are only too obvious today as also are its vain attempts to hide them under anachronistic Edwardian postures. Its 'skills', the traditional skills that Oakeshott makes so much of, have 'become mere manners, and its manners, increasingly, affectation 'Gone are the virtues of its 'whole cumulative tradition', 'those of agrarian squirearchy and industrial laissez-faire', and only the vices are left: 'universal dilettantism and anachronistic economic liberalism'. And this when the situation that confronts this elite is one of unprecedented crisis, 'a general malady of the whole society, infrastructure and superstructure—not a sudden breakdown, but a slow, sickening entropy.[45]

The recognition that traditionalism, including the traditional social and political hierarchies, will not do has today penetrated into the darkest recesses of the English mind. Confronted with the contemporary crisis, though not really understanding it, even a Macmillan felt compelled to tell a Conservative audience:

This country has got to be prepared for change...we are still as a nation too set in our ways, too apt to cling to old privileges, too unwilling to abandon old practices that have outlived their usefulness ...there are too many demarcation lines, social and industrial—one might almost say a sort of caste system.[46]

But what the practitioner of conservatism can clearly see, the philosopher of conservatism does not. Or, perhaps, he will not. For with Oakeshott, in the final analysis, political philosophy has nothing much to do with political practice. The philosopher, his occasional flirtations with the 'vulgar' notwithstanding, is really 'never concerned with a condition of things' at all!

XI

What is true of Oakeshott's elitism in fact true of his conservatism as a whole, understood whether as 'a disposition' or 'a doctrine'. Whatever its value as a negative gesture in defence of the *status quo* this conservatism has little positive relevance to contemporary social and political reality, to the *real* needs and possibilities of a society in the mid-twentieth century.

It may perhaps be claimed that Oakeshott's teaching has a relevance, at least in theory, to the situation of a well-ordered and affluent society. But apart from the question whether any society can afford to do for long without new ideas or significant change—both of which Oakeshott generally frowns upon—without becoming hopelessly stagnant, it is, to say the least, highly doubtful if any contemporary society, certainly not the British or the American which Oakeshott presumably has in mind, is well-ordered or affluent enough to do so. As a matter of fact these as well as the other societies of more advanced capitalism in the west could today do with a great deal more of reason and radical change, even revolutionary change, than is generally admitted by their apologists. And as for the other societies of the non-socialist world—'the socialist societies' I regard as on principle committed to both reason and change[47]—particularly the colonial, neo-colonial, and post-colonial societies, it is obvious that Oakeshott's teaching has no relevance to their situation at all.[48] For here, more than anywhere else, men need not so much to cultivate 'the conservative disposition' which Oakeshott so loves and lauds, as to put on 'the heroic character' which he so distrusts and denigrates. Here they must move both 'fast' and 'far' if they would move at all and not stagnate in conditions of utter poverty, wretchedness and exploitation, if their societies are not to remain, in Basil Davidson's phrase, 'a mere peripheral fragment of the rich man's world'. Here men need all the reason they can muster and all the revolution they can make, for they have not only to win or defend their freedom but also build socialism or, in a fundamental sense, they will have won and built nothing at all.[49]

But it is not the specific problems of change in different contemporary societies or the overall revolutionary compulsions of our age—which may well go down in history as the age of transition from capitalism to socialism—that I propose to discuss here. This is neither possible, nor very necessary for my purpose to do so. What I want to raise here are two issues of a general nature which are more immediately germane to my theme.

I suggest, in the first place, that while Oakeshott's conservatism may indeed have some relevance or appropriateness to the circumstances of a society which is static or slow-changing or which deliberately chooses to be stagnant or closed, it has none at all to those of a scientific and industrial society such as every contemporary society either is, to a greater or lesser degree, or, for understandable reasons, wants to be. It has certainly no relevance to the circumstances of a freely competitive capitalist society to which Oakeshott is professedly committed and whose defence and conservation is the purpose of his political philosophy in so far as it has any conscious social or political purpose.[50] Such a society simply cannot exist without rapid change or disturbance, it 'cannot exist without constantly revolutionizing the instruments of production, and thereby the relations of production, and with them the whole relations of society'.[51]

Marx and Engels had pointed out this change 'constant revolutionizing of production' and 'uninterrupted disturbance of all social conditions'—as one of the distinguishing features of modern capitalist society, and had contrasted it with the 'condition of existence' of the societies that had gone before.[52] But what they wrote of capitalist society is in fact true of every modern society based on science and technology. And what particularly needs to be noticed is that never before in human history has change been so obvious, so profound and all-pervasive a fact of human existence, in all spheres; as in the mid-twentieth century. Speaking of this change Robert Oppenheimer writes:

This world of ours is a new world, in which the unity of knowledge, the nature of human communities, the order of society, the order of ideas, the very notions of society and culture have changed, and will not return to what they have been in the past. What is new is new not because it has never been there before but because it has changed in quality. One thing that is new is the prevalence of newness, the changing scale and scope of change itself, so that the world alters as we walk in it, so that the years of man's life measure not some small growth or rearrangement or moderation of what he learned in childhood, but a great upheaval.[53]

What positive relevance to the reality of this world does Oakeshott's conservative traditionalism have—a traditionalism which is so full of fear and distrust of change, which understands change essentially as something 'to be suffered' or, at most, to be 'accommodated' to, which regards it 'always, in the first place, as deprivation', as 'a threat to identity', as 'an emblem of extinction' itself?

Change, it has been suggested above, is the very law of existence of contemporary scientific and industrial society—the capitalist which Oakeshott admires or the socialist which he abhors, or any other. But in recognising this one must remember that this change is not to be blamed, as Oakeshott does, on rationalism. It springs rather from deeper causes, from the very nature of such a society. But—and this is important—it certainly gives new value and significance to human reason, to the knowledge which man has. For this change has to be understood and coped with, it has to be planned and directed to proper human purposes. It is thus that human reason or knowledge itself becomes a most potent factor of social and historical change. Oakeshott recognises, with Burke and most conservative political philosophy since, the vital connection between rationalism and radical change between reason and revolution. He does in his own way recognise the fact that reason and change invariably go together, that they always involve and implicate each other: to know is to plan change consciously, and in order to cope with change, to plan. It consciously, that is, purposefully, one has to know. This fact Marx too had recognised. But a thinker, scholar and 'man of science', Marx was 'above all a revolutionary' as Engels has told us;[54] a philosopher, he was also fully aware of 'the liberating quality of practical activity'. In Marx, therefore, this recognition, when combined with a revolutionary's truly humanist acceptance of change, led to an acceptance of reason also. It led Marx to affirm that the function of reason, which is philosophy, is not merely to interpret the world but to change it,[55] that reason as philosophy is nothing if it is afraid to be revolutionary.[56] With Oakeshott, however, it is different, for Oakeshott is by choice a conservative. In Oakeshott, therefore, the recognition mentioned above, when combined with a conservative's essentially anti-humanist commitment to the *status quo*, leads, inevitably, to a commitment against reason also. It leads Oakeshott to seek, in an effort to deny reason its true function, to emasculate it into an 'abridging' and 'abbreviating' caricature of itself. It is thus that rejecting change, Oakeshott comes to reject reason also; and this rejection of reason, in turn, tends to justify his prior rejection of change. It is thus that traditionalism and anti-rationalism reinforce and validate each other in Oakeshott's conservatism, that fear of change and hostility to reason come to be the characteristic features of Oakeshott's political philosophy as a whole.[57]

But fear of change and hostility to reason, deep distrust of one and an equally deep scepticism about the other, together with that 'reconciliation' with the past, or 'love' and 'respect for what is dead', which Oakeshott is always urging upon us, can hardly be regarded as an appropriate disposition with which to face and cope with the problems of change today, the problems of the present and future development of human society. Such a disposition, 'the conservative disposition' as Oakeshott calls it, is in fact most inappropriate. Possessing this disposition Oakeshott not only fears and distrusts change in general, but also fails or refuses to take a positive, meaningful note of *the change of our time*. The outcome is obvious. What Oakeshott's philosophy really succeeds in doing is to obscure, both the significant *choices* this change confronts us with and the unprecedented *opportunities* it offers.[58]

The other issue I want to raise relates to the fact that the process of social and historical development regularly gives rise to situations—we speak of these situations when we legitimately speak of 'crisis', or 'bankruptcy', or 'breadown', or 'collapse', or 'degeneration', etc.—when radical, even revolutionary, changes are called for in a society. Oakeshott's teaching completely fails to understand, accommodate or provide for either such situations or such changes. It is simply irrelevant to the problems of such situations and changes.

In thinking of such situations, there, is, of course, always 'this consideration', as Dr. Johnson once put it, 'that if the abuse be enormous, nature will rise up and claiming her original rights overturn a corrupted political system'. But what I have in mind at the moment are not so much the 'abnormal' as the more normal or organic causes which give rise to such developments, to situations of real crisis in a society. In other words, what has to be recognised is that such situations arise from time to time, as part of the regular dialectics of social and historical process. Their causes are of course varied, extremely complex and at different levels. At the most general or fundamental level, Marx, for example, located them in the fact that 'at a certain stage of their development, the material forces of production in society come in conflict with the existing relations of production, or—what is but a legal expression for the same thing—with the property relations within which they had been at work before.' 'From forms of development of the forces of production, these relations turn into their fetters.' And these fetters have to be broken, 'burst asunder', if the further material and moral progress of society is to be ensured.[59]

Thus, according to Marx, arise situations of deep social crisis, of social revolution itself. At such times the particular interests of the ruling class, vitally interested, as its prime beneficiary, in the preservation of the existing pattern of social and property relations, come into conflict with the interests of society as a whole, which interests demand a fundamental change in these relations, in the now relatively obsolescent socio-economic structure.[60]

A veritable gulf opens at such times between society's potentiality and its performance in satisfying human needs. And not 'small and slow changes', which do not endanger the existing pattern of social relations and which the ruling class is therefore always prepared to admit, but fundamental;, revolutionary changes in this pattern become imperative if the society is not to stagnate and decay, if the existing and maturing possibilities for society's further advancement, for further growth and development of all its members are not to be sacrificed in favour of the interest of the dominant class in the continuation of the established social order.[61]

Marx's analysis of social and historical change is not what we are immediately concerned with. This analysis is; of course, central to any real understanding of the nature and problems of contemporary change—and this is as true of change in the more advanced societies of capitalism as in any other. But I have made a reference to it only in order to focus attention on the fact—and this is what we are primarily concerned with here—that whatever their causes, ultimate and immediate, and whatever their specific nature, situations of deep economic, political and social crisis are today, as in the past, an integral part of social and historical development. These situations can occur in different spheres and at different levels of life of a society, and they can as well take the form of 'a sudden breakdown' as of 'a slow sickening entropy', or may have the elements of both. The important point is that they always demand precisely those large-scale changes, 'consciously planned and deliberately executed', which Oakeshott's conservatism simply does not permit; they may demand even revolutionary changes. The full poverty of Oakeshott's empiricistic traditionalism, its utter inadequacy, even dangerous irrelevance, when confronted with such situations is too obvious to be dilated upon. Suffice it to state that in a situation of real crisis, a purely pragmatic policy, a policy of unprincipled 'pursuit of intimations', could well turn out to be only an exercise in futility, which may even prove fatal. And to the extent such a policy, a policy of 'small and slow changes' which Oakeshott permits, succeeds, it may well condemn a society to a greater or lesser degree of stagnation, condemn it to stagnate into what C.P. Snow has called an 'existential' society.[62] Needless to add this inability or refusal to change radically, to change 'in the significant sense' as Snow puts it, is bound to impose, as it always has, a very heavy cost on its victims, the poor and underprivileged classes of such a society.

It seems to me that Oakeshott's conservatism, with its aversion to 'innovation'—'innovating', he insists, is 'always an equivocal enterprise'—and its preoccupation with the worth of 'the merely traditional, customary or habitual', completely misses the truth of Bacon's aphorism that 'the forward retention of custom is as turbulent a thing as an innovation' (*On Innovations*). In its satisfaction with the present—occasional reference to the 'voice' of future notwithstanding—and its obsessive concern for the conservation and continuity of the existing order, it is altogether oblivious of what Jawaharlal Nehru once referred to as the 'terrible costs of not changing the existing order'. It is so taken up with the desire only 'to move together', that it ignores altogether the desirability, imperative on occasion, of moving both 'fast' and 'far'. It simply refuses to recognise that there are times in social and historical development, times of real crisis, when the 'existing arrangements' of a society are indeed found to be unworkable and intolerable, when the old and the traditional, in thought and in practice, becomes really moribund, when traditions inherited from the past turn into empty shadows of themselves, incapable of giving guidance to men who still so desperately cling to them, and when, therefore, the 'traditional ways', including all 'politics piously attached to traditional ways', which Oakeshott commends, have indeed nothing to offer and the only way out is a new way out; when men must perforce leave 'the known' and 'the familiar' behind and 'sail uncharted seas'—yes, 'navigate the unknown'. Above all, Oakeshott's conservatism gives no sense of being aware of the fact that given the crisis as well as the scientific and technological revolution of our time, 'if we do not know how to make large-scale changes of our choosing, then we probably never will, since large-scale changes *not* of our choosing seem so liable to come and break us.'[63]

There is no doubt that Oakeshott's political philosophy, at its best, recognises and does full justice to the slow and continuous, the quantitative or evolutionary, aspect of the process of social and historical development. But it completely fails to recognise and do justice to the 'jerky' and 'discontinuous', the qualitative or revolutionary, aspect of this process. Oakeshott seizes upon one aspect, the former, and treats it as if it were absolute. He in fact elevates this one-sidedness to the status of a theory—his theory of traditionalism as a defence of conservatism.

But, then, it is one thing to make a theory and quite another to make it true also, make it true in this case of a political reality which faces us at every step with the fact or choice of radical, revolutionary changes. It is not surprising therefore that confronted with this reality, with the social and historical experience of our time, Oakeshott's traditionalism shies away from it; seeing the terrible, yet terribly magnificent countenance of change in the mid-twentieth century,[64] it grows suspicious and fearful of change itself. In theory it fights 'logical' battles against it. In practice it ends up preaching a do-nothing conservatism of 'pursuit of intimations'.

This do-nothing conservatism Oakeshott buttresses with what is virtually a know-nothing theory of knowledge. The two, as suggested earlier, go together, they continuously justify and validate each other in Oakeshott's social and political philosophy. It may be that a society which is static and stagnant, deliberately or otherwise, will be able to get along with the help only of the 'practical' or 'traditional' knowledge which Oakeshott has to offer. But men in any other society, certainly in a modern, science and technology-oriented society, need to have lots more to be able to cope with its problems successfully. They need all the knowledge they can have, above all the higher scientific knowledge about the dynamics of social change, to be able to direct the processes of change to their own ends, to 'design and execute', in a collective organised manner, large-scale changes of their own choosing.[65]

If I have insisted that men are today not devoid of scientifically valid knowledge about society and social change, this does not in any way imply an underestimation either of the present limits of this knowledge or of the urgency of acquiring much more of it. This insistence becomes necessary only in view of the scepticism which is today prevalent in western philosophy, both academic and not so academic. Theories, more or less sophisticated, abound, as Dunham has told us, 'which preach paralysis—which tell us that we can't know or can't do'. Scepticism is in fact the vogue today, the academic fashion *par excellence.* And the power of fashion is great. Oakeshott himself is very much in the fashion. But fashion, in philosophy at least, is never something merely frivolous or fortuitous. It is always 'a true and revealing thing'. And contemporary scepticism is truly revelatory, at the philosophical level, of the dominant conservative or 'existential' mood of the societies of western capitalism. This scepticism thus lacks *real* validity and we must reject it. Today we do possess sufficient knowledge, with a reasonably high degree of reliability, about man and society, and about the dynamics of social change, to be able to plan and execute large-scale changes of our own choosing. Only we must learn to value what we have and choose to use it with courage and confidence.[66]

What we need, in other words, is to adopt a positive attitude to both social change and human knowledge. We need to possess as never before 'a sense of change as a progressive factor in history, and belief in reason as our guide for the understanding of its complexities.'[67] Thus alone can we direct change to our chosen purposes, and 'plan for both security and freedom' for ourselves in a world full of unprecedented change and flux.[68] Merely to 'love' the past, or to enter into 'partnership' with it, or to somehow 'keep afloat' in the present, has never been deemed enough by men. It is certainly not enough for us today. It is perhaps not even possible. Today more than ever before, we need to win knowledge and understanding of our past and present in order to save the present and build a better future on it. We need to acquire all the knowledge we can and use all the knowledge we have in order to survive the change of our time and give it the quality of progress. This is as much our right as our responsibility.

Suspicious of social change and sceptical about human reason, Oakeshott would deny us this right and responsibility. He chides the rationalist for not knowing 'that the world did not begin in the twentieth century'. But, then, 'nor did human knowledge and understanding which have *made* the world what it is today. What is more, Oakeshott himself seems to forget that the world does not end in the twentieth century either.

NOTES AND REFERENCES

1. Barrows Dunham, 'The Love of Wisdom: A Marxist, Meditation,' *loc. cit.*, pp. 202-3. It should be noted that by 'narrow' Dunham alludes 'not to the number of postulates beneath the theory, but to the range of reference in the postulates'.
2. In a footnote Oakeshott writes:

   > The Russian Revolution (what actually happened in Russia) was not the implementation of an abstract design worked out by Lenin and others in Switzerland: it was a modification of *Russian* circumstances. And the French Revolution was far more closely connected with the *ancien regime* than with Locke or America.

   Oakeshott offers this statement which is certainly true but true only as far as it goes as an argument to prove that even 'serious political crisis' occurs always within a tradition and not without it, and that its resolution, through 'even the most serious political upheaval', is never anything but traditional political activity. In fact this statement proves nothing of the sort. One might indeed ask, for example, whoever said that the Russian Revolution was 'the implementation of an abstract design worked out by Lenin and others in Switzerland'? The really important issues here are two which Oakeshott's traditionalist empiricism evades. In the first place, it was not 'an abstract design' but a *theory*—call it Marxist or scientific —which guided Lenin's actions, and *guided them successfully* because it reflected more or less truthfully the real causal relations of the objective reality constituted by '*Russian* circumstances'. In the second place the'modification'involved was something *revolutionary* and not traditional; of necessity 'closely connected' with the old and traditional, it was yet a *revolutionary transformation* of the old and traditional '*Russian* circumstances'—the new in human society, as in nature, necessarily based on or determined by the old, or carrying it forward transformed, is yet *genuinely new.* These are also the issues, generally speaking, in the French Revolution which, certainly 'far more closely connected with the *ancient regime* than with Locke or America', was yet a *revolutionary transformation* of this regime, and one that was influenced very powerfully by ideas from 'Locke or America'. Needless to add these are precisely the issues which Oakeshott systematically obscures here as also elsewhere in his essays.

3. Lord Hugh Cecil wrote that 'it is an indispensable part of an effective resistance to Jacobinism that there should be moderate reform on conservative lines' (*Conservatism*, London, 1912, p. 64).
4. It may be (as already noticed in Ch. I, section III; above) that scepticism about human reason or knowledge is itself an argument for such political conservatism: since we do not know enough, or lack the required knowledge, we are simply not in a position to do much or better and must avoid making risky large-scale experiments. Such, for instance, is the logic behind Popper's plea for piecemeal social engineering as against large-scale—'utopian' he also calls it—social engineering ('At present, the sociological knowledge necessary for large-scale engineering is simply non-existent' *The Open Society and its Enemies*, Vol. 1, p. 162). Oakeshott's radical scepticism concerning human knowledge, implied in his attack on rationalism, can certainly develop a full-fledged argument along the same lines: since 'Rationalism', including even scientific theory, cannot be a valid guide in politics and since 'from a practical point of view .. the style of politics which approximates to pure empiricism' is only 'an approach to lunacy'—as Oakeshott rightly holds it to be—empiricism of tradition alone is left for man to turn to for guidance in political activity. And it can be argued that such traditionalism which, as Perry Anderson put it, 'sanctions the present by deriving it from the past' and 'shackles the future by riveting it to the present'—does not allow any other politics than the conservative.

But while Oakeshott may well lay claim to this argument, as he indeed does on a number of occasions, in support of conservatism, his more basic and comprehensive argument concerning the logical inevitability of traditionalism simply rules it out as irrelevant and unnecessary.

It may also be contended that, according to Oakeshott, in politics we need to work with a knowledge that fully consults tradition and experience, that 'the right conduct of policy 'requires' knowledge, as profound as we can make it, of our tradition of political behaviour', of 'the character of the society' and its 'permanent interests and direction of movement',— 'a profound knowledge' indeed of 'a concrete, coherent manner of living in all its intricateness'. And it can be argued that this, in some sense at least, makes the traditional or conservative style inevitable in politics.

But this knowledge, no matter how one interprets 'tradition', is as necessary for the radical or revolutionary style as for any other, and it may not always indicate only 'slow, small changes' as necessary or desirable. This argument, therefore, by itself proves nothing whatsoever in favour of traditionalism or conservatism being the only possible or permissible style in politics.

5. For this the reader may consult, for example, William J. Newman, *The Futilitarian Society*, New York, 1961.
6. A notable exception, interesting as well as instructive, is Karl Popper's defence of the essentially conservative 'piecemeal social engineering' in terms of reason (see his *The Open Society and its Enemies*, and *The Povery of Historicism*). Popper of course presents his teaching as something liberal and not conservative. But this only shows how low indeed the mighty have fallen since the days when Acton spoke (in 1887) of 'The Revolution, or as we say Liberalism'.

E.H. Carr has pointed out that 'in our day, what survives of liberalism has everywhere become a conservative factor in society' (*op. cit.*, p. 148). C. Wright Mills noticing the same fact wrote that 'in advanced capitalist societies, the ideological and intellectual functions performed by nineteenth century conservatism are now usually performed by liberalism' (*The Marxists*, p. 18). Once a radical, even revolutionary, creed, all that is now left to liberalism is the sort of 'piecemeal tinkering' and muddling through' which Popper advocates. This is a sign not of maturity or the coming of age of liberalism as an ideology, but of its decline and loss of force as a dynamic of social change with the decline of the class and the socio-economic order whose ideological product it originally was.

One would enthusiastically welcome and endorse Popper's defence of reason and his ever so firm and principled rejection of irrationalism in every form. But the difficulty with his teaching is that he assigns to reason an extremely limited role. He permits it to operate only within the assumptions of the existing societyany questioning of its fundamental presuppositions or ultimate purposes is simply tabooed. The result is that his practical conclusions come to be largely indistinguishable from those of a professedly conservative philosopher like Oakeshott, who disparages reason and speaks entirely in terms of tradition.

Popper argues in terms of reason and as a liberal for 'piecemeal social engineering'. Oakeshott rejects altogether 'this assimilation of politics to engineering' as 'the myth of rationalist politics', and argues instead in terms of tradition and as a conservative for a politics of 'pursuit of intimations', which according to him allows only 'slow, small changes'. Popper has himself warned us that 'we must guard against the danger of being impressed by mere words', and that 'nothing depends upon words, and everything upon our practical demands or upon the proposals for framing our policy which we decide to adopt' (*The Open Society and its Enemies*, Vol. 1, pp. 89, 91). Thus looked at there is apparently not much to choose between the reason-based liberalism of Popper and the tradition-based conservatism of Oakeshott.

As a matter of fact while fundamentally disparaging reason, even Oakeshott concedes the need for a certain amount of 'reasoning' and 'convincing' in exploring, eliciting and pursuing 'intimations', in practising the traditional style of politics. But, as he makes it abundantly clear, this 'reasoning' and 'convincing' has to take place entirely *within* the closed system of presuppositions and expectations of what he calls the 'existing arrangements' of a society. In other words, reason, when at all permitted in politics, must function in complete bondage to 'tradition'.

Thus Popper, and Oakeshott when he permits reason in politics, whatever other differences they may have—and I do not by any means regard these as unimportant—both subordinate reason in different ways, and to a lesser or greater extent, to the assumptions of the established social and political order. In doing so they both emasculate it. They obscure or altogether deny the real power and function of reason which consists in confronting reality—natural, social and political—courageously and continuously. Reason must do so, or else cease to be reason and become mere 'common sense' or 'practical intelligence', content only to 'tinker' and 'muddle through', or to 'abridge' and 'abbreviate'—that is mere caricature of itself.

E.H. Carr's comment in this connection is very relevant. He writes:

> But this subordination of reason to the assumptions of the existing order seems to me in the long run wholly unacceptable ....Progress inhuman affairs, whether in science or in history or in society, has come mainly through the bold readiness of human beings not to confine themselves to seeking piecemeal improvements in the way things are done, but to present fundamental challenges in the name of reason to the current way of doing things and to the avowed or hidden assumptions on which it rests (*op. cit.*, p. 150).

7. Leo Strauss, *Natural Right and History*, Chicago, 1953, p. 6.
8. T.E. Utley says: 'In him is contained all that is necessary to political salvation. "Back to Burke" ought still to be our motto. Read and re-read the *Reflections on the Revolution in France*: this is an exercise that should be performed at least once a year' (The State and the Individual', a lecture published in the Conservative Political. Centre's *The Good Society*, London, 1953, p. 41).
9. I.L. Horowitz has very well illustrated this for America in his 'The New Conservatism', *loc. cit.*
10. See Russell Kirk, *The Conservative Mind from Burke to Santayana*, Chicago, 1953, from which the ideas quoted in the text are taken. Nothing new, such ideas are characteristic of the dominant trend in conservative thinking today. In fact they are among the very small number of basic ideas which, though differently formulated—F.J.C. Hearnshaw's 'twelve principles of conservatism' (*Conservatism in England*, London, 1933), Russell Kirk's 'six canons of conservative thought' (*op. cit.*), Clinton Rossiter's' "twenty-one points" of the conservative tradition' (*Conservatism in America*, New York, 1955), etc.— constitute the hard core of contemporary conservative social and political thought.
11. C. Wright Mills thus summarises the position of this more orthodox conservatism: Tradition is sacred; through it the real social tendencies of Providence are displayed; therefore, tradition must be our guide. Whatever is traditional represents the accumulated wisdom of the ages, and more: it exists by "divine intent"' (*The Power Elite*, New York, 1959, p. 327).
12. It was the essential intellectual and ideological poverty of much of modern conservatism which provoked C. Weight Mills to write, perhaps with some exaggeration but certainly not without truth, that 'conservatism is a defensive gesture of businessmen and politicians who would defend the *status quo* but who are without ideas with which to do so'. He noted that 'wherever "conservatism" prevails as the ascendant ideology of a state in power—as in Franco's Spain, Verwoerd's South Africa, Salazar's Portugal, or the Trujillos' Dominican Republic it rests more upon police power than upon ideological consent' (*The Marxists*, p. 18).
13. C. Wright Mills, *The Power Elite*, p. 327.
14. J. Stalin, *op. cit.*, pp. 570-5.
15. *The new*, here as elsewhere, is of course always based on and determined by the, old but it is nonetheless new and cannot be treated merely as a continuation of, or an addition to, the old and

the traditional. Nor is it right to ignore this aspect of change in human affairs by insisting on assessing the human situation always only in empiricist, or quantitative terms, by arguing as, for example, Oakeshott does, that 'the new is (always) an insignificant proportion of the whole', and, therefore, never to be much preferred to the old. It can be at times new and significant enough to change the essential quality of the whole, and, therefore, men seeking it may well be willing to stake their very lives on it.'

16. Marx, *A Contribution to the Critique of Political Economy*, p. 12.
17. J. Stalin, *op. cit.*, p. 580. Stalin wrote:

    New social ideas and theories arise only after the development of the material life of society has set new tasks before society, But once they have arisen they become a most potent force which facilitates the carrying out of the new tasks set by the development of the material life of society, a force which facilitates the progress of society. It is precisely here that the tremendous organizing, mobilizing and transforming value of new ideas, new theories, new political views and new political institutions manifests itself. New social ideas and theories arise precisely because they are necessary to society, because it is *impossible* to carry out the urgent tasks of development of the material life of society without their organizing, mobilizing and transforming action. Arising out of the new tasks set by the development of the material life of society, the new social ideas and theories force their way through, become the possession of the masses, mobilize and organize them against the moribund forces of society, and thus facilitate the overthrow of these forces, which hamper the development of the material life of society.

18. Marx, 'Critique of the Gotha Program' in Marx and Engels, *Selected Works*, Vol. II, p. 21.
19. Engels, Ludwig Feuerbach in *Reader in Marxist Philosophy*, p. 97. Engels goes on:

    Each stage is necessary, and therefore justified for the time and conditions to which it owes its origin. But in the newer and higher conditions which gradually develop in its own bosom, each loses its validity and justification. It must give way to a higher form which will also in its turn decay and perish.

20. For a discussion of the traditionalist politics as recommended by Oakeshott see also S.I. Benn and R.S. Peters, *Social Principles and the Democratic State*, London, 1963, pp. 312-8.
21. Oakeshtott adds: 'and consequently, relevant political reasoning

will be the convincing exposure of a sympathy, present but not yet followed up, and the convincing demonstration that now is the appropriate moment for recognizing it'.

The 'relevant political reasoning' or 'convincing' that Oakeshott here allows may indeed look like a backdoor admission of reason into a system of politics which intitially claimed to have expelled it through the front door, and which really has no room for it. And in its logic this 'reasoning', or 'convincing', if conducted seriously, may even prove disruptive of Oakeshott's traditionalist conservatism, for there is no inherent reason why it must indicate only 'small and slow' and not radical or even revolutionary changes. But, then, one must remember that in Oakeshott's own scheme of things, whatever 'reason' is admitted in politics is subordinated completely to the 'existing arrangements' of a society, it is put in abolute bondage to 'tradition' and thus really reduced to a mere caricature of itself. Such an admission of reason, therefore, does not in any meaningful sense modify Oakeshott's basic anti-rationalism in politics.

22. Marxist rationalism, as already suggested, does not take its stand on 'fixed' human needs, 'preconceived' purposes, 'preordained and inevitable' ends, 'final' goals or 'destination,' or on 'abstract' and 'eternally valid' ideals. On the contrary, it seeks, and seeks continuously, to relate all these to the process of social and historical development. It seeks to elaborate the definition of social needs, purposes, ends or goals which are objectively achievable in terms of the stage of historical development reached by a society; it seeks for the historical occasion and conditions which make the human ideal feasible, which make, for example, socialism not only desirable but necessary and *possible* also. C. Wright Mills wrote:

    > The distinctive character of Marx's 'scientific socialism'... lies in this: his images of the ideal society are connected with the actual workings of the society in which he lived. Out of his projections of the tendencies he discerns in society as it is actually developing, he makes up his image of the future society (the post-capitalist society which he wants to come about) (*The Marxist*, p. 81).

23. Even a passing look will make clear the existence of widely divergent political traditions in a modern society, the traditions of different classes and even of different sections within the same class. Among these, one may note, for example in England, the conservative and liberal traditions, the radical democratic tradition of what Raymond Williams calls the 'Long Revolution', and

numerous traditions of working-class politics; in France, several traditions of not only reaction, but of the Revolution too; in Russia, within socialism itself, the traditions of Lenin and Stalin, to say nothing of what the Chinese call 'modern revisionism'; in America a tradition of even anti-traditionalism, so baffling for the Oakeshottian thesis; in India, the Gandhian tradition, the 'moderate' and 'extremist' traditions of different hues, and the traditions of caste-cum-communal politics; and everywhere the traditions of war and peace, imperialism and anti-imperialism, reaction, reform, and revolution, etc., etc.

24. For a discussion of the difficulties of the idea of treating politics as tradition, and for a sympathetic critique of conservatism— 'this good friend of politics', Crick calls it— see also Bernard Crick, *In Defence of Politics*, Pelican, 1964, pp. 111-23.
25. Marx, *The Eighteenth Brumaire of Louis Bonaparte*, p. 16. That is why, pleading for a little 'less reverence for tradition' as such, J.H. Plumb writes: 'Old, complex, tradition-haunted societies find change as difficult to make as aged rheumatoid arthritics to move; old men, however, die and are replaced, but in old societies young men grow up, frustrated, crippled, distorted by them' (*op. cit*, p. 10). See also Karl Popper, 'Towards a Rational Theory of Tradition', *The Rationalist Annual*, 1949.
26. Made aware of the difficulty arising from the plurality of political traditions in a 'single community', Oakeshott seeks, in an additional note to the original essay on 'Political Education', to provide a somewhat more concrete and firm basis to his argument about the 'singleness' of a society. He now makes law do duty for tradition. After insisting that 'the absence of homogeneity does not necessarily destroy singleness', he writes: 'What we are considering here is a legally organised society and we are considering the manner in which its legal structure (which inspite of its incoherencies cannot be supposed to have a competitor) is reformed and amended'.

    This sudden faith in law may appear rather intriguing but is not entirely unexpected. For such recourse to law is nothing uncommon in the political theory of the *status quo*. Only in case of Oakeshott it creates more problems than it solves. It implies, in fact, a tacit abandonment of the principle of tradition. What is more, law, with its comparatively rigid and inflexible nature, far from helping to prop up the sort of argument Oakeshott wants to build up, deprives it even of the obvious advantages flowing from the 'pre-eminently fluid' and amorphous quality of his concept of tradition.

One wonders if in his search for greater realism, having moved in his political theory from tradition to law, Oakeshott will advance still further to recognise force as the ultimate basis of the unity or 'singleness' of the contemporary class-divided 'political community' called 'the state'? We know, of course, that in conservative political practice, at least, such progress has not been rare.

27. It maybe noted that Marx regarded socialism not as something 'premeditated' or 'merely imposed upon the situation' from 'outside', but as something that '*emerges* from the capitalist society'. And an important part of the socialist argument runs characteristically in terms of 'the incompatibility of social production with capitalist appropriation' and the consequent 'social antagonism' (Engels), of 'the productive forces developing in the womb of bourgeois society (creating) the material conditions for the solution of that antagonism' (Marx), of socialism that 'looks out at you through all the windows of capitalism' (Lenin), etc., etc.

28. Barrows Dunham writes:

    This theory, which is one of Aristotle's most important contributions to human thought, really states the essence of all good planning. We have first the analysis of the objective situation, then the determination of a policy exactly suited to it, then the carrying out of the policy in action. The situation thus serves as a standard by which all proposals can be tested, and the fact that the situation is objectively real ensures protection from wishful thinking. To act upon decisions thus reached is indeed to act, as Aristotle would say, like a 'man of practical wisdom' (*Man Against Myth*, p. 108).

29. This sort of difficulty is implicit in most advocacy of small-scale change which puts such change in more or less arbitrary opposition to the large-scale. Popper's distinction, for example, between the two methods and two types of change, between the permissible 'piecemeal social engineering' and the impermissible 'utopian social Engineering' is also drawn in the same question-begging manner (see *The Poverty of Historicism*, section: 'Piecemeal versus Utopian Engineering'). As a consequence, his preference for the former, from the point of view of logic, is as arbitrary as that of Oakeshott. To the extent Popper disallows the 'attempt to draw a precise line of demarcation between the two methods', or puts 'no limits to the scope of a piecemeal approach' or suggests that it is 'a difference not so much in scale and scope as in caution

and in preparedness for unavoidable surprises', he really abandons his entire argument for the permissibility of *only* 'piecemeal social engineering', 'small-scale experiments' and 'piecemeal tinkering' and 'muddling through', all of which he otherwise so defends and lauds.

The arbitrariness of the procedures of Oakeshott and Popper suggests that the only changes possible and permissible in a society are, perhaps, those which they approve of!

30. Oakeshott, of course, denies the imputation that his politics means doing nothing, that according to him 'the office of government is to do nothing'. Generally 'averse from change' and 'averse from innovation', and having, unlike the 'Rationalist', 'nothing to do with innovations designed to meet merely hypothetical situations', Oakeshott nevertheless 'has room for other thoughts'. What are these 'other thoughts' of Oakeshott, what according to him 'shall be on the agenda of reform' in contemporary England? In a passage, where arguing that 'government is providing rules of conduct' he makes one of his all too rare forays into the realm of fact, Oakeshott thus answers this question:

> The current condition of human circumstances is one in which new activities (often springing from new inventions) are constantly appearing and rapidly extend themselves, and in which beliefs are perpetually being modified or discarded; and for the rules to be inappropriate to the current activities and beliefs is as unprofitable as for them to be unfamiliar. For example, a variety of inventions and considerable changes in the conduct of business, seem now to have made the current law of copyright inadequate. And it may be thought that neither the newspaper nor the motorcar nor the aeroplane have yet received proper recognition in the law of England; they have all created nuisances that call out to be abated. Or again, at the end of the last century our governments engaged in an extensive codification of large parts of our law and in this manner both brought it into closer relationship with current beliefs and manner of activity and insulated it from the small adjustments to circumstances which are characteristic of the operation of our common law. But many of these Statutes are now hopelessly out of date. And there are older Acts of Parliament (such as the Merchant Shipping Act), governing large and important departments of activity, which are even more inappropriate to current circumstances. Innovation, then, is called for ....

Some 'other thoughts' and 'innovation' indeed, for England in the mid-twentieth century!

31. In a set of notes, The Pursuit of Intimations', now added to his original essay on 'Political Education', Oakeshott tries 'to remove some of the misunderstandings it provoked' on its first publication. But really he does not succeed in doing anything of the sort. For he complains of 'unfortunate misreading', denies the criticism his essay provoked, repeats his own argument with little that is new or helpful, attacks 'Rationalism' again and in the usual terms, and finally advises the critics 'to think again' Instead of answering any of the questions asked, Oakeshott ends these notes with a rhetorically belligerent question of his own: 'Do you want to be told that in politics there is, what certainly exists nowhere else, a mistake-proof manner of deciding what should be done?' The reader will easily recognise in it a resort once again to that dogmatically sceptical all-or-nothing style of argument which pervades so much of Oakeshott's philosophy and which helps him evade so many real and awkward questions.

    Now unless one believes *a priori* that Oakeshott's opinions are unchallengeable, this sort of attempt 'to remove misunderstandings' will simply not do. I would suggest that Oakeshott's repeated failure to be positive, here as elsewhere, his inability to offer some constructively helpful guidance or programme, is, in its own way, an evidence for the now commonly recognised fact that conservatism, whether old or new, has been rarely a positive creed, a positive enunciation of principles, purposes and programmes. It has always been primarily a 'defensive', a truly 'negative' reaction—a reaction, generally speaking, against the main direction of social and historical development of our times. Once it was a reaction against the French Revolution and the Enlightenment principles of democracy, equality and social justice. More recently, it has been a reaction against the Russian and later the Chinese Revolutions, and against socialism and communism and, of course, the continuing principles of the earlier radical-democratic traditions.

    In this connection see, for example, Samuel P. Huntington's 'Conservatism as an Ideology' in *The American Political Science Review,* Vol. LI, No. 2, June 1957. Huntington points out that 'the only threat extensive and deep enough to elicit a conservative response today is the challenge of communism'. Incidentally, speaking of 'the threat' of communism to 'the most liberal institutions in the world', that is, the American, Huntington gives a call to liberalism in America to liquidate itself, at least for the duration of the threat', for the sake of defending 'the achievements of American liberalism': 'This defense requires American liberals to lay aside their liberal ideology and to accept the values of conservatism for the duration of the threat'!

In a 'Communication' on this article, in *The American Political Science Review* Vol. LI, No. 3, September 1957, Murray N. Rothbard very rightly points out that Huntington's article is a cogent demonstration of the fact that conservatism 'can only be a purely *situational* rather than ideational ideology—a defense of any existing institutions against fundamental challenge'. The New Conservatives, he suggests, are quite clear about the nature of the enemy—and this is not communism alone; according to Rothbard, it is even more democratic socialism, socialism and democracy and even New-Fair Deals at home. But they are quite vague about their positive purposes, even about what they positively wish to defend: 'They are not really *defending* any more, if they ever did;, they are fighting against trends which have already and increasingly prevailed'. Rothbard adds that 'they can unite only in opposition to the enemy, and never on the positive advancement of a consistent creed, their public stance tends always to seem purely "negative" and situational'.

Apropos Huntington's call to American liberals, Rothbard writes:

> The true conservatives in America today are the defender: of the current *status quo*. The fact that so many former liberals have shifted to the 'conservative' mantle is highly significant, for it seems to mean that liberals have begun to lose faith in the liberal ideology, and must therefore turn to tropistic conservatism as a final defense of what is. But if historical precedents are prophetic, this means that liberalism is doomed and that either communism or one of the ideational creeds of the Right opposition bids fair to become the 'wave of the future:

32. Locke, *Essay Concerning Human Understanding*, p. 87.
33. Alfred Cobban, *loc. cit.*, p. 337. He adds: That is what the decline of political theory means in practice'.
34. Pointing out that the concept of 'pursuit of intimations' is 'political romanticism at its purest', Colin Falck writes: 'Oakeshott would deny that he intends this as an apology for the kind of political irrationalism that has its ultimate expression in the charismatic leader and the fascist state; but what matters is that this is the actual tendency of his argument' (*loc. cit.*, p. 70).

35. The generally conservative character of contemporary American political theory is clearly expressed, among other things, in the fact that, as James Petras has pointed out (*loc. cit.*, in it the concept of 'consensus' and the allied concepts of 'equilibrium' and 'balance' have virtually swamped the concepts of 'cleavage' and 'conflict'. Almond even speaks, like many other sand much in the manner of earlier German conservative idealists, of 'a sense of community over and above political decisions' (Almond and Verba, *Civic Culture*, Princeton, 1963, p. 490). Almond regards this 'sense of community' beyond politics as the best safeguard against the disruptive threat of mass politics in a community, against the involvement of the ordinary citizen in more dangerous mass movements which may threaten the established 'consensus' or 'equilibrium' or 'balance' of a community—which community in the case of Almond and also others, we must remember, is a *capitalist* community, full of cleavage and conflict, and essentially irrational and unjust.
36. See, for example, Quintin Hogg, *The Case for Conservatism*, Penguin Books, 1948. Insisting on 'harmony, not struggle' as the 'ruling' principle of conservative political thinking, and rejecting as 'superficial' any analysis of politics in terms of classes or 'the so-called class struggle' he writes: 'Conservatism derives its inspiration and seeks to base its policy on what Conservatives believe to be the underlying unity of all classes ...their ultimate identity of interest, their profound similarity of outlook, ...(p. 31).
37. It was this assumption of a pre-given unity or harmony in society which, being basically false, prevented Burke ultimately from giving a true explanation of the revolution in France. He indeed condemned the Revolution—and condemned not the excesses but the revolution itself as an excess which sought to settle matters with the *ancien regime* outside the framework of tradition and convention. But given the assumption concerning the basic unity or harmony of the French society, he could only explain it as the product of the false and pretentious theories of the *Philosopher*, rather than recognise it as springing, along with the theories of the Philosopher, from the class-divided and conflict-ridden matrix of this society itself. In other words, Burke saw the revolution but misunderstood it. Oakeshott with the same assumption but with a reductionist empiricism which dismisses all theory as ineffectual 'abridgement' and 'postscript', cannot even genuinely misunderstand a revolution. Helped by his curiously inflated concept of tradition, he simply refuses to see one—unless, of course, it be 'a genuine cataclysm'!

38. Discussing elitism in contemporary conservative philosophy in America, I.L. Horowitz writes:

    The new conservatism is in theory a series of footnotes to Platonist teachings. And it should not be overlooked that the present output of 'defenses' of Platonism (John Wild, *Plato's Modern Enemies and the Theory of Natural Law*, 1953; Ronald B. Levinson, *In Defense of Plato*, 1953, etc.) parallels efforts in other areas of thought to reduce the history of culture to the history of conservatism (*loc. cit.*, p. 11).

39. Burke's identification of the three groups on either side is rather interesting. The not so subtle insinuation is that in human society 'the wiser, the more expert, and the more opulent' are all one and the same group of people, and 'the weaker, the less knowing, and the less provided' are one and the same also. Thus does Burke seek to provide—through simple semantic magic—an easy defence and justification of the unjust and iniquitous economic, social, and political divisions existing in society. It is obvious, however, that such people or groups do not necessarily go together. The briefest appeal to facts and logic will expose the utterly arbitrary character of these seemingly very clever identifications.

    Burke is, however, not the only thinker to indulge in this sort of argument. Many others, including Lecky for example, have spoken of 'the wise and the rich' and 'the foolish and the poor'. And there is Herbert Spenccr who, in the more elaborate argument of his *Social Statics*, identified the biologically fit, the economically successful, and the morally good, on the one hand, and the biologically unfit, the economically unsuccessful, and the morally bad on the other. As a matter of fact the treatment of property as 'a surrogate for virtue' or as an evidence of wisdom has been quite common in social and political philosophy since the days of Plato and Aristotle. Needless to add that the purpose in all cases is not any different from Burke's, namely the defence and justification of the socially-produced unjust divisions in society—nor the argument any more sound.

40. C. Wright Mills wrote:

    Conservatism in its classic form is of course traditionalism become self—conscious and elaborated, argumentative and rationalized. It also involves some 'natural aristocracy'. Sooner or later all those who relax the grand tension of human rationality must take up the neo-Burkeian defense of a traditional elite, for in the end, such an elite is the major premise of a genuinely conservative ideology (*The Power Elite*, p. 326).

41. One might add, though, that if Oakeshott were not so 'sceptical' or 'modern', and if he had taken his conservatism more seriously, he would have found it necessary to do something more to make his elite acceptable to the masses, to provide it with 'stronger' support, as it were, as, for example, Plato (myth), or Aristotle (teleological-sociology), or Burke (religion), or fascism (race or nation) did.

    As it is, Oakeshott supports his elite with a few rather shaky 'logical' props only.
42. It is interesting to note that Oakeshott's account of human situation, of 'human activity and intercourse' to be more precise, suggests a super-elite, situated far above the political elite. This is the elite of 'philosophy' regarded as an activity of pure contemplation. This represents in another form and at another level the same basic divisions among men which have been referred to in the text. The 'philosophic' elite of Oakeshott, however, is occupied, not with meditation on nature or society, not with 'knowing'—an activity which according to him is 'boring' when not 'vulgar', and always futile—but with 'contemplating and delighting', with 'making and entertaining mere images'.
43. As, for example, C. Wright Mills has done in *The Power Elite* for the U.S.A.; and more recently W.L. Guttsman has done, though less definitively because of his narrow 'academic' approach and lack of necessary socio-historical depth or perspective, in *The. British Political Elite*, London, 1963, for England. See in this connection also Tom Nairn, 'The British Political Elite', *New Left Review*, No. 23, January February 1964, which also contains highly perceptive comment on Guttsman's otherwise significant book.
44. Anthony Sampson, *Anatomy of Britain*, Hodder and Stoughton, 1962, p. 638.
45. Perry Anderson, *loc. cit.*, pp. 50-2.

    Anderson writes:

    > It is in the political field proper that the present crisis has, of course, produced its most spectacular—if also in a sense superficial—manifestations. The debilitating palpitations of economic policy, the continuing duet of speculation and slums in urban life, the ignominious fiascos in military policy, the colossal humiliation of rejection from the Common Market, the scandals which followed it: all these were the outward signs of the inner disarray—and then demoralization—of the governing class of England, confronted with a world which had passed it and all its monuments by (pp. 52-3).

46. Quoted by Anderson, *ibid.*, p. 52.
47. This does not in any way imply that all is always well with the practice of these societies.
48. Consider, for example, the situation of a society thus described by President Sukarno: '...a nation who have in the first place been economically exploited and oppressed by imperialism...a nation that has lived on two-and-a-half cents per person per day, a nation that eats today and doesn't know where tomorrow's meal wil come from, a nation dressed in tatters, a nation living in broken-down hovels, a nation living in poverty and destitution...' (quoted by Brian Simon, The Present Predicament', in *The Challenge of Marxism*, p. 22). What relevance indeed does Oakeshott's conservatism have to the problems of such a society?
49. President Sukarno, in his above-mentioned speech, very rightly concluded that the only hope of progress for such societies today lies in socialism, that People in such societies 'cannot be otherwise than inspired with socialism'. Needless to add, 'inspirtation' alone is not enough, they must struggle and build too; they must really *move*, and move both *fast* and *far*, otherwise they will reach nowhere at all. 'Socialism is not a policy for the timid', Lange used to say. And he was right in more than merely economic sense.

    As a matter of fact the need for socialism is today imperative even in the economically more advanced capitalist societies of the west, in view of the fact that the essential irrationality of capitalism—that is, its inherent inability to make a *socially rational use of productive resources* to provide for the fullest possible growth and development of man—is becoming daily more pronounced. A *socialist* change in these societies is necessary, in other words, to alter in a fundamental manner the inhuman priorities of capitalism that Galbraith has deplored, though not explained (see *The Affluent Society*, Pelican, 1962); to stop capitalism's ever expanding waste of productive resources in both public and private sectors that Tsuru and Baran have so well exposed (see their contributions to *Has Capitalism Changed? An International Symposium*, edited by Shigeto Tsuru, Tokyo, 1961); to ensure that the scientific and technological revolution, which has just begun, proceeds, both at home and abroad, constructively and not destructively (see, for example, S. Lilley, *Automation and Social Progress*, London, 1957); and, above all, to eliminate the basic inhumanity of capitalism as. a 'socio-economic system and, thus, ensure the recovery of an *alienated* man and society, the evidence for which alienation is written large in the pages of contemporary sociological and psychologial literature of the capitalist societies (see, for example, Fritz Pappenheim, *The Alienation of Modern Man*, New York, 1959, and Eric and Mary Josephson, ed., *Man Alone: Alienation in Modern Society*, New York, 1962), and of which Marx wrote so brilliantly, and prophetically, in his *Economic and Philosophic Manuscripts of 1844*.

On the general question of the need for socialism today see Paul A. Baran, *The Political Economy of Growth*, New Delhi, 1958, and Paul A. Baran and Paul M. Sweezy, *Monopoly Capital*, New York, 1966.

50. In this connection it is well to note that while occasionally conceding the need to restrain 'the indecent competition', Oakeshott thoroughly disapproves of developments like the decline of pure competition, the emergence of 'the welfare state', etc.
51. Marx and Engels, *Manifesto of the Communist Party*, p. 45.
52. They had written:

    Conservation of the old modes of production in unaltered form was, on the contrary, the first condition of existence for all earlier industrial classes. Constant revolutionizing of production, uninterrupted disturbance of all social conditions, everlasting uncertainty and agitation distinguish the bourgeois epoch from all earlier ones. All fixed, fast-frozen relations, with their train of ancient and venerable prejudices and opinions, are swept away, all new-formed ones become antiquated before they can ossify. All that is solid melts into air, all that is holy is profaned, and man is at last compelled to face with sober senses his real conditions of life and his relations with his kind (*ibid.*, p. 45).
53. Quoted by Max Ways, 'The Era of Radical Change', an article reprinted from *Fortune* in *Span*, December 1964, p. 23.
54. Franz Mehring, *Karl Marx*, London, 1951, p. 532.
55. Marx wrote: 'The philosophers have only *interpreted* the world in various ways; the point, however, is to *change* it' (Theses on Feuerbach', *Reader in Marxist Philosophy*, p. 318).
56. See, for example, Marx's 'A Contribution to the Critique of Hegel's Philosophy of Right'. Marx speaks of 'the doctrine that *for man the supreme being is man*', and of 'the *categorical imperative to overthrow all conditions* in which man is a debased, enslaved, neglected and contemptible being.' In the realisation of this revolutionary imperative, according to Marx, 'the proletariat finds its *intellectual* weapons in philosophy', just as 'philosophy finds its *material*

weapon in the proletariat'. Speaking of *'the emancipation of man'*, he wrote: 'The *head* of this emancipation is philosophy, its *heart* the *proletariat*. Philosophy cannot realize itself without the transcendence (*Aufhebung*) of the proletariat, and the proletariat cannot transcend itself without the realization (*Verwirk lichung*) of philosophy' (*Early Writings, op. cit.*, pp. 251, 257).

57. It is in this context that we can also understand the contemporary conservative attack upon democracy, upon the democratic principle itself, wherein we are often told that democracy is 'out' because it leads to 'the tyranny of majority', 'dictatorship', 'communism', '1984' and all the rest of it. Lord Percy (in his *The Heresy of Democracy*) has even argued that democracy, in any thorough going form, all the way from the Augustinian Church to comprehensive schools, must lead to totalitarian dictatorship.

   Behind this attack on the democratic principle lies the fear of radical change in the interests of the common people which popular or radical democracy must always imply. It is this fear which explains both the attack on reason and the attack on democracy which so characteristically go together in contemporary conservative philosophy. In this connection the observations of T.E. Utley, one of the better known conservative theorists, are quite interesting. He writes:

> It is the main theme of almost all intelligent writing about politics today that our contemporary troubles arise from the eighteenth century and are attributable to the rationalist tradition in political theory and the most popular minor theme is that majority rule, as an institution, has a permanent and increasing tendency to produce either dictatorship or bankruptcy or both (quoted by John Strachey, *Contemporary Capitalism*, London, 1956, pp. 270-1).

   Obviously, according to Utley, the best way to avoid 'dictatorship', to say nothing of 'bankruptcy', is to institute, well in advance, an elitist minority rule!

58. In doing this Oakeshott's philosophy is no exception. This is in fact what most contemporary philosophy seems to have done. Certainly so far as 'the mainstream of recent formal and fashionable philosophy' is concerned, it has, as Gellner points out, 'consisted, in the main, of devices for ignoring change, and thus obscured rather than illuminated the choices we face' ('Crisis in the Humanities and the Mainstream of Philosophy', *loc. cit.*, p. 81).

   On 'the loss of the pervading sense of a world in perpetual motion' among the intellectuals and political thinker; of the

English-speaking world in this era of rapid, revolutionary changes, Carr's comments are quite apposite. Pointing out the accompanying loss of faith in reason, he writes:

> It is, however, not the waning of faith in reason among the intellectuals and the political thinkers of the English speaking world which perturbs me most, but the loss of the pervading sense of a world in perpetual motion. This seems at first sight paradoxical; for rarely has so much superficial talk been heard of changes going on around us. But the significant thing is that change is no longer thought of as achievement, as opportunity, as progress, but as an object of fear. When our political and economic pundits prescribe, they have nothing to offer us but the warning to mistrust radical and far-reaching ideas, to shun anything that savours of revolution, and to advance—if advance we must—as slowly and cautiously as we can. At a moment when the world is changing its shape more rapidly and more radically than at anytime in the last 400 years, this seems to me a singular blindness, which gives ground for apprehension, not that the world-wide movement will be stayed, but that this country—and perhaps other English-speaking countries—may lag behind the general advance, and relapse helplessly and uncomplainingly into some nostalgic backwater (*op. cit.*, p. 151).

59. Marx, *A Contribution to the Critique of Political Economy*, p. 12. One of the basic arguments for socialism today is that the new forces of production being made available by contemporary scientific and technological advance demand, for their proper, rational utilisation, a corresponding change in the relations of production of capitalism. As S. Lilley writes: 'There is no ultimate escape from the fact that capitalism, well though it worked in its time, is not a suitable economic structure for making beneficial use of the advanced techniques of today and the even more advanced techniques of tomorrow .... There is no ultimate way forward except that of changing the whole economic system into a socialist one' (*op. cit.*, p. 213).
60. This conflict of interests is inevitably reflected in the ideological sphere and the mainspring of social change is to be found in the ideas and ideologies which express the radical or revolutionary requirements of the new situation.

    Making the distinction between 'two kinds of ideology—ideologies which *obscure, mystify reality* and ideologies which *lay bare, reveal reality,*' Lange writes:

> The class whose social existence is based on the relations of production which are at odds with the requirements of the development of the productive forces, together with the strata whose position is linked with a superstructure which cannot survive if the relations of production are changed, tend to obscure, to mystify reality, trying in this way to weaken the forces demanding the alteration of social relations (*op. cit.*, p. 330).

61. Paul Baran, 'On the Nature of Marxism, *loc. cit*. At such historical junctures the confrontation of social reality with reason, a really objective inquiry into society and its development, makes clear the need for fundamental revolutionary changes. It reveals not only the irrationality of the existing social order but also the principle and the possibility of a better and more rational social order. It thus 'becomes at once one of the most responsible activities of the time and one of the most powerful engines of humanism and progress'. But, for the same reason, it also becomes a highly suspect and dangerous activity from the point of view of the existing social order. Pointing this out Baran writes:

> It is precisely then that the confrontation of reality with reason is proscribed by the ruling class, is persecuted as subversive by its police, is condemned as sacrilegious by its priests, and is decried as metaphysical and unscientific by its ideologists (p. 262).

62. C.P. Snow, *Science and Government*, London, 1961, p. 80. Snow expresses his concern over the fact that the more advanced societies of capitalism in the west are fast becoming 'existential'. Speaking of 'our dangers and our losses of hope', he writes:

> One of those dangers is that we are beginning to shrug off our sense of the future. This is true all over the West. True even in the United States, though to a lesser extent than in the older societies of Western Europe. We are becoming existential societies—and we are living in the same world with future-directed societies. This existential flavour is obvious in our art. In fact, we are becoming unable to accept any other kind of art. It is there to be seen in quarters much nearer the working mechanism of our society, in the deepest of our administrative arrangements .... We seem to be flexible, but we haven't any model of the future before us. In the significant sense, we can't change. And to change is what we have to do (pp. 79-80).

63. M.O. Milligan, *loc. cit.*, p. 57.
64. In a brief but brilliant sketch, in the concluding chapter of *What is*

History? Carr has well brought out the nature and dimensions of contemporary change. Pointing out that in the change of our times 'the social revolution and the technological revolution and the scientific revolution are part and parcel of the same process', Carr writes:

> The middle years of the twentieth century find the world in a process of change probably more profound and more sweeping than any which has overtaken it since the mediaeval world broke up in ruins and the foundations of the modern world were laid in the fifteenth and sixteenth centuries. The change is no doubt ultimately the product of scientific discoveries and inventions, of their ever more widespread application, and of developments arising directly or indirectly out of them. The most conspicuous aspect of the change is a social revolution comparable with that which, in the fifteenth and sixteenth centuries, inaugurated the rise to power of a new class based on finance and commerce, and later on industry.

Carr draws our attention particularly to two aspects of this historical change. It is 'a change in depth, and a change in geographical extent', both implying a tremendous 'expansion of reason', that is, 'increase in the numbers of those who learn to think, to use their reason'.

With regard to the first aspect Carr points out that functions and powers of reason have come to be extended to increasingly new spheres of human existence. Man today seeks through conscious exercise of reason not only to harness the forces of nature to his purposes, to transform his natural environment, but also to reshape his society in a planned manner, to transform his social environment as well. He writes:

> The primary function of reason, as applied to man in society, is no longer merely to investigate, but to transform; and this heightened consciousness of the power of man to improve the management of his social, economic and political affairs by the application of rational processes seems to me one of the major aspects of the twentieth-century revolution.

Of the other aspect Carr writes: The second aspect of the progressive revolution through which we are passing is the changed shape of the world .... After some 400 years the world centre of gravity has definitely shifted away from Western Europe.' Pointing out that 'Western Europe, together with the outlying parts of the English-speaking world, has become an appanage of the North American continent, or, if you like, an agglomeration in which the United States serves both as powerhouse and as control-tower' and that 'it is by no means clear that the world centre of gravity now resides, or will continue for long to reside, in the English-speaking world with its Western European annex', Carr writes: 'It appears to be the great land-mass of eastern Europe and Asia, with its extensions into Africa, which today calls the tune in world affairs'.

One might add, with reference to the first aspect of today's historic change pointed out by Carr, that the fullest extension of reason to the management of economic and social arrangements of society is precisely what socialism, in one of its central features, meant to Marx. Marx wrote that socialism is nothing but 'the fact that socialized man, the associated producers, regulate their interchange with nature rationally, bring it under their common control, instead of being ruled by it as by some blind power, that they accomplish their task with the least expenditure of energy and under conditions most adequate to their human nature and most worthy of it' (*Capital*, Vol. III, Kerr edn., p. 954).

'But', Marx immediately added, 'it always remains a realm of necessity. Beyond it begins that development of human power, which is its own end, the true realm of freedom, which, however, can flourish only upon that realm of necessity as its basis'.

65. Speaking of change in contemporary society and of human responsibility in this regard, Max Ways clearly recognises the need of knowledge to cope with 'the radical change around us'. He in fact attributes the growth in recent years of what he calls 'the knowledge industry', the remarkable growth of activities concerned with 'the production', more particularly with 'the processing and distribution of knowledge—all the teaching, the textbooks, the journalism, the advertising, and other forms of communication', to the need of coping with the problems created by 'radical change as a condition of life' (*loc. cit.*).

I cannot here go into the merits of Max Ways argument as a whole. But what he says about 'the knowledge industry, its general relevance notwithstanding, calls for some critical comment. It seems to me that his use of the term 'knowledge' is rather loose and ambiguous. If not open to downright objection, it certainly demands that very serious qualifications be made. For much of what Max Ways includes in 'the knowledge industry' —much of journalism, advertising, various communication media like cinema and television, etc., to say nothing of certain sorts of teaching and textbooks has often enough hardly anything to do with knowledge, its production, processing or distribution, as we rightly understand these. Much of it even involves—for example, in political journalism and commercial advertising—a gross abuse of knowledge, of reason and rational processes. It involves large-scale exploitation of unconscious psychological urges of the masses, a trading on their irrationalism, and really constitutes techniques not of communicating or distributing rational, scientific knowledge, but of what Oscar Wilde once described as 'hitting below the intellect'. (Adlai Stevenson, who was twice a victim of these techniques during his Presidential election campaigns in the United States, once sorely complained: The idea that you can merchandise candidates for high office like breakfast cereal ...is the ultimate indignity to the democratic process' (quoted in Vance Packard, *The Hidden Persuader.*, Penguin, 1961, p. 164).

Putting it briefly, what Max Ways euphemistically calls 'the knowledge industry' is quite often only 'the opinion business', or 'the persuation industry' as Pearson and Turner have called it in their book of the same title, which manipulates the public for hire in the interests of the rich and powerful, of the ruling classes of a monopoly capitalist society. And not a few of the persons employed in Max Ways' 'knowledge industry', far from being the proud producers, processors or distributors of *knowledge*, far from being knowers or thinkers, seekers or guardians of truth, are really poor 'persuaders', open or hidden, conscious or unconscious, in the service of the *status quo* and its system of privilege and private profit.

66. One might add that in doing so we must not either fight shy of Marxism and the knowledge it makes available or possible, or ever forget what Whitehead, believing in man's ability to control his world, always used to point out: 'to give up solving problems because they are difficult is treason to the human race'.
67. Carr, *op. cit.*, p. 148.
68. One would fully endorse Popper's proud and passionate plea in this regard. Speaking of 'the cross of humaneness, of reason, of responsibility', which we must carry 'if we wish to remain human', he writes: 'We must go on into the unknown, the uncertain and insecure, using what reason we may have to plan for both security and freedom' (*The Open Society and its Enemies*, Vol. I, p. 201).

3

Of Economics and Politics

Oakeshott's fear and suspicion of change is, in the final analysis, only a corollary of his basic commitment to the *status quo*, to the contemporary capitalist society. Illustrative, as it were, of his satisfaction, even if somewhat bored and ambiguous, with things as they are, of the nature of his sympathies as well as his prejudices, and of the limits of his sociological insight and comprehension, are Oakeshott's two essays, 'The Political Economy of Freedom' and 'On being Conservative.' Here Oakeshott for once deals, more or less concretely, with some of the basic issues of contemporary economics and politics. These essays lack the usual subtlety and sophistication of Oakeshott's argument. But they are nevertheless significant because they make explicit the sort of political commitment which lies behind his more abstract, and occasionally even obscure, 'academic' or 'philosophical' essays, wherein he is professedly concerned only to 'analyse' and 'understand', to 'describe' and 'explain', and not to 'recommend' a 'programme or policy' or to offer 'warrants for conduct'. It is clear, however, from our discussion so far, that despite his repeated and emphatic disclaimers of evaluative or prescriptive intent—which sometimes make one feel that he is perhaps protesting too much—Oakeshott's so-called 'descriptive' or 'explanatory' exercises contain not only substantial political doctrine but also one which is comfortably conformist and conservative in its practical implications.[1] The two essays now under consideration throw important light on the nature of this doctrine. They directly reveal not only what

Oakeshott does or does not permit in politics but also the sort of practical purposes which his philosophy as a whole may be said to serve.

'The Political Economy of Freedom' was written, it is well to remember, in 1949, with a Labour Government in power in England. Oakeshott, 'a genuine libertarian', apparently felt that the very hand of tyranny was upon his country. And he moved into the battle in defence of 'liberty' with a characteristically conservative invective, reminiscent in many ways of Burke's performance in another age.

In this essay, Oakeshott proclaims his 'love', indeed his 'passion for liberty', at a time when, he bemoans, 'other loves have bewitched us'. He speaks of 'the leaders of fashion, the intellectual dandies of the Fabian Society' and 'their hastily composed syllabus of errors', of '"this sophisticated generation", which knows all the answers but is sadly lacking in education'. He rails against 'the influence of misguided journalists and cunning tyrants', 'the small vocal section of our society', who dare put 'freedom of speech' above 'the right to private property' —'the major part of mankind', Oakeshott insists, 'has nothing to say; the lives of most men do not revolve round a felt necessity to speak'. He informs us that 'with eyes focussed upon distant horizons and minds clouded with foreign clap-trap, the impatient and sophisticated generation now in the saddle has dissolved its partnership with its past'—a partnership which Oakeshott tells us elsewhere not even the most violent revolutionaries can ever succeed in dissolving. And he gives the solemn warning that 'the government of a collectivist society can tolerate only a very limited opposition to its plans; indeed, that hardwon distinction, which is one of the elements of our liberty, between opposition and treason is rejected: what is not obedience is sabotage'.

All this Oakeshott writes not about some Jacobin or Bolshevik dictatorship, but about a Labour Party, whose difference from the Conservative Party, that is any *real* difference, has persistently eluded scholars. Only recently, for example, Robert McKenzie has informed us that between these two rival contenders for political power in England 'the "agreement on fundamentals" is today very nearly as great as it has ever been in the modern history of British politics![2] One indeed wonders, therefore, what Oakeshott must really think of *his* Conservatives!

'Collectivism', Oakeshott tells us, is one of 'the two great contemporary opponents of libertarian society', the other being what he calls 'syndicalism'. 'Collectivism' is in fact the 'enemy' of a 'free society' which is attacked and pilloried throughout this essay. And, according to Oakeshott, 'collectivism in the modern world ...stands for a managed society, and its other titles are communism, national socialism, socialism, economic democracy and central planning'. The making of even elementary distinctions is of no importance at all in Oakeshott's social and political theory!

Liberty, Oakeshott repeatedly insists, depends above all upon the maintenance of 'the right to private property'. He in fact makes the two, liberty and private property, virtually synonymous with each other. Oakeshott simply does not know, or perhaps he does not care to know, either the mass of unfreedom which capitalism—as a system of private property and wage slavery that throws men at the mercy of the blind forces of the market—produces at all levels in society, or, how often and how easily in our time liberty has been crucified, as Caudwell once put it, 'upon a cross of gold'![3]

Speaking of 'private property' and of every man's 'right' to it, Oakeshott informs us that there are no 'categorical distinctions' between 'different kinds of property', between 'personal and real property, chattels, property in a man's own physical and mental capacities and property in the so-called means of production'; they are all 'forms of power', and 'incidentally spring from the same sources, investment, inheritance and luck'. We are thus all of us property owners, and, therefore, free—the capitalist exploitation and wage-slavery is, presumably, only 'so-called'!

Oakeshott writes of 'a right to private property...which allows to every adult member of the society an equal right to enjoy the ownership of his personal capacities and of anything else obtained by the methods of acquisition recognised in the society'. This certainly seems to secure for all, at any rate for the bulk of humanity, at least one 'equal right'—the right to be exploited!

Oakeshott further tells us: 'a man is not free unless he enjoys a proprietary right over his personal capacities and his labour', and 'no such right exists unless there are many potential employers (or purchasers) of his labour'. Freedom, he therefore concludes, 'implies private property in resources other than personal capacity'. In other words, the capitalist, according to Oakeshott, is a capitalist—for the sake of the worker's freedom![4]

Oakeshott goes on: 'All monopolies are prejudical to freedom; but there is good reason for supposing that labour monopolies are more dangerous than any others'. 'Their appetite for power is insatiable', their activity simply 'scandalous'. 'A society in the grip of such monopolies', Oakeshott says, 'would enjoy less freedom than any other sort of society'. One may, therefore, well begin the fight for freedom, as, for example, the fascists did, by breaking up the trade unions!

As if all this were not enough Oakeshott informs us that 'the labour monopoly', apart from being 'more subversive of freedom' than any other, is also 'dangerous because it demands enterprise monopoly as its complement. There is a disastrous identity of interest between the two kinds of monopoly ....Indeed, the conflict of capital and labour ...is merely a sham fight'. Sham too, therefore, according to Oakeshott, is labour's fight for socialism, and the sooner it is abandoned altogether the better for all concerned![5]

There is no end to plain prejudice and economic naivety, 'no end to the clap-trap—to borrow a phrase he himself is fond of using against his opponents—in Oakeshott's discussion of the problem of freedom in contemporary capitalist society.

Oakeshott, no doubt, recognises the existence, owing, among other causes, 'to the negligence of past generations', of 'an accumulated mass of maladjustment' in this society. He even concedes the necessity of an attack on it—this 'attack upon the accumulated maladjustments in our society and upon our real problems', he says, 'is certainly long overdue'. But what really interests him is something different. He asserts that 'the task to which this generation is called is not the much advertised "reconstruction of society" but to provide against the new tyrannies'. And the provision he makes at the end of his long argument, the magic-formula he rediscovers and recommends for the preservation of liberty in a capitalist or any other society is 'the establishment and maintenance of effective competition' by means of 'appropriate legal reform'.

Oakeshott informs us of what according to him 'every school boy used to know', namely that 'if effective competition is to exist it can do so only by virtue of a legal system which promotes it, and that monopoly has established itself only because the legal system has not prevented it'. Urging 'the libertarian', therefore, not to 'think it beyond the capacity of his society to build upon its already substantial tradition of creating and maintaining effective competition bylaw', he recommends a so-called 'positive programme of *Laissez Faire*' aimed at 'making competition effective', at 're-establishing a diffusion of power'. 'Restraint of trade must be treated as a major crime', Oakeshott tells us, and 'private monopoly in all its forms is to be suppressed'—though Oakeshott hastens to add that above all 'the monopolies and the monopolistic practices to be destroyed are monoplies of labour'.

Such is Oakeshott's answer to the problem of 'the political economy of freedom'. One cannot help pointing out that if Oakeshott's is indeed the answer to the problem of liberty in a contemporary society—which fortunately, it is not—then liberty is, if not impossible, certainly in permanent jeopardy, in every modern industrialised society. Oakeshott would, of course, readily concede this with regard to a socialist society, for such a society is by definition 'collectivist' and therefore not 'free'. But what Oakeshott, with singular blindness to the facts of real life, seems unable to see is that this is no less true of a private property-based capitalist society, if the growth of 'enterprise monopoly' in this society, for example in the U.K., is any indication,[6] to say nothing of the growth of trade unions, of what Oakeshott chooses to call 'labour monopolies'. The utter ineffectiveness of anti-monopoly legislation in England, or in the U.S.A. and elsewhere, has clearly shown that the attempt to curb monopoly by law is futile. It has in fact only further underlined the fact that all reform of capitalism—conservative, liberal or labourite, legal or moral or any other—is really a labour of Sisyphus that never ends and relative to needs and possibilities makes little if any progress.

One final word before we leave Oakeshott on the subject of freedom. Oakeshott, it is clear, wants freedom through competition, through 'the maximum diffusion of power' of a competitive capitalist society based on a virtually unfettered, 'least qualified', 'right to private property'. But he wants such competition and such a society without that, according to Oakeshott, freedom-negating 'concentration of power' which inescapably goes with them. In other words, Oakeshott wants competition without the monopolies, the 'great and dangerous concentrations of power', which competition in a capitalist society inevitably breeds; and he wants the capitalist society without that working class organisation which the class struggle inherent in such a society equally inevitably brings into existence. He, thus, wants the impossible.

But, then, this is what all good bourgeois, unable or unwilling to look beyond the bourgeois horizon, do. Marx once wrote of them: 'They all want competition without its tragic effects. They all want the impossible, namely, the conditions of bourgeois existence, without the necessary consequences of those conditions'.[7]

II

Oakeshott's attack on 'collectivism', is little better than the 19th century critique of Lecky and Spencer, carried forward in our time, among others by Hayek,[8] to the effect that all social-welfare oriented planning, all state or any other form of social intervention in the economic field in the public interest, is a dangerous erosion of individual intitiative and freedom, that socialism is nothing but the road that leads to slavery or serfdom. True to form, Oakeshott sees in collectivism, or central planning or economic democracy or socialism, one of the great sources of political evil in the contemporary world. It is certainly the greatest single threat to freedom in a society. It involves not only 'wastefulness, frustration and corruption', but also, and more than anything else, 'servility' and certain loss of 'freedom'. 'Collectivism and freedom are', Oakeshott tells us, 'real alternatives—if we choose one we cannot have the other'. Furthermore its claims to promotion of public welfare are spurious. 'The only "welfare"it is capable of pursuing—a centralized, national "welfare"—is hostile to freedom at home and results in organized rivalry abroad.' Collectivism is in fact 'inherently warlike'. It means not only permanent 'international disharmony' but also 'war'—so Oakeshott goes on in denunciation of collectivism.

Against this 'collectivism', Oakeshott defends capitalism as a system of private property and market competition, using in the course of this defence all the ancient cliches—about men not being 'children in *statu pupillari* but adults' capable of 'making choices for themselves' and doing things 'on their own account', about 'freedom', 'free way of living', and 'free play of human choice' that the capitalist system provides, about the 'proprietary right over personal capacities and labour' that men enjoy or 'the self-government', 'initiative' and 'inventiveness' that men exercise under this system, etc., etc.[9]

In attacking 'collectivism' in this manner,' and defending 'freedom' as it obtains in capitalist society, what Oakeshott in fact does, particularly in his essay 'On being Conservative', is to restate the entire theory of the negative-liberal state which was first fully elaborated in the late 18th and early 19th centuries, of course, on the basis of the developments, practical and theoretical, of the preceding period.

Oakeshott thus points out 'the kind of limited but necessary service a society may expect from its government', and this is 'merely to rule', 'to prevent coercion', 'to keep its subjects at peace with one another in the activities in which they have chosen to seek their happiness', to ensure 'orderly and peaceable behaviour' among them. 'The image of the ruler', he informs us, 'is the umpire whose business is to administer the rules of the game, or the chairman who governs the debate according to known rules but does not himself participate in it'.

Government, Oakeshott repeatedly tells us, 'merely pursues

peace'. Its is a 'specific and limited activity, namely the provision and custody of general rules of conduct'. It seeks only to 'adjust' the interests of its subjects, 'to resolve some of the collisions which (the) variety of beliefs and activities generates' in a society, 'to preserve peace...by enforcing general rules of procedure upon all subjects alike'. It has no other function to perform, certainly no social or political or economic function of any importance—though Oakeshott relents a little to allow 'the maintenance of a stable currency' as '(perhaps the only) specifically economic activity appropriate to government'. To postulate any positive or 'substantive' functions is to be guilty of entertaining 'vain and dangerous expectations', it is to harbour the illegitimate desire to 'impose' one's own 'dream' on others, to betray the itch, as it were, for what Oakeshott ridicules as 'this jump to glory style of politics', although he concedes that 'there is much in our circumstances to provoke it'. Oakeshott warns most categorically against 'putting too high a value on political action and placing too high a hope in political achievement'. He insists that 'governing' must be 'understood to be a secondary activity' which only seeks 'to restrain, to deflate, to pacify and to reconcile', that 'the proper attitude of government towards the current condition of human circumstance is one of acceptance', that its attitude towards society as a whole, towards the beliefs or activities or aspirations of the people must be one of indifference' and 'inertia', of 'mockery' and complete 'scepticism'. The model for Oakeshott always remains 'the integration of activity which competition (the market) provides'.[10]

Oakeshott thus resurrects for our benefit the entirely anachronistic theory of the nature and functions of political authority which first arose in England as a characteristic ideological product of the period of the rise of modern capitalism. The origins of this theory can be traced back to the 17th century, in Hobbes and in Locke, but its clearest expression came later, in the 18th and 19th centuries, in the writings of Adam Smith, Jeremy Bentham and the Philosophical Radicals, followed by Herbert Spencer and others. Resting basically on the notion, born of capitalist market economy, of society existing as a more or less automatic balance of individuals, classes, or interests—a notion which was often supported by references to 'Providence' or 'unseen hand', or 'natural harmony', and was always relied upon to defend or justify an extreme form of individualism, 'possessive individualism' Macpherson has called it—this theory grew up as an integral part of classical liberalism as the latter arose to become the dominant ideology of the new capitalist social and political order. As a typical product of the times, it reflected what were historically the most important and vocal interests of the period, namely the rising middle or capitalist class interests. The specific political form it assumed, particularly in the wake of the Industrial Revolution, was that of a carefully elaborated theory of the state which, while regarding the state as an instrument of society as a whole, took an extremely limited, a wholly negative or 'police' view of its functions.

But if this theory showed the fullest awareness of the needs and interests of the rising propertied classes, particularly of the new industrial capitalist class, it was characteristically blind to the needs and interests of the common people, particularly of the new working class, immediately the worst victims of the industrial revolution, of the new capitalist social order.[11] It is not surprising, therefore, that even as this theory established its transient sway, it came under heavy fire. Convinced socialists like Marx or later William Morris, for example, assailed not only the theory but the entire underlying notion of the state as a neutral 'supra-class' agency simply serving the interests of the whole society; they rejected such a notion as completely false in the circumstances of a capitalist or any other class divided society.[12] Others, Southey and Arnold, Carlyle, Ruskin and Dickens among them, were not interested in the theory but were deeply disturbed by the immediate practical consequences flowing from it, by the terrible social effects of unrestrained industrialism. They lodged powerful, passionately eloquent protests against this industrialism. While many of them assailed capitalist industrialism and *laissez faire* mainly on moral and aesthetic grounds, others also clearly understood and criticised the disastrously negative nature of the emergent liberal ideology. Carlyle, in his characteristic manner, ridiculed its wisdom as 'anarchy plus a constable'. And all these critics demanded a sane, a more positive and constructive approach to the problems of post-Industrial Revolution England.

We have come quite some distance since then. The last hundred years have seen, not only in England but in the other economically advanced societies of the capitalist world as well, the slow and tortuous, and invariably belated, development of 'social services', 'social welfare measures', or 'social policy programmes' of all sorts, to help the more unfortunate victims of the irrationality and exploitation of capitalism, and to provide, however inadequately, for some at least of the needs, private and public, created by unplanned industrialism and economic change, needs which the profit-oriented economy of these capitalist societies has been, on its own, unable or unwilling to provide for. This development has meant over the years a definite transition from the so-called 'negative' to the 'positive' state. It has reached its practical consummation in what has come to be known as 'the welfare state' and found its best theoretical expression in what has come to be known as 'the liberal-democratic theory'.[13] But while ' "Welfare Statism", either as an established fact or as a political objective', is a common phenomenon of all capitalist societies in the west today, and has come to be duly endorsed, even if grudgingly at times, by most western political theorists, 'whether on the right or left politically',[14] it has not meant any modification of the basic irrationality or inhumanity of capitalism. This irrationality springs, inevitably as it were, from the very nature of capitalism as a system of private property, profit-making and exploitation. The essential irrationality or inhumanity of capitalism has, therefore, remained. It has in fact become still more pronounced with the passage of years. By altering some of its forms, by mitigating some of its worst manifestations through a patch-work of welfare measures, 'the welfare state' has only smoothed over the class antagonisms, prevented the class-struggle from assuming sharper revolutionary forms and thus ensured a better functioning of the existing economic and social system, a strengthening of the basic institutions of capitalism. It has acted, as John Saville says, as a 'shock absorber'[15] and thereby contributed not to any transformation but only to the continued survival of the essentially unjust and irrational capitalist social order.[16]

In fact the central issue before the more advanced societies of capitalism in the west today is whether to remain satisfied with what little has been achieved, or can be achieved, within the essentially capitalist limits of 'the welfare state' or to go beyond it. The issue has become central not only because of the most glaring inadequacies of 'welfare capitalism' even under the most favourable circumstances, but also because of the tremendous scientific and technological advance of our time, which is making it both possible and necessary for us to go boldly forward, beyond the 'welfare state', beyond, as some others have put it, the 'liberal democratic society'.

There is no doubt, of course, that the smug and complacent among contemporary social and political thinkers, those committed irrevocably to the established order, have been willing to rest content with what has been achieved, with the so-called 'welfare state'[17] They have not only settled down, as Barrington Moore Jr. puts it, 'to a stolid acceptance of things as they are',[18] but also proceeded to rationalise and justify this truly 'stolid' acceptance: they have seized upon the development of 'the welfare state' in the more advanced societies of western capitalist democracy[19] as the occasion and the excuse to proclaim the 'triumph of the democratic social revolution', and with it 'the end of political ideology' itself in these societies.[20] But there have been others, scholars with finer sensibilities, deeper sociological insight and an infinitely superior sense of history—Cole, Tawney, Laski, Wright Mills, Richard Titmuss and C.B. Macpherson among them—who have been fully conscious of the limits of 'the welfare state', of 'the liberal-democratic society', and who have, therefore, boldly looked forward to a transcendence of these limits, a transcendence which in the circumstances of today can only be socialist in its nature and scope. This is indeed what the real needs of men and the new possibilities of the objective situation imperatively demand in the mid-twentieth century.[21]

The need for a socialist transcendence of the capitalist limits of the modern welfare state has now been obvious for a long time.[22] But it has become all the more urgent today in view of the scientific and technological advance of our time, which is issuing, among other things, in what has been called 'the second industrial revolution'—a revolution which has just begun but is rapidly gathering momentum, and whose social consequences are likely to be every bit as farreaching as those of the first industrial revolution. This scientific and industrial revolution, the enormous advance it implies in the development of new productive forces or techniques, is in fact daily exposing the essential irrationality of capitalism, its inherent inability, 'the welfare state' notwithstanding, to satisfy basic human needs and provide for the fullest possible growth and development of man, to secure rational utilisation of the productive resources for the advancement of human welfare at home and abroad. In so doing the scientific and technological revolution is indicating the clear need for a basic change in the production or property relations of the societies of capitalism so that the resources now becoming available, along with those already existing, may be used for genuinely human ends and for the benefit of mankind as a whole.[23]

The new scientific and technological advance is indeed opening up magnificent new vistas of progress for mankind. It has brought us at last to the threshold of transition from a civilisation of scarcity to a civilisation of abundance, making possible for the first time the full recognition of the worth and dignity of human personality, the realisation of man's unlimited potentialities for knowledge, enjoyment and creation. But it needs no deep analysis to recognise that these possibilities will not be automatically realised and that the capitalist ownership and control of key economic resources is the main obstacle to such a realisation. The entire history of capitalism, in fact, warns us that under this system, given its motivating principle of profit-making and there can be no other motivating principle under capitalism—the fruits of the introduction of new industrial techniques have never fallen automatically to the community as a whole.[24] On the contrary, these techniques have invariably been turned into instruments for still more intensified exploitation of workers at home and abroad. It is not likely to be any different with the new techniques of today, those born of what has been called the 'Cybernation Revolutions.'[25] It will be no different unless, as urged by the radical or the socialist, the *capitalist* limits of the modern welfare state are transcended. This transcendence, in fact a fully socialist ownership of the means of production, is necessary if the scientific and technological revolution now taking place is to proceed constructively and not destructively; if 'the new wave of industrialism' is to lighten the burden of common working people at home and abroad and not find, as the old one did, only its victims among them; if the promethean fire of expanding human knowledge which should be given for the benefit of mankind at large is not to be used, as always in the past, only to stoke up the furnaces of private privilege and profit, or, even worse, to make wars.[26]

Oakeshott, it is obvious, belongs with neither the radicals nor the complacent ones of contemporary social and political theory. Professedly anti-socialist and therefore opposed to any planned progress into the future, he is also, unlike the smug and complacent ones, largely oblivious of or indifferent to the actual, existential needs of the present. What is really worth noting, however, is the fact that like 'the smug conservatives, tired liberals and disillusioned radicals' of 'the end of ideology' chorus, he too is unaware of the significance of the tremendous advance of modern science and technology,[27] of its likely social consequences, particularly under capitalism, and, above all, of the possibility this advance holds for the first time of building a civilised society free from the taint of class-division and oppression and exploitation of man by man, of creating what Marx called a 'truly human society'[28] He is totally unaware of the change in our thinking that the scientific and technological revolution of our time calls for, and the added urgency it gives to the need not only of what Titmuss calls 'redistributive social justice', of making greater investment in people and social services, of introducing greater *moral* purpose in the social and economic arrangements of our society, but even more of putting these arrangements on a *firm moral basis* by establishing the social ownership of the means of production, which alone makes *possible* a truly rational planning of production and distribution of goods and services for the welfare of all the members of society, for guaranteeing them, in Engels' words, 'the completely unrestricted development and exercise of their physical and mental faculties:[29] Though living in the mid-twentieth century Oakeshott is strangely oblivious of both its needs and its possibilties. Or, perhaps, unlike his smug and complacent contemporaries, he somehow senses the revolutionary, 'future-directed' implications of these needs and possibilities and shrinks back, dismayed, into the past. Despairing of the future, the present itself, he seems to feel, can be salvaged only with the help of an appeal to the past. And committed as he is to the present, to the existing bourgeois society, Oakeshott turns for its defence and justification to its past, to the great age of the bourgeoisie, the age of triumphant *laissez faire* and its political expression, the negative liberal state.[30]

III

In defending the bourgeois society as it does, in defending and justifying 'the current condition of human circumstance', the 'existing arrangements' which constitute the bourgeois social order, Oakeshott's political philosophy betrays an amazing lack of sense of history and contemporary socio-political reality, of what Carr has called 'the pervading sense of a world in perpetual motion'. For, in a fundamental sense, not only to the much-maligned rationalist but also to men in general, 'nothing (certainly no social and political order) is of value merely because it exists', or even 'because it has existed for many generations'. 'Familiarity', however valuable otherwise, by itself indeed 'has no worth'. In human affairs 'nothing' indeed is or can be 'left standing for want of scrutiny' for long. The mere existence, or continued survival of a social and political system has never been deemed sufficient to justify or legitimatise it. The 'existing arrangements' of a society have never been accepted, certainly not for long, 'simply because they are current' or 'are afoot'. On the contrary, men, in the course of their long history, have always subjected them to critical 'scrutiny', to scrunity in the light of reason, that is to say, in terms of the ability, or inability, of these arrangements to satisfy human needs, to provide for the growth and development of man. This has been an indispensable condition of all social and historical progress. To help and guide in the carrying out of this 'scrutiny' has been the function of all progressive thought from its earliest beginnings. To continuously confront reality with reason, as Baran puts it, in order to establish the principles of and the road to a better social order, to systematically struggle against all that obscures people's view of the social reality and destroys their awareness of the conditions and prerequisites for their best possible growth and development, has been the great, in fact the only true function of all fruitful intellectual endeavour. It has been the paramount task indeed of the intellectual in social and historical progress, in the forward movement of mankind.[31]

Oakeshott is not only indifferent to or oblivious of all this, he also fails to recognise the simple historical facts that the 'existing arrangements' he so doggedly defends and would like to see perpetuated for ever, were themselves once born of precisely that historical 'conjunction of dreaming and ruling' which he condemns as 'tyranny',[32] that 'the current condition of human circumstance' whose 'acceptance' he so strongly urges upon every one was itself once, not only 'a dream', but also one which was, in a real sense, 'imposed upon everybody', and that the first and the most fundamental function of a government is to make this 'dream' work, to continue its 'imposition' on those of its subjects who are still unwilling to accept it or who have other and, perhaps, better 'dreams' of their own.

Oakeshott completely fails to see that the government of a class-divided society is not, it simply cannot be, a neutral agency, an 'umpire' or 'a referee' as he calls it, raised far above this society's conflicting class and sectional interests, and acting always only as an instrument of some *mystique* of the interests of this society as a whole.[33] Questionable at all times, such a notion makes little, if any, sense in a society characterised by such deep class-divisions and by so great a concentration of economic power as is the present day monopoly capitalist society in the west.[34] In this society—'our society', Oakeshott fondly calls it 'the rules of the game' that he makes so much of, are, appearances apart, rather heavily loaded against the overwhelming majority of its members. To keep 'the game' going, to 'govern' it 'according to the rules' is therefore really 'to participate' in it, 'to prevent coercion' is itself coercion of another sort. 'Merely to rule' in such a society, 'to keep peace', is both to 'impose' and to 'take sides'.

IV

It is interesting to note that, relying mainly on ideological resources from the past, Oakeshott also has occasional recourse to the idiom of contemporary political theory. But, like much of this theory, or 'science' as its authors prefer to call it, he does so without really confronting the contemporary political reality, the political reality of contemporary capitalist society. He raises, particularly in his discussion of the problem of freedom in capitalist society, the question of political power in this society. But after the manner of most academic political theory which makes 'power' the central category for purposes of political inquiry, or works with 'the power hypothesis' so-called, Oakeshott's argument remains preoccupied mostly with power *as such*, with power in the abstract. The sociology of power, its social content or determinants, the nature, sources, ends or purposes of political power in a class-divided society, power as exercised by specific social groups or classes *over* others in order to maximise their advantages, these and similar issues are simply swamped by the implicit assumption of power as a generalised phenomenon, characterising any society, which is either very properly 'diffused' or 'balanced' between different interests, organised sections or countervailing forces of society, or very improperly 'concentrated' so as to constitute a threat to freedom in society. Used in this manner 'power' is too formal, too highly generalised, even if supposedly 'neutral' or 'scientific' a concept to be really fruitful in any social or political inquiry.[35] The use of this concept certainly cannot claim, so far, to have contributed much that is new or significant to our knowledge of important political realities.[36] Oakeshott's passing flirtation with this concept, which runs pretty much to form, is no different in its outcome. It results, not unexpectedly, in a characteristic evasion of the more important issues raised by his own argument.[37]

Oakeshott speaks, in the course of his argument concerning freedom, of 'limited' and 'unlimited power', of 'dispersion' and 'concentration' of power, of 'moderation' and 'sharing' of power, etc., etc. He diagnoses 'the absence from our society of overwhelming concentrations of power' as 'the most general condition of our freedom', and pronounces 'the diffusion of power' to be absolutely 'inseparable from freedom'. He lauds, on the one hand, the 'balance' of power in his society—'with us power is dispersed among all the multitude of interests and organizations of interest which comprise our society'—and finds in this 'balance', among other virtues, the true secret of what he calls 'our freedom'. On the other hand, he speaks, almost inevitably as it were, of the 'fear' and 'threat' of power, and tends to regard freedom and power as mutually exclusive and irreconcilable entities. He, therefore, rigidly opposes one to the other, that is, 'freedom' to 'power', an abstract 'freedom' to an equally abstract 'power'[38] In so doing, like most other liberal-conservative political theorists who argue in the same manner,[39] Oakeshott not only by passes the more important problems of *freedom* in contemporary capitalist society, but also avoids coming anywhere near asking the more fundamental questions about *power* in this society, about the real nature, centre and function of political power in the societies of monopoly capitalism today—questions, speaking more generally, such as *what* is power, *whose* power is it, *which* ends does it serve and over whom is it exercised? Needless to add, political theory, at its best, has always asked and sought to answer these questions.[40]

One cannot help concluding that Oakeshott's political theory, whatever positive political theory there is in Oakeshott, hardly ever comes to grips with the basic political or socio-economic issues of contemporary capitalist society. On the rare occasions when Oakeshott manages to raise these issues in a fundamental manner, he ends up only lauding the sacrosanct virtues of this society's competitive adolescence. As an answer to the very real problems of this society; he can do no better than dig up the commonplaces of a bygone era, proved false by more than a century of historical and political experience, and offer them as the very latest in political wisdom [41] All this hardly merits serious consideration. Oakeshott could certainly have done with a little rationalism himself, with some scientific theory which takes one behind the appearance or form of things to their nature, their essential reality. As it is he is seldom, if ever, able to go behind the appearance or form of things, economic or political.[42] I shall be content, therefore, to leave the subject with two very general observations only. In the first place, I suggest that the sort of society, capitalist, Oakeshott upholds (one of rapid and uninterrupted change) and the sort of politics, conservative, he recommends (one of fear and distrust of change) are so incompatible with each other that his prescription of the politics of 'pursuit of intimations' for a more or less competitive capitalist society, not only looks like an exercise in utopianism, but is also an indication of his failure to understand the real nature, 'the character' as he calls it, of this society. In the second place, I suggest that Oakeshott's failure to understand 'the character' of the capitalist society, perhaps, also explains why he can still less understand either the movement which is seeking to overthrow or transform this society, namely socialism, or the theoretical expression of this movement, namely the scientific materialist rationalism which is what Marxism is.

NOTES AND REFERENCES

1. It is nowadays generally recognised, as Gellner has observed, that the philosophical' or 'conceptual' investigations' are seldom or never separable from either substantive ones or from evaluation... In fact, "analyses" almost always plainly do have evaluative implications' (*Words and Things*, pp. 263-4). And Bernard Crick has rightly pointed out that 'academic conservatism' is very often 'a great smuggler of content and substance under the guise of talking simply about method, education, and philosophy' (*In Defence of Politics*, p. 19).

These observations seem to apply fully to the more important 'philosophical' or 'academic' essays of Oakeshott. The two essays now being discussed only serve to bring out much more dearly the 'substantive' or 'evaluative implications', the 'content and substance', of Oakeshott's philosophy as a whole.

2. R.T. McKenzie, *British Political Parties,* London, 1955, p. 581. McKenzie writes: After he had examined the Conservative and Liberal Party organizations almost half a century ago, A.L. Lowell wrote: "Both are shams, but with this difference, that the Conservative organization is a transparent, and the Liberal an opaque sham." It can be argued that if the word "Labour" is substituted for "liberal" there is a sense in which Lowell's remark is equally appropriate today' (p. 581).

   It will not be irrelevant to point out that today similar situation obtains in several other bourgeois-democratic political communities of the west, on both sides of the Atlantic. Most western political theorists are in fact generally agreed that today 'the differences between the left and the right in the Western democracies are no longer profound', that 'the ideological issues dividing left and right (have) been reduced to a little more or a little less government ownership and economic planning', and that it really makes no difference 'which political party controls the domestic policies of individual nations' (S.M. Lipset, *Political Man*, London, 1960, pp. 404-6). Herbert Tingsten goes even further to point out that 'the great controversies have... been liquidated in all instances', and that the actual words "socialism" or "liberalism" are tending to become mere honorifics, useful in connection with elections and political festivities' ('Stability and Vitality in Swedish Democracy', *The Political Quarterly*, No. 2, 1955, p. 145).

   This is a development which, among other things, makes nonsense of the cliche, so beloved of academic political science, that the existence of two or more opposing political parties offers voters a real choice between alternative programmes and is, therefore, the *sine qua non* of democratic form of government. This apart, I venture to suggest that this very significant development is an expression, at the political party level, of the same dominant conservative or 'existential' mood of the societies of western capitalism, which, at the philosophical level finds expression, among other forms, in deep scepticism about human reason or knowledge. It is indicative not so much of the Right becoming 'progressive' or 'forward-looking', as of the established Left, for various historical reasons, surrendering its position, politically as well as ideologically, and coming to accept the legitimacy of the bourgeois social order.

3. Of course, always, 'In the name of personal freedom' (*The Concept of Freedom*, London, 1965, p. 75). Caudwell's essays are among t he best studies of the Marxist concept of freedom.

   The moral validity of Marx's condemnation of capitalism as a system of unfreedom and the universal moral element in his own concept of freedom is thus acknowledged by Jacques Maritain in *True Humanism*: Marx, he writes, 'had a profound intuition, an intuition which is to my eyes the great lightning flash of truth which traverses all his work, of the conditions of heteronomy and loss of freedom produced in the capitalist world by wage slavery, and of the dehumanization with which the possessing classes and the proletariat alike are thereby simultaneously stricken' (quoted by Harry Slochower, *No Voice is Wholly Lost*, London, 1946, pp. 220-1).

   Incidentally, Slochower's excellent chapter, The Marxist Idea of the Universal Man', is one of the earliest discussions, in the English language, of the powerful humanist theme in Karl Marx, wherein he draws attention to Marxism's 'absolute notion of man', 'its anti-totalitarian concept of the individual', and 'the humanistic criterion of its ethics', which critics have so often missed or obscured.

4. This is, incidentally, nothing new or original. As long ago as 1848, Marx and Engels thus summed up the wisdom, 'the last word', of what they called 'conservative or bourgeois socialism': the bourgeois is a bourgeois—or the benefit of the working class' (*Manifesto of the Communist Party*, p. 84).

5. One must concede, however, that this Oakeshottian wisdom has today come to be widely accepted not so much by the capitalists as by the 'socialists' in the 'more advanced' societies of western capitalism. Some years ago, G.D.H. Cole expressed the opinion 'that in the countries of Western Europe, Socialism is dissolving even as an ideal related to current practice' (*Forward*, 8 March, 1952). A little later Richard Crossman informed us that for most European socialist leaders, socialism has become a 'Utopian myth ...often remote from the realities of day-to-day politics' (*Encounter*, May, 1954). Crossman also expressed the view that if socialism was not being thrown overboard altogether it was only because a political party 'can never afford to scrap its central myth'.

   While the 'practical minded' British socialists have managed to abandon their socialism with the help of such inanities as Herbert Morrison's: 'Socialism means the assertion of social responsibility for matters which are properly of social concern' (quoted by S. Aaronovitch, *Monopoly*, London, 1955, p. 171), others, for example, the 'theoretically inclined' German socialists, have done the same in the name of principles like 'free economy', 'free competition', 'free enterprise', 'property-owning society with equal opportunities for all', etc. etc.—principles whose utter vacuity in societies of monopoly capitalism should be plain to anyone with eyes to see. They have indeed jettisoned the 'old (socialist) catchwords' like class struggle, social ownership of the means of production, etc., but only to load themselves up with the still older capitalist cacthwords (see R. Palme Dutt, *The Internationale*, London, 1964, Chap. XIV).

This abandonment of socialism, or, more comprehensively, the failure of the irrationality of capitalism in these societies to give rise to a movement for the more rational order of socialism, is a very significant development which Marx did not quite foresee but which is certainly amenable to a Marxist explanation. Paul Baran, in an analysis of the causes underlying this development, focusses attention particularly on the expanded role that bourgeois ideology has come to play in the course of the last hundred years and recognises in this development, among other things, the succumbing of important sections of the socialist movement in the west to the dominant bourgeois ideology.

Bourgeois ideology, Baran writes no longer serves merely as a break on people's striving for a better society, it no longer represents merely a barbed wire entanglement keeping people from satisfying their basic needs and potentialities—it has now reached what may be called its ultimate target: it has crippled that striving itself, it has driven a powerful wedge between human *needs* and human *wants*.' Not only has the mentality of the dominant class become undisputedly the dominant mentality—this was to be expected and was fully foreseen and analysed by Marx and Engels—but 'with bourgeois taboos and moral injunctions *internalized*, people steeped in the Culture of monopoly capitalism do not want what they need and do not need what they want'.

Baran points out that Marx and Engels 'much as they were aware of the plasticity and moldability of human nature, seriously underestimated the extent to which man's wants can be influenced and shaped by the social order within which he is enclosed. And, collaterally, giving capitalism only a relatively short life, they could not possibly anticipate the scope and the depth of *habit* formation resulting from centuries of capitalist development.'

But this abandonment of socialism, or the absence of a significantly powerful socialist movement, is no argument for the rationality or the desirability of capitalism. On the contrary.

Just as protracted addiction to alcohol or to narcotics leads sooner or later to disaster, so a prolonged divergence between the *needs* of men and their *wants* cannot but result in catastrophe. The failure of an irrationally organized society to generate internal forces pressing towards and resulting in its abolition and replacement by more rational, more human social relations results necessarily in economic stagnation, cultural decay, and a widespread sense of despondency. Such a society—even if once the most advanced in the world—loses its position of leadership, slides into the backwaters of historical development, and turns into a breeding ground of reaction, inhumanity, and obscurantism ('Crisis of Marxism?' *Monthly Review*, October 1958, pp. 232-3).

Baran holds that Marx's analysis of the essential irrationality of capitalism has not been vitiated, let alone refuted, by subsequent events and developments. Arguing that the basic irrationality of capitalism, though it has altered some of its forms, is now even more pronounced and has proved incurable by 'assorted medications prescribed from time to time by social reformers of all kinds', and that socialism is the only rational exit' from the impasse into which capitalism has driven mankind, history's next and necessary step demonstrated to be so 'not only by theoretical reasoning but by vast historical experience', Baran writes:

> Yet ...the proletariat in the advanced capitalist countries has not developed in the way anticipated by Marx. Bad as its condition has been, it was able to rise above the inescapable, unvarnishable, imperative misery' which was observed by Marx, and which he expected would be accentuated with the passage of time. Although its social and cultural existence is in essence as inhuman as it was in Marx's time, it has largely failed to 'win the theoretical awareness of its loss' and has tended to succumb to bourgeois ideology and to adjust itself to its degradation. What Marx misjudged, in other words, is the intensity and speed with which the irrationality of capitalism would give rise to a movement powerful enough to carry out a socialist transformation of society. Yet serious as this miscalculation undoubtedly is, it should not even be mentioned

> in the same breath with the fallacy committed by those who consider the weakness or even absence of socialist movements in some countries to be a proof of the rationality, an argument for the desirability, or a sign of the progressiveness of the capitalist order. That position is no more defensible than would be the view that an inability of a human body to resist tuberculosis, however caused, furnishes a proof of the harmlessness or even usefulness of that illness. Both errors reflect essentially the wish being the father to the thought. The former, however, stems from insufficient appreciation of the obstacles barring the road to socialism, and—even if causing sometimes grave political errors—does no irreparable harm to the cause of reason. The latter, on the other hand, results inevitably in surrender to bourgeois ideology, in apologetics for the capitalist system, and in the abandonment of the struggle for a better society ('On the Nature of Marxism', *loc. cit*, pp. 267-8).

Baran very rightly suggests:

> It would be parochial and myopic, however, to judge the prospects of socialism in the world solely on the basis of the conditions prevailing in the countries of monopoly capitalism. Throughout world history those nations have led in progress in which the irrationality of the social order gave rise to powerful counteracting movements. It was Lenin's genius to have recognized that in the age of monopoly capitalism and imperialism this function of leadership would be taken over by the nations inhabiting the colonial, dependent, and underdeveloped countries. Bearing the brunt of the irrationality of the capitalist system, not having been exposed to the same extent as the advanced capitalist countries to the debilitating and demoralizing impact of capitalist 'culture' and bourgeois ideology, some of these nations have already revolted and others are revolting against the irrationality of the capitalist order and now march at the head of history's forward movement. Within a historically short time it will be in these countries that the tone of the world's further development will be set, while the countries of monopoly capital will first lag behind and then eventually be swayed by the force of example and by the slow but irresistible process of osmosis ('Crisis of Marxism?' *loc. cit*., pp. 233-4).

6. On the growth of monopoly, amazing concentration of personal wealth and increasing inequality in the U.K., see

S. Aaronovitch, *Monopoly*, London, 1955, and *The Ruling Class*, London, 1961; W. Mennell, *Takeover*, London, 1962; R.M. Titmuss, *Income Distribution and Social Change*, London, 1962.

7. Letter to P.V. Annenkov, 28 December, 1846, *Selected Correspondence 1846-1895*, p. 15.
8. See F.A. Hayek, *The Road to Serfdom*, London, 1944. One is also reminded of a Barry Goldwater warning true Americans 'not to stagnate in the swamp land of collectivism'.
9. Erich Fromm's comment on this kind of argument is very apposite: 'The cry for individual initiative as an argument for Capitalism is at best a nostalgic , yearning and at worst a deceitful slogan used against those plans for reform which are based on the idea of truly human individual initiative' (*The Sane Society*, London, 1963, p. 356).
10. It is interesting to note that in the view Oakeshott generally takes of man, society and politics, he shares his assumptions with Thomas Hobbes, his favourite philosopher, on whom he has written with great perception. Macpherson, in his study of the seventeenth century political theory (*The Political Theory of Possessive Individualism*, London, 1964), has summed up these assumptions, which are 'peculiarly appropriate to a possessive market society', as possessive individualism': the conception of individual as essentially the proprietor of his own person or capacities, owing nothing to society for them,' of freedom as 'a function of possession', of society as consisting of 'relations of exchange between proprietors', of politics as 'a calculated device for the protection of this property and for the maintenance of an orderly relation of exchange', etc., etc. What Macpherson says of 17th century liberalism is true of all political theory based on such or similar assumptions. He writes: 'The greatness of seventeenth century liberalism was its assertion of the free rational individual as the criterion of the good society, its tragedy was that this very assertion was necessarily a denial of individualism to half the nation' (p. 262).

    Macpherson's book, which has been hailed as an attempt to rescue the intellectual products of the early, heroic bourgeois epoch in England from 'the suffocating weight of a historical academic commentary', not only focusses attention on the unifying assumption of possessive individualism behind 17th century English political thought but also points to its persistence as the source of the 'dilemma' or difficulties' of modern, liberal democratic theory. He argues that 'central difficulties of liberal-democratic thought from John Stuart Mill to the present might be better understood if they were seen to have been set by the persistence and deep-rootedness of that assumption' (see his concluding chapter: 'Possessive Individualism and Liberal Democracy'.

11. There is great truth in Barrows Dunham's observation on Philosophical Radicalism. He remarks that, its achievements notwithstanding, it 'was radical only toward the gentry; toward the masses it was philosophical' (*Thinkes and Treasurers*, p. 22).
12. The primary or classical Marxist view on the subject of the state in capitalist society was formulated by Marx when he wrote in the *Communist Manifesto*: 'The executive of the modern state is but a committee for managing the common affairs of the whole bourgeoisie'; 'Political power, properly so called, is merely the organized power of one class for oppressing another' (pp. 43, 72). Marx, however, never set out a comprehensive and systematic general theory of the state. Some scattered references in Marx and Engels and discussion of only a few basic issues by Lenin (see particularly his polemical *The State and Revolution and The Proletarian Revolution and the Renegade Kautsky in Selected Works*, Vol. II, Moscow, 1947) have left it one of the least satisfactorily treated subjects in Marxism. It is therefore necessary to point out that while it is certainly true that *in general* the state in a capitalist society serves the interests of the ruling class, centered basically in the preservation of the system of capitalist exploitation, it does not mean that every action of the state is immediately or directly or solely so determined. It is not only that the state has to constantly act or intervene, apparently against capitalism but really on its behalf, to alleviate the anarchy of the market, to prevent major depressions, or to save capitalism from its own self-destructive consequences. In any given situation the course followed by the state is also influenced, of course within limits set by the basic need of preserving the capitalist order, by factors like conflicts between the long run and short run interests of the ruling class, between the interests of the ruling class as a whole and of its particular sections or between particular interests of its different sections, by the pressure of other classes and the necessity of making concessions to them, by ideological considerations of different sorts by errors of economic or political policy etc., etc. In other words, Marxist theory of the state in capitalist society has nothing to do with the vulgar notion often attributed to Marx— as, for example, by Deane, when he speaks of 'the simple and

monolithic Marxist analysis of the state' (*op. cit.*, pp. 153-69)—that the state always and everywhere and automatically, in a simple, mechanical or predetermined manner, serves 'the sole purpose of defending the interests of the ruling class'.

On certain secondary but highly significant aspects of Marx's view of the state see Ralph Miliband and Marx and the State' in *The Socialist Register 1965*, edited by Ralph Miliband and John Saville, London, 1965.

For the views of William Morris on the state see E.P. Thompson, *William Morris, Romantic to Revolutionary*, London, 1955, pp. 790-95.

13. The fours behind the process of historical development of 'the welfare state' have been varied and complex. 'Fear of social revolution, the need for a law-abiding labour force, the struggle for power between political parties and pressure groups, a demand to remove some of the social costs of change —for example, industrial accidents—from the backs of the workers, and the social conscience of the rich all played a part' (Richard Titmuss, 'The Limits of the Welfare State', *New Left Review*, No. 27, September-October 1964, p. 34).

Of decisive *political* significance in this process has been the continuous and often very bitter struggle waged by an increasingly organised and enfranchised working class through its political parties and trade unions, not only on its own behalf but also on behalf of other underprivileged sections of capitalist society. Of decisive *economic* significance in this process has been the unprecedented expansion of material production in these societies on a continuing capitalist or capitalist-cum-imperialist basis. The development of democratic rights and institutions–which again had to be fought for and won by the working masses—and of Keynesian theory and techniques also played a notable part in the historical evolution of 'the welfare state'.

The political theory reflecting, aiding and consolidating, or guiding this evolution over the last hundred years and more is expressed in the 19th century in the writings, among others, of J.S. Mill and T.H. Green, who taking into account the claims of rising dcmocracy gave classical liberal theory a positive turn and content and, as Macpherson says, 'between them' set the pattern of English liberal democratic political theory from their time on'. In the twentieth century its important figures have been liberals like Hobhouse, Barker and MacIver and radicals and socialists like Lindsay, Tawney, Cole and Laski. On the development, as also the contemporary dilemma, of liberal-democratic theory, see C.B. Macpherson, 'Post-Liberal Democracy?' *loc. cit.*).

14. Richard Titmuss, 'The Limits of the Welfare State,' *loc. cit.*, p. 29.
15. John Saville, 'The Welfare State, An Historical Approach', *New Reasoner*, No. 3, 1957-58.
16. There are of course others who have seen more positive meaning in the development of 'the welfare state' than is suggested in the text or warranted by the facts of the case. Gunnar Myrdal, for example, has written: 'In the last half century, the state, in all the rich countries in the Western world, has become a democratic "Welfare State", with fairly explicit commitments to the broad goals of economic development, full employment, equality of opportunity for the young, social security, and protected minimum standards as regards not only income, but nutrition, housing, health and education, for people of all regions and social groups' (*Beyond the Welfare State,* London, 1960, p. 45).

Baran has commented that so far as the richest capitalist country, the United States, is concerned this view 'is applicable only partly and only with major qualifications'. He finds the performance of the American capitalist economic system, when judged by the two distinct, though closely interrelated, criteria of 'fullness of employment' and 'goodness of employment' of available productive resources, to be seriously wanting. Pointing out the existence of a permanent and sizeable 'industrial reserve army', massive squandering of resources observed on every side, massive and persistent poverty, and 'in addition to this, all of society...ill-educated, exposed to a deblitating barrage of fraudulent politics, stupefying entertainment, inspirational rackets, and demoralizing press and comic books', he asks: 'What remains then but a mirage of the. "democratic welfare state"' ('Social and Economic Planning', *Monthly Review*, March 1965).

See also Harry Magdoff, 'Problems of United States Capitalism' in *The Socialist Register 1965*, wherein he points out that despite the important reforms introduced by the New Deal in the 1930s, the political acceptance of the "welfare state", the tremendous advance in productive capacity, and the very sizeable expansion of inner markets, no less than two-fifths of the nation still live in poverty or in a state of economic deprivation in the U.S. (p. 72).

Magdoff argues that this results from 'the behaviour of the market system itself', from 'the operations of a private market economy that creates and continuously refreshes the sources of poverty'. Pointing out 'the need for a new type of industrialization and a reconstruction of the physical wealth of the society', Magdoff says that, the magnitude of the problems being what it is, 'the various proposals for even radical tinkering with the existing economic set up are akin to the romantic and utopian ideas of an earlier era.'

17. These are the theorists who have seen in the emergence of 'the welfare state' the elimination of all 'fundamental' issues from 'domestic politics', indeed the liquidation of 'the great controversies' and 'genuine political alternatives', and who hold or endorse the view that henceforth the only issues are whether the metal workers should get a nickel more an hour, the price of milk should be raised, or old-age pensions extended' (see S.M. Lipset, *op. cit.*, pp. 403-17).
18. Barrington Moore Jr., *Political Power and Social Theory*, Harvard University Press, 1958, p. 183).
19. The conventional usage, academic as well as non-academic, generally drops the prefix capitalist and prefers the simpler but obviously deceptive phrase 'Western democracy'.
20. The end of ideology' has been, along with 'the decline of political theory', a much canvassed theme in recent political theory, particularly mid-fifties onwards. See, for example, Lipset, *op. cit.*, ch.: 'The End of Ideology?' Verney, *op. cit.*, ch.: 'Government and the Political Process'; Daniel Bell, *The End of Ideology: On the Exhaustion of Political Ideas in the Fifties*, New York, 1962, particularly the epilogue: 'The End of Ideology in the West'; F.M. Watkins, *The Age of Ideology: Political Thought; 1750 to the Present*, Prentice Hall, 1964, ch.: 'Conclusions'; etc., etc.

Notwithstanding the differences, more or less important, between the various exponents of this theme, Lipset is a good representative here. In proclaiming 'the end of political ideology' in the more advanced societies of 'Western democracy', he writes: 'the fundamental political problems of the industrial revolution have been solved: the workers have achieved industrial and political citizenship; the conservatives have accepted the welfare state; and the democratic left has recognized that an increase in over-all state power carries with it more dangers to freedom than solutions for economic problems. This very triumph of the democratic social revolution in the West ends domestic politics for those intellectuals who must have ideologies or utopias to motivate them to political action' (*op. cit.*, p. 406).

Titmuss draws attention to many important questions of facts and values which these sweeping conclusions leave unexamined:

'To what extent are they based on the real facts of income and wealth distribution, property, power and class? Has 'The Welfare State" abolished poverty, social deprivation and exploitation? Has man a greater sense of social control and participation in the work and life of his community? What will be the human consequences of further social and technological changes?'etc., etc. In a sharp comment on Lipset's thesis he says: 'As a generalization it is conceivable that this statement may serve as a summing-up for the 1950's in the history books of the next century. But from the perspective of 1960 it is, to say the least, a dubious proposition' ('The Limits of the Welfare State', *loc. cit.*, p. 31).

In this essay Titmuss examines some of the basic assumptions behind the thesis put forward by Lipset. He points out that this thesis is unhistorical in that it assumes that the "industrial revolution" was a once-and-for-all affair' and ignores not only the evidence concerning the growth and role of monopolistic concentration of economic power and the continuing problems of social disorganisation and cultural deprivation, but also the growing impact of automation and new techniques of production and distribution—'without a major shift in values, an impoverishment in social living can only result from this new wave of industrialism'. Also, 'conceptions of what constitutes "citizenship" for the worker require to be related to what we now know about man's potential and his basic social and psychological needs, they cannot be compared with conditions of industrial slavery in the nineteenth century'. Further, the problem of the distribution of income and wealth, far from being either solved or of insignificant proportions and posing no threat to democratic values, is daily growing worse, if the evidence concerning increasing concentration of wealth (and wealth still bestows economic and political power) and the growth of inequality is any indication— 'No political utopia since Plato has envisaged such degrees of economic inequality as permanent and desirable states for men'. Above all, the establishment of social welfare, far from necessarily or inevitably contributing to free human development, to 'the spread of humanism and the resolution of social injustice', may be and has often been used simply as an instrument of economic growth benefitting only a minority, or made to serve military, even racial ends, used to narrow allegiances and not to diffuse them; it may thus serve as a link in a system of 'individual gain and political quietism, fostered by the new feudalism of the corporation'.

The fundamental issue, Titmuss says, is the objective at which social welfare must aim: 'to universalize humanistic ethics and the social rights of citizenship or to divide, discriminate and compete?' Suggesting that 'the conventional criteria of capitalism, a system which by its very nature distributes resources... on the basis of success and failure in economic competition', and not of human needs, can secure only the latter objective, Titmuss argues for an abandonment of these criteria, 'the pseudo-moral principles', as Keynes once put it, 'which have hag-ridden us for 200 years (and) by which we have exalted some of the most distasteful of human qualities into the position of the highest virtues'. He points out particularly that the new developments in the field of science and technology are making 'the conventional criteria of capitalism'—criteria which Lipset and Oakeshott in their different ways defend and justify—largely irrelevant and are demanding 'a major shift in values', they are demanding the production and distribution of social services 'according to needs in place of the principle of productivity and performance in a market economy', as is the case at present. He writes:

> We shall need different rules domestically to live by... Indeed, our societies in Britain and the United States are already in need of them. In no other way in the long run will it be possible for us to prevent the deprived and the unable from becoming more deprived and unable; more cast down in a pool of apathy, frustration, crime, rootlessness and tawdry poverty (*loc. cit.*, p. 37).

21. C.B. Macpherson, in his 'Post-Liberal-Democracy'?' *loc. cit.*, speaks of 'the doubtful adequacy of liberal-democratic society even in the most advanced conditions'. He writes of 'the market system' of capitalism that, the welfare state notwithstanding, 'there is no reason to expect that the wants and tastes which it satisfies will reflect or permit that full development of the individual personality which is the liberal-democratic criterion of the good society.' He in fact urges us to give serious thought as to 'whether it is any longer possible for us to move towards our goal within the pattern of the market society', and whether meaningful liberty can much longer be had without a much greater measure of equality than we have hitherto thought liberty required'.

    It is with the consideration of these and similar questions that Macpherson links not only the need for 'a transcendence of capitalism', for 'post-liberal democracy' but also the need for 'a post-liberal democratic theory', for 'a revolution in democratic consciousness —'if we are to avoid being caught up ourselves in the backwash of the revolutions in the rest of the world'. Only thus can the hopes and possibilities of today be realised and man's aspirations through the epochs past, including the bourgeois epoch itself, fulfilled.

It is obvious that this is a task which contemporary liberalism, with its timid and shrunken apologetics for the existing order and the utterly parochial proclamations of 'the end of ideology', has hardly the vision or the courage to undertake. Only socialist thought as the true heir of the best elements in classical liberalism can help carry out this task. Macpherson has, therefore, well emphasised that in going beyond liberal democracy, in theory as well as in practice, 'we should not shrink from either the populist teaching of Rousseau or the radical teaching of Marx ....we may have more to learn from them than we think. 'It may even be', he adds, 'that the utility of Marxism as a means of understanding the world is increasing over time.'

Titmuss also writes, in concluding his argument for a transcendence of the *capitalist* limits of the welfare state, that the answers to the problems of this transcendence will come from the socialists who will reunite ethics to politics and define the tasks ahead 'in the language of equality'. He adds: 'The answers will not come and, indeed, logically cannot come from those who now proclaim "the end of political ideology" ('The Limits of the Welfare State', *lot. cit.*, p. 37).

'The end of ideology' is in fact itself only an ideology of conservatism today. In a scathing comment on 'the end of ideology' academicians —'the NATO intellectuals' with their 'intellectual celebration of apathy'— C. Wright Mills wrote: 'The end of ideology is a slogan of complacency, circulating among the prematurely middle-aged, centred in the present, and in the rich Western societies ....It is a consensus of a few provincials about their own immediate and provincial position'. Mills defined 'the end of ideology' as an ideology of political complacency which seems the only way now open for many writers to acquiesce in or to justify the *status quo*.' Describing these writers as 'status-climbers', he wrote that 'the most immediately important thing about the "end of ideology" *is* that it *is* merely a fashion, and fashions change' ('The New Left', in *Power, Politics and People: The Collected Essays of C. Wright Mills*, edited by Irving Louis Horowitz, New York, 1963, pp. 249, 251).

It is significant that 'the end of ideology' academicians, while proclaiming 'the end of ideology' in the west, concede, in fact insist on, the need for ideology in the rest of the world. Lipset, for example, argues, and most others would agree with him, that while within 'stable and affluent' societies of the west 'serious ideological controversies have ended', 'ideology and passion' are no longer relevant and politics has lost all 'ideological excitement', there is still a need for intense political controversy and ideology' in other parts of the world, particularly in 'underdeveloped countries' like India, Ghana, Ceylon, Burma etc., in the interests of the larger fight' against world communism. 'Ideology and passion', we are told, 'are clearly needed in the international effort to develop free political and economic institutions in the rest of the world', or, as Daniel Bell puts it, to defend 'some old verities', 'the verities of free speech, free press, the right of opposition and of free enquiry', and to fight against 'the suppression of liberties in the new states'.

As to what sort of ideology in defence of free political and economic institutions' Lipset would permit to 'allies' of the west in these countries—the 'radicals, probably socialists'—this can be gauged from the fact that he characterises any attack on domestic capitalists, foreign investors, or the machinations of the departed imperialists as finding 'a scapegoat'! One must, however, admire Lipset for the frankness of his advice to these 'our allies in the underdeveloped countries', who 'hope to compete with the Communists'. He warns them that they must not accept, not openly at least, 'the arguments of Western socialists that the West has changed, that complete socialism is dangerous, that Marxism is an outmoded doctrine', etc.; otherwise they may never acquire or retain 'a popular following'!

All this only proves that while many of these theorists may have indeed become aware of 'the uselessness of vulgar Marxism', of 'easy "left" formulae for social change' as Bell puts it, they continue to remain unaware of the still greater uselessness of anti-communism in the world of today. What is more, faced with or frightened by revolutionary change–' "the Communist Challenge" as it is very properly called' (Verney); 'the have-nots, inspired by revolutionary ideology', 'superior in numbers and enthusiasm', 'the real nightmare of twentieth century politics' (Watkins)—they never tire of giving us warnings against 'the rhetoric of revolution' (Bell), but without ever realising the utter parochialism and irrelevance of 'the liberal rhetoric' they themselves practise.

C. Wright Mills was very right in pointing out that nowadays liberalism, 'as ideology and as rhetoric' is, at home, 'much more useful as a defence of the *status quo* —in the rich minority of nations, and of these nations before the rest of the world —than as a creed for deliberate historical change'; that 'to the world's range of enormous problems, liberalism responds with its verbal fetish of "freedom" plus a shifting series of opportunistic reactions'. He had concluded that the most grievous charge today against liberalism and its conservative varieties is that they are so utterly *provincial*, and thus so irrelevant to the major problems that must now be confronted in so many areas of the world' (*The Marxists*, pp. 30-31).

22. Even friendly critics have been compelled to recognise the glaring social inadequacies of the so-called 'welfare capitalism' and the utterly irrational composition and social direction of production and distribution under it. J.K. Galbraith, for example, writing, in *The Affluent Society* of the wealthiest country of capitalism today, the U.S.A., notes its obvious 'failure to invest in people' because of the gross social imbalance' of its economy: its strong bias toward production of private consumer goods, no matter how frivolous or even injurious, and away from public services, no matter how necessary or beneficial, resulting in a strange combination of starved community services with extravagant private consumption, of public squalor with private opulence.

It is really interesting that in order to remedy this situation all that Galbraith offers is a call to scrap the old outmoded economic theories and ideas, the conventional wisdom' as he calls it, born of a period of economic scarcity, for new ideas suited to the needs of 'the affluent society', which demand the diversion of resources from production and distribution of private consumer goods or frivolities to provision of public services that satisfy vital social needs. This, obviously, is easier said than done. There is no doubt, of course, that capitalist economy may on occasion—in order to ward off a crisis or to sustain its prosperity or to maintain its growth rate, ctc.,—accept such and similar ideas and make necessary institutional and ideological adjustments. In times of crisis even far reaching concessions may very expediently be made to them. But this does not last for long, nor ever go deep enough to touch the basic irrationality of the system, which as a whole continues to function on the basis of 'conventional wisdom', that is, the central motivating principle of profit-making. As a *capitalist* system, it can function on no other basis. And what Galbraith calls 'conventional wisdom not merely a set of outworn ideas and prejudices, which the capitalist class is itching to get rid of on the advice of the well-meaning liberals. It is rather the ideological mask of very powerful vested interests, 'the righting creed', as Sweezy and Huberman once put it, 'of a class-conscious minority which understands the nature of its privileges and means to protect them'. What is more, this minority has truly formidable means of doing so.

What the situation, therefore, demands is far more than a setting up of new ideas, however eminently reasonable or intrinsically valid they might be. It demands the decisive breaking down of the entrenched power of the interests behind the old ideas. This means socialism. Only socialist ownership of the means of production can help break decisively with the value system of private profit-oriented ownership, and alter in a fundamental manner the irrational and inhuman priorities of capitalism. Only thus will it become possible to make a rational and purposeful use of the productive resources, 'their studied and rational use' as Galbraith says, which ensures that our production and distribution satisfy the real, truly human, needs of men in a modern society.

For a critical comment on Galbraith's argument see Michael Lipton, 'The Mythology of Affluence', *New Left Review*, No. 35, January-February 1966. Suggesting that the Galbraithian attitude is unsound in its theoretical basis, careless in its empirical analysis and harmful in its political consequences', and that Galbraith 'buries theory and fact in a half-baked mythology of affluence', Lipton particularly underlines the fact that in holding that wrong doctrines, not sectional interests, are the main cause of social evils', Galbraith ignores 'the realities of power', 'the pwerstructure that perpetuates proved abuses, stifles industrial democracy and numbs social feeling'. For a fuller discussion of the subject see Tom Kemp, 'Galbraith as Prophet of, American "Neo-Capitalism"', *Science and Society*, Vol. XXIX, No. 4, fall 1965. Commenting on Galbraith's argument in defence of capitalism, Kemp points out that Galbraith 'leaves out of the picture altogether the exploitative nature of capitalist society and the political consequences which flow from it', that he 'refuses to make a full qualitative assessment of American society' and that he 'avoids a deep analysis of power relations'. Arguing that 'the relevant problems with which Galbraith does not deal, by reason of his limited perspective, are legion', Kemp underlines the apologetic' character of Galbraith's argument as a whole: 'Scientific method and science itself are renounced in favor of comforting sophistries and evasion of the main case against capitalism'.

To criticise the argument of Galbraith, however, is not to deny that even within the limits of capitalism itself much more can be done to mitigate the economic and social consequences of its irrationality, or that a better balance can be achieved ——Sweden is a case in point between social and private needs. For the sake of argument, one could go still further and concede the possibility of acceptance, by the oligarchy which controls the resources and surpluses of society under capitalism, of the proposal recently put forward by the authors: of 'The Triple Revolution' in the USA who, making a powerful indictment of America's present sorry situation, of its poverty amidst affluence, have suggested that in view of the 'Cybernation Revolution' now underway, society should guarantee an adequate income as a matter of right' to all its members. But it is not difficult to see that given the *essential* irrationality and inhumanity of capitalism and the *mores* and values of a market society, even this would mean not the much hoped for social and moral regeneration but only a streamlining of the present patchwork of welfare measures, which would still further dull men's striving for a more rational and human social order and reconcile them with a society which even at its best, and no matter how productive it becomes, must remain one of class division and exploitation, of social and cultural deprivation, of inequality at once culturally degrading and morally repulsive, and of alienation. It would thus serve, as religion often does, only as an opiate of the people tending to strengthen the *status quo*. And its beneficiaries would still remain really the victims of an irrational and unjust social order, men alienated from their *human* essence, from their rightful inheritance of freedom, of happiness and justice, of knowledge, enjoyment and creation. If happy, they will be 'happy' only as willing slaves are; if cheerful, they will only be 'cheerful robots' as C. Wright Mills would describe them (see *The Sociological Imagination*, ch: 'On Reason and Freedom').

See also Erich Fromm, *The Sane Society*. Fromm points out how 'alienation and automatization' are already leading to an ever-increasing insanity. Life has no meaning, there is no joy, no faith, no reality. Everybody is "happy"—except that he does not feel, does not reason, does not love.' Fromm writes: 'In the nineteenth century the problem was that *God is dead*; in the twentieth century the problem is that *man is dead*. In the nineteenth century inhumanity meant cruelty, in the twentieth Century it means schizoid self-alienation. The danger of the past was that men became slaves. The danger of the future is that men may become robots' (p. 360).

This is the reason why it is all the more important today, to affirm the necessity of a socialist transcendence of the capitalist limits of the welfare state, the necessity of socialism in the sense of a socialist ownership and use of the means of production. This is an absolutely necessary condition, though admittedly not a sufficient condition, of being able not only to fully develop and utilise the expanding productive resources for the benefit of whole society, but also to go beyond it to realise for all men the conditions of genuine *human* existence, to realise a productive cultured community of free and equal human beings in which, as Marx and Engels once put it, 'the free development of each is the condition for the free development of all' (*Manifesto of the Communist Party*, p. 72).

23. The inherent irrationality of capitalism, particularly of monopolistic and oligopolistic capitalism, is today nowhere more evident than in the fact that it has increasingly become 'an economy of waste', an economy of 'institutionalized wastes' where automatically expanding waste in the private or business sector (ever-proliferating sales organisations, tremendously expanded and expensive advertising campaigns, 'acceleration of obsolescence', etc.) goes hand in hand with deliberately organised waste in the public or governmental sector (ever-increasing arms expenditure, sky-rocketing military budgets, prosecution of imperialist or counter-revolutionary wars in Korea, Malaya, Kenya, Algeria, Angola, Congo, Vietnam, etc.)

It can be, and has been in fact, argued that the capitalist-democratic state, interested in the stability and smooth functioning of the system as a whole, can, aided by Keynesian techniques—whose efficacy up to a point is not to be denied —use the economic surplus generated by a capitalist economy rationally and purposefully, to secure not only work and livelihood but also a fuller and more meaningful life for men, at home and abroad. But this is no more than saying that if capitalism were something other than what it actually is there would be no need to change it.

Writing of the United States, 'the principal citadel of capitalism today', Paul Baran draws attention to its ever-expanding waste in the private sector. 'tremendously expanded (and expensive) sales organizations, advertising campaigns, public relations programs, lobbying schemes ...a continuous, relentless effort at product differentiation, model variation and the invention and promotion of fancier, more elaborate, more sumptuous, and more expensive consumer goods'. But pointing out that not all the recklessly multiplied waste of the business sector and the rampant growth of the system's unproductive sector are able to provide sufficient drainage for the overwhelming economic surplus generated by today's vastly developed forces of production, Baran writes:

> Nor are other more or less automatically functioning mechanisms of surplus absorption—capital exports, corporate outlays on research and development, and the like— powerful enough to solve the problem. A conscious effort at utilization of the economic surplus is indispensable if its congesting effects are to be kept with in tolerable limits, if depression and unemployment are not to be allowed to assume major proportions and thus to endanger the stability of the economic and social order. Such a conscious effort can be undertaken only by the government.

The government in capitalist society, however, is not constituted in a way to promote, the purposeful and sustained employment of the economic surplus for the advancement of human welfare. The powerful capitalist interests by which it is controlled, as well as its social and ideological make-up, render such a policy most difficult if not entirely impossible. It is unable to control the practices of Big Business, let alone invest directly in productive enterprise, since this would be manifestly in conflict with the dominant interests of monopolistic and oligopolistic corporations. It is barred by the values and *mores* of a capitalist society from large-scale spending on welfare objectives (at home and abroad). Thus even a liberal, progressive administration tends to seek salvation in military spending adding in this way deliberately organized waste in the government sector to automatically expanding waste in the business sector ('Reflections on Underconsumption', *Has Capitalism Changed?* pp. 155–60). See also Paul M. Sweezy, *The Present as History*, New York, 1953, particularly essays on 'Recent Developments in American Capitalism' and 'An Economic Program for America'.

Elsewhere, discussing the interaction of various forces at work in the capitalist economy, Baran points out that 'the very survival of monopoly capitalism becomes increasingly dependent on squandering of resources and on accelerated preparation for war'. He writes:

Except during wars and their aftermaths, the interaction of all these forces creates a vast potential overflow of the economic surplus which means underproduction, underconsumption, and underinvestment, or—what is the same underemployment of men, underutilisation of productive capacity, and depression. The only remedy for this persistent malaise that is available to monopoly capitalism is further multiplication of waste in both the private and the public sectors of the economic system. The utter irrationality of this 'cure' is just as obvious as it is clear that the only *rational* solution is social planning of production and distribution of goods and services. Such social planning is impossible, however, without social ownership of the means of production, without a socialist transformation of society. The *need* for this transformation was never more firmly established than it is now, for never was the gap between society's potentiality and society's performance so immense as it is in monopolycapitalism's present stage. Witnesses to this need are the squalid slums, the poverty and the illiteracy that are the lot of millions of families in the wealthiest country of the world; the moral, cultural, and intellectual decay gripping the entire advanced capitalist world; and—last but not least—the misery of hundreds of millions of people in the underdeveloped countries whose fate could be drastically changed if only a fraction of the resources continually wasted in the United States were to be used to help overcome their backwardness.

Nor can there be any doubt about the *urgency* of the replacement of monopoly capitalism by socialism. Indeed, every year lost means premature death and immeasurable suffering for millions of people in the entire world. Every year lost increases the mortal danger that capitalism may plunge into the last act of its dialectical drama and seek salvation in a thermonuclear holocaust ('Crisis of Marxism?' *loc. cit*, pp. 228-9).

The scientific and technological revolution of our time only underlines the need for as well as the urgency of the replacement of capitalism by socialism.

24. This is not to deny that in each case in the end there was a general improvement in the living standards. But then this improvement was never the most evident immediate effect. It came as a result of bitterly fought class struggles on the part of the working people, and *after* dragging them through large-scale unemployment, misery and suffering, and has always remained, relative to needs and possibilities, grossly inadequate.

25. The evidence for this statement is there for all to see. In fact there is bitter irony in the fact that a kind of development which men have so long dreamed about has come to be regarded, all round, with deep fear, apprehension and anxiety. At home, in the very citadel of capitalism, we already have Walter Reuther asking, in a speech to the United Auto Workers in 1961, the question: 'Why is it that automation's bright promise of abundance and creative leisure has been transmuted into the nightmarish mockery of mountainous inventories of unsold goods and the barren corroding idleness of unemployment?' (quoted by John Eaton, 'Labour and the Technological Revolution', *Labour Monthly*, January, 1965, p. 35). Abroad, in Asia, Africa, and Latin America, we have the spectacle of the world's strongest capitalist power engaged in playing the terrible, and terribly ignominious, role of what Issac Deutscher has called 'world's gendarme of counter-revolution', desperately seeking to preserve the 'free world' as a freely exploitable area in which giant American corporations can do business on their own terms.

    The answer to Reuther's question as also to the situation both at home and abroad can be found, one might suggest, with the help of the concepts which Marx developed (see, for example, Ch. III, section XI, above). The source of trouble lies is the very nature of capitalism as a system of private property and profit-making, in the use of society's economic surplus by private persons or groups for private ends, an arrangement that rests on the foundation of private ownership of the means of production. The remedy obviously involves the substitution of public for this private ownership. When JeaaPaul Sartre recently argued— 'Why I Will Not Go to the United States', *The Nation*, 19 April, 1965— that American war in Vietnam makes 'brutally evident that American society as such has an imperialist base' and that 'American policy cannot be changed short of a complete turnover of American society, his argument applied not only to Vietnam or American foreign policy but also to every important problem of American society today—be it poverty, racism, low-level citizenship, alienation, etc.

26. That the scientific and technological revolution of our time is demanding a collateral social revolution has been thus argued by a scientist:

    A new scientific and industrial revolution is not in itself a sufficient guarantee of universal well-being. It certainly cannot be a substitute for social revolution, and we delude overselves if we imagine any such choice is open to us. The major significance of the increasing power of science and technology is that it must make more urgent the demand for a revolutionary change in social structure.

Only a socialist revolution will serve. The fantastic potential of the new techniques can only be controlled to give us a maintained increasing national wealth, with the degree of planning of industry and trade that is only possible with the social ownership of national resources. And only is social ownership have we any guarantee that the increased wealth will appear in the form of a general enjoyment of prosperity, rather than luxury, power and privilege for the few (E.V. Rowsell, 'Science, Revolution and Politics', *Marxism Today,* November 1964, p. 338.

See also J.D. Bernal's contribution to the collection of essays published in his honour, *The Science of Science,* edited by Maurice Goldsmith and Alan Mackay, Pelican, 1966. Bernal points out that 'the scientific and computer age is necessarily a Socialist one.'

27. F.M. Watkins is a typical example here. He dearly recognises that the modern ideologies arose 'as an accompaniment of the Industrial Revolution', as the necessary products of a period of rapid change and radical adjustment and of high hopefulness that goes with advancing science and technology, etc. There can be no doubt', he says, 'that the rise of ideology was from the beginning associated with, and has at all times been much affected by, the Industrial Revolution' (*op. cit.,* p. 2). But, significantly enough, Watkins completely misses the meaning of the present day 'industrial revolution', of the unprecedented advance of science and technology in our time.

    It is equally significant that Daniel Bell, another exponent of 'the end of ideology' theme, can today only remind us of Machiavelli's statement, made in an altogether different context, that 'men commit the error of not knowing when to limit their hopes' (*op. cit.,* p. 393).

28. For Marx the abolition of capitalism or the establishment of socialism does not by itself usher in the 'truly human society', it only makes it possible. What is more, material fulfilment is for him only the condition, the necessary basis, and not the sum, of man's 'spiritual', that is 'truly human' fulfilment. The vision which underlies his life-work, from the early 1840's to the end, is the vision of 'human emancipation'. His was a powerful plea to replace the pitiable, fragmentary and self-alienated existence, which is man's lot in a class-divided and exploitative society, with

a truly rich human life; his was an assertion of life abundant against mere existence.

At the heart of Marx's thought is his deep concern for man and his future. Central to his criticism of capitalism is the idea (elaborated particularly in his early writings such as *On the Jewish Question, Contribution to the Critique of Hegel's Philosophy of Right; The Economic and Philosophical Manuscripts of 1844, The Holy Family,* etc.) that man, stripped of 'his human essence' when he first tell into the class of the exploited, faces 'the destruction of all humanity' in him under capitalism. The process of capitalist exploitation, with its attendant 'greed and the war between the greedy— competition', not only holds the entire society, the capitalist as well as the worker, in its irresistible compulsive grip and at the mercy of the blind forces of the market, it also transforms free creative self-activity of man into alienated labour, it reduces man himself to a commodity. It 'estranges man from nature, from himself, his own active functioning... from his *universal essence*... It makes his *essence* into a mere means for his existence...it estranges... his spiritual, his human essence ..:(it results in) the alienation of *man* from *man;* Capitalism tears up 'all genuine bonds between men' and replaces them by selfishness, dissolving 'the world of men into a world of atomized individuals, hostile towards each other'. It leaves 'no other nexus between man and man than naked self-interest, than callous "cash payment"' and resolves 'personal worth into exchange value'. The very things which were once 'communicated, but never exchanged; given, but never sold; acquired, but never bought—virtue, love, conviction, knowledge, conscience, etc.-' now become marketable and pass 'into commerce'; 'the *divine* power of money' overturns and confounds 'all human and natural qualities' in the market place. There comes to be generated a savage lust for money and property, a maniacal obsession with the accumulation of capital a veritable fanaticism of appropriation. A massing wealth becomes the supreme objects of human endeavour and the final criterion of human success. The emphasis is on acquisitiveness and the only success that matters is the success of the market place, resulting in 'that whole system of appetites and values' which 'with its deification of the life of snatching to hoard, and hoarding to snatch' leaves, as Tawney wrote, 'a taste as of ashes on the lips of a civilization which has brought to the conquest of its material environment resources unknown in earlier ages, but which has not yet learned to master itself' (*Religion and the Rise of Capitalism,*

Pelican, 1948, p. 280). And all this leaves man, even the so-called rich man of capitalism, 'ever poorer as a mass', robbed of real life and crippled in his inner being.

In pointing out the alienating, depersonalising and dehumanising consequences of capitalism, Marx particularly focused attention on the fact that for all the glorious human senses, whose concrete and active exercise alone constitutes the true content of a genuinely rich human life, capitalism substitutes a single abstract sense, the sense for property, a particular, historically transient substitute sense which plays havoc with human personality and plunges man, in the words of Ladislav Stoll, 'into the terrible inner sickness of a dehumanised world'. Marx wrote: 'In place of *all* these physical and mental senses there has ...come the sheer estrangement of *all* these senses—the sense of *having*. The human being had to be reduced to this absolute poverty in order that he might yield his inner wealth to the outer world' And he insisted that 'the transcendence of private property is therefore the complete *emancipation* of all human senses and attributes.' He spoke of communism, 'the *actual* phase necessary for the next stage of historical development in the process of human emancipation and recovery', 'as the *positive* transcendence of *private property as human self estrangement,* and therefore as the real *appropriation of the human* essence by and For man; communism therefore as the complete return of man to himself as a *social* (i.e., human) *being*—return become conscious, and accomplished within the entire wealth of previous development.' Marx added: 'What is to be avoided above all is the reestablishing of "Society" as an abstraction *vis-a-vis* the individual. The individual *is the social being*. His life ... is therefore an expression and confirmation of *social life*' (*Economic and Philosophic Manuscripts of 1844,* Moscow, n.d., pp. 98-114).

What this 'transcendence of human self-estrangement' means, what Marx meant when early in his life he wrote (in *Economic and Philosophic Manuscripts of 1844*) that 'communism equals humanism', and towards the end spoke (in *Capital*, Vol. III) of 'the true realm of freedom which makes possible 'that development of human power, which is its own end', what vision of the genuinely rich human life lay behind his life-long struggle for socialism—this has been well expressed by Ladislav Stoll. Pointing out that in place of many-sided, active, concrete appropriation of life and the world, through which the individual says not only "I see, I hear; I smell, I taste, I touch," but also "I work, I study, I love, I admire, I struggle for a happier tomorrow"—in place of all this wealth of emotion capitalism makes one single emotion supreme: "I have Stoic writes:

> The truly human way of appropriating the world's riches is that by which man really overcames the world, in other words, with all his senses, concretely. And here it is not a question only of the five physical senses, for unlike the animals man has a whole series of glorious human senses, not only the senses of sight, hearing, smell, taste and touch, but also a sense for music, A sense for poetry, a sense for the plastic arts, a sense for science, a sense for mathematics, a sense for history, crystalography, etc. etc. It is only when a man begins to satisfy the needs of these glorious human senses, which one and all are the product of historical development, that he can appropriate to himself all the beauties of the world and become genuinely rich (*Face to Face with Reality*, Prague, 1948, pp. 29-30).

The humanist theme in Marx, the theme of 'alienation', has evoked deep and widespread interest is the west during the past two decades. Marx's early writings, where he first developed this theme in elaborate critical studies of the philosophies of Hegel sad Feuerbach have beep the subject of innumerable books and essays in recent years. This interest, whatever its causes, beats witness to the deep crisis of contemporary capitalist culture and civilisation, manifested in the emergence of 'alienation' as a major and ever-worsening social phenomenon in the societies of modern capitalism. This phenomenon finds expression in man's growing sense of anomie and estrangement, of isolation, loneliness and homelessness, of hostility and frustration; it has resulted in a society really sick with these and a hundred other social and psychic ailments born of the essential irrationality of capitalism, sick with apathy and boreoom, with 'other directedness', conformism and self-abasement, with insanity and crime and widespread dehumanisation. (The evidence for this phenomenon is written large in contemporary sociological and psychological literature, in the writings, for example, of Wright Mills, David Reisman. Vance Packard, William Whyte, Erich Fromm, Karen Horney and others).

Alienation under capitalism as a system of private property, competition and exploitation is today far more pronounced, far more inclusive and monstrous, than when Marx first wrote about it. Of the several non-Marxist commentators Fromm, perhaps, best recognises not only Marx's brilliant insight into human condition in bourgeois society, but also the value of his argument for 'human emancipation', for 'the unfolding of man', 'the all round development of the individual', through a socialist transformation of this society. (This does not mean that Fromm's interpretation is otherwise not open to serious criticism). Pointing out that Marx 'represented the flowering of Western humanity', that he 'represented the Western tradition in its best features: its faith in reason and in the progress of man', Fromm writes: 'Socialism, for Marx, is a society which permits the actualization of man's essence, by overcoming his alienation. It is nothing less than creating the conditions for the truly free, rational, active and independent man; it is the fulfilment of the prophetic aim: the destruction of the ideals., ... For Marx, the aim of socialism was freedom ...based on man's standing on his own feet, using his own powers and relating himself to the world productively' (*Marx's Concept of Man*, with a translation from Marx's *Economic and Philosophic Manuscripts* by T.B. Bottomore, New York, 1961, p. 61)

Apropos the non-Marxist western scholars' newly-discovered interest in young Marx and his writings, one must say that this interest is very welcome. Some of these scholars have indeed shown a real desire for understanding, and they have often written with sympathy and perception. Nevertheless it is rather amusing to find so many of them trying, some of them so very desperately, to separate Marx from himself and from Marxism—to separate the young Marx from the old, the 'idealistic', 'freedom-loving' Marx of *Economic and Philosophic Manuscripts* from the supposedly cynical and disillusioned Marx of *Capital*, Marx the humanist from Marx the revolutionary and an advocate of class struggle, Marx from Engels, and, of course, from Lenin and Mao Tse-tung and the contemporary communist movement!

29. Engels' argument for socialism is as, if not more, valid today as when it was first formulated nearly ninety years ago. Speaking of 'the expanding force of the means of production' bursting asunder 'the bonds imposed upon them by the capitalist mode of production', Engels wrote:

> Their release from these bonds is the sole condition necessary for an unbroken and constantly more rapidly progressing development of the productive forces, and therewith of a practically limitless growth of production itself. Nor is this all. The appropriation by society of the means of production puts an end not only to the artificial restraints on production which

> exist today, but also to the positive waste and destruction of productive forces and products which is now the inevitable accompaniment of production ....Further, it sets free for society as a whole a mass of means of production and products by putting an end to the senseless luxury and extravagance of the present ruling class and its political representatives. The possibility of securing for every member of society, through social production, an existence which is not only fully sufficient from a material standpoint and becoming richer from day to day, but also guarantees to them the completely unrestricted development and exercise of their physical and mental faculties—this possibility now exists for the first time, but it *does exist*.

The seizure of the means of production by society puts an end to commodity production, and therewith to the domination of the product over the producer. Anarchy in social production is replaced by conscious organisation on a planned basis. The struggle for individual existence comes to an end. And at this point, in a certain sense, man finally cuts himself off from the animal world, leaves the conditions of animal existence behind him and enters conditions which are really human. The conditions of existence forming man's environment, which up to now have dominated man, at this point pass under the domination and control of man, who now for the first time becomes the real conscious master of Nature, because and in so far as he has become master of his own social organisation. The laws of his own social activity, which have hitherto confronted him as external, dominating laws of Nature, will then be applied by man with complete understanding, and hence will be dominated by man. Men's own social organisation which has hitherto stood in opposition to them as if arbitrarily decreed by Nature and history, will then become the voluntary act of men themselves. The objective, external forces which have hitherto dominated history, will then pass under the control of men themselves. It is only from this point that men, with full consciousness, will fashion their own history; it is only from this point that the social causes set in motion by men will have, predominantly and in constantly increasing measure, the effects willed by men. It is humanity's leap from the realm of necessity into the realm of freedom (*Anti-Duhring*, pp. 310-12).

In judging the *possibilities* inhering in socialism one must remember that the development of socialism in the Soviet Union, carried out under exceptionally difficult and unfavourable circumstances, has been much distorted and has not yet gone far enough —it has in fact still a long way to go—to reveal the full advantages of socialism. The historical conditions surrounding the first great experiment in building socialism: Russia's past history and habits; its vast peasant environment of rural idiocy and lack of democratic consciousness and traditions; the need for rapid industrialisation beginning from scratch in an illiterate and technically backward society; constant military, economic and political pressure of hostile, counter-revolutionary western capitalist encirclement; therefore, the necessity of building socialism not on the achievements of capitalism, except when borrowed or copied, and not with the help of the more advanced societies but in the teeth of their opposition; serious theoretical or ideological errors and weaknesses, together with the character of the men who led, etc.—all these have left their mark—how permanent it is too early to say—on what has been built in the Soviet Union. They have produced their inevitable distortions, and there own forms of alienation also. The historical context and character of the Russian experiment in socialism must therefore always be borne in mind. But in so doing one must also recognise that the Soviet achievement is there, and though historically conditioned it holds promise of altogether errand exciting vistas that await a society moving into socialism today, particularly if it does so from a comparatively more advanced economic, political and cultural bane, vistas that will open up to an affluent *socialist* society in a world at peace, and which are absolutely impossible for a capitalist society no matter how affluent it becomes.

One must therefore add that critics, including many socialists, betray an amazing lack of historical sense when they see only the negative elements in the Russian experiment, and in so doing fail to recognise the historic *socialist* achievement of the Soviet people, particularly as it followed upon the failure of socialism to come to power in the more advanced capitalist societies. As Anna Lousie Strong, speaking of 'the evils' that have gone with the Russian experiment, wrote: 'Most of all, they came because the democratic and technically developed working class of the West left the first building of socialism to an illiterate, technically-backward peasant people, who knew that they were not ready for the task and yet who built' (*The Stalin Era*, Calcutta, 1957, p. 10).

30. In doing this Oakeshott only proves the truth of C. Wright Mill's observation: 'As an intellectual articulation, the conservative mood

is merely a reformulation of classic liberalism in the entirely unclassical age of the twentieth century; it is the image of a society in which authority is at a minimum because it is guided by the autonomous forces of the magic market' (*The Power Elite*, p. 336).

Obviously, Oakeshott is no isolated phenomenon. While he is content only to repeat some of the basic propositions of classic liberalism, others, in Their defence of the *status quo*, have argued far more elaborately on the basis of these very old and antiquated premises. It is this which has compelled C.B. Macpherson to write that while 'we do need a post-liberal democratic theory' today, 'what we have now is not post-liberal democratic theory, but recessive liberal theory. It would be nearer the mark to call it pre-democratic liberal theory' ('Post-Liberal Democracy?' *loc. cit.*)

James Petras, in his essay on 'Ideology and United States Political Scientists', points out that 'of the ideologies current in the social science field the most popular and pervasive appears to be that which espouses stability and whose major theoretical anchor is the concept of "equilibrium" or "balance"' (Dahl, Berelson, Almond and others). This is accompanied naturally by what Petras calls 'the broker view of the state'. The state, they hold, is a neutral agency, not committed to any particular group or class in society; 'or perhaps ...it is so committed that it is not questioned', says Petras. And it is significant that 'the equiliberal view of society and its functioning "balance" is underwritten by a strong undercurrent of Burkean and conservative values'.

In his critical survey of the 'ideology' of American political scientists, James Petras points out that whatever their differences they are all 'subsumed under a set of common assumptions about American politics which limit the debate and, in a sense, overwhelm it'. Virtually all of them 'accept the social-economic institutional structure and theorize on the basis of it.' Their main consideration 'in drawing up their theories of democratic politics is derived from and is located in the "ongoing system".' Their concern is primarily 'with equilibrium and the preservation of the dominant institutions, elites, and interests of society'. This is most evident in the fact that 'whenever democratic theory comes into conflict with contemporary reality, the theory is discarded, modified, or adjusted to fit the requirements of the system'. In other words, the values of these 'scientists' are derived from the functioning of contemporary institutions, though 'this value assessment is frequently obscured by the "objectivist" stance of "functional requirements"'. Naturally, almost all of them avoid 'discussion of socio-economic issues in politics': There has occurred an alienation of politics from society', a regression towards 'formalism of political science'. 'A related common element is a Hobbesian fear of mass movements, large-scale change and conflict'. The great psychological unifying force among them is 'their reverence for the present'. And their 'psychic attitude of fear-repression towards "society" and social conflict becomes sublimated into reverence deference to the political sphere: This results in an 'authority fixation' through which 'creeps the authoritarian principle', and their work comes to represent 'the convergence of elitism and formalism, focusing on problems of leadership and organisation... without relating this to *who* leads *whom*, and for *what* in terms of society and social values.' This is really the 'reduction of politics to organizational and leadership criteria for functioning in the ongoing system.' In the process 'what remains of democratic theory is some of the language; the substance is completely alien' *loc. cit.*, pp. 207-9).

31. When Marx wrote (in the *Deutsch-Franzosische Jahrbucher*, 1844) that 'we do not seek to anticipate the new world dogmatically, but rather to discover it in the criticism of the old', and accordingly set himself the task of criticising the existing world, the task of 'ruthless criticism of everything that exists, ruthless in the sense that the criticism will not shrink either from its own conclusions or from conflict with the powers that be', he may well have formulated the credo of the intellectual for our time. Marx not only formulated the credo and established it on a firm scientific-materialist basis, he also practised it with brilliant success. Subjecting the 'existing arrangements' that constituted the capitalist society to ruthless *rational* criticism, he demonstrated, in the very midst of its first great celebration, and its advance over feudalism notwithstanding, capitalism's inherently irrational, contradictory and conflict-laden nature, and evolved, concomitantly, the concrete and historically relevant notion of a more rational social order which he spoke of as socialism or communism.

Interpreting Marxism as 'a philosophical position the fundamental principle of which is continuous, systematic, and comprehensive *confrontation of reality with reason*', Baran has drawn attention to the fact that it was Marx's achievement not only to discover the law of historical development but also 'to lay bare the part played in its operation by fruitful intellectual endeavour to define and continuously redefine the meaning of reason, to assess and continuously reassess the structure of reality—confronting systematically the one with the other, pointing out the shortcomings of the concrete, specific reality in terms of equally concrete, equally specific standards of reason. Remaining realistic, because it derives its frame of reference from the study and observation of the attained stage of historical development, and retaining the courage to be utopian because its sets its sights on the not yet realized but already visible potentialities of the future, such intellectual effort performs an overridingly important function: it serves as a guidepost to the next steps in mankind's forward movement' ('On the Nature of Marxism', *loc. cit.*, p. 262).

Elsewhere, in his brilliant and passionately written essay, 'The Commitment of the Intellectual' *loc. cit*, Baran discusses 'the place and the function of the intellectual in society', a subject which is of profound relevance to the situation in contemporary social science. Baran makes a very meaningful distinction between 'the intellect worker' and 'the intellectual'. He tells us that under capitalism the intellect worker is really 'a technician', 'typically the faithful servant, the agent, the functionary, and the spokesman of the capitalism system', who 'takes the existing order of things for granted and questions the prevailing state of affairs solely within the limited area of his immediate preoccupation'. His 'preoccupation is with the job in hand', with 'the rationalization, mastery, and manipulation of whatever branch of reality he is immediately concerned with' and not with 'the meaning of his work, its significance, its place within the entire framework of social activity'. 'His "natural" motto is to mind his own business, and... to be as efficient and as successful at it as possible'; 'he is not concerned with the relation of the segment of human endeavour within which he happens to operate to other segments and to the totality of the historical process'. 'The concern with the whole' he leaves to others, and in so doing 'he *eo ipso* accepts the existing structure of the whole as a datum and subscribes to the prevailing criteria of rationality, to the dominant values, and to the socially enforced yardsticks of efficiency, achievement, and success.' Taking an agnostic view of the ends themselves, he makes a fetish of 'ethical neutrality', of his abdication, *qua* scientist, expert or scholar, of all 'value judgments', an abdication which 'amounts in practice to the endorsement of the *status quo*, to lending a helping hand to those who are seeking to obstruct any change of the existing order of things in favour of a better one.'

Against this 'what marks the intellectual and distinguishes him from the intellect workers and indeed from all others is that his concern with the entire historical process is not a tangential interest but permeats his thought and significantly affects his work.' The intellectual systematically seeks 'to relate whatever specific area he may be working in to other aspects of human existence. His is the effort 'to *interconnect* things' and it is this effort which identifies 'one of the intellectual's principal functions in society: to serve as a symbol and as a reminder of the fundamental fact that the seemingly autonomous, disparate, and disjointed morsels of social existence under capitalism—literature, art, politics, the economic order, science, the cultural and psychic condition of people—can all be understood (and influenced) only if they are clearly visualized as parts of the comprehensive totality of the historical process.' For him 'the truth is the whole' as Hegel put it—a principle which carries with it 'the inescapable necessity of refusing to accept as a datum or to treat as immune from analysis, any single part of the whole.' It is thus wholly inadmissible for him 'to refrain from laying bare the complex relations between whatever phenomenon happens to be at issue and what is unquestionably the central core of the historical process: the dynamics and evolution of the social order itself. He will aim at not merely seeking truth 'about things that do not matter', but at 'telling the truth about what *does* matter, seeking the truth about the whole, and uncovering the social and historical causes and interconnections of the different parts of the whole', even though this be 'decried as unscientific and speculative' and 'punished by professional discrimination, social ostracism, and outright intimidation'. Pointing out that 'the desire to tell the truth is therefore only *one* condition for being an intellectual' and that 'the other is courage, readiness to carry on rational inquiry to wherever it may lead', Baran concludes:

An intellectual is thus in essence a *social critic*, a person whose concern is to identify, to analyze, and in this way to help overcome the obstacles barring the way to the attainment of a better, more humane, and more rational social order. As such he becomes the conscience of society and the spokesman of such progressive forces as it contains in any given period of history. And as such he is inevitably considered a 'trouble maker' and a 'nuisance' by the ruling class seeking to preserve the *status quo*, as well as by the intellect workers in its service who accuse the intellectual of being utopian or metaphysical at best, subversive or seditious at worst (p. 10).

The relevance of all this for contemporary social science is obvious. The intellect worker, more often than not, belongs with that tradition in social science which is the tradition really of *adjusting* science to existing social reality of *apologetics* in the broad sense of the term, of social interpretation only, a tradition which has today found a typical expression in so much of the work of the so-called 'behavioral sciences' in the United States and elsewhere. He accepts; more or less timidly, 'the existing structure of the whole as a datum', taking the existing order of 'facts' for granted and the existing order of 'values' as somehow beyond rational inquiry. As a 'specialist' or an 'expert' he concerns himself only with unrelated aspects of society or politics, with minor problems, often with the trivialities of contemporary social and political life. The intellect worker thus, while enjoying a comfortable and lucrative conformity, only serves the *status quo* and the powers that be—justifying this, if need be, with all sorts of 'methodological' or 'philosophical' or even 'scientific' reasons.

The intellectual on the other hand belongs with the classical tradition in social science. In his search for truth, he rejects positions such as the 'methodological nominalism' of Popper, or what has been called the 'abstracted empiricism' of the behavioral sciences which, by treating any serious concern with 'the whole' as 'unscientific' or 'metaphysical' or even 'mystical', rule out any truly critical or rational study of the social wholes or structures, and thereby not only make 'the existing structure of the whole', the contemporary capitalist society, immune against serious scientific scrutiny but also involve an abdication of the true function of social science.

The intellectual seeks to perform this function, he carries out such a critical scrutiny and in so doing carries forward the great tradition of social criticism, the classical tradition in social science, which has always been concerned, among other things, with historical systems or social structures (the 'wholes', which are of course always relative, transitory unities), with vital issues and with truth 'about what *does* matter', with knowing how and why 'facts' and 'values' have come to be what they are and with changing or developing these 'facts' and 'values' in a more humane and rational direction, with an unremitting search for the principles of and the road to a better social order.

32. One may point out that in noticing the 'tyranny' involved in this 'conjunction', Oakeshott puts his finger, inadvertently of course, on a fact of great historical importance. This is a 'conjunction'

that has always gone with such fundamental social changes as we do not go back upon and which have therefore inevitably demanded 'tyranny' for their consolidation. Witness the 'tyranny' of the regimes that have followed a revolution—in England in the 17th century, in America and France in the 18th century, in Russia and China in the 20th century, etc.

33. Oakeshott's theory of the state and government is, as already suggested, only a rehash of the classical liberal theory of state as a neutral and 'supra-class' entity, representing the interests of the society as a whole, with its corollary that the state apparatus is a neutral instrument impartially serving the government of the day, whatever its political complextion. This theory has little basis in reality, the development of democracy notwithstanding. Democracy is rightly to be valued, fought for and defended by the people; its preservation and extension is indeed of the utmost importance for the advancement of their interests. But the fact remains that in a capitalist society the state, even 'the democratic state', *in the ultimate analysis*, cannot but represent the political power of the economically dominant class. It is in fact the means by which the capitalist class maintains and perpetuates its rule. And 'political democracy' by itself does not prevent the state from functioning in this manner. See, for example, James Harvey and Katherine Hood, *The British State*, London 1958, where the authors, endeavouring to look below the surface of British democratic institutions, have argued that, fundamentally speaking, the British State represents the political power of monopoly-capitalism, that while an '*appearance* of neutrality' is carefully kept up, 'the machinery of the State has been shaped and developed by the capitalist class as an instrument to safeguard and promote the capitalist mode of production,' and that 'the various organs of the State arc clearly linked together, so that the armed forces, the police, the foreign and home civil service, and the legal system, as well as the Cabinet, form parts of a single whole through which the monopoly capitalists exercise poetical power' (pp. 281, 283). See also H.J. Laski, *The State in Theory and Practice*, London, 1935, and *Parliamentary Government in England*, London, 1938.

It is not necessary to go into the merits of the above argument to point out at least one thing the socialists who accept the liberal theory of a neutral and 'supra-class' state are bound, sooner rather than later, to come to grief. Such at least has been the historical experience. Marx had emphasised that the working class cannot use the *capitalist* state-apparatus, evolved for preserving capitalism, for the entirely different purpose of building socialism. He wrote that 'the working class cannot simply lay hold of the ready-made state machinery, and wield it for its own purposes' (*The Civil War in France*, in Marx and Engels, *Selected Works*, Vol. I, Moscow, 1950, p. 468). This one thing, he insisted, was decisively proved by the Paris Commune of 1871.

Nearly fifty years later the controversy between Katusky and Lenin tuned precisely on this point, when Lenin, with Mane, declared that it was necessary for the working class not to take over but to break up the existing capitalist state machine and to establish one of its own in order to defend the revolution and to build socialism (see V.I. Lenin, *The Proletarian Revolution and the Renegade Kautsky*). The success of the Bolsheviks in Russia, though dogged by other problems, fully vindicated the views of Marx and Lenin.

The socialists in Germany, however, denied this Marxist teaching. They came into power after the first world war, but only to be thrown out of it by the Fascist counter-revolution some years; later: This is what they wrote alter the event:

> The political transformation of 1918 ended up in a counter-revolutionary development ....The Social Democratic Party...took over control of the State without opposition, sharing it as a matter of course with the bourgeois parties, the old bureaucracy and even with the reorganised military forces. *That it should have taken over the old machinery of government virtually unchanged was the great historical error committed by a German Labour Movement which had lost its sense of direction during the war* ('The Battle of Revolutionary Socialism and its Objective': Manifesto of the Executive of the German Social Democratic Party, published in the Karlsbad Neuer Vorwarts, January 28, 1934—quoted by R. Palme Dutt, *Fascism and Social Revolution*, London, 1935, p. 283).

One must, however, add, in fairness to historical truth, that behind this error lay the still more fundamental 'error': a simple lack of faith in socialism. These socialists did not use their power to do the necessary things, political and economic, to introduce socialism reform and transformation of the old state apparatus, break up of the great landed estates, socialisation of the giant capital is combines etc.— 'not only because the Social Democratic leaders were afraid to do them, but also because they did not want to. They feared the collapse of the existing society much more than they hoped for a really new social order; and because of these fears they betrayed the revolution and helped to bring the Republic to its dismal collapse' (G.D.H. Cole, *A History of Socialist Thought*, Vol. IV: *Communism and Social Democracy, 1914 -1931*, Part II, London, 1961, p. 893).

The experience, however partial and limited, of successive Labour governments with the old State apparatus in England only underlines the validity of the argument above. Thomas Balogh has recently pointed out ('The Apotheosis of the Dilettante', in *The Establishment*, edited by Hugh Thomas, London, 1959) that a Labour Government needs to create, through appropriate civil service reform, its own state apparatus, its own 'Establishment', so to speak, which will be sympathetic and not opposed to the radical or socialist ends it may want to pursue;. This 'cannot, by itself, create the basis for a successful Socialist government, but, Balogh says, this is 'one of the most essential and fundamental preconditions' of such a government.

All this, of course, assumes that one day even a Labour Government in England would have faith and courage enough to want to be 'a successful Socialist government'!

34. The existence of monopolies, of vast concentrations of effective wealth in the more advanced societies of capitalism, predicted long ago by Marxists, is denied by few today. It is also generally conceded that those who control this wealth may be said to have economic power, and one which is generally inclined to be socially irresponsible. But what the liberal or social democratic political theory insists upon is that over and above this economic power and opposing it, is the political power of the state, the power of democracy, which can not only check and control this economic power but also subordinate it decisively to the interests of the people as a whole, which the *democratic* State represents. This is the most widely accepted thesis in the academic circles today. But this thesis is not so self-evident as its wide and uncritical acceptance would seem to suggest.

One does not need to dispute either the importance of democracy as the best general form or method of government yet devised by man or its great value for the common people who won it at great cost and through long and bitter struggles, in order to point out its limitations in a class-divided capitalist society—limitations which Bagehot well expressed in his own engaging manner when, early in the life of modern democracy, that is, in a more honest age, he wrote (in *The British Constitution*) that 'democracy is the way to give the people the greatest illusion of power while allowing them the smallest amount in reality'. What is more, a form of political power, democracy does not exhaust its content; political power is certainly much more than a matter of enjoying formal political rights, casting of votes, securing electoral majorities or pursuing proper legal or constitutional procedures, etc., most valuable though these and other related things are. Any meaningful and realistic treatment of the concept of political power today mast reckon, among other things, with the full dimensions of economic power in a modern capitalist society, no matter how democratic it is formally or politically, and with the nature and organisation of the state apparatus of coercion still provides the ultimate boat of sovereignty in the modern state, whose possession and control indeed constitutes, in the last resort, the final form of political power, oven though, one must readily concede, we are by no means constantly at the last resort. In other words, one must recognise that in contemporary capitalist democratic society the economic power is real enough— in the affluent society, *no* government is able to give orders to big business', R.H.S. Crossman has recently informed us; that there is a monopoly control of press, television and various other media of mass expression, of 'the opinion business' or 'the persuation industry' as it has been called, which gives great power to manage and manipulate the people, to engineer the consent of men itself; that apart from the poetical control which monopoly capitalism directly exercises through political parties and government, it is mostly its representatives, men trained and sharing in the outlook of the ruling class, who occupy leading positions in the State apparatus, in the apparatus not only of governmental policy-or-decision-making, but also of coercion and control. It would therefore seem that those who have economic power have very real political power also. The state, even the democratic state, is very much their state—it continues to be that 'whole complex of practical and theoretical activities with which the ruling clues not only justifies and maintains its rule but manages to win the active consent of the governed' (Antonio Gramsci, *The Modern Prince and Other Writings*, London, 1957, p. 182).

As a matter of fact the more discerning of contemporary social and political theorists, who still hold on to the notion of two separate contending or countervailing powers: or social forces, are increasingly coming to recognise the very real threat which the oligopolistic economic power poses to the continued existence of whatever political power democracy represents in a modern capitalist society.

John Strachey, for example, speaks of two ultimately incompatible features of western capitalist society, the growing concentration of economic power and what he calls the growing 'diffusion' of political power. Democracy and monopoly capitalism—last stage capitalism', he calls it—thus 'pull in opposite directions'. Their co-existence constitutes a state of antagonistic balance', it is 'a co-existence in tension'. And this co-existence, he says, can hardly be permanent or indefinite. One or the other must gain 'decisively'. 'In the end the power of contemporary democracy must encroach upon capitalism', and transform it, 'or, alternatively, capitalism must encroach upon democracy' and completely subvert it. Such is the 'hitherto unresolved' contradiction at the base of the more advanced capitalist-democratic societies of the west, and Strachey points his warning finger at 'the experience of the first half of the century'. (One is reminded of Laski writing nearly two decades earlier of 'the uneasy marriage between capitalism and democracy' which Fascism sought to dissolve in favour of capitalism—*Grammar of Politics*, London, 1938, p. xv. See also his *Democracy in Crisis*, London, 1933). For fascist totalitarianism had its roots in precisely that concentration of economic power which is the principal feature of contemporary capitalism.

Strachey himself does not apprehend, for reasons which are far from convincing, a 'direct' or 'frontal' attack on democracy; but he makes pointed reference to the indirect and 'subtle' encroachment and subversion, which is going on all the time and which if it 'did not encounter successful opposition, would spell out the end of effective democracy'. He writes: 'What is not only likely but inevitable —indeed it is taking place without ceasing is an attempt, largely unconscious, on the part of capital, highly organised and integrated in oligopolies, to manipulate and distort, and if necessary frustrate, the workings of contemporary democracy to its own advantage' (*Contemporary Capitalism*, pp. 254-6).

Recognising the limitations of political democracy, Benn and Peters, in their well-known textbook, write:

> Nevertheless, the Marxist is right so far: legal forms of election, freedoms of speech, publication, and association may not be enough in themselves to warrant calling a state a democracy.

If the idea behind these forms is frustrated by economic power, government may be sensitive only to the interests that wield it, and the state would be a disguised oligarchy (*op. cit.*, pp. 339-40).

Needless to add, to speak of government of an oligarchy, however disguised, as an 'umpire' or a refer', as Oakeshott does, makes no sense at all.

35. This criticism would teem to apply, to an extent, even to some of the better, and better knows, works in the field of contemporary political science, such as, for example, Lasswell and Kaplan, *Power and Society: A Framework for Political Enquiry*, Yale University Press, 1950; or G.E.G. Catlin, *Systematic Politics*, London, 1962.

    In his article 'Some Note on the Concept of Power', *Political Studies*, Vol. XI, No. 2, June 1963, P.H. Partridge has subjected the contemporary use of the concept of 'power' to criticism from another angle. Pointing out that 'power is a concept or phenomenon, too amorphous, sprawling or chameleon-like ever to be amenable to exert identification', he writes that this concept is not likely to be a fruitful concept in the explication of the "power structures" of actual societies; perhaps what is called for is a great deal of analysis in the sense of breaking up and discrimination, and the substitution of more manageable concepts for the portmanteau concept of power.'

    See also Arnold Brecht's brief comment suggesting that 'the general concept of power' is 'inept to supply an adequate basic unit in political theory (*op. cit.*, pp. 345-8).

36. On the contrary, the increasing formalism of political science in this and several other respects, its preoccupation with 'power' more or less in the abstract together with the persistent effort to view the question of power, consciously or otherwise, only from above, that is, from the point of view of the ruling classes and often enough only in order to rationalise 'elitism', and not from below, that is, in terms of the hopes and aspirations, or even fears, of the common people—which common people are generally treated merely as obeying or rebelling, as either apathetic low-level citizens, which is very much welcomed, or as representing the potential threat of mass politics which is very much feared — all this has contributed its share to the perpetuation of a situation which provoked C. Wright Mills to remark that 'much political science has of late been irrelevant to understanding important political realities, but not irrelevant to the scientific applauding of official policies and defaults' (*The Sociological Imagination*, p. 84).

37. If the concept of 'power' has been none too fruitful in contemporary political theory, the collateral concept of balance of power', which is so common in contemporary American political science and which Oakeshott too flirts with, has not done any better either. On this Petras writes:

The notions of 'equilibrium' and 'balance', perhaps more than any other, have distorted the perception of political scientists. The real political question begins, not ends, when one mentions 'balance'; balance of power in whose favor? As Mills noted: "Balance of power" implies equality of power and equality of power seems wholly fair and even honorable, but in fact, what is one man's honorable balance is often another's unfair balance. Ascendant groups of course tend readily to proclaim a just balance of power and a true harmony of interests, for they prefer their domination to be uninterrupted and peaceful' (*The Power Elite*, p. 246). In fact, the 'balances' are so drawn as to cover up essential imbalances that exist in society among social classes, races, and sectors of the country: the imbalances caused by the 'economically determined class lines' in American society where, as Kolko notes: 'On the one hand, nearly one-half of the population is financially able to meet only its immediate physical needs, and the larger part of the group, nearly one-third of the nation, are in want of even basic necessities. On the other hand, a small section of the population, at most, the top tenth, lives in the prosperous and frequently sumptuous manner that mast social commentators ascribe to the large majority of Americans' (G. Kolko, *Wealth and Power in America*, New York, 1962, p. 128); the 'imbalances' caused by racial discrimination and segregation .... Imbalances are created by the malfunctioning of the economic system where productive facilities are unused, where demand (popular needs) is seriously curtailed and where unemployment includes at least six per cent of the labor force; imbalance exists between expansion in some areas of the country and the absolute decline and impoverishment of others; ... This is far form complete list, but it includes major societal data that must be explained. These disequilibria generate conflict, challenge existing society, present problems to the system generate issues and even, at this point, creep into the major political arenas. By the equiliberals' very commitment to the values of stability and system maintenance, these problems and issues are minimized or repressed. Their 'deductive pluralism' prevents the equiliberals from seeing the undemocratic features of the society, the lack of responsiveness of institutions and practices to societal need. Hypotheses see such as 'democracy' become untenable; they are made to do the work and provide the emotive labels for activities which do not correspond to the 'appropriate' reality ....The failure of institutions to function as they are supposed to is obscured by the redefinition of concepts and the repression of issues and problems. The imbalances mentioned above become 'unproblems' as they do not fall within the purview of the analytic concepts; or only a small aspect of an imbalance is caught and presented as a marginal phenomenon....

The 'balances' of the equiliberals are at best one-sided explanations of limited areas of society; this one-sidedness fails to account for the issues and problems, the elements of disequilibria which present the problems of politics, the areas of issue gestation, the substance of political life.

Petras adds that the implications of equiliberal thought are really much more profound than simply this misperception of reality. For what they (Almond, Dahl and their disciples) have in effect done is 'to redefine the concept of democracy to fit the institutional demands of the present system'. They have so confused 'the terms democracy and stability', assuming them to be synonymous, that 'the stabilizing of the *status quo* is identified with democracy.' The paradoxical consequence of this confusion of values is 'a society billed as the paradigm of democracy but with a minimum of democratic citizens' (*loc. cit.*, pp. 213-5).

38. That such is the general character of Oakeshott's argument is in no way disproved either by his professed aversion to 'abstraction' in such matters, or by occasional statements to the effect that the question 'what is a free society?' if proposed abstractly', opens the door 'upon a night of endless quibble, lit only by the stars of sophistry'.

39. This approach to the problem of freedom in contemporary society is quite common with western political theorists of liberal-conservative persuasion today. Lipset, for example, has told us in a typical argument, already noticed in another context, that these theorists are agreed 'that an increase in over-all state power', whatever 'economic problems' it may claim to solve, carries with it serious 'dangers to freedom' (*op. cit.*, p. 406). Popper has gone so far as to suggest that it was Plato who by asking the question: 'Who should rule?' created a lasting confusion in political theory.

For this, according to him, put the question of unchecked political power or sovereignty at the centre of political theory, whereas the really fundamental question—in the interests of freedom and democracy, above all—is that of controlling and checking political power, of how 'rulers can be prevented from doing too much damage' (*The Open Society and its Enemies*, Vol. I, pp. 120-5).

This manner of argument is really part of a much wider contemporary phenomenon, of what Kettle has called 'this twentieth-century suspicion of power'? Today, as Cobban too has pointed out, men increasingly see power as a force they did not create, do not understand and cannot control, as something outside of them which masses them, the individual atoms, together, hurls them about and even disintegrates them (*loc. cit.*, pp. 326-7). This profoundly pessimist dislike and fear of power together with the sense of man's essential helplessness in face of it, which today pervades so much of the liberal consciousness, is not to be understood merely as a reaction against widespread abuse of power in our time. Its roots lie deeper in the loneliness inherent in the bourgeois-liberal outlook, which always sees man *primarily* as an isolated, atomistic individual, and only secondarily as member of a social group, a loneliness intensified, perhaps, by a sense of living at the end of an epoch. 'Power is bad', we are told, the true villain of political and perhaps every other piece—a view which is expressive of so many fears and prejudices of the intellectual in capitalist society. But if this suspicion of power thus becomes articulate in the intelectuals, it quite often evokes a very sympathetic response from the common people also in whose awareness power, economic as well as political, has for so long been the prerogative of the exploiting classes and therefore associated 'predominantly with ruthlessness, self-seeking and chicanery and scarcely at all with principle and responsibility'; who, given the undemocratic practice of even the most democratic capitalist society, 'have comparatively little sense of the possibilities of a responsible use of power', of being able to so participate in its exercise as to control their own destiny, who, in other words, have the knowledge and the feeling that ultimately it is *They* who have the power and who rule. Power is seen as *Their* power and therefore felt to be bad. On the question of the intellectuals and power, see Arnold Kettle, 'Communism and the Intellectuals', in *The Challenge of Marxism*.

These general considerations apart, it seems to me that the poser freedom *versus* power, in whose terms so many western social and political thinkers discuss the question of freedom today, is not only highly abstract but arbitrary also. Within the broad ideological context mentioned above, this approach stems, in part, from the false atomistic view of man and society and the collateral laissez faire view of government and political authority, which lie at the base of much of social and political thought of these thinkers. In part it also reflects the refusal of these thinkers to understand what Cole pointed out when he wrote that 'there are more kinds of tyranny and oppression than the political, and more kinds of freedom than the liberal-democratic freedoms that are rightly valued in the countries of the West' (*op. cit.*, p. 894). And on the whole the most that can be said for this approach, in theory at least, is that it may be relevant to the situation of men and societies that are comfortable and affluent. But then universally comfortable and affluent societies simply do not exist, not yet. Therefore, in practice, and particularly in relation to the situation of under-privileged men and societies, this approach is largely meaningless. A more meaningful approach, and one particularly relevant to the needs of men and societies now emerging into history, will not only restore such questions as '*whose* power is it?' and '*what* purposes does it serve?' to their rightful place in political theory, but also recognise that Popper's two supposedly different and even mutually exclusive questions are really parts of a single fundamental question: Men need to have power, often great power, for they have to achieve great human purposes which alone can give meaning and content to their freedom, and men also need to check and control this power *in relation* to these purposes, so that its serves only to give meaning and content to their freedom. Viewed from this angle the repetition of such well worn assertions as Acton's 'all power corrupts; and absolute power corrupts absolutely' is not very meaningful or illuminating. At any rate the truth of the latter part of this assertion must not blind us to the absolute pointlessness of the former, which is really tantamount to saying that all action or doing, and therefore living itself, corrupts. You cannot live by the principle 'all power corrupts' unless you have decided to do nothing and therefore have nothing, no freedom either. To regret power or to condemn it, to try to avoid it or to seek its absence or destruction, is therefore both meaningless and futile, and all this certainly does not mean freedom. In other words, it is wrong to treat freedom and power as mutually exclusive values. Besides, one must always remember that there are more dimensions to human freedom than the liberal-democratic or the conservative thinker generally shows himself to be aware of. And even with regard to 'the liberal democratic freedoms', there was Laski who argued (in *I Believe: The Personal Philosophies of Certain Eminent Men and Women of Our Time,* edited by Clifton Fadiman, New York, 1939) that 'liberty has no meaning save in the context of equality' and that 'equality, also, has no meaning unless the instruments of production are socially owned'—an argument which has the clear implication that the road to freedom lies *through* power which can establish this socialist ownership.

All this is only to suggest that the problem of freedom in contemporary society is far too complex and concrete to be comprehended and settled in terms of the abstract poser 'freedom *versus* power', and that we need to build a concept of freedom which is based not on escaping from power as the liberal-conservative thinker is often asking us to do, but on making a wise, responsible and effective use of power. Abstraction for abstraction, 'freedom *through* power' is any day more meaningful, and certainly more relevant to the needs of the vast majority of men and societies in the world today. For these men and societies need not only freedom but *also* power, power to make their freedom come true.

40. An inquiry today which asks these questions in the best tradition of social and political criticism in the west, a truly scientific inquiry into the location, nature, purpose and legitimacy of political power in the societies of monopoly capitalism, into the real problems of power or freedom or democracy under capitalism, an analysis, in other words, of the real situation, as it is and as it is developing, in the 'more advanced' societies of the capitalist world, may well reveal behind the facade of freedom and democracy, of 'free political and economic institutions' that Lipset speaks of (*op. cit.*, the concluding chapter) of 'the parliamentary and presidential systems of government' that Verney makes so much of (*op. cit.*, the concluding chapter), something of the ugly political reality of these societies: at the top 'an elite of power', men wielding unheard of power, economic, political and ideological, and wielding it above all in the interests of monopoly capitalism both at home and abroad; at the bottom mass-like people, economically dependent, politically powerless and ideologically disarmed, and manipulated constantly for hire; and the political community, as a whole, essentially undemocratic in its practices, largely apathetic, fragmented and stereo-typed, bearing little resemblance to the

image of a 'fret' or 'open' society that its apologists are all the time trying to project. And in so doing, in searching out the real centre of power and in revealing its true nature and function, such an inquiry may also indicate the imperative need to struggle against this power concentrated in the hands of a few in the societies of monopoly capitalism. Such a struggle is today indeed necessary not only to defend, against the threat of this power, whatever freedom and democracy there is, but also to extend and give a fuller meaning to this freedom and democracy by abolishing *this* power altogether.

But such an inquiry is, obviously, a dangerous undertaking, dangerous to the powers that be and, therefore, to those who may undertake it. It is always a dangerous thing to look too closely into the workings of the capitalist society. Fashionable exercises in a politically conformist scepticism, or in an 'end-of-ideology' complacency, or in a surface-scratching and socially impotent 'science of politics', are any day safer, and materially more rewarding too. Scholars have spoken in recent years of 'the decline' of political theory in the west. The evidence suggests that much of this political theory would rather decline than take up risky undertakings!

Focussing attention on 'the major issue facing political science: its relationship to the world at large', Arnold A. Rogow has pointed out that, in the United States, '*certain* vital research areas and topical questions are being neglected by the profession'. He notes 'the increasing tendency of the profession to engage in major research on minor or peripheral problems'. Speaking of the causes, he refers to the fact that 'the current political and social atmosphere does not encourage the forthright exploration of certain problems', and adds: 'I do not refer only, or even mainly, to McCarthyism and the loyalty investigations, but to the general climate of conservatism, opportunism, careerism, and "togetherness". The McCarthys are much less representative of our time than the Herman Wouks, the Norman Vincent Peales, and the man in the gray flannel suit. Like every one else in the middle class, the political scientist is togethering it around the barbecue pit, and the barbecue pit is not the best vantage point from which to examine the major national problems and issues'.

Rogow also writes:

> Given the prevailing mood, it is not always easy, or 'safe' to confront 'great issues'. For various reasons those who hold power in the nation and the world are not eager to be identified,

> or subjected to critical scrutiny. No serious researcher need be told that it is extremely difficult, if not impossible, to obtain information about certain organizations and activities, as a consequence of the wall of silence, secrecy, and security that has been created. Such research, moreover, often lacks pay-off value with respect to career interests—a consideration that younger, less secure members of the profession, especially, are inclined to take into account. I have seen more than one letter circulated in which acceptance of, or at least a record of silence about, the *status quo* appears to be a condition for academic employment (*loc. cit.*, pp. 771, 775).

41. This is nothing very surprising though. Pointing out that the sceptic's or the empiricist's indifference or aversion to theory can be carried too far, that scepticism or empiricism (and, therefore, an empiricist scepticism such as Oakeshott sports) can itself become a dogma and 'that way lies despair, mysticism and the mutilation of the intellect'— John Strachey has written:

> In Britain and America we are only too ready to make a virtue out of our own intellectual laziness, and to plume ourselves, not only on freedom from enslavement to 'a theory', which is prudent, but on sheer ignorance of political and economic theory in any shape or form. The sceptical and empirical tradition, pushed to this point, degenerates into mere illiteracy . . . . As Keynes wrote in a justly famous passage, a 'know-nothing', contemptuous, attitude to theory results merely in abject unconscious dependence upon some half-understood, vulgarised version of the dominant theory of the day before yesterday (*op. cit.*, pp. 15-6).

42. Marx once wrote that 'all science would be superfluous, if the appearance, the form, and the nature of things were wholly identical' (*Capital*, Vol. III, p. 951).

4

Of Scepticism in Politics

Oakeshott has been widely regarded, praised or condemned, as a conservative thinker. There is no doubt about his basic commitment to bourgeois society. He attacks rationalism and persistently mocks the radical and the revolutionary. In advocating traditionalism he defends even 'the merely traditional, customary or habitual' in political life. His political philosophy, thus, not only satisfies the very real appetites and prejudices of the average conservative, it also lends powerful ideological support to the established social and political order. He may, therefore, well be considered a philosopher, albeit a trifle unconventional, of modern conservatism. But a characterisation of Oakeshott as a conservative conceals, perhaps, about as much of his social and political philosophy as it reveals. This is so not because Oakeshott's conservatism deliberately eschews 'a creed or a doctrine' and speaks only of 'a style or disposition of thought', but because Oakeshott's scepticism, the philosophic basis on which his conservatism rests, goes far beyond 'rationalism in politics' to reach its ultimate target in politics itself. It is in a fundamental sense destructive of, all politics, including the conservative.

According to Oakeshott politics is not to be taken to seriously or hopefully, it is not something to worry or feel strongly about. There is nothing much here worth doing or achieving—there simply are no real possibilities in politics. You may, of course, engage in it, but 'for its own sake' and should be quite content if it helps you in 'merely passing the time.'[1] As a matter of fact to expect anything more from politics is sheer folly—though a youthful one, if that is any consolation! Oakeshott writes:

> Coming to be at home in this commonplace world qualifies us (as no knowledge of 'political science' can ever qualify us), if we are so inclined and have nothing better to think about, to engage in what the man of conservative disposition understands to be political activity.

Politics is, thus, never anything more than acceptance of things as they are, than somehow 'coming to be at home in this commonplace world'. It is indeed the toleration of 'what is abominable', and a thoroughly 'humdrum' affair, though Oakeshott adds, out of consideration for the conservative politician perhaps, that it 'need not be despicable'. And you engage in politics only if you 'are so inclined and have nothing better to think about'. After all, Oakeshott seems to say, it takes all sorts to make up 'this commonplace world' —or, perhaps, to make this world 'commonplace' therefore why not the conservative politician too![2]

After this it need suprise no one when Oakeshott informs us that 'politics is an activity unsuited to the young'—unsuited 'not on account of their vices but on account of...their virtues'. For them 'life is a dream' and 'everything ...a possibility'. They simply lack the mood 'which this manner of politics calls for', 'the mood of indifference' which is obviously not 'easy to acquire or to sustain'.

It is this mood of quiet indifference, utterly pessimist in its loss of every dream and destination, and laden with a sense of the ultimate purposelessness of politics, which pervades Oakeshott's well-known passage:

> In political activity; then, men sail a boundless and bottomless sea; there is neither harbour for shelter nor floor for anchorage, neither starting place nor appointed destination. The enterprise is to keep afloat on an even keel; the sea is both friend and enemy; and the seamanship consists in using the resources of a traditional manner of behaviour in order to make a friend of every hostile occasion.[3]

Under the circumstances one might well ask the question: why 'keep afloat' at all? And why indeed 'on an even keel'? Oakeshott evidently believes that it is necessary not only 'to keep afloat' but also 'to keep afloat on an even keel'. He evidently does not want the boat either to rock or to sink. In other words, Oakeshott assumes that it is necessary at least to maintain the established order and to keep it going as it is. But this assumption only reflects an *a priori* belief in; the value of social and political stability. While ostensibly only 'describing', or 'understanding or explaining' political activity, Oakeshott seems to have smuggled in a general prescriptive principle of the highest importance. And this is rather interesting. For it means that after having first ridiculed and then dismissed 'freedom', or 'equality', or 'social justice', or 'the public good', or 'happiness or prosperity' as 'abstract ideals' or 'abstract "principles"', as so many rationalist 'generalities' or 'plebeian "causes"', Oakeshott himself has in the end fallen for one of these, namely 'stability'. Only unlike the rationalist, he feels himself under no obligation to justify his choice on rational or any other grounds. It appears that 'Rationalism' is after all inescapable and, what is more, also permissible—but only in the service of conservatism.

In thus affirming the absolute and unconditional value of social and political stability, Oakeshott is only doing his duty to the conservative cause—causes, it seems, are 'causes', and like much else 'plebeian' and 'vulgar' only when they are not conservative. But this duty done Oakeshott continues with the main task of demolishing *all* causes in politics. He proceeds to develop his scepticism concerning politics to its logically inevitable nihilistic end. In doing so he again warns us against 'the illusion that in politics there is anywhere a safe harbour, a destination to be reached or even a detectable strand of progress', and concludes with the final assertion, the ultimate in political wisdom that Oakeshott's philosophy has to offer: 'The world is the best of all possible worlds, and *everything* in it is a necessary evil.

This *everything*, I presume, includes the rationalist and his politics too, which Oakeshott has been all along so vehemently and it now appears quite needlessly denouncing. And it equally inevitably appears to exclude the need even for 'slow, small changes' of the traditionalist conservative. At the end of our long journey with Oakeshott we have indeed reached 'a final destination', where nothing seems to matter, where to do or not to do is all the same, and where, therefore, there is no politics, no political theory—and no 'pursuit of intimations' either![4]

Such is the special quality of Oakeshott's political philosophy as a conservative, in so far as it is still legitimate to regard him as one. His acceptance of the bourgeois society is sincere enough, he would defend it and see it conserved fundamnentally as it is. Unwilling to look beyond its horizon, he cannot ever subject it to anything more than the most superficial criticism. But equally sincere it seems is his disillusionment with this society. If he is unable to reject it, he is yet genuinely bored with and indifferent towards this society—which, I submit, is the other reason why Oakeshott does not ever subject it to anything more than the most superficial criticism. His voice indeed says 'yes' to bourgeois society but it appears somehow to leave him cold and unconvinced; his soul echoes, however feebly, an unmistakable 'no'. His commitment to bourgeois society, his commitment as a conservative, thus turns out to be half-hearted and ambiguous. Highly sensitive, profoundly sceptical, and too much of an individualist, Oakeshott is really unable to conform to the *actual*, existential political needs of the bourgeois order. He is certainly unwilling to climb into the Establishment or to serve, except perhaps once in a while when the itch for the 'vulgar' becomes really irresistible, in the company of those academicians whom Loren Baritz once referred to as the 'servants of the established power'—though he too has to earn his living, like the rest of us.

But unable to commit himself unambiguously to bourgeois society, Oakeshott is equally unwilling to choose the only real alternative; disparagingly he calls it the 'heroic' alternative. Criticise and occasionally even condemn it he may, but Oakeshott would not seriously challenge or fight the ugly reality of contemporary bourgeois existence. He is ever 'suspicious of those who offer us more; those who call upon us to make great sacrifices and those who want to impose upon us an heroic character'. Since Oakeshott has a *priori* refused to learn any lesson from history, past or present, he simply cannot believe that men are as much capable through their conscious, clear-eyed, free choice, of this 'heroic character', of 'destruction and creation', as they are of the much eulogised 'conservative disposition', of 'acceptance or reform', and that men need to be capable of both in order not only to survive, but also to give to this continuity of survival its specific human quality, progress.

Thus unable or unwilling either to accept or to reject, in a fundamental manner, the reality of contemporary bourgeois existence, the only alternative left to Oakeshott, his own 'free' choice, as it were, the only one he ever really feels positive or enthusiastic about, is that of with drawal—withdrawal into a nihilism of bored indifference towards man and his concerns, and beyond it into a lonely and lost subjectivism of an inconsequential philosophy of 'making and entertaining mere images'. This is apparently Oakeshott's own private 'short cut to heaven', his search, in mid-twentieth century, for immortality *a la'* Aristotle.[5] To Oakeshott this may appear to be 'salvation' enough, but his fellowmen may well be forgiven if, unable or unwilling to thus find an escape, they see in it only a futile gesture of protest, if not the act of desertion itself.[6]

NOTES AND REFERENCES

1. Oakeshott defines 'conservative disposition' as a disposition 'merely to enjoy' what an activity offers 'for its own sake'. Concerning what this disposition permits in, or expects from, politics, an analogy which Oakeshott gives is quite revealing. Speaking of activities 'that may be engaged in, not for a prize, but for the enjoyment they generate, and for which the only appropriate disposition is the disposition to be conservative', Oakeshott writes:

   Consider fishing. If your project is merely to catch fish it would be foolish to be unduly conservative. You will seek out the best tackle, you will discard practices which prove unsuccessful, you will not be bound by unprofitable attachments to particular localities, pieties will be fleeting, loyalties evanescent; you may even be wise to try anything

> once in the hope of improvement. But fishing is an activity that may be engaged in, not for the profit of a catch, but for its own sake; and the fisherman may return home in the evening not less content for being empty-handed. Where this is so, the activity has become a ritual and a conservative disposition is appropriate. Why worry about the best gear if you do not care whether or not you make a catch? What matters is the enjoyment of exercising skill (or, perhaps, merely passing the time), and this is to be had with any tackle, so long as it is familiar and is not grostesquely inappropriate.

2. Criticising optimistic idealism and high hopefulness—'dreaming' as he calls it—of 'the rationalist politics', Oakeshott writes: 'Like men born in prison, we are urged to dream of something we have never enjoyed (freedom from want) and to make that dream the foundation of our politics.'

   According to Oakeshott, it seems, the proper thing to do would be, to forget all about freedom—from want or any other—and settle down to make the prison itself a permanent home!
3. We have Alfred Cobban's very interesting comment on this, which brings out the real meaning of the Oakeshottian understanding of politics as 'the pursuit of intimations'. Cobban does not mention Oakeshott by name. But pointing out that analogies are really the camouflage of loose thinking, he explores what he calls 'the image of political life which emerges from the prevailing tendencies in political thought', in which the state appears as a ship in the sea of politics, with no port of embarkation or destination, tossed in unending meaningless motion, and manned by a crew who in their sole endeavour to keep it afloat have little to help them save their own traditional seamanship. 'A depressing picture', Cobban says, 'perhaps dreamed up by some remote philosopher who has seen the ships scudding by from the lantern-room of a dead lighthouse, dead because he has carefully extinguished the light.' He comments:

   > One thing is missing from the picture. It is missing from contemporary politics also. This ...is the idea that the ship is going anywhere. A sense of direction is lacking, a feeling of purpose. That, I think, is what the decay of political theory means in ordinary terms to the ordinary man. Does it matter? If we were all of us, all our time, porkers not even from the sty of Epicurus, perhaps it would not: our purpose would beset by something outside ourselves, and it would be just as well that it should not be revealed to us in disturbing detail. Such, of course, may be the facts of the case; but rightly or wrongly

the human mind demands something more than living from trough to snout... (*loc. cit.*, p. 336).

4. 'A depressing doctrine, it will be said, Oakeshott himself readily concedes about his teaching. But he adds immediately that 'if it suggests that the politics are, *nur fur die Schwindelfreie*, that should depress only those who have lost their nerve'.

   Brave words and sentiments these but they sound familiar. Despite their undercurrent of a certain tongue-in-check scepticism, they have about them the authentic flavour of the commonplace maudlin posturing of all effete and dying social systems. This is not the first time, nor the last, that a pessimism, in its utter indifference and loss of hope and purpose, has compelled if not its own formal denial, at least a posture of false bravado and fake defiance. Haven't we heard before, the profoundly pessimist philosopher of *The Decline of the West* prophesy doom and yet declaim: 'Only dreamers believe that there is a way out', 'optimism is cowardice', 'our duty is to hold on the last position, without hope, without rescue', etc., etc.

   Incidentally, Spengler spoke of intellectualism as a 'weed of the pavement' and represented yet another form of revolt against reason in our time.

5. It is symptomatic of the deep crisis of the ancient city-state, and of the hopelessness of Plato's and Aristotle's love for it, that in the end both of them virtually turn *away* from it. Plato comes to find the ultimate fulfilment of life and philosophy in the essentially religious and mystical, the wordless', experience of contemplation of the Idea or Form of the Good', and Aristotle in an activity of thought about thought, which, being akin to God's 'activity of immobility', 'thinking of thought itself constitutes man's sole claim to immortality. And in a pathetically noble sentence in his *Ethics* Aristotle admonishes mortal man to 'be as immortal as possible'.

6. Oakeshott's position as a whole, particularly the view he takes of politics and political theory or philosophy, contrasts very sharply with what Cobban has called 'the tradition of Western political thought'. 'The greater political thinkers of the past', Cobban points out, 'wrote with a practical purpose in mind. Their object was to influence actual political behaviour. They wrote to condemn or support existing institutions, to justify a political system or persuade their fellow citizens to change it: because, in the last resort, they were concerned with the aims, the purposes of political society...' (*loc. cit.*, p. 330).

   These political thinkers or philosophers wrote because they were above all 'concerned with a condition of things' and not, as

Oakeshott claims, 'only with a manner of explanation'. Of necessity concerned with what Oakeshott today calls the 'manners' or modes of thought', they yet thought like citizens, genuinely solicitous for the present and even more the future of their society. Sabine has well pointed out that 'those who are genuinely indifferent about the future do not take the trouble to make political theories, and those who do take that trouble usually care intensely about something' ('What is Political Theory?', *loc. cit.*, p. 5). Whatever their persuasion, these thinkers and philosophers cared intensely about man and his concerns, they were always with him, even if they could not always be said to be *for* him. They possessed political conscience and were deep and bold in their commitment. They were neither above the battle nor indifferent to its outcome. They always sought to come to grips with the practical world, with the significant problems of their age. In political theory they sought answers to these problems, they sought knowledge which may serve as a guide to human action in this world. 'Theory exists'. Andrew Hacker writes, 'because there stave been men of intellect who saw politics as real problems which cried out for solutions' (*Political Theory*, p. 20)

It is clear that Oakeshott repudiates the great tradition of western political thought, as many others, too, have done in our time. Harold Laski was a notable exception. Of him, while disagreeing with his analysis or his conclusions, Cobban writes:

> Among recent political thinkers, it seems to me that one of the very few, perhaps the only one, who followed the traditional pattern, accepted the problems presented by his age, and devoted himself to the attempt to find an answer to them was Harold Laski ....I think that he was trying to do the right kind of thing. And this, I suspect, is the reason why, practically alone among political thinkers in Great Britain, he exercised a positive influence over both political thought and action (*loc, cit.*, p. 332).

Now it may be that Cobban is all wrong about Laski and about 'the tradition of Western political thought', and Oakeshott is right, for all his love of tradition, in repuditating at least this one tradition. Maybe the greater political theorists of the past were really mistaken, and we should indeed deplore their 'vulgar', 'vocational' disposition. But we could still, perhaps, feel humble and be a little grateful to them at least for their having taken politics seriously and produced the classics thereby providing for scepticism in political philosophy, and, the irreverent might cynically add, for our jobs in the universities too!

5

In Lieu of a Conclusion

At the beginning of this essay it was pointed out that philosophical reflection on politics or any other subject is never a uniquely self-generated or self-determined intellectual exercise. Attention was also drawn to the connection which of necessity obtains between philosophy and society, between the philosopher and the world he lives and philosophises in. There is no doubt, of course, that a philosophy is in part determined by its inherent logic, by rational and empirical considerations intrinsic to it. But it is not entirely, nor often even mainly, so determined. As Gellner has emphasised:

> People do not think in a vacuum, and even if the content and direction of their thought is in part determined by rational considerations, by where the wind of argument and the force of reasons and evidence drive them, these factors never uniquely determine what people think. By this I mean not that people are incapable of overcoming their emotional, non-rational inclinations (this may or may not be true as well), but that it is in the very nature of thought that its course is not rigidly dictated by some inherent rules. Some evidence may be incontrovertible and inescapable, some inferences cannot be resisted, and in those cases 'we can no other'. But the choice of problems, the choice of criteria of solutions, of rigour, of permissible evidence, the selection of hunches to be followed up and of those to be ignored,...all these matters which make up a *style* of thought or the spirit of the times, are not dictated by an immovable reason, and they are at the very least influenced by the social and institutional milieu of the thinker.[1]

The social and institutional milieu, the entire set of historically evolved conditions which constitute the social being or existence of a period, thus exercises great selective and formative influence over the philosophies or systems of thought of that period.[2] It determines to a significant degree not only the content and direction of a philosophy or a system of thought but even more its socio-historical role and consequences.

There is no doubt, again, that an inquiry into the social origins or significance of a philosophy does not, and cannot, provide an answer to the really important question: is it true or false? The truth or falsity, and the consequent acceptance or rejection, of a philosophy is never a matter merely of its origin or import. It is a matter really for an independent inquiry which focusses attention on questions of logic, evidence, and truth, and looks for the grounds on which a philosophy may be accepted or rejected as being more or less true or false. But a reference to the social origins of a philosophy, to 'the unconscious motives and determinants in the social habitat of the thinker',[3] a reference both to the socio-historical conditions in which a philosophy rises and gains acceptance and to its social role and practical consequences, does help us to understand it better. This reference certainly does not detract from the importance of a philosophy. On the contrary it serves to establish its full meaning and larger significance. What is more it enriches our comprehension of a philosophy by helping us to explain and understand its ambiguities and contradictions, its inevitable rationalisations and distortions, its elements of 'illusion' and 'false consciousness', and all other seemingly queer features which can be neither rationally justified nor empirically validated.

A social analysis or diagnosis is thus at all times a true and helpful procedure in the study of a philosophy or a system of thought. It is particularly so in case of Oakeshott's philosophy which is so fantastically queer at times, and whose nihilistic queerness virtually swamps the few genuine insights it has to offer. Our inquiry into Oakeshott's philosophy so far has been concerned mostly with the question of its truth or validity. And I have sought to assess the truth or validity of this philosophy on rational and empirical grounds. A socio-analytical inquiry, an inquiry into its sociology, so to speak, is now not only in order or legitimate but also necessary to achieve a better definition of the meaning and significance of Oakeshott's philosophy for our time.

An inquiry of this nature, to be adequate, requires more patient and painstaking work than can be undertaken here. It is in fact a task for the social historian. But for the tentative social analysis or diagnosis which I want to offer, and which alone can be attempted here, something quite modest should suffice. I opened this essay with a passing reference to the historical context and meaning of certain developments in the field of contemporary political theory and practice, developments to which, generally speaking, Oakeshott's philosophy and politics may be said to belong. Later, while subjecting this philosophy and politics to critical scrutiny, I have on occasion also drawn attention to their historical background and social or practical consequences. It would suffice for my purpose to bring these stray arguments together and conclude this essay with another brief reference to the sociology, to the socio-historical context and significance of Oakeshott's philosophy as a whole.

How, then, shall we sum up, in social and historical terms, the philosophy and politics of Professor Oakeshott? How are we to understand, explain or interpret Oakeshott's philosophy as a socially significant phenomenon? Where do we put it on the map of contemporary social and political thought and how do we assess its socio-political role and significance? What experience, what hopes and fears indeed, does this philosophy 'abridge' and 'abbreviate', and what world does this experience reveal? And how shall we relate this experience and its 'abridgement', the whole style and content of thought that is Oakeshott's, to the social and political reality of our world, to the thought and spirit of our times?

Oakeshott denies reason, and distrusts and disparages it, in an era of social and scientific revolutions which have meant an unprecedented expansion of reason in the world, and which bear eloquent testimony to its unlimited power not merely to understand, explain or interpret but even more to change and transform man's world in accordance with his wishes and interests. Betraying a singular lack of sense of history, he pleads for a change fearing, tradition-bound conservatism in the midst of a world-wide process of change which is probably more profound and sweeping than any since medieval society broke up to give birth to the modern world. He nurses a strange scepticism about human knowledge, ridicules his age as one 'over-impressed with its own accomplishment and liable to those illusions of intellectual grandeur which are the characteristic lunacy of post Renaissance Europe', and warning us against 'the exaggeration of Bacon's hopes' wants us to take to heart only 'the scepticism of Descartes'; this at a time when the achievements of human knowledge, in determining and winning human objectives, have made it possible for us to realise even the most exaggerated of Bacon's hopes, 'and thus render ourselves the masters and possessors of nature' as Descartes so clearly foresaw more than three hundred years ago.[4] In opening up magnificent new vistas of progress for mankind, these achievements of human knowledge—in the domains of nuclear energy, electronics and technology (automation and cybernation), biochemistry, space exploration and so on—represent a development which man has so long hoped for and dreamed about, and which holds promise of a life far richer and happier than any that man has ever dared put into his utopias. But Oakeshott can today only warn man against 'dreams', against 'vain and dangerous expectations'. His thoughts stay riveted to the *status quo*, and to 'the present' only.[5] He defends and justifies an unjust and irrational social order, the capitalist order of profit, privilege and minority rule, whose continued existence is turning man's hope into fear and anxiety, his dream into a nightmare, and the promise of a new life into a threat, a deadly nuclear threat, to the very existence of human life on this earth. Oakeshott's attack on rationalism and his advocacy of traditionalism are only two aspects of this defence and justification of the *status quo*. But his sceptic's attack on rationalism, rapidly reducing reason to an 'abridging', 'abbreviating' and 'abstracting' caricature of itself, soon reaches the point where it becomes an attack upon systematic thought' itself, an attack which Whitehead once characterised as 'treason to civilization'.[6] And his conservative's advocacy of traditionalism, urging upon us the need to live in the present, 'to live at the level of one's own means' and to 'recognise the circumstance' and be content with 'what we can get', soon reaches the point where interest even in the present is lost. Oakeshott finds its problems to be perennial 'predicaments' and its evils to be 'necessary'. It appears drained of all value or purpose, it becomes an aimless and destination-less, truly 'floating' present. And the only value or purpose seemingly left is in the Oakeshottian injunction 'to love the past'—an injunction which, Carr tells us, 'may easily be an expression of the nostalgic romanticism of old men and old societies, a symptom of loss of faith and interest in the present or future'.[7] Oakeshott is indeed left without any genuine interest in the future also. For him a veritable gulf opens up between 'the actual' and 'the possible', between 'the present' and 'the future', resulting in a fear of, or an indifference towards, the future, 'the unknown' as he also calls it, which all his Burkeian rhetoric about 'partnership' between the past, present and future but ill conceals. The enterprise being only 'to keep afloat', all talk of reaching somewhere, as of coming from anywhere, is 'out'. That there is any destination to be reached is an 'illusion'; we are simply not going anywhere, not any longer, at any rate!

Men have no future, nor has their socio-historical development any 'pattern or purpose', or 'progress', or 'even a detectable strand of progress'. Oakeshott banishes the very idea of progress from human history, an idea which only the other day Bury called the 'animating and controlling idea of western civilization';[8] which is, in fact, 'the synthesizing idea' of all civilisation, 'the one certain judgment of value that can be made about history'.[9] Oakeshott thus banishes future, that is human progress, from history; and this at a time when men in most places have seen their future and seen it work too, when content no longer to somehow 'keep afloat' in the present, to be creatures merely of custom and tradition, they are fast moving into this future, they are *progressing*, through terrible yet magnificent struggles, through reverses and defeats no less than through victories, into a *socialist* future, where, at last, 'men will share the planning of their happiness, even as they will share the happiness they plan'.[10] Oakeshott not only rejects and fights this future, which is already here as the *next* destination of man in a future of infinite progress, with it he rejects and fights all ideals and aspirations also. To him man's ideals and aspirations are only so much 'idolatry' and 'clap trap', so many sedimented and sterile 'abstractions', sheer intellectual confusion when not downright hypocrisy. He ridicules the pursuit of ideals as 'the pursuit of perfection as the crow flies', as 'the project of finding a short cut to heaven', as the search for 'a premeditated utopia' or 'a permanently impregnable society', etc., etc. He thus mocks men's pursuit of 'the better' as an utterly ignorant presumption when men have gained a heightened consciousness of their powers, and have indeed reached out to grasp 'the better' successfully, when in fact they are everywhere realising old ideals and making new ones for themselves. Oakeshott fails to recognise that ideals or utopias or dreams, 'as the expression of rational possibilities', are not only 'an integral feature of purposive living' but also 'essential conditions for man's development'. And he is unaware of the fact that 'the neglect of the ideal leads only to the covert practice of giving to the present an ideal significance it does not possess'[11] He denies the simple historical truths that vision of 'the better' not only prevents man's submission to evil as something necessary or inevitable, it also makes possible what, we call human achievement; that, as men, we must not only 'dream of freedoms we have never enjoyed' but also, if we would progress, 'make that dream the foundation of our politics'; and that man's attempt to reach beyond himself, to transcend his limits, is not an ignorant presumption but his proud privilege and destiny, the very essence and affirmation of his humanity. Oakeshott not only denies all this but if history, especially that of recent times, bears witness to these truths, he does not hesitate to say 'no' to this history itself. Pessimistic as he is about western civilisation in general, he is in utter despair about its development 'particularly in the last four centuries', centuries which have been almost universally regarded, their darker aspects notwithstanding, as the finest, the most brilliantly creative and hopeful period of the western, indeed of all civilisation so far, and have been so regarded for their dominant humanist belief in reason, science, and progress, for precisely that which Oakeshott so persistently denigrates, repudiates, and condemns.[12]

Such are the more important ideas of Oakeshott that immediately demand our attention. How are we to analyse and diagnose them in social and historical terms? How indeed shall we understand, explain or interpret them and the nihilistic scepticism pervading the entire philosophy of Oakeshott, scepticism which seeks to deprive politics of all purpose and philosophy, including political philosophy, of all wisdom, which seeks to drive out ideals and aspirations from ethics, meaning and progress from history, cognition and truth from poetry, the world and its knowledge from science, and reason from almost everywhere, which seeks to rob nearly every activity of man of its essential human character?

Many are the easy answers that immediately suggest themselves especially if, determined not to look beyond Oakeshott himself, one tends to regard his philosophy as a unique, or uniquely self determined phenomenon. May be it is the passing aberration of an individual mind, albeit a mind of great senstivity and brilliance. Or may be we have here a case of that 'half-way coherent conservatism' which in our time has often taken the form of what Wright Mills once described as 'mere eccentricity'. Or, perhaps, it is yet another example, of course a truly sophisticated one, of that desperate straining after originality or novelty, of that 'gimmickry', which is one of the more amusing, and in its own way quite instructive, features of academic social and political theory today.[13] Or, perhaps, in his avowed preference for 'contemplating and delighting' as against 'inquiry or argument', for 'conversation' as against 'argumentative discourse', Oakeshott has gone in, like many other contemporary philosophers, for learned frivolity, for a highly sophisticated exercise in what Gellner would call 'conspicuous triviality', which is fully aware of its inconsequential nature and irrelevance and which, therefore, leaves his philosophy a subject fit more for 'contemplating and delighting' than for argument, explanation or interpretation. Or, perhaps, as claimed by his admirers, Oakeshott's philosophy is indeed a 'rich store-house of highly original ideas', so original that they, for the most part, defy understanding or interpretation, turning it almost inevitably, as it were, into misunderstanding or misinterpretation.

One could think of more such interpretations. These interpretations may or may not have their elements of truth, but they do, in their own way, draw our attention to a certain specifically unique quality of Oakeshott's ideas. But to rest content with such interpretations, or even to develop them along more positive lines (as can certainly be done), to emphasise only the uniqueness, the 'highly original' or 'unconventional' nature of Oakeshott's philosophy, is to be blind to its true meaning. It is to rob Oakeshott's philosophy of its larger social meaning and signficance, which meaning and significance it certainly possesses. The argument of this essay has already made this abundantly clear. In concluding this argument, I again venture to suggest that in all its uniqueness, originality or unconventionality, in its obscurity as well as its lucidity, in its simplicity as much as in its esoteric and occasionally even obscurantist sophistication, Oakeshott's thought belongs fully to the times. Even if it is regarded as 'a sort of truancy', it is a truancy within the thought of our age and, as an *ideal* phenomenon, it reflects—perhaps unconsciously and, therefore, with all the greater *fidelity* a most significant aspect of the *real* life of our times:

An important segment of the thought of our age, particularly in the western world, is today characterised by a general retreat from reality and from reason,—'a twentieth century intellectualism' which is full of 'disillusionment, or even despair, of reason' as Karl Popper once put it. There is profound scepticism about systematic thought concerning 'the world of things', which often slips into belief in the essential incomprehensibility of this world. Irrationalism has emerged as a significant philosophical position, postulating either the fundamentally irrational nature of reality itself or the complete inadequacy of the categories of reason to comprehend it; thereby, fostering obscurantism and reaction all around. A regression in philosophy, indeed a *contraction* of thought has occurred, resulting in a general reluctance to raise or confront fundamental issues in every field of human inquiry: in philosophy, for example, where the desire to know and understand the world has come to be regarded as 'an outdated folly', and the philosophers, abandoning the world and its problems, have withdrawn into 'an arid desert of linguistic conundrums'; or in political theory where pronouncements, complacent or apprehensive, abound about 'the end of ideology' and 'the decline' or even 'death' of political theory; or in historiography and philosophy of history where any search for laws and generalisations, for meaning, purpose or progress in history, is decried as 'metaphysical' and 'unscientific'; or in the social sciences in general where so many social scientists, instead of subjecting the irrationality of contemporary bourgeois reality to scientific scrutiny *adjust* their science to this reality to produce only *insignificant* truth or somewhat significant *apologetics*, and thereby prove that they are bourgeois first and social scientists only a long time afterwards. There is widespread fear of change, expressing itself in a wave of ultra conservatism which arbitrarily contrasts 'the practical' or 'the concrete' with 'the ideal' or 'the abstract', which disavows ideas and ideals, and condemns all radicalism, all striving for a better, more humane and rational social order, as 'utopian' or 'subversive'. The established capitalist order is defended in the name of tradition, or religion, or scepticism, or 'freedom', or plain utilitarianism; popular democracy is rejected as impossible or undesirable, and the rights and authority of the ruling elite are labouriously justified. There is not only a waning of faith in reason as the instrument of social change and a loss of the concept of change as progress; reason, change and progress are also often identified with socialism and a struggle is waged against all of them simultaneously. There is an yearning for the past too, and a significant tendency to trace the origin of almost all contemporary evil back to the Renaissance and the post-Renaissance period. And, above all, there is a general leaning towards nihilism, a mood of doubt and disillusionment, of 'meaninglessness and despair in all realms of life' (Paul Tillich), 'an overwhelming feeling' that 'something's wrong', that 'somehow we have lost our way' (James Reston), all of which is faithfully reflected, for example, in contemporary literature which is so full of themes of bitterness, boredom and neurosis, of guilt and remorse, of renunciation and evasion, of brutality, violence and death, and which in giving expression—at times with rare analytic intelligence and sensitiveness—to 'the helpless, despairing disgust with life in our time' bears witness to the terrible inner sickness of an alienated and dehumanised world.

These are some of the more important developments in the social and political thought, in the ideological superstructure, of the societies of more advanced capitalism today. These developments are ideologically, and even more socially, supplementary; they generally justify and reinforce each other and in their totality constitute a highly significant social phenomenon. Oakeshott, it is clear, shares in these developments, of course in his own way; his philosophy, its uniqueness notwithstanding, is a part of this social phenomenon. And it is here that the real meaning and significance of Oakeshott's philosophy has to be ultimately sought. For this highly significant social phenomenon is, as always, the product and expression of a fundamental change taking place in the world in the twentieth century, a change which Mumford has described as 'the active disintegration of Western civilization'.[14]

Ours is on the whole an age of progress, an age of unprecedented scientific and social advance. Carr has spoken of 'our twentieth-century revolution' is which 'the social revolution and the technological revolution and the scientific revolution are part and parcel of the same process'. Cobban has called this 'an age of revolutions'. Occurring in such an age, the aforesaid social phenomenon, so characteristic of twentieth century bourgeois ideology, bears all the marks of a real *trahison des clercs*. What progress there has been for mankind as a whole in our times and how bourgeois thought and practice have been busy fighting and writing it off; what hopes and possibilities life today offers for the advance of the whole of mankind and what fears and anxieties, what retreats, indeed, fill the multiform bourgeois thought and ideology today—a thought and ideology which is, at its best, aware of the dilemmas and tragedies of the contemporary world but which, unable or unwilling to accept an explanation that involves revolutionary social change, retreats inevitably in the direction of pessimism, of irrationalism, obscurantism and reaction, and thus becomes itself as limited, as frustrated and irrational, as the world it fails or refuses to understand or change!

One remembers another time and another age when capitalism was in the ascendant and bourgeois thought and ideology had an altogether different ring about it, the ring of humanist optimism, of profound though not easy confidence in man and his future. One is indeed reminded of the great tradition of human thought which was once the tradition of the rising bourgeoisie and is so no longer, the tradition of faith in reason, science and progress, in the greatness of man and the powers and potentialities of the human race, in man's ability to know and master his environment, to fight and win a more rational and just world for himself—a tradition which other people, other classes now uphold and carry forward.

Could it be, then, that Oakeshott's philosophy is only a minor ideological episode of the period of the decline and disintegration of capitalism?

NOTES AND REFERENCES

1. Ernest Gellner, *Words and Things*, p. 229.
2. Herbert Spencer once said: 'Ideas wholly foreign to this social state cannot be evolved, and if introduced from without, cannot get accepted, or if accepted die out' (quoted by Maurice Dobb, *op. cit.*, p. 228).
3. Karl Popper, *The Open Society and its Enemies*, Vol. II, pp. 251-2.
4. Descartes, *Discourse on Method*, in *Philosophical Works*, edited by E.S. Haldane and G.R.T. Ross, Cambridge 1931, Vol. I, p. 119.
5. This, incidentally, reminds one of what Hobbes, living in another age of revolutionary crisis, wrote: 'The present ought always to be preferred, maintained, and accounted best; because it is against both the law of nature, and the divine positive law, to do anything tending to the subversion thereof' (*op. cit.*, p. 361).

6. A.N. Whitehead, *Adventures of Ideas*, Pelican, 1948, p. 191.
7. E.H. Carr, *op. cit.*, p. 20.
8. J.B. Bury, *The Idea of Progress*, London, 1920, p. viii.
9. J.H. Plumb, *op. cit.*, pp. 34, 42.
10. Barrows Dunham, *Giant in Chains*, p. 17.
11. Lewis Mumford, *op. cit.*, pp. 10, 13. Emphasising the 'quality of self-transcendence' in man's nature, Mumford points out that man, 'the unfinished animal', is 'ever reaching out into the unknown' and that 'man's higher development has been due to his unwillingness to accept the limits of the outer world as his own ultimate boundaries.'
12. Oakeshott is not alone in his attack on the post-Renaissance development of western civilisation. Many others in our time have shared in this attack which often amounts to cutting off the branch on which one is sitting. There is, for example, Arnold Toynbee (*A Study of History*), who speaks of 'the crime of our sixteenth and seventeenth century ancestors' and condemns particularly the Reformation and the French Revolution—those landmarks in the struggle for human liberation—together with the rise of democracy which followed, as the root cause of the contemporary moral and political crisis. Toynbee would have us renounce it all and retrace our steps to seek salvation 'in the arms of an ancestral church' (the Church of Rome), or, possibly, in the arms of some universal church of the future, capable of combating what Toynbee describes as 'the recrudescence of idolatry in the peculiarly vicious form of Man's corporate worship of himself.'
13. Research projects on all sorts of fanciful themes; laboured exercises in originality and empty or formal ingenuity; pretensions of *expertise* that so overawe the non-expert; the academic pose born of the notion that to be readable or understandable is to be superficial; elaborate vocabularies and involved manners of speech and writing, full of turgid and polysyllabic verbiage; 'the academic prose' so-called, Malcolm Cowley's 'socspeak', which at times degenerates into weird and unintelligible jargon and needs to be translated into English before it can be understood, a prose which has often less to do with any complexity of subject matter or profundity of thought and a great deal more with the academic's desire for easy prestige and status and which occasionally even serves as a cover for genuine mediocrity; etc. etc.—these are common phenomena in contemporary social science, especially in the USA (On this see, for example, C. Wright Mills, *The Sociological Imagination*). In a passing reference to this

situation Saul Landau has spoken of 'the plodding research and lack of imagination that passes for scholarship at our institutions of higher learning'. He writes:

> The intellectual quest of most professors and up-and-coming graduate students is to discover the gimmick that will capture the imagination of the Ford Foundation directors. They justify feeble intellectual efforts by referring to the world body of scientific knowledge that they are adding to; in reality they are contributing assorted and irrelevant statistics or fancy words to the ever increasing mound of academic rubble (*Science and Society*, Vol. XXVIII, No. 4, Fall 1964, p. 478).

One might add that this style of academic work, speech and writing, financially well-backed as it is like most things American, is catching on in other places too.

More seriously I would suggest that in this laboured search for 'originality', in the scholar's desire to have a private social science of his own, as it were, lies one of the more important causes of the lack of advance in contemporary social science. 1n this connection what Shigeto Tsuru says of economics is true of all social sciences, including political science. Pointing out that ecnomics, as a discipline in social science, 'has not attained that degree of unified, systematic maturity which would evoke unqualified respect for its specialists', he writes:

> 'Economists themselves are partly to blame for this state of affairs. Instead of being satisfied with adding as tone or two to the common edifice, too many of them, especially good ones, have been prone to build one's own which by nature of the case could never be complete even with assiduous buttressing by their faithful disciples. Thus 'a new name for an old thing' reappears in an endless train (*op. cit.*, p. i).

14. Lewis Mumford, *op. cit.*, p. 391.

PART II

Marxism and Politics

The doctrine that man is the highest being for man, i.e. the categorical imperative to overthrow all conditions in which man is a humiliated enslaved, despised and rejected being.

In place of the old bourgeois society, with its classes and class antagonisms, we shall have an association in which the free development of each is the condition for the free development of all.

I call revolution the conversion of all hearts and the raising of all hands in behalf of the honour of the free man.

Karl Marx

6

Concerning Marxism*

> We do not set ourselves up against the world in doctrinaire fashion with a new principle: Here is the truth! Here you must kneel! We develop new principles for the world out of the principles of the existing world...
>
> It is the great advantage of the new movement that we do not seek to anticipate the new world dogmatically, but rather to discover it in the criticism of the old... It is not our task to build-up the future in advance and to settle all problems for all time; our task is ruthless criticism of everything that exists, ruthless in the sense that the criticism will not shrink either from its own conclusions or from conflict with the powers that be...
>
> **Karl Marx**

In humankind's centuries-old effort to understand society and to change it for the better on the basis of this understanding, Marxism is possibly the most ambitious and yet a genuinely modest exercise, so far. It is ambitious not only in the extraordinary sweep and power of its explanatory theory, its truth, but also in its actual historical achievement. Peter Laslett, no Marxist himself, has pointed out that the teachings of Marx 'have proved more successful than any other set of doctrines which the West has brought forth, swifter and more final in its conquest of the world than ever Christianity was.' Marxism's

---

* These are passages excerpted from the author's *Of Marxism and Indian Politics.*

explicit commitment and claim to truth is particularly significant today when, under cover of a seemingly scientific scepticism, and in different, more or less sophisticated, guises (including, most recently, 'the discourse theory') relativism in matters of truth or knowledge has emerged as a new orthodoxy among bourgeois philosophers and social scientists, and not among them alone. Theories abound today which, as Barrows Dunham has put it, 'preach paralysis—which tell us that we can't know or can't do.'

At the same time, Marxism is extraordinarily open, and very modest indeed in its claims, contrary to the conventional belief, the familiar caricature of Marxism as a rigid, closed system already in possession of 'the truth', a set of scriptures as it were—a caricature compounded of its opponents' distortions and nurtured by certain trend within Marxism itself. *De omnibus dubitandum* ('Doubt everything') was Marx's favourite methodological principle. And breaking sharply with the received tradition from Plato to Hegel, and in a truly remarkable statement for their age, the Darwinian age drunk with the achievements of science, or reason as they also called it, the founders of Marxism proclaimed: 'the generations which will put *us* right are likely to be far more numerous than those whose knowledge we...are in a position to correct;... the stage of knowledge which we have now reached is as little final as all that have preceded it.' Engels in fact specifically wished that their followers 'would not pick quotations from Marx or from him', as if from sacred texts, 'but would think as Marx would have thought in their place'. He had insisted that 'it was only in that sense that the word *Marxist* had any *raison d'etre*...

This scientific resilience, this openness to 'correction', is really the strength of Marxism and not its weakness, except to religious minds. Behind it lies an explicit assumption about the growth of human knowledge, about the continuous struggle of men and women to acquire a better, more true, understanding of the world. To question the signature of Marx in the course of this struggle, to seek to 'put *him* right' if need be, is not to deny Marx but to enter into the freedom of his Marxism...

Marx was not a system builder, nor his Marxism a positivist science. And it needs to be remembered that his theoretical work is, in a most important sense, 'an unfinished project'. So much of what Marx expressely wished to write to ensure a clearer or fuller understanding of his ideas—for example, on philosophy (Hegel), or political theory (the State), or at least 'two or three printer's sheets' on method (Dialectics), and much else—remained simply unwritten. Part of the explanation lies in the inescapable, near-exclusive, concern of the mature Marx with his work on 'Economics' as he called it, which yet remained unfinished... More specifically, Marx's treatment of politics, ethics, literature, culture, in fact of the realm of the non-economic in general, remained largely *untheorised* by him. Quite understandably, therefore, Marxism has its limitations and inadequacies, its ambiguities and 'silences' or 'empty spaces'; there are many loose threads, the argument often yielding large questions, rather than providing neat answers... This is indeed as it should be. Yet, it needs to be recognised that most critiques of Marxism are simply nihilistic, born of an implicit, utterly unscientific, 'all-or-nothing' attitude. For the fact remains that Marx opened up the continent of social sciences, as Althusser stated it years ago. It is not merely that 'Marx's combination of insight and method permanently altered the manner in which reality would thereafter be perceived', as Heilbroner has argued more recently; it is that none has provided, so far, a better method of understanding this reality, the reality of society and historical processes. Marxism has gained for us knowledge of the structure and dynamics of social formations, past and present, particularly the contemporaneously dominant capitalist social formation, better than anything bourgeois social science has to offer...

As Marxism views it, society is not merely an aggregate or random togetherness of parts, factors, levels or instances. It is a social whole, or totality, a historically specific structured interdependence of parts, with an economic-structural base and loaded with contradictions that account for its dynamics, its concrete *over-determined* historical development. In other words, this determination, insofar as we must use the term, is neither unique, nor is it to be understood in any economic or class reductionist manner; it is something far mare complex and problematic, realised on an economic base, but through any number of interactions and mediations. The important point is that the parts, aspects or instances, generally referred to as superstructure, along with their contradictions, are not some epiphenomenal manifestations of the economic base. On the contrary, they may and often do have an autonomous, irreducible, historically specific existence of their own. But this is an existence of dialectical, determined and determining, relationships to each other and to the social whole. And the dynamics of this existence, the working out of their contradictions, is most decisively *conditioned* by the basic economic contradictions, the structural logic of the economic base. One might add, it is only within the necessities and constraints of the given objective, economic-structural situation, within 'this determination by the economic in the *first* instance', that whatever happens, including a revolutionary transformation of the economic-structure itself, is *ultimately* determined by the activity of men in pursuit of their ends...

Viewed thus, the political as a whole is the realm of the contingent, of historical conjunctures and changing balance of social forces, a realm of *real* choices and possibilities; and for that very reason devoid of the certainties and predictabilities that politics as 'social science' seeks. Yet, as suggested earlier, these choices and possibilities arise and exist *within* the necessities and constraints of the given objective situation, above all, the economic-structural situation, which sets their context, outer limits and parameters. The economic defines as it were the terrain, the 'conditions of existence', the horizon of the non-economic, including the political; without this emphasis on the role of 'the economy' Marxism would be theoretically indistinguishable from any other 'sociology'...

Within the framework of the reasonably adequate scientific generalisations that Marxism provides about the structure and dynamics of society (which encompass state and politics too), and within the more limited range of the necessities and possibilities of revolutionary and non-revolutionary practice of politics it suggests, we can, given the requisite data and delicacy of analysis, still make more or less valid, historically specific, explanatory statements about what is generally seen and understood to be *politics*. (Incidentally, 'political scientists' are still having a lot of problems with defining the object of their learned attentions). But this latter exercise possibly cannot add upto anything that can be legitimately called *science*. To phrase it a little differently, in politics as elsewhere, men and their choices, all the diverse factors, elements or variables, constituting as it were the *subjective* dimension of society, always a most vital part of social reality, are yet not calculable as the *objective* dimension is. In a famous passage, Marx himself drew attention to the *differing* amenability of the levels of *base* and *superstructure* in society to scientific treatment. Speaking of the historical transformations set off by the conflict between 'the material productive forces of society' and 'the existing relations of production,' involving both 'the economic foundation' and 'the entire immense superstructure,' Marx wrote: 'In considering such transformations, a distinction should always be made between the material transformation of the economic conditions of production, which can be determined with the precision of natural science, and the legal, political, religious, aesthetic or philosophic—in short, ideological forms in which men become conscious of this conflict and fight it out.' Obviously, this fight and its outcome cannot be determined 'with the precision of natural science.' Elsewhere, even as he insists that 'the history of all hitherto existing society is the history of class struggle,' Marx immediately points out that this struggle 'each time ended, either in a revolutionary reconstitution of society at large, or in the common ruin of the contending classes.' There are thus no promises of inevitability or guarantees of victory in Karl Marx's politics, only *strong* probabilities and *real* possibilities. Men and women choose and act, but the outcome, the outcome of concrete historical class struggles, is not predetermined, cannot be predicted in advance, least of all with the certainty of natural science. Thus understood, the historical process, in a most meaningful sense, remains open, relatively undetermined. It shall be *ultimately* determined by the activity of men in pursuit of *their* purposes, an activity in which men continually seek to materialise their freedom...

It needs to be emphasized that Marxism is social science not for peers or for policy-makers; it is social science at the service of the people, the exploited and the oppressed. And insofar as it seeks knowledge of a social formation as a whole, add recognizes the decisive importance of its 'economic basis' or structural necessity, it carries with it the imperative, the *other* necessity, that Marxist, political practice be revolutionary. It is not for nothing that Marx insisted: 'the working class is revolutionary or it is nothing'. ...

Marx's scientific and revolutionary projects are not merely interconnected, they grow into each other and together they put politics at the centre of social practice for our times. (At least that is how Marx understood it and one may legitimately note a divergence between Marxism as Marx himself practised it and a certain kind of contemporary Marxist scholarship). Given a Marxist understanding of the structured nature of the totality and the crucial role of 'the economy' in it, any fundamental, revolutionary change in society involves as a necessary, though not sufficient, condition, a changing of .its economic structure, of its *real basis*—if I may, contrary to fashion and in a confession of 'orthodoxy' still use that much maligned concept. Hence the centrality of politics as *revolution in Marx*—'Revolution is the highest form of class struggle'. In this sense, the sense in which ' Marx was before all else a revolutionist', politics, not economics, has primacy in Marxism. And the obvious corollary is that in the absence of a revolutionary politics changing the economic-structural basis of society, the logic of its economic structure shall assert itself, all politics will remain super-structural in its *essential* nature and outcome. This is the basic, a determined and determining choice in politics, within which other, more or less important, choices occur. Such is the dialectics of economy and politics in the social science of Karl Marx...

To put the argument in more general terms, Marxism, as science, seeks knowledge of the necessity underlying the historical processes for enhancing the freedom for *praxis*, for not foreclosing but liberating human practice, for free choices by men, free not in some abstract or metaphysical sense, but in the only possible *human* sense of men choosing and acting with the fullest possible knowledge and consideration of this necessity, the objective situation or circumstances. Such is the dialectics of men and circumstances, freedom and necessity, of revolution and science in Karl Marx. Moreover, it is of the nature of the structured and changing character of the social process that the relation between freedom and necessity, the ratio between them, varies from one period to another in the development of society. And taking everything into consideration, it seems to me that ours is pre-eminently an age of freedom, of revolutionary praxis. The altenative is mankind's rapid descent into another age of barbarism....

7

Of Marxism Today*

We do not set ourselves up against the world in doctrinaire fashion with a new principle: Here is the truth! There you must kneel! We develop new principles for the world out of the principles of the existing world...

It is the great advantage of the new movement that we do not seek to anticipate the new world dogmatically, but rather to discover it in the criticism of the old... It is not our task to build up the future in advance and to settle all problems for all time; our task is ruthless criticism of everything that exists, ruthless in the sense that the criticism will not shrink either from its own conclusions or from conflict with the powers that be...

KARL MARX

In humankind's centuries-old effort to understand society and to change it for the better on the basis of this understanding, Marxism is possibly the most ambitious and yet a genuinely modest exercise, so far. It is ambitious not only in the extraordinary sweep and power of its explanatory theory, its truth, but also in its actual historical achievement. Peter Laslett, no Marxist himself, has pointed out that the teachings of Marx 'have proved more successful than any other set of doctrines which the West has brought forth, swifter and more final in its conquest of the world than ever Christianity was.' Marxism's explicit commitment and claim to truth is particularly significant today when, under cover of a seemingly scientific scepticism,

---

* Excerpt from the preface for a friend's forthcoming book, introducing Marxism.

and in different, more or less sophisticated, guises (including, most recently, 'the discourse theory'), relativism in matters of truth or knowledge has emerged as a new orthodoxy among bourgeois philosophers and social scientists, and not among them alone. Theories abound today which, as Barrows Dunham has put it, 'preach paralysis—which tell us that we can't know and can't do.'

At the same time, Marxism is extraordinarily open, and very modest indeed in its claims, contrary to the conventional belief, the familiar caricature of Marxism as a rigid, closed system already in possession of 'the truth', a set of scriptures as it were—a caricature compounded of its opponents' distortions and nurtured by certain trends within Marxism itself. *De Omnibus dubitandum* ('Doubt everything') was Marx's favourite methodological principle. And breaking sharply with the received tradition from Plato to Hegel, and in a truly remarkable statement for their age, the Darwinian age drunk with the achievements of science, or reason as they also called it, the founders of Marxism proclaimed: 'the generations which will put *us* right are likely to be far more numerous than those whose knowledge we... are in a position to correct; ...the stage of knowledge which we have now reached is as little final as all that have preceded it.' Engels in fact specifically wished that their followers 'would not pick quotations from Marx or from him', as if from sacred texts, 'but would think as Marx would have thought in their place'. He had insisted that 'it was only in that sense that the word *Marxist* had any *raison d'etre...*'

This scientific resilience, this openness to 'correction', is really the strength of Marxism and not its weakness, except to religious minds. Behind it lies an explicit assumption about the growth of human knowledge, about the continuous struggle of men and women to acquire a better, more true, understanding of the world. To question the signature of Marx in the course of this struggle, to seek to 'put *him* right' if need be, is not to deny Marx but to enter into the freedom of his Marxism.

But Marx has been subjected to a questioning and denial of another, essentially nihilistic, sort. History of Marxism is well illustrative of Hobbe's observation that if geometrical axioms were to be 'a thing contrary to any man's right of dominion, or to the interest of men that have dominion', even these would be, if not disputed, certainly sought to be suppressed—if necessary 'by the burning of all books of geometry'! Marxism arose as a challenge to all the established authorities—economic and political, intellectual, ideological or academic. It is not surprising, therefore, that they all reacted with hostility. Hence the continuous effort to ignore Marxism, to denigrate and distort it, to 'refute,' 'reject' and 'dismiss' it, and the periodic announcements of its death and final demise over the last hundred years and more. But Marxism has not merely survived, it has succeeded to an unusual degree to achieve, across all barriers, a genuinely global presence and influence, compelling even so hostile a critic as Leopold Schwarzschild to write: 'if a name had to be found for the age in which we live, we might safely call it the Marxian era'. Marxism has indeed become, as Sartre once put it, the 'necessary' philosophy of our time. Significantly enough, Marxism is even paying the penalty for its 'success'—namely, its cooptation by alien elements. It is not so much a question of the rapidly spreading, confused and confusing, use of Marxian language, categories and concepts in bourgeois social and political theory. Really significant is the fact that so much of what goes by the name of Marxism nowadays has little or nothing to do with Marxism as Marx himself understood or practised it. Witness, for example, 'the theoreticist deluge' of academic Marxism in the West in recent years; or, more specifically, the fast flourishing theoretical school called 'post-Marxism', which has, in the name of openness, of updating Marx's supposedly antiquated method and theories, virtually abandoned, via diverse routes or forms ('Analytical' or 'Neoclassical' or 'Game-Theoretic' or 'Rational Choice' Marxism, etc.), even the basic or 'central' Marxist positions. It may have served to light up and clarify many issues, but it has certainly defused Marxism of its revolutionary content and transformed it into so many safe, academic exercises. Why so many of the scholars involved still insist on describing themselves as Marxists—even if only of some qualified 'post-

Marxist' variety—is, obviously, not an intellectual matter only. It is far more a matter of social history, as Hal Draper has argued. It certainly indicates an awareness of the intellectual and moral authority Marxism continues to enjoy despite its many enemies and critics, 'funereal,' or any other. Besides, Norman Geras has suggested, the 'post-Marxist' tag certainly has a nicer ring to ears than the alternative 'ex-Marxist'; it evokes the idea of forward movement, of 'going beyond', of 'an upto-the-minute thinker', rather than, as does the latter, of a change of colours, if not of downright renegacy itself!

Much of this Marxism is practised, as already mentioned, in the name of 'openness' as against 'orthodoxy'. Now, the value or importance of 'openness' is almost impossible to overrate today in view of the long and persistent tradition of a certain other practice of Marxism, which has been, 'officially' or otherwise, dogmatic and sectarian, 'economistic', 'deterministic' or 'scientistic', often reducing Marxism to a political catechism, the ossified 'commonsense' of the average Party cadre, or sanctifying it as the legitimising ideology of a movement or social order, especially in the countries of 'actually existing socialism' but elsewhere also, etc., etc. There is certainly a need for 'openness' in the context of all this and so much else that has disfigured and stultified Marxism in our times, resulting in repeated failures to respond effectively to the changing historical situations and to particular national conditions, as, for example, in India. But as Stuart Hall has pointed out, 'openness' is not a self-evident or self-validating good. And at a time when anything and everything claims the fashionable mantle of Marxism, and so many Marxists are busy revising it out of existence, a certain orthodoxy, a commitment to 'Marxism of Karl Marx', I believe, is not only in order, it is necessary, if one would take the issues of *socialist* theory and practice seriously.

This is not to deny that there are problems with the theory and practice of Marxism. Marx was not a system builder, nor his Marxism a positivist science. And it needs to be remembered that his theoretical work is, in a most important sense, 'an unfinished project'. So much of what Marx expressely wished to write to ensure a clearer or fuller understanding of his ideas —for example, on philosophy (Hegel), or political theory (the State), or at least 'two or three printer's sheets' on method (Dialectics), and much else—remained simply unwritten. Part of the explanation lies in the inescapable, near-exclusive, concern of the mature Marx with his work on 'Economics' as he called it, which yet remained unfinished, the high, exacting standards he set himself for any serious scholarly or theoretical work, intense practical activity and involvement with men, politics and movements the world over, besides long years of poverty, privation and ill-health, 'the humiliations, torments and terrors', the '*petites miseres* (small wretchednesses)', as Marx himself wrote, of the daily struggle for sheer physical survival, and always the demands, and still more the hazards, of the life of a revolutionary.... This apart, while we certainly have an authentic, even if somewhat partial, expression of the views of Marx, as of Engels, in works which were put out under the writer's own control, duly corrected and revised for publication, we do need to take note of *the specific nature* and therefore the precise *theoretical* status or quality of their other works, the early as well as the latter ones, which have come down to us, scattered and translated, over a long period of time. These include writings of all sorts: numerous articles and journalistic, even hack, pieces; addresses, proclamations, speeches and statements for particular occasions, situations or audiences; unpublished or unpublishable manuscripts, finished and unfinished or fragmentary; extensive correspondence with diverse addressees, obviously not intended for the eyes of others; private notes and workbooks, often in a personal 'shorthand' and meant only for the writer's own use later on, etc., etc. More specifically, Marx's treatment of politics, ethics, literature, culture, in fact of the realm of the non-economic in general, remained largely *untheorised* by him. Quite understandably, therefore, Marxism has its limitations and inadequacies, its ambiguities and 'silences' or 'empty spaces'; there are many loose threads, the argument often yielding large questions, rather than providing neat answers... This is indeed as it should be. Yet, it needs to be recognised that most critiques of Marxism are simply nihilistic, born of an implicit, utterly unscientific, 'all-or-nothing' attitude. For the fact remains that Marx opened up the continent of social sciences, as Althusser stated it years ago. It is not merely that 'Marx's combination of insight and method permanently altered the manner in which reality would thereafter be perceived', as Heilbroner has argued more recently; it is that none has provided, so far, a better method of understanding this reality, the reality of society and historical processes. Marxism, has gained for us knowledge of the structure and dynamics of social formations, past and present, particularly the contemporaneously dominant capitalist social formation, better than anything bourgeois social science has to offer. Given its powerful analytical method, it could even be, Macpherson has suggested, 'that the utility of Marxism as a means of understanding the world is increasing over time'—and 'the world' includes, I would like to make clear, not only the advanced capitalist countries or India and the so-called Third World, but the world of 'actually existing socialism' also, with its troublous past, continuing problems, and the truly historical predicament today.* And insofar as we really 'go beyond' Marx, we go with him and not against him or away from him.

---

* Incidentally, in a Marxist understanding of transitions between historical epochs the transition from capitalism—via 'socialism' which Marx never saw as a distinct form of society in its own right—to a communist civilization, is not to be viewed, nationally or internationally and at any stage, as a peaceful or unproblematic, unilinear process, free of contradictions and conflicts, social or class antagonisms, something impelled forward entirely by the forces of 'scientific and technological revolution'. On the contrary, in some ways comparable to the passage, through centuries, from the feudal to the capitalist civilization, though qualitatively different from it in its exceptional revolutionary character—'the most radical rupture' Marx called it—this transition is bound to involve, as it already has, even wars and civil wars, revolutions and counter-revolutions. In general, it should be viewed as a long period, contradictory and conflict-laden, 'the period', as Marx put it, 'of revolutionary transformation of the one (capitalism) into

Marxism, however, is not about understanding the world only, it is even more about changing it; it is about communism as human liberation, that is, men and women at last coming to appropriate the world with all their glorious *human* senses—or, as Marx himself described it, 'the *definitive* resolution of the antagonism between man and nature, and between man and man', indeed 'the realm of freedom... beyond the sphere of actual material production (where) begins that development of human energy which is an end in itself' . Hence the primacy of politics, not economics, in Marxism and the fact that Marx was, by vocation, a revolutionary. Philosopher, economist, historian, and so much else, Marx was indeed 'the man of science', said Engels. He had, however, immediately added: 'But this was not even half the man.... For Marx was before all else a revolutionist.... Fighting was his element. And he fought with a passion, a tenacity, and a success such as few could rival'. Indeed, it is this revolutionary, fighting commitment and a certain moral passion that goes with it, which gives its special quality to the life and work of Karl Marx, to *his* Marxism He recognised for himself and for others the liberating quality of practical activity, the purifying power of revolutionary action in transforming the very nature of those involved in it. I think Teodor Shanin is very right in insisting that revolutionary ethics was as central as his historiography to Marx's political judgement, and to the practice flowing from it. It is necessary to recover and emphasise this today when, in moving away from the 'economistic' or 'scientistic' images and versions of yester years, so many are seeking to turn Marx into an abstract savant or a humanist philosopher, and Marxism into a modern metaphysics or scholastic exercises in analytical philosophy.

---

the other (communism)', characterised at every stage by bitterly fought class struggles with their inevitable victories and defeats, retreats and advances, ups and downs of all sorts—provided, of course, that the irrationality of continued existence of capitalism does not in the meantime plunge mankind into a new barbarism, that of an ecological disaster, if not of a nuclear holocaust itself. The issue, indeed, remains 'socialism or barbarism'.

Marx would have dismissed it all with amused scorn, and he certainly would have had no difficulty in understanding all this. Very early, while at school, Marx had put 'working for humanity' at the centre of his values for life. Years later, speaking of Feuerbach's preoccupation with philosophy, he wrote to a friend that Feuerbach's weakness was that 'he refers too much to nature and too little to politics.' For Marx, on the other hand, philosophy had to be realised through politics, then and ever afterwards. This indeed is the meaning and message of his famous pronouncement: 'The philosophers have only *interpreted* the world, in various ways; the point is to *change* it. Politics, for Marx, is the cutting edge of this change, of any and every social revolution. Hence the primacy of politics, that is, revolutionary politics, in Marxism—at least in Marxism as Karl Marx understood it and practised it.

8

Politics—The Dialectics of Science and Revolution in Karl Marx*

Now, in whatever manner one describes or phrases this problem concerning Marx and politics, or Marxism's understanding or explanation of politics, a discussion in this area needs—among other considerations like the unfinished nature of Marx's theoretical work (especially as it affects politics), the intellectual ethos of his time, what he was arguing with or against, etc. –to take notice of two positions in Marxism, which are also integral to each other. These are Marx's absolute Promethean conception of man ('free, conscious activity is man's species character')[1] *and* his life-long commitment to revolution (a 'man of science... Marx was before all else a revolutionist'—Engels).[2] One implication is obvious. Marx's scientific project, the explanatory exercise, I suggest, fully accommodates these positions and thus leaves different areas of human activity, including politics, that are often loosely defined as 'non-economic' or 'non-material', relatively open, end undetermined in a manner as to be not entirely amenable to *law-like* generalisations, to *scientific explanation* as it is properly understood.

Marx's scientific project was focussed on understanding the society he wanted to overthrow; it is a reconstruction of the way capitalism as a system arises, functions and develops, and prepares the necessary, though not sufficient, objective conditions for a transition to the higher, more rational form of

* Excerpt from comments made at a seminar, *Teaching Politics* (1986).

society, a Communist society. In this scientific/explanatory enterprise, Marx's method is a model of the practice of materialist dialectics. Thus, the key concepts in his social-scientific theory involve viewing society as a whole, as a *totality* (complex and differentiated, a historically specific structured interdependence of parts), which is loaded by the predominance in the long run of one part within it, the economy ('the mode of production', and more precisely, *the economic structure*), and which is characterised by *contradictions* (principal or structural, and other equally specific secondary ones within and between the various parts) that account for its dynamics, its concrete *over-determined* historical development. Even as he emphasised the special role of the *economy*, 'the direct relationship of the owners of the conditions of production to the direct producers... which holds the inner-most secret, the hidden foundation of the entire social structure',[3]—without which emphasis Marxism would be theoretically indistinguishable from any other 'sociology'— and, more specifically, sought to lay bare 'the economic law of motion' of capitalism, Marx aimed at achieving through 'successive approximations' from different perspectives, a 'mirrored' version of the concrete reality of capitalist social formation as a whole. It is part of the story of Marx's unfinished project that, concerned with *all* of capitalism, he lived long enough to view it only from the vantage point of capitalist economics (even that incompletely). A fuller version or understanding would require that it be viewed from the vantage points of other parts also, of capitalist politics, ethics, ideology, culture, etc. Therefore, Marxian explanation of politics requires that, as against the fragmented and surface studies of contemporary political science, the problems of this area be handled in such a way as to illuminate the character of the capitalist system (including its politics) as a whole, in all its structured interconnections and movement—the whole shaping and expressing itself through the parts, and the parts, even as they represent and bear the signature of the whole, constituting, in their inter-relatedness, the specific unity that makes it a whole, *the* whole and no other. This goes for the study of any given social formation. For Marxism, 'the truth is the whole', as Hegel put it;[4] and in Marxism, as Marx insisted, one seeks to move from 'the appearance, the form' to 'the nature of thing.'[5] Such is the cardinal methodological thrust behind Marxism's social scientific enterprise, its search for dialectical knowledge as against positivist science.

This Marxist approach or perspective avoids the major *empiricist error* and the minor *holist error* characterizing most contemporary writing on politics within the discipline of political science and outside. (The former error, found typically on the Right, lies in grasping things only in their appearance and isolation, while the latter error, found typically on the Left, lies in missing out on the richness of the mediations that constitute the whole). Though not written as exercises in social science scholarship, one could draw attention in this connection to what are now rightly recognised as the *political* writings of Karl Marx: *The Class Struggles in France, The Civil War in France,* etc., and above all *The Eighteenth Brumaire of Louis Bonaparte* which is a model, as it were, of the treatment of politics in Marxism. Here we have, along with a wealth of other insights, Marx's full recognition and masterly exposition, in a Marxian perspective, that is, *within* the objective conditions structurally constituted by the prevalent mode of production, of the realm of the political, of the class struggle at the level of politics—at a particular juncture in the history of France. Though one must add that just as Marx's proposed work on *The State* never came to be written, Marx's treatment of politics, as of the realm of the non-economic in general, remained largely *untheorised* by him.

In this context, the phrase 'relative autonomy of politics', its value against economic and class reductionism apart, *could* be more misleading than helpful in understanding or explaining politics in a given social formation; it easily tends to give rise to mutually reinforcing empiricist and liberal-reformist errors. On the other hand, 'relative autonomy of the state' is a meaningful concept denoting as it does state's *possible* autonomy in a particular historical situation, from any given class or classes, economically dominant or otherwise. However, the state is not autonomous from the socio-economic structure of a class-divided society which it essentially serves. The state remains, always, the organiser of society in the interests of the class (exploitative) structure as a whole.[6]

Marx's scientific and revolutionary projects are not merely interconnected, they grow into each other and together they put politics at the centre of social practice for our times. (At least that is how Marx understood it and one may legitimately note a divergence between Marxism as Marx himself practised it and a certain kind of contemporary Marxist scholarship). Given a Marxist understanding of the structured nature of the totality, and the crucial role of 'the economy' in it, any fundamental, revolutionary change in a society involves as a necessary, though not sufficient, condition, a changing of its economic structure, of its *real basis*, if I may, contrary to fashion and in a confession of 'orthodoxy' still use that much-maligned concept. Hence the centrality of *politics* as *revolution* in Marx ('Revolution is the highest form of class struggle').[7] In this sense, the sense in which 'Marx was before all else a revolutionist', politics, not economics, has primacy in Marxism. And the obvious corollary is that in the absence of this revolutionary politics changing the structural base of society, the logic of this base shall assert itself, all politics will remain superstructural in its essential character and outcome. This is the basic, a determined and determining choice in politics, within which other, more or less important, choices occur. Such is the dialectics of the economy and politics in the social science of Karl Marx.

Viewed thus, the political as a whole is the realm of the contingent, of historical conjunctures and changing balance of social forces, a realm of *real* choices and possiblities; and for that very reason devoid of the certainties and predictabilities that politics as 'social science' seeks. Yet, as suggested earlier, these choices and possibilities arise and exist *within* the necessities and constraints of the given objective situation; above all, the economic-structural situation, which sets their context, outer limits and parameters. The economic defines as it were the terrain, the 'conditions of existence', the horizon of the non-economic, including the political. Though, it must again be stressed, it does not in a direct, or *reductionist* manner determine it. This determination, insofar as we must use the term, is far more complex and problematic, achieved through any number of mediations, horizontal, vertical and across each other. To put the argument differently, the superstructural instances, the parts or levels of the uneven and differentiated unity that a social formation is, along with the contradictions that characterize them, are not some immediate or epiphenomenal manifestations of the economic-structural base. On the contrary, they may and do have, each one of them, an autonomous, irreducible, and historically specific existence. But this is an existence of dialectical, determined and determining, relationships to each other and the whole. And the dynamics of this existence, the working out of their contradictions, is ultimately and most decisively conditioned by the structural logic of the given mode of production and the basic contradictions that constitute it. Thus, whatever happens, every complex historical effect or outcome, is 'over determined' in the Althusserian sense. As Marx himself put it: 'the concrete is the product of many determinations.'[8] Furthermore, for Marxism the working out of the structural necessity, the determination by the economic, is not unique. It is essentially a *correspondence* and, therefore, variable. For example, speaking of 'the political form of the sovereignty-dependency relationship,' *i.e.*, 'the specific form of the state', Marx wrote: '...due to innumerable different empirical circumstances, natural conditions, relationships among races (tribes, & c.), outside historical influences, etc., the same economic basis same in terms of the main conditions—can show endless variations and gradations in the phenomenon, which can be made out only by analysis of these empirically given circumstances.'[9]

It needs to be emphasised that Marxism is social science not for peers or for policy-makers; it is social science at the service of the people, the exploited and the oppressed. And insofar as it seeks knowledge of a social formation as a whole, and recognises the decisive importance of its 'economic basis' or structural necessity, it carries with it the imperative, the *other* necessity, that Marxist political practice be revolutionary. It is not for nothing that Marx insisted: 'the working class is revolutionary or it is nothing'.[10]

It is true that there are problems with the theory and practice of Marxism as social science. But it is also true that most critiques of Marxism in this area are simply nihilistic. Notwithstanding the limitations and inadequacies, even ambiguities, and the unfinished nature of his theoretical work, Marx did open up the continent of social sciences; and Marxism has provided better knowledge concerning the structure and dynamics of social formations, particularly the capitalist social formation, than anything bourgeois social science has to offer. Equally important is Marxism's explicit assumption about the *growth* of human knowledge. As Engels put it: 'the generations which will put *us* right are likely to be far more numerous than those whose knowledge we...are in a position to correct...the stage of knowledge which we have now reached is as little final as all that have preceded it.'[11]

Pursuit of Marxism as 'science', especially during certain phases of historical development, does tend to produce a loss of revolutionary perspective, its replacement by a complacent concern with 'the historical necessity' at work in the social process. Such, for example, was the Marxism dominant in the Second International; 'irresistable...natural necessity' having made socialism 'something *inevitable*' (Kautsky),[12] it simply turned its back on the other necessity, which is yet a free choice, namely, a revolutionary struggle for socialism. Lenin's repudiation of *this* Marxism was in the authentic tradition of Marx himself whose political theory and, still more, political practice throughout his life, never countenanced such deformation of Marxism into an evolutionist, deterministic metaphysics. At other times, a valid, Marxist recognition of the 'historically progressive' character of certain phenomena (men/women, movements, economic developments, etc.) has been deemed excuse enough to eulogize and extend support to them in a manner as to go soft on the exploiting classes, even to the point of rallying behind them in the name of Marxism. Marx would have none of such political opportunism either. It was on this issue that he, along with Engels, broke publicly with the Lassalleans in Germany and later (1881), apropos Russia, spoke with unconcealed scorn of 'Russian capitalism admirers.'[13]

(Apropos India, we may today well speak of 'Indian capitalism admirers', the apologists for 'progressive capitalism', 'independent capitalist development', 'selfreliant economic growth', 'independent economic/national development', etc.). Marx was always allergic to and contemptuous of such doctrinaire or, shall we say, 'scientific' Marxism. If Marx sought to discover the necessity underlying contemporary socio-historical process, it was to establish the objective context or terrain of his political struggle, and to define its revolutionary thrust; and when he recognised the historical progressiveness of certain roles or developments, it was as *fait accompli,* without approval but with all their advantages and drawbacks, so as to make the best possible use of the new starting points or opportunities provided by them for the prosecution of his own political purpose, his uncompromising struggle aimed at overthrowing the system of exloitation and oppression that is capitalism progressive', 'self-reliant' or any other. In this sense, Marx's practice of science was always subject to the logic of his political position, of the choice he had already made in the fight between the people and those who oppress and exploit them. And he had chosen to stand by the people. A political position for Marx was not a matter of scientific analysis—economic or social or historical; it was, always and above all, taking of sides in the on-going lass war.

To put the argument in more general terms, Marxism, as science, seeks knowledge of the necessity underlying the historical process for enhancing the freedom for *praxis,* for not foreclosing but liberating human practice, for freeer choices by men, free not in some abstract or metaphysical sense, but in the only possible *human* sense of men choosing and acting with the fullest possible knowledge and consideration of this necessity, the objective situation or circumstances. Such is the dialectics of men and circumstances, freedom and necessity, revolution and science in Karl Marx. Moreover, it is of the nature of the structured and changing character of the social process that the relation between freedom and necessity, the ratio between them, varies from one period to another in the development of society. And taking everything into consideration, it seems to me, that ours is pre-eminently an age of freedom, of revolutionary praxis. The alternative is mankind's rapid descent into another age of barbarism.

Within the framework of the reasonably adequate scientific generalisations that Marxism provides about the structure and dynamics of society (and which encompass state and politics also), and within the more limited range of the necessities and the possibilities of revolutionary and non-revolutionary practice of politics respectively, we can, given the requisite data and delicacy of analysis, still make more or less valid, historically specific, explanatory statements about what is generally seen and understood to be *politics*. (Incidentally, 'political scientist's are still having a lot of problems with defining the object of their learned attentions). But this latter exercise possibly cannot add up to anything that can be legitimately regarded as *science*. I have already suggested as much earlier on. To phrase it a little differently, in politics as elsewhere, men and their choices, all the diverse factors; elements, variables constituting, as it were, the *subjective* dimension 'of society, always a most vital part of social reality, are yet not are calculable as the *objective* dimension is. In a famous passage, Marx himself drew attention to the *differing* amenability of the levels of *base* and *superstructure* in society to scientific treatment. Speaking of the historical transformations set off by the conflict between 'the material productive forces of society' and 'the existing relations of production,' and invoving 'the economic foundation' and 'the entire immense superstructure,' Marx wrote: 'In considering such transformations, a distinction should always be made between the material transformation of the economic conditions of production, which can be determined with the precision of natural science, and the legal, political, religious, aesthetic or philosophic —in short, ideological forms in which men become conscious of this conflict and fight it out.'[14] Obviously, this fight and its outcome cannot be determined 'with the precision of natural science.' Elsewhere, even as he insists that 'the history of all hitherto existing society is the history of class struggle,' Marx immediately points out that this struggle 'each time ended, either in a revolutionary reconstitution of society at large, or in the common ruin of the contending classes.'[15] There are thus no promises of inevitability or guarantees of victory in Karl Marx's politics, only *real* possibilities and *strong* probabilities, Men and women choose and act, but the outcome, the outcome of concrete historical class struggles, is not predetermined, cannot be predicted in advance, least of all with the certainty of natural science. Thus understood, the historical process, in a most meaningful sense, remains open, relatively undetermined. It shall be *ultimately* determined by the activity of men in pursuit of *their* purposes, an activity in which men continually seek to materialise their freedom. And it is quite possible and probable that some time in the course of this determination, politics itself shall wither away and with it the need for explaining politics, scientifically or otherwise.

All this may sound rather dismal to those in the profession who, subject to the 'functional rationality' permeating the discipline, are committed to the search for 'a science of politics'. But do we really want it to be otherwise? I think not. Especially so if *freedom* is indeed 'the essence of man' and if our prime commitment is for man, as indeed was the proud and passionate commitment of Marx who spoke of 'the categorical imperative to overthrow all conditions in which man is a humiliated, enslaved, despised and rejected being';[16] who laughed at 'the so-called "practical" men with their wisdom' and wrote: 'If one chose to be an ox, one could turn one's back on the sufferings of mankind and look after one's own skin';[17] who, writing to an old friend, expressed his contempt for the philistines who 'consider people like you and me immature fools who all this time have not been cured of their revolutionary fantasies';[18] and who, even as he argued that while 'people make their own history...they do not make it just as they please,'[19] and always warned against utopianism and Blanquism in the movement, yet stood up magnificently in defence of the Paris communards for 'storming heavens,'[20] and scorned the socialists who 'keep themselves within the limits of the logically presumable and of the permissible by the police'... [21]

I would like to conclude by pointing out, for whatever it is worth at this stage of the extreme 'specialization', 'professionalisation' and 'vocationalisation' of the social science disciplines, that it is this commitment that gives its special quality to the scholarship of Karl Marx. Typical of this 'man of science' is his response to the news of the great run his theories were then having in Czarist Russia. On December 14, 1882, Karl Marx, old, sick and dying, thus wrote to his daughter Laura Lafargue: 'Nowhere is my success more delightful to me; it gives me the satisfaction that I *damage* a power which, besides England, is the true bulwark of the old society' (*emphasis added*).

Yes, *damage* is the word. How much of even Marxist scholarship can claim this quality for itself today?*

REFERENCES

1. K. Marx, *Economic and Philosophic Manuscripts of 1844.*
2. F. Engels, *Speech at the Graveside of Karl Marx.*
3. K. Marx, *Capital,* Vol. III.
4. G.W.F. Hegel, *Phenomenology of Mind.*
5. K. Marx, *Capital,* Vol. III.
6. See Hal Draper, *Karl Marx's Theory of Revolution,* Vol. I, II, III, Monthly Review Prees, 1977+. This is possibly the most outstanding work to date on Marx's political theory including his theory of the State.
7. K. Marx, *Poverty of Philosophy.*
8. K. Marx, *Grundrisse, Introduction.*
9. K. Marx, *Capital,* Vol. III.
10. K. Marx's letter to F. Engels, 18 February, 1865.
11. F. Engels, *Anti-Duhring.*
12. Quoted by Lucio Colletti, 'Bernstein and The Marxism of The Second International' in *From Rousseau to Lenin,* Monthly Review Press, 1968.
13. 'Marx-Zasulich Correspondence' in Teodor Shanin, *Late Marx and the Russian Road, Part II,* Routledge Kegan and Paul, 1984.
14. K. Marx, *A Contribution to the Critique of Political Economy, Preface.*
15. K. Marx and F. Engles, *Manifesto of the Communist Party.*

---

* It is part of the sociology of Marxism that in recent years, so often, it has come to be reduced to a subject for academic study in the universities, with strong fragmentist, scholastic and theoreticist deformations; or as in the countries of 'actually existing socialism', and even elsewhere, to a legitimising ideology.

16. K. Marx, *A Contribution to the Critique of Hegel's Philosophy of Right.*
17. K. Marx's letter to S. Meyer, 30 April, 1867.
18. K. Marx's letter to J.P. Becker, 26 February, 1862.
19. K. Marx, *The Eighteenth Brumaire of Louis Bonaparte.*
20. K. Marx's letter to L. Kugelmann, 12 April, 1871; *The Civil War in France.*
21. K. Marx, *Critique of the Gotha Programme.*

PART III

STATE AND DEMOCRACY IN INDIA

History does nothing, *it* 'possesses no *immense wealth, it 'wages* no *battles'* . *It is* man—*real, living man—who does everything, who acts, possesses and fights; history is* nothing but *the activity of man, pursuing his aims.*

Men make their own history; but they do not make is just as they please; they do not make it under circumstances chosen by themselves, but under circumstances directy encountered, given and transmitted from the past.

World history would indeed be very easy to make, if the struggle were taken up only on condition of infallibly favourable chances.

Do not say that social movement excludes political movement. There is never a political movement which is not at the same time social.

It is only in an order of things in which there are no more classes and class antagonisms that social evolutions *will cease to be* political revolutions.

Marx

Without revolutionary theory there can be no revolutionary movement.

Lenin

Marxism is above all a method of analysis—not analysis of texts, but analysis of social relations.

Trotsky

9

Of Reservations*: A View from the Far-Left

The issue of job reservation for the Other Backward Classes (OBCs) and the agitations around it have, for the time being at least, swamped about everything in large, mostly northern parts of the country, pushing even the Gulf crisis into second place in the concerns of our people, especially the ruling elite and the intelligentsia allied with it. 'Are you for reservations or against?' is the question flung at you everywhere; and it is very much a loaded question which, however you answer it, leaves you looking damned—and so many seek an opportunist escape from their 'yes' or 'no' with a qualifying 'but...' Yet another example indeed of how the dominant bourgeois politics has come to define and pre-empt the terrain of political debate and action in contemporary India. Even the Left is busy answering *this* question, and in a manner *they* want it, and then trying to save its face, whatever Left-face it is still left with, by invoking the essentially farcical notion of 'economic criteria', etc.

During those heady, rebel days in the late sixties, students of Paris used to ask of everyone who would address them: 'Where do you speak from?' A necessary question when in our argumentation, almost always and in everything, so much is most illegitimately taken for granted, so much done to obscure

---

* Speech at a symposium, Lady Shri Ram College, New Delhi, August 1990.

that there are other, different ways of looking at things. I learnt to answer this question very early in my academic career when I discovered that I was perhaps the only teacher with a 'bias' at Delhi University—the others were assumed to be objective, impartial, truly academic simply because they were not even aware of this question. I mention this because the sharpest, at times almost hysterical, criticism of the new policy has come from those speaking from the standpoint of a most uncritical nationalism, and as if no other standpoint is possible. At stake, we are told, is 'the very future of India as a nation'. The new policy is 'an assault on Indian nationalism'. It will 'legitimise caste and perpetuate it', 'divide and disrupt our national polity', *mandalise* it—yes, that is the word for the impending disaster. The 'nationalist edifice' built through painstaking efforts of the 'founding fathers' and others, over these forty long years and more, will be destroyed. 'Subversion of public institutions' will be accompanied by a reversal of 'India's march to a modern nationhood', setting it instead on the road to become 'a nation of backwards', etc, etc. We simply cannot afford it!

A plausible argument for such a standpoint, and *seemingly* quite persuasive. Seemingly, because having lived reasonably happily with caste all these years, its hideous reality in rural India notwithstanding, and having equally happily countenanced its manipulation in the political practice of the ruling classes and the social scientific analyses of its scholars, the nationalist elite or intelligentsia are arguing as if caste or casteism is something just invented by the Mandal Commission or V.P. Singh. Seemingly also because the argument proceeds entirely oblivious of the fact that even without the OBCs coming in, over these years, our public institutions have come to be well and properly subverted and the Indian polity dangerously divided and fragmented. Indian capitalism, with its structural logic, has already caused 'a corrosive dualism' and produced 'two nations' in our society that scholars of the eminence of V.K.R.V. Rao, K.N. Raj and Sukhomoy Chakrabarty have written of; it has exacerbated all the old divides and fissures and, given its somewhat lumpen-comprador character, generated a whose lot of explosive material which is today lying all around us, especially in the urban areas. And ruling class politics, its leadership increasingly inept and opportunist in recent years, has been busy, as it were, doing nothing but turning issues into problems and problems into one tragic crisis after another. With the current controversy we are witness to yet another issue erupting as a crisis, yet another fissure in our society becoming still more of a running sore. Not something entirely unexpected. Only three years back, apropos the 'Punjab problem', I had pointed out: 'It is fashionable these days to speak of India as "a nation-in-the-making". One might add that if you leave it to the ruling classes, India may well be on its way to be "a nation-in-the-unmaking".'

This is only to suggest that there is a different, better standpoint for looking at things—from below and not from above. Better because it is more truthful, more revealing of the situation in our country, the Mandal Commission and all that. We need to look beyond 'the nation' at the Indian people, at what India's *national* economy and politics have done to our people at the end of these forty-three years. For that is how Punjab and Kashmir and a myriad other problems of our polity have come to be. That is how only the other day a Rajiv Gandhi thought nothing of using the divisive potential of communalism, enacting the Muslim Women's Bill on the one hand and unlocking the Ram Janmabhoomi-Babri Masjid complex and *shilanyas* at Ayodhya on the other, for petty political purposes—of course in the name of 'secularism', of *'sarva dharma sambhav'* and 'communal amity'! And now, a V.P. Singh has no compunction in trying to tap the divisive potential of casteism, with Mandal's Report and OBC reservations, for purposes which are no different or better—only the plea this time is 'social justice', it is 'helping the poor' and 'duty to the downtrodden'! Needless to add, the victims all the time are precisely these 'poor and downtrodden', of all communities and castes, so much in the news these days, who have not so far found a place or representation either in 'our national economy' or in 'our national politics' except as objects of exploitation and manipulation, barring where they have learnt to stand up and struggle for their own interests.

'The truth is the whole,' Hegel had insisted. Facts and arguments about the Mandal Commission, its report and recommendations, are now well-known and they hold together. The important thing is to know *how* they hold together, they are part of which larger story. Apart from what I have already stated about Indian economy and politics, I would like to offer, very briefly again, a few additional considerations which I believe go into constituting 'the whole' which is this job-reservations story. You can surely add some more and establish the interconnections yourself.

All 'compensatory opportunity' or 'affirmative action' by way of reservations involves discrimination against others, and this discrimination, however justified, invariably gives rise to resentment among them, to a certain sense of injustice. When reservations were first provided for the Scheduled Castes and Scheduled Tribes, forty years ago, it was a different India altogether. The sense of injustice involved was, *then*, easily bearable. There was the elan born of a successful freedom struggle, notwithstanding the partition and other problems with the settlement of 1947. A general hopefulness about the future was combined with the extraordinary legitimacy of the new rulers who had a certain vision and whose promises about this future, as embodied in the Indian Constitution, were widely trusted. And there was an universal, almost guilty, recognition of the injury, oppression and exploitation which the Scheduled Castes and Scheduled Tribes had collectively suffered over the centuries, which justified measures of special consideration for them. The reservations were, therefore, easily acceptable, especially so when they were stated and believed to be only a short from affair.

This acceptability, however, has been declining over time. And now, forty years later, the situation is entirely different. Even as dreams and hopes of those early years have all but vanished for most Indians, the rulers have lost their vision and are not left with much legitimacy either that could entitle them to demand sacrifices of others. There is widespread cynicism and hopelessness about the future and an youth ever haunted by the spectre of unemployment—there is frustration and despair, and much ignorant, impotent anger. And among the beneficiaries of the new reservation policy, those likely to corner its benefits, are the economically better-off, locally dominant sections of the OBCs who, far from being victims of any collective oppression, are today themselves oppressors and exploiters of the rural poor, notorious for committing the worst atrocities against landless scheduled caste labourers and others.

Understandably, therefore, the resentment and the sense of injustice this time is deep and, to put it mildly, far less bearable. It has in fact exploded in a spontaneous protest of massive proportions, especially in the north, on the part of those directly affected in an adverse manner—the students and the educated urban youth. And the protest has continued unabated, even if its future is uncertain. Devoid, so far, of any larger vision or ideological perspective, often far from healthy and at times blatanly casteist, mostly urban and unorganised and therefore more open and vulnerable to lumpen, anti-social, and questionable political elements, the protest is yet, in its own way, legitimate and, whatever its inherent limitations or ultimate outcome, threatens to leave behind, as I have already mentioned, yet another running sore in our polity. The implementation of the earlier policy has been called into question and, with a few, even the principle of job reservation itself. And the logic of the anti-reservationist argument today is no worse than that of the reservationist, now or over the years—even the much canvassed argument, that in view of the limited number of jobs involved the real benefits or stakes are 'psychological' and not substantive, whatever its validity, has begun to work for both sides.

This is a fact of some importance. Given the nature of the immediate issue, a contention over job-reservations in a situation of shrinking job opportunities, and given also the dismal quality of thought and action on both sides and the competitive ethos—'war of everyone against everyone' is how Hobbes described it—of our possessive market society, and a poor one at that, the current contention brings to mind an observation Marx once made, of course, in a different context. 'Between two equal rights,' he had said, 'force decides.' But a decision in this case, whatever it is, will resolve no real problem, this contention can only be debilitatory of 'the system', however one defines it.

Reservationist enthusiasts have been hyperbolic about 'a fight between the rich and the poor', the 'risks', 'necessary costs' of 'social revolution', etc. More modestly, they have sought to see the contention as something akin to class war, if not class war itself—and a certain learned but laboured theorising has not been wanting which insists on presenting it as a distinctive 'Indian form of class conflict'. Now caste, with its social, economic and ideological aspects a most important part of Indian social reality, certainly has a very significant class dimension to it. But it is well to recognise that, whatever other problems we may have with the concept of class, it is an economic structural concept, and class struggle, with the requisite class consciousness, aims at an economic restructuring; its successful outcome, a genuine social revolution, resolves the basic economic structural contradictions of society, opening the way to its further progress. Notwithstanding a certain caste class overlap in our society, a caste and caste consciousness-determined conflict has no such possibilities at all. Even of class struggle Marx had pointed out in *Communist Manifesto* that it can end 'either in a revolutionary reconstitution of society at large, or in the common ruin of the contending classes'. With the current contention, the first possibility simply does not exist; there is only the certainty of a 'common ruin' insofar as real issues or basic contradictions are displaced or distorted, consciousness further corrupted, and a radical restructuring of society which alone could ensure jobs for all prevented from becoming what is should be, the key concern of the thought and action of the contending youth on either side.

There is logic on both sides, but also a great deal more of cant and hypocrisy and self-deceiving rhetoric—around 'social justice' etc. in one case and 'merit and efficiency' etc. in the other.

Reservations over these forty years have hardly provided much social justice to the masses of the poor and oppressed among the Scheduled Castes and Scheduled Tribes in our country. A small, better-off and influential section among them, monopolising the benefits available, has established itself as a self-perpetuating elite which, even as it has *moved up* in society, given the dominant ethos of this society, also *moved away* from its own people, but without giving up their use and manipulation to further promote its own interests, in politics and elsewhere. As public servants, being 'more representative' has not made its members any more responsive to the needs of the people, their own or any other. Reservations have ended up only as an exercise in *tokenism* which, benefitting a few at the top, leaves the vast masses below worse off than before, but facilitates their cooptation into the system and their availability as a political constituency for the concerned elite. The vast masses of the Scheduled Castes and Scheduled Tribes are worse off because, being among the poorest and most oppressed, but thus coopted and therefore disarmed ideologically and politically, they continue to remain the worst victims of the oppressive and exploitative logic of the socio-economic development in our country. For the ruling classes as a whole, this *tokenism* has served well as an easy device, very cheap and safe too, to secure a certain legitimacy for themselves, collect votes from time to time and, perhaps, salvage some of their conscience as well. This has been the experience with such policies, always and everywhere. There is no reason, none at all, why it should be any different with the new policy of job reservations for the OBCs.

I would like to add that over the years such policies have provided an excellent alibi for the ruling classes to avoid carrying out those *other* promises that free India's Constitution made to our people forty years ago, which would have given real relief to the vast masses of our Scheduled Castes, Scheduled Tribes and the poorer OBCs. I am not here referring to the tall propositions of the Preamble and the Directive Principles of State Policy—that at any time would be expecting too much of our post-Independence rulers. I have in mind much simpler things like effective land and tenancy reforms and protection of the tribals' right to land and forest, abolition of bondage and implementation of minimum wage laws, universal elementary education and adult literacy, ban on child labour, minimum of shelter and health services in the rural areas including safe drinking water in every village, a firm and honest execution of anti-poverty programmes, etc., etc. Such a programme or practice would have not only directly improved the living conditions of the common people in our villages and elsewhere but also enabled a larger number from among the disadvantaged groups to gain even from the reservation or similar policies of 'affirmative action'.

It should be obvious that I am not arguing against such policies. Welcome even as gestures or *tokenism*, their positive effect is not to be denied, they do make for certain economic and even more social gains, however limited or marginal these may be. I have only sought to suggest their inadequacy as well as essential nature even as a partial answer to the problems of the poor and oppressed in our society, or as a means of dispensing social justice to the tong deprived and disadvantaged sections of our people. And implicit in my argument is also a plea for so reviewing and rationalising these policies that, even within their limitations, they are more effective and benefit a larger number of those concerned. Incidentally, a thought persists: if reservations are indeed *the* answer and the means, what of women who undeniably, in their overwhelmingly large numbers, are the most oppressed and disadvantaged section of our society? The new reservation policy may well leave them still more disadvantaged.

With the anti-reservationists the rhetoric has been over 'the principle of equality of opportunity', 'merit and efficiency', the issue being, *a la* Kaka Kalelkar, not job for someone but 'the service to be performed', etc., etc. And they certainly seem to have succeeded in persuading themselves. In any case it is gratifying to see the dear old liberal elite and its intelligentsia recall 'principles' even if it is a bit late in the life of our republic—a bit late, for so many of these principles appear to have been lost somewhere along the way during these forty three years of freedom and 'nation-building'. Equally gratifying, incidentally, is the sight of liberal scholars discovering, after their decades-long affair with 'modernity' that was caste, some merit at least in class—they call it 'economic criteria' these days.

'Equality of opportunity' in a caste and class-divided, increasingly inegalitarian society? —the notion is simply impossible to sustain. Again, in such a society, 'merit' is a questionable quantity even at the best of times. Now, with widespread corruption and nepotism, venality and sundry manipulations, it has been for long only an euphemism for self-perpetuating privilege and private aggrandisement. Many of the 'meritorious' have never heard of idealism and, once in service, the growing ignorance and illiteracy soon come to be covered up and well-sustained by the smugness and conceit of the arrived. 'Efficiency', when not merely routine bureaucratic functioning, is mostly self-serving or practised in the service of the powers that be. A job is not merely a job any more, far less 'the service to be performed'. It has become a means of what has been well-described as 'rapid private accumulation'. And surely 'the public servant' has something to do with the increasing use of 'state as private property' in India too, much in the manner of many third world countries. Besides, who does not know of the nexus between the civil servant, the businessman and the politician, with the criminal chipping in at the appropriate level, often at the level of the politician and that other well-known 'public servant', the police. And it is the common people who are invariably at the receiving end. For them the public servant combines his callousness with arrogance of power and all pervasive corruption. It is a Rajiv Gandhi who has informed us—and he should know for it is his party which has ruled this country most of the time since that early 'tryst with destiny'—that even of the funds allocated for direct poverty alleviation, eightyfive per cent have never reached the people. Some 'leakage' this on the part of our public servant and his cronies! Liberal rhetoric notwithstanding, the fact is that like the Indian economy, the Indian state too has been anti-people. Far from being a solution to anything, it is a part of almost every problem that our people face today. With new reservations, what the OBC elite is claiming is only its share of what is up for grabs here, private accumulation and all, an opportunity, at last, to also 'serve the people.' Who can deny it the right to make its contribution to the oppressive mess that the Indian state and our public services are today?

This is not to argue that 'merit', 'efficiency' or 'competence,' or 'the service to be performed,' etc. are no consideration at all. It is only a plea for less cant and hypocrisy on the subject, and for recovering at least some of these lost principles and putting them at the service of our people, if possible. And a certain possibility is always there—there are no dead-end situations in real life, ever. Besides, to argue in more theoretical terms, its class character notwithstanding, the modern state is yet an arena of class struggle, an arena for intervention on behalf of the people. Thus, even today, within the present state-system in India, there are men and women of great ability who, still honest, idealistic and dedicated, really serve, and try to stand by the people. I know, for I have known some of them since they were my students at Delhi University. I will only add that most of them do not belong to the Scheduled Castes, Scheduled Tribes or OBCs. Honesty, idealism or dedication, holding on to principles or sensitivity for human considerations, are not a matter of birth or caste. The essential correlations here lie almost entirely elsewhere.

Incidentally, far too many reservationist luminaries, Prime Minister V.P. Singh downwards, have been making light of the issue of efficiency or professional competence. Oftentime they have done it as part of their spurious radical rhetoric, a certain populist myth making about the 'deprived' and the 'downtrodden', which, incidentally, many on the Left, who should know better, also indulge in. This mythmaking, however, is not my concern just now. Only the issue of competence is. And here it will not be out of place to mention a proposal made by people who are knowledgeable about these things. If questionable in some ways, the proposal is not, at the moment, without its merit either. We are told that it is these ministers and sundry other VIPs who virtually monopolise the limited facilities at the All India Institute of Medical Sciences and other reputable hospitals at Delhi. It is proposed that henceforth let there be one exclusive hospital, meant only for them. And it should be staffed entirely by those who have come in or up via the reservation quotas!

A while ago I had spoken of 'the OBC elite', and this is an important part of the larger story of the contention over job-reservations today. As already noticed, among the beneficiaries of the new reservation policy are certian sections of the OBCs—the upwardly mobile intermediate castes—who have gained much from India's development process, especially its zamindari abolition, green revolution, and other state-subsidised policies in the agricultural sector. As new-rich peasants, they constitute a part of the emerging class of *kulaks*, who are today a powerful, aggressive social force in large parts of the country, particularly the north, with much economic and muscle power, though without much inhibition or scruples about its use, and possessing the ability to mobilise a large caste-class constituency for electoral and other purposes. First emerging at the state-level power structure in 1967, they have now, after a brief stint around 1977, finally arrived at the centre of political power in the Indian Union with the elections of 1989-90. They are naturally desirous of consolidating their economic and political power and pursuing their interests more effectively by securing a grip on the Indian state, its organs of governance and various public services. The Indian state has certainly served their class interests well, so far, as it has served even better, the interests of the exploiting classes in the industrial or business sector, together with those of the associated professionals, politicians and others—the major beneficiaries of the present social and economic order. Having arrived at the Centre by virtue of the extant democratic process, this class of rich peasants is now seeking a direct share in the power and the pie that is the Indian state today. For them, a section to begin with, reservations *a la* Mandal may serve as one bid, however weak and partial, to thus come *into* the administratives structure of the Indian state. Just as an anti-English campaign could be, in its own way, another. And more bids are likely, including the demand to include more of them in the list of OBCs.

If at one level the contention is over scarce jobs, at another, in the context of the conflict of interests *within* the classes dominant in our society, it is as if a new rural elite is challenging the position, power and privileges of the old, established, predominantly urban elite, which has administered this country since independence. The old elite is claimed to be 'national', 'pan-Indian', 'enlightened', 'secular', 'liberal', and so on. But, the veneer may be there and a certain outward sophistication, these values find little genuine expression in its public performance or treatment of the people. The new claimant is being denounced as 'casteist', 'parochial', 'obscurantist', 'communal', 'socially reactionary', and so on. But, true or not, this is hardly likely to make much difference so far as the common people are concerned.

I wish we had other choices. This lack of choice in fact points to a most singificant aspect of the contemporary situation in our country. I had hinted at it right at the beginning of this presentation. It is a mark of the dominance of the ruling class politics in India over these forty years—after an early, much confused, Communist protest and the surrender and suppression of the great Telengana struggle—that it has always succeeded in effectively defining and pre-empting the terrain of Indian politics, setting the parameters of intellectual discourse and political action, imposing its own issues and choices, concepts, language codes and forms of politics on others, in the process appropriating, marginalising, and suppressing whenever necessary, those of any kind of alternative radical or revolutionary politics, which has thus survived only at the fringes of Indian polity.

Once, during the golden age of the post-colonial state, 'the Nehru era', it was 'national development', 'parliamentary politics' and the 'nationalist discourse' ('nationalism', 'nation-building', 'we' and 'they', whoever *they* be, 'imperialism', Pakistan, etc.) which successfully appropriated even concepts like 'socialism' or 'social transformation' —completely obscuring the class character of the settlement of 1947 and the consequent reality of an India-specific *capitalist* development, and marginalisg all genuine radical or revolutionary thought and action. In the more recent, crisis-ridden period, while the old discourse and political practices have limped along—setting 'the agenda for the nation,' etc.—and 'Boat Club politics' has acquired a new importance, it has been, as defined by *them*, the ruling classes, terrorists versus the nation, secessionism or unity and integrity of India (accompanied by an unparalleled fetishism of the Constitution), communalism or secularism, violence or democratic politics, the National Front or the Congress-I, etc., etc. And now true to form the issue is reservation versus ant-reservation, which could be caste versus caste too, or, as with so many, caste versus the nation, and so on. Once again the issues or problems are so posed and argued as to rule out any alternative discourse or politics. The larger context and the deeper determinant interconnections of social reality are obscured, the issues or problems are dissociated from all considerations of class structure, class domination, or ruling class politics, pushing people out of the picture, along with all radical or revolutionary choices—they are simply not allowed to arise as real, historical passibilites. Thus pushed out, the people continue to pay the price of ruling class politics and suffer—in Punjab or Kashmir, through communalism or casteism, under the National Front government or that of the Congress-I, with reservations or without them, and, increasingly, even in 'democratic politics'. In a more lucid, obviously Marxist moment, Nehru had once spoken of 'terrible costs of not changing the existing order'. Today this is true in more ways than the one he had in mind when he said this.

In conclusion, what does one immediately suggest, and what does one hope for? It is obvious that politics is where the answer to the present crisis is to be found, as also the answers to the other problems besetting our society today; politics is indeed the arena of struggle for India's future. I believe that it is possible for the present-day rulers, as it is always possible for the ruling classes, to practice better politics, if only for their own sake—there is only *conditional* determinism here, but no inevitabilities. Therefore let them hold their hand on the Mandal Commission Report and seize the opportunity provided by this crisis to assess the experience so far and review the entire scheme of reservations to make it more effective, that is, more rational and just and, therefore, more beneficial for the groups concerned—and do this in the light of legitimate criticism and suggestions on issues like criteria, enumeration, entry, qualifications, promotions, dereservation, ceiling, etc., so that the resentment and the sense of injustice of the protesting students and youth becomes more bearable and the reservations more fair and easier to accept. Let these rulers, for a change, look beyond plain thinking and short-term gains, electoral or any other, and act according to some principles. Let them honour their own Constitution a little more to fulfil some at least of its *other* promises that I have spoken of earlier. They could well begin by taking serioulsy the reports of their Commissioner for Scheduled Castes and Scheduled Tribes, giving due recognition to the recommendations made therein and to their repeated indictment of the governments at the Centre and in the States for persistenly violating the letter and the spirit of the Indian Constitution. They must remember that, after all, in an important sense, it is still *their* system, so far. And it already has too many fissures become explosive, too many running sores, and has been much too badly damaged and subverted, institutionally and otherwise, in recent times. Let them eschew further damage and subversion, the adding of yet another running sore. This will make life a little easier for them, and for our people too. Though, I must add, it will also make the situation somewhat less unfavourable for the emergence of real, more basic issues, for a genuinely radical politics which our people are today desperately in need of.

Far those who represent or would practice this radical politics, the Left as it is called—I wish the protesting students and youth belonged here, but they don't, and this is their tragedy and part of the tragedy of the Indian people today—the present crisis provides yet another opportunity to undertake a serious self-critical review of its current theory and practice. Let it not remain content with operating on the terrain of bourgeois politics only, responding to the issues it presents, accepting the choices it offers, and succumbing to the corruption of consciousness all this involves, in the process not only getting marginalised again and again but also losing the revolutionary commitment and elan that defines it as Left. It is time the Left sought to establish and function on its own terrain, the terrain of independent class-based people's politics which, even as it confronts bourgeois politics on the latter's terrain, knows how to pose *its own issues, its own way*, before the people, present them with genuine choices, and, most important, organise them to fight around these issues, in defence of their own choices, for not some phoney electoral gains but real political advance.

A difficult task but not impossible. Possibilities are far more open today, and one always hopes. But if, for whatever reasons, the task is still deemed impossible, I can only respond, again with those rebel students of Paris who had insisted: 'Be a realist, attempt the impossible!' This is indeed what the situation demands. People must begin to take over from the ruling classes before it is too late.

10

Terrorism, State Terrorism and Democratic Rights*

It is a privilege for me to be addressing this inaugural session of the Seventh State Conference of the Andhra Pradesh Civil Liberties Committee (APCLC) at Karimnagar, home of the great Telengana Struggle which, regardless of what happened to it afterwards, yet has a message, and the promise of other possibilities, for the people still struggling for a better life in this country, in Andhra Pradesh and elsewhere. I have my memories of those youthful years as a full-time Communist activist. It is a privilege also because the APCLC is no longer just another civil liberties organisation; today it is a movement, a movement of exceptional significance, representing as it does an outstanding example of effective people's intervention in the life and politics of our country—all the more exceptional and significant for the paucity of its material resources and the heavy odds against which it has to work.

Not formally associated with any democratic rights organisation, I have admired your work from a distance, as have many others. And everywhere in this country your courage, commitment and struggle have been a source of inspiration to those actively engaged in defending people's democratic rights or civil liberties. Among them are friends in the People's Union for Democratic Rights at Delhi, who have specifically asked me to convey their fraternal greetings to this Conference.

---

* Inaugural address at the Seventh State Conference of the Andhra Pradesh Civil Liberties Committee, Karimnagar, April 1991.

You have been admired and sought to be emulated but, together with other democratic rights organisations; you have also been criticised and condemned. Even as the Indian state and ruling class politics have been rapidly degenerating into a lawful as well as lawless authoritarianism in recent years, especially repressive when people protest or seek to organise and struggle, thereby making the presence and work of democratic rights organisations all the more necessary and urgent, though more risky also, these organisations have come to be regularly reviled and run down, not only by the ruling elite or those manning its state apparatuses but also by others in all sorts of other places, especially the media.

The critics claim to be independent and impartial, above party, politics or classes; even more than 'law and order' they speak in the name of 'the nation', 'the unity and integrity of India.' It has become customary for them to refer to democratic rights organisations, with ill-concealed hostility and unease, as 'a nuisance', 'do-gooder groups', 'the self-styled do-gooders', 'so-called defenders of civil liberties', 'these worthy organisations', and so on. At other times these are protrayed, attacked or dismissed, as 'front organisations' —for 'anti-national forces', 'terrorists' or 'scessionists', or, as in case of the, APCLC, 'the Naxalites', etc.

I am not going to speak of the increasing importance, despite all the odds and all these critics, of your struggle in defence of democratic rights in our essentially undemocratically constituted society which, with its multiple crises, is daily becoming more undemocratic and oppressive for the people. There is more to learn from you here than to teach you. Nor is it for me to make a critical assessment of your work and offer suggestions—you are in every way better placed and equipped to undertake this exercise, and this is indeed what you shall be doing at this Conference. As a concerned citizen who believes that the issues of Terrorism, State Terrorism and Democratic Rights involve us all, today more than ever before, even if in apparently different ways, I shall be content to make a few observations on *how to think* about these issues, in the hope that a little more clarity here may lend a little more effectiveness to our struggle in defence of people's democratic rights. If there is something of the teacher or the academic about my argument, I can only ask you to overlook it as an occupational hazard, for this is how I have mainly functioned over the last forty years and more. Though, I would like to reassure you, it is not going to be an academic' or 'scholarly' exercise. I shall try not to be boring and I shall also avoid the jargon, the 'ifs' and 'buts', the Aesopian or 'now black, now white' manners of expression that sophistication in academic scholarship seems to entail these days. I will try to speak as simply and clearly as possible for I do want to be understood.

Mine will be in fact a straight forward political and partisan exercise in the sense that in a class divided, exploitative society like ours all worth while thinking *is*, inevitably as it were, political and partisan. In such a society, on all important issues, in philosophy as in real life, neutrality is an illusion. Here everything said or done, or left unsaid or undone, helps one side or the other. And so it is with the issues of terrorism and democratic rights. I will readily concede that what I am going to say is nothing new or original. If, nevertheless, I have considered this exercise worthwhile, and chosen to so speak today, I could perhaps, in justification, appeal to Goethe who had asserted: 'One must from time to time repeat what one believes in, proclaim what one agrees with and what one condemns'.

How does one think? The question is important, whatever the issue or the area of one's concern, because on this thinking, on the nature and adequacy of the understanding it provides, depends the nature and adequacy, the ultimate effectiveness, of how one acts in the matter. It is our diagnosis of a disease which determines its treatment. In the same way, it is our explanation or understanding of social reality, any aspect of it, which indicates the prescription, the necessary purposeful action on our part. An explanation thus always has a 'value-slope', it determines the prescription as well.

Bourgeois social science, seeking to become 'truly scientific', has often so debated this issue as to ignore or effectively deny this dependence or determination. It has in fact sought to drive a wedge between explanation and prescription, between 'facts' and 'values', and made much of the dogmas of 'value freedom' or 'ethical neutrality' in social scientific enterprise. (As George Catlin once put it: 'There is always a demand that the professor of the social sciences shall become a political eunuch'). Much of this debate has been a wasteful exercise, illustrative only of a certain philosophical illiteracy among the social scientists concerned. This is not the place or occasion to explore the philosophical or methodological issues involved in this debate, issues which are necessarily political also. I have written and spoken of these elsewhere. Here I will make only two points which are immediately relevant to my argument.

In the first place it needs to be recognised that the issue of democratic rights directly impinges upon human interests in our society, one way or the other. Therefore disputation and conflict over them should not be a matter of any surprise. Centuries ago, the English philosopher Thomas Hobbes had, with characteristic insight, pointed out that if geometrical axioms were to be 'a thing contrary to the interest of men that have dominion', even these would be 'if not disputed, yet by the burning of all books of geometry, suppressed, as far as he whom it concerned was able'. Hobbes' insight in fact goes deeper to touch on a problem at the very heart of social sciences: truth here is always partisan. Unlike the physical or natural sciences which are fairly neutral politically, the social sciences, concerned as they are with class-divided societies, are full of political dynamite.

Truth here is not only partisan but also dangerous for the dominant classes, for it tends to affect their interests adversely. Truth becomes a matter for disputation and, if need be, suppression and therefore also difficult to acquire. This is perhaps the most important reason—another, closely related to it, is its philosophical or methodological orientation—why so much of social science, far from being concerned with truth, is only so much *apologetics* for the established order, serving to secure or engineer the consent of men and women for it, which has led Noam Chomsky to describe its practitioners as 'a secular priesthood' and, given its increasingly esoteric sophistication, weired and unintelligible jargon —'socspeak', Malcolm Cowley called it—and often obscurantist ideological role in society, compelled Stanislav Andreski to even write of 'social sciences as sorcery'.

Be that as it may, our concern here is with democratic rights of the people. And the point is that they involve human interests, they do adversely affect the interests of those who have dominion in our society. Hence the disputation around them, and their attempted suppression by the powers that be, suppression of the truth historically embodied in democratic rights. So it has been in the past, and so it is today, in our own troubled times.

My second point is theoretically the more important one. If our explanation always has a 'value slope', if it is decisive in suggesting the prescription, the purposeful human intervention on our part, then, obviously, it matters *how* we generally go about explaining or understanding things. In other words, we need to be self-consciously aware of our philosophical or methodological orientation, or, if I may put it that way, aware of the 'philosophy' we have for coming to terms with the reality around us.

This indeed matters. It is this vital issue that the rebel students of Paris raised in the late sixties, when they asked of everyone who would speak to them: 'Where do you speak from?' They had well grasped the fact that everyone has a position to speak from, a philosophy so to speak, whether one knows or acknowledges it or not. Because everyone needs to have it to be able to live minimally as a human being.

To live postulates coping with the reality of the world around us. To cope or come to terms with this reality, to relate to it in an intelligent, purposive manner, we need to make sense of this reality. And this we do by explaining or understanding it as best as we may. Thus arise our most general ways of seeing and comprehending things, 'our more or less open, more or less clearly or consciously formulated assumptions, opinions, beliefs, principles, attitudes towards life, on which we habitually act, by which we indeed live' —this is our philosophy. Philosophy thus understood is a precondition for any kind of *sane* existence in the world. It is in this sense that we indeed live by thinking, by ideas even more than we live by bread. That is why there is none so poor as not to have a philosophy of his own, just as there is none so rich either as to be able to do without one. As A.E. Taylor pointed out long ago, the choice here is not whether one has a philosophy or not but only what kind of philosophy one does or shall have.

'What kind of philosophy'—this immediately draws our attention to an important dimension of the philosophic situation around us. It is a fact that people have generally found the social reality around them rather difficult to cope with, for throughout recorded history and in our own times, it has been an ugly and painful reality, the reality of a class-divided, exploitative and diversely oppressive society. A genuinely *human* coping would be to seek to change it into a more humane society. But such an effort to change requires, at the very least, a true explanation of things as well as guts to act in a revolutionary manner—a combination rather rare to come by in real life. Unable to change it, the people learn to accept this ugly and painful reality—but they can do so only by interpreting it differently, often in a necessarily false manner. Necessarily, because the strain of a true explanation coupled with the inability to carry out the change it demands is simply too much to bear.

In a sense, unable to change the *objective* reality around them, people so change themselves *subjectively*, thinking-wise, as to be able to accept this reality, with the least socio-psychological strain. Unable or unwilling to think of themselves as exploited or victimised by an unjust society and yet incapable of doing anything much about it, the people, especially the poor and oppressed, have generally found it more comforting, certainly less punishing, to think of themselves as correctly placed by a just society—and here the Will of God, law of *karma*, vagaries of fate, teachings of various religions and 'the enshrined wisdom' of assorted moral philosophies, they all help. If the risks involved in the discovery of truth about a class-divided society have persistently pushed social sciences in the direction of *apologetics* and even 'sorcery', the difficulties involved in changing such a society have left their massive mark on social thinking in the form of flourishing social myths, and any number of limited, mistaken or false philosophies. Limited, mistaken or false philosophies or ideas have helped the common people everywhere to survive, to live on without going insane. The majority of our own people, the other half of 'the Indian nation', are even today living more by such ideas than by bread—the bread is simply not available most of the time, unlike the ideas which are always there to help interpret and accept its non-availability. It is thus that they come to accept the ugly and painful reality of their poverty and oppression as part of a natural or divinely ordained arrangement of things.

It is one of the many ironies of their life that while the heads of the poor and oppressed are indeed their own, physically, the ideas in their heads belong to others, they correspond not to their own interests, but to the interests of the rich and powerful in society who oppress and exploit them. In this sense, the poor and oppressed are really the philosophers of the rich and powerful, all the time reinforcing the latter's domination over themselves.

But this is not the case with only our supposedly ignorant or illiterate common people. So many of us, in our half of 'the nation', may be thinking more consciously, but we generally do so with 'a false consciousness' in the sense that we are not aware of the real origins of our ideas, the practical-political interests they correspond to, or whom they really serve. All too often, even as we too find it comforting to go along with God, *karma*, fate, religious or moral teachings and the rest of it, we live our daily life by the prevalent 'philosophy of common sense' —'what can one man do', 'men are selfish by nature', 'the poor have always been with us', 'Indians are all corrupt', 'politics is dirty business', 'there is much to be said on both sides', etc. etc.—which helps us evade real issues, difficult choices, all social responsibility, and accept or endorse the established order of things.

I might add, the situation in the academy and such other places is hardly any better, only the evasion and the acceptance or endorsement is more subtle and sophisticated. The philosophic underpinning of most of what goes on in our schools and universities only ensures that 'the educated' are duly socialised into the existing social order, that is, come to feel 'at home with exploitation and domination'...Indeed all of us, 'the illiterate', and 'the educated', the academic and the scholar, the intellectual and the journalist, the democratic rights activist and his critic, need to answer the question: 'Where do you speak from?', 'Whose philosopher you really are?'

'Where do you speak from?' is an important question for the democratic rights activists for it points to the need of having a philosophy or methodological orientation which is as rational and scientific as they can possibly make it, in order to ensure greater clarity and effectiveness for their struggle. But the question is important for their critics also, perhaps more so because they are generally far less aware of the issue involved, sharing as they do, despite pretensions, in the currently dominant mode of thinking in our society. And this mode as a rule, Marx had pointed out, is the mode of the dominant classes. These classes, no doubt, always have their 'hired prize fighters'. But the critic may well discover that even when he is *subjectively* most honest and upright, the position from which he speaks is limited, mistaken, or even false in a manner as to yield prescriptions and politics which correspond to the interests of those who have dominance in our society and that these interests demand a defence and justification of the state's current assault on the demoratic rights of the Indian people.

How does the dominant mode of thinking deal with the issues of terrorism, state; terrorism and democratic rights? And how do *we* need to think about them? I shall take a quick critical look at the basic limitation of the dominant mode in its treatment of terrorism and democratic rights; state terrorism is simply an 'unproblem' for it—it stands understood and justified as a corollary of its treatment of the problem of terrorism. State terrorism is something which only needs to be defended. My critical comment shall also be suggestive of a different, more adequate way of thinking about these issues.

The dominant mode of thinking is really the mode of commonsense, which furnished with academic frills has even come to be raised to the status of 'Method' in social sciences. Its is a loudly proclaimed 'clearheaded' concern with 'here and now', with 'hard facts' and 'things as they are', that refuses to look deeper into them or go beyond them—any such effort would be dismissed as impermissible 'metaphysics'. In one sense such concern is justifiable, indeed necessary, for this is where the search for all scientific understanding begins. It begins, but does not end here. 'Sound commonsense' of the dominant mode, however, stays put with the immediate and the obvious, .the apparent or the visible, with facts apart from other facts. The complexity of things, phenomena and processes is itself sought to be reduced, abstracted and isolated into 'facts' and treated as given once for all, outside of their history and their more or less important interconnections. 'The immediately observable, measurable *fact*' becomes 'that Moloch', as Paul Baran once put it, 'which is always seeking to devour analytic thought in contemporary social science'. It has certainly served to obscure social reality, 'the nature of things', as Marx called it, for things or facts exist, above all, in their history and their interconnections. In fact, the more of this history and interconnections one is able to grasp, the more of truth one has.

Let me illustrate with a couple of very simple examples. It is customary with economists and politicians of different hues to regularly refer to the fact of our surplus foodstocks as a sign of success, indeed the growing health of our economy and society—gone are the PL-480 days of foodgrain imports. This appears quite obvious and convincing. But seen in relation to only one other fact (I am leaving out the rest), that nearly half our population regularly goes without food, that we are unable to bring our surplus food and our own hungry people together, these stocks would be indicative of something entirely different, they are far more the sign of a failure, indeed a certain shameful sickness of our economy and society. Incidentally, however you define this failure or sickness, it has something to do with the much celebrated 'market-friendliness' of our economy and society.

Again, it is customary in our country, with its 'spiritual traditions', to see and speak of 'charity' as a virtue, the mark indeed of a good man who cares for his soul and a good society. This too appears obvious enough. But next time you are in the mood to look after your soul, try giving charity to your best friend—and the truth will be out! Even a cursory search for its history and, interconnections will reveal that charity implies a society which has degenerated into one of gross inequality, of givers and takers of charity. Recognised thus, 'charity' represents a certain sickness in human relations, its prevalence is far more the mark of a bad society. In a society of equals there will be no such virtue as charity. Those still retaining their souls—for souls too are a matter of history and interconnections —will have to look for other devices to arrange for their well-being in the hereafter.

Engels had something to say about the way of thinking or apprehending the world which I have been discussing. He chose to describe it as 'the metaphysical mode of thought'. In that masterpiece of popular exposition of Marxism, *Anti-Duhring,* which, despite its critics, all sorts of 'Marxist', 'ex-Marxist' or 'post-Marxist' experts, remains unrivalled in its elucidation of the Marxist way of thinking, Engels noticed that 'at first sight (the metaphysical) mode of thought seems to us extremely plausible because it is the mode of thought of commonsense'. But he found it to be 'one-sided, limited; abstract' because it studies things 'in their isolation, detached from the whole vast interconnection of things; and therefore not in their motion, but in their repose; not in their life, but in their death'. He added:

> In considering individual things it loses sight of their connections; in contemplating their existence it forgets their coming into being and passing away; in looking at them at rest it leaves their motion out of account; it cannot see the woods for the trees.

And so it is with the metaphysical mode's treatment of the issues of terrorism and democratic rights.

Armed actions—protests, resistance or struggles—in different parts of the country, in Punjab, Kashmir and Assam, Andhra Pradesh and Bihar, the North-East, and .elsewhere, which have mostly come to be described as 'terrorism', have an extraordinary variety about them As *Indian* phenomena, they do share a certain social-material basis and historical context and they have all arisen within an ongoing structure of economy, politics and power-relations, often in response to an utterly unscrupulous and myopic ruling class politics. But they have in each case a specificity of causation and characteristics; each expresses its own kind of grievances against and alienation from the system and the powers that be; each poses a challenge to the Indian state but a different kind of challenge; each seeks a different kind of future for itself, and so on. The armed aspect which they share notwithstanding, they represent social and political developments of great significance, each distinct from the other.

All this and more is of decisive importance for any proper understanding of the ongoing 'terrorist violence' in India. But in the metaphysical mode of thought all this and more is precisely what comes to be ignored, all distinctions are blurred or obliterated, and everything, all such protests, resistance or struggles are simply lumped together into one omnibus thing called 'terrorism'. The obvious and visible similarities are focussed upon and a certain autonomy which their violent dimension necessarily comes to acquire is inflated into an independent factor, indeed their defining characteristic, as if this violence has no social basis, has nothing at all to do with the economy of the country or its politics, including politics of the ruling classes. Violence is simply abstracted from its varied histories and still more varied interconnections, isolated and reduced to produce an essentially depoliticised composite phenomenon and its equally depoliticised composite image, 'terrorism', complete with bombs, landmines and rocket-launchers, the AK-47s and Kalashnikovs, and 'the dreaded terrorist', an image suggestive of only ruthlessness and inhumanity, delinquency, irrationality and fanaticism and, of course, foreign linkages.

'Terrorism' now is simply a resort to senseless, utterly uncivilised forms of violence, a foreign inspired social or political deviance. It becomes a label of defamation, a means of ostracising those branded as 'terrorist', excluding them from any human standing. They are the 'outsiders', 'foreign agents', a menace to an otherwise peaceful and orderly society. The image is indeed powerful, evoking fear and hostility, which are then sought to be reinfored with the help of equally abstract, mechanically posed counter-images of 'non-violence' and 'democratic politics', 'the rule of law' and a fetishised 'Constitution'; 'judicial processes' and 'law-abiding ordinary people' and so on, including the almost mythical 'national mainstream', which nobody knows what it is and where it flows. Academic scholarship, indigenous or foreign-aided, lends its prestige and sophistication to this construct of 'terrorism' as it comes to be nicely aligned with the demand of the establishment for an exclusive focus on violence or the threat of violence.

It is this essentially depoliticised image or construct of 'terrorism' and 'the terrorist' which is then promoted by the state through the massive regime of modern propaganda servicing it today—its own electronic devices, with television bringing the image visibly alive right into our homes, and the rest of public and private media, including 'the national press'. A nationwide 'selling of terrorism' takes place. The selling certainly has its variety and flexibility, but underlying it is the media's ready adoption of the official identification of terrorism and the terrorists. As issues of history and socio-political basis are pushed out of consideration, the discourse comes to be confined almost entirely to ways of meeting a self-evident terrorist threat to society.

Simultaneously, state terrorism is not seen as another form of 'terrorism', it is rationalised and defended, public sanction secured for it, as a means of countering this threat. Compelled to admit the obviously lawless and terrorist acts of the state, they are justified simply as necessary counter-terrorism. We are even informed that terrorism is a world wide phenomenon now, just like corruption. But, given the priorities of the ruling classes, while nothing much can or need be done about corruption, terrorism has to be ruthlessly put down. There is no escaping from this responsibility, even if you insist on calling it 'state terrorism'. If the deeper, more specific factors underlying 'terrorism' still come up for consideration, they are either dismissed as no longer relevant or sought to be taken care of by that very common and characteristically evasive response: 'Of course, but...' The argumentation turns into a feat of system-supportive word-management, almost an intellectual legerdemain. It is thus that the depoliticised abstraction 'terrorism', well-manipulated by the powers that be, comes to serve the most brutal form of ruling class politics—state terrorism.

The manipulation is facilitated by the fact that all the 'mainstream' political parties, including those of the established Left, come to subscribe to this depoliticised image. Their continuous contention for power in the state notwithstanding, they have a consensus here—shared by the assorted image and opinion-makers—based upon everybody's commitment to nationalism of one kind or the other. Nationalism as an ideology covers up the essential character of Indian social reality whence 'terrorism' ultimately springs, and helps unite the large social audience behind the ruling class politics in a war against terrorism.

Occasionally there is the appeal to the deviant to give up the bad and violent new ways and rejoin 'the national mainstream', as if some morality play is on. But the appeal s neither meant nor taken seriously. In the 'national consensus', the 'terrorist' remains and has to be treated as an 'outsider', an enemy, a threat to the nation, its unity and integrity. There is intermittent talk of 'political solution', 'restoration of the political process', 'political and economic initiatives' and 'packages' of all sorts—the less the ruling classes have to offer the more their emphasis on 'packaging' these days. But this remains so much rhetoric, mere ploys in a deadly political game. Overwhelmed by their own image of 'terrorism', and their ineptitude and opportunism as well; the powers that be are simply incapable of any such initiatives.

Perhaps a policy of drift has its own advantages. In any case, a political solution is impossible for them until they recognise 'terrorism' as a *genuine political problem*—rather a set of political problems, problems with history and interconnections, becoming daily more difficult *politically*. Despite noises to the contrary, it continues to be seen primarily as a 'law and order' problem. 'Firm action', 'the hard option' persists as the only viable solution, 'a more meaningful alternative' indeed. Counter-terrorism reappears, again and again, as the easier option for the ruling classes. The vested interests that have grown around this option, involving the police and paramilitary forces, bureaucracy, politicians and sundry other dubious elements, only facilitate the persistence of this option—and state terrorism continues. Ever new justifications are found for it, including its currently fashionable rationalisation as a means of creating those ever elusive 'conditions', 'congenial atmosphere' they also call it, for a political solution.

But there is no *real* solution or success in this option. On the contrary, as I wrote four years back, apropos the emerging state terrorism in Punjab: 'Its success, such as it may be, will turn out be even worse in its consequences than its failure.' The politics of state terrorism in Punjab has only ensured the total alienation of the Sikh people—not with the Khalistani militants, they are today even less with the Indian state. And, except for some odd pitifully small ultra-Left groups, no other politics is in sight. Therein lies the tragedy of Punjab today—a tragedy for the Sikhs, the Punjabis, including Hindus, and the Indian people as a whole.

State terrorism as a political option has fared no better in Kashmir or elsewhere in the country; it has produced only tragedies for the people. Yet the powers that be, in government or in opposition, may criticise or condemn, even 'flay' each other *factionally*, they don't know and can't do anything different or better. Even the best they can offer, but in their ineptitude and factious lack of will do not, is only a cooption or accommodation within their own, brand of 'democratic politics', which is incapable of confronting the really important issues underlying the explosive presence of 'terrorism' in different parts of the country today. They can only seek to hide the utter bankruptcy of their option by still more vigorous nationalist posturing. Not only does the rhetoric around 'the nation' or 'the unity and integrity of India' grow louder, there are new warnings against 'undermining the morale of the police force' or 'tarnishing the image of the army.', etc. etc.

Bankruptcy of this option apart, it does have its own advantages for the ruling classes. It is not merely a question of their different political formations or groups within them, 'patriots' all, playing their petty political games with 'terrorism' or terrorism-related 'nationalism' in their quest for power in the state. Far more important is the fact that a situation of terror and counter-terror, despite the risks involved, yet serves their more basic class needs. For one thing, it facilitates the ongoing ideological manipulation of the people; the bogey of 'secessionism', 'destabilisation', 'threat to unity and integrity of India', etc. is invoked to divert people away from their own concerns and mobilise them behind ruling class politics. People's own politics, their struggles for a better life are delegitimised as inopportune in the prevailing, supposedly temporary, situation; even the suspension of democratic rights, for the duration, is demanded. For another, this situation provides the ruling classes with additional pretext and public sanction to further expand and strengthen the repressive state apparatuses and use them to defend their general class interests in the name of fighting terrorism or even otherwise.

Thus, we have new laws like Terrorist and Disruptive Activities (Prevention) Act (TADA), which in its attack on democratic rights undermines almost every safeguard provided by the Indian Constitution and violates all principles of liberal jurisprudence and natural justice—its definition of terrorist and disruptive activities is wide enough to cover anything and everything that those in authority may choose to find embarrassing, inconvenient or undesirable. And we have more of modern, better equipped security forces, army's active involvement in 'civilian conflict' and state's everyday resort to extra-legal means—and a people socialised into accepting every new inroad and expansion of state apparatus as necessary in 'national interet'. This state apparatus, thus refurbished ideologically and materially augmented, and rationalised as 'a bulwark against terrorism', is now available for use against not just the 'terrorists', but others also, above all, the people struggling in defence of their interests and for a more just and equitable social existence.

And it has been so used against every form of democratic movement, popular struggle or social activism; against trade unions and striking workers, and those seeking to defend the environment; against women and dalits protesting the atrocities committed on them; against the landless and the adivasis engaged in a battle of survival; against journalists and academics, poets and cultural workers, in fact anyone deemed inconvenient or undesirable by the state, including of course the civil rights activists. Such has been the experience not only in Punjab, Kashmir and Assam, Andhra Pradesh and Bihar, or the North-East, but everywhere else in the country. Not surprisingly, even those who opposed the new legislation and repressive practices when in opposition have found selective recourse to them useful when in power themselves—among the victims have been the Opposition members in Congress-I ruled States and Congress-I members in the States ruled by the Opposition, but, needless to repeat, the common people and those struggling with or for them in all the States. It is thus that state terrorism, spreading within democratic forms and without them, is contributing to the rise of an authoritarian, ever more repressive and anti-people state in India. And when the civil or democratic rights organisations protest and seek to intervene on behalf of the people against this growing terrorism or lawlessness of the state, they are seen as 'a nuisance', dismissed as 'do-gooders', denounced as 'front organisations', and finally, identified with 'terrorism' itself, condemned as 'anti-national'.

If 'things', abstracted from thir concrete socio-historical existence, come to be easily depoliticised, 'their mental images', that is, 'ideas', too may come to be subjected to a similar treatment. It is thus that alongside the depoliticisation that 'terrorism' represents, we are witnessing an increasing depoliticisation of the idea of democratic rights into a rapidly spreading version of 'human rights'.

Lewis Namier, whose work gave rise to a whole new school of history-writing, argued for and practised a historiography which pushed ideas out of history. He sought a history voided of ideas and, as a conservative, a politics voided of 'political philosophy', of 'programmes and ideals'—he hailed such politics as a token of 'greater national maturity'. In a parallel development in philosophy, scholars have sought to push history, as well as politics, out of ideas. Philosophy properly understood and practised is analysis, which easily becomes a timeless elucidation of ideas or concepts. Ideas are divorced from things they represent, concepts from the reality they are the concepts of ideas and concepts extrapolated from their concrete existence, their historical context or socio-economic interconnections, are transformed into weightless counters which are then manipulated at will, by themselves or in arbitary conflation with other such idea-counters, generally in the service of conservative, often admittedly anti-radical, politics.

In political philosophy proper this is well exemplified in the work of Isaiah Berlin, Karl Popper or Michael Oakeshott in their treatment of the ideas or concepts of 'liberty'—'negative' and 'positive', 'historicism' and 'open' or 'closed' society, or 'rationalism' and 'tradition', respectively. Such treatment, especially as analysis, has indeed served as an antidote to sloppiness in our thought and expression, it has helped light up many dark corners, resolved ambiguities of language and argument, and generally made for greater precision and clarity in our thinking. But if 'one-sided, limited, abstract' concern with *facts*, as they *appear* to be, has been a Moloch 'seeking to devour analytic thought in contemporary social science,' such philosophical exercises in their flight from the real world, the world of facts as they *really* are, have tended to denude social thinking of its substantive empirical content and ethical concern.

In any case, an atemporal, dehistoricised treatment of an idea or a concept easily makes for its 'depoliticisation'. And it is in this manner that the conept of democratic rights or civil liberties is undergoing a certain depoliticisation these days. As history and politics are pushed out of it, what is emerging is a particular, abstracted and almost bloodless, use of the term 'human rights'. 'Human rights' has been a much used tern for a longtime, essentially expressive of same or similar concerns as democratic rights or civil liberties and for certain purposes its use is indeed most appropriate. But it always had a certain history-and-context-lessness about it, referring as it does to that rather abstract category 'human being'. Thus amenable to easy dehistoricisation, it is a *particular*, dehistoricised and therefore depoliticised version of human rights' which has come into circulation with remarkable speed and strength in recent years, its trajectory rather closely related to that of the other abstraction, 'terrorism', produced by the metaphysical mode of thinking.

As with 'terrorism' in one way, now with 'human rights' in another, economic-structural basis of democratic rights, the concrete historical, political and cultural context of their existence as well as the state's attack on them, is obscured. Conflicts in society and the processes generating them which are always historically specific and the equally specific contradictions between the people and the state which make democratic rights an important issue in real life, come to be pushed out of consideration. The rough and troublesome specificities of situation and struggle, conflict and confrontation smoothed out, an universalised abstraction, 'human rights' takes over, leaving everyone free to make moral demands, pass ethical judgements, or play politics in its name. These 'human rights' won't hurt anyone, least of all those who deny or violate the democratic rights of the people. The violation of democratic rights can in fact go hand in hand with a defence of 'human rights'. The worst violators of the one the world over can parade themselves as the best defenders of the other, and this in pursuit of world domination. A Reagan or a Bush comes to stride as the man for our times...

Thus sanitised from the grim reality of life, from the economy and politics of our essentially undemocratic times, 'human rights' increasingly becomes an eminently fit subject for discourse, and a little later, almost inevitably, for discourse over changing terms of discourse! It is indeed in this way that 'human rights' as a subject for study is arriving on the academic scene the world over, characteristically devoid of any concern for the people or involvement with democratic rights movement: departments and courses at universities, long or short-range research projects at centres old and new, foreign sponsorship and funding, especially by the American agencies well-known for their role in such matters in Latin America and elsewhere in the Third World, 'human rights' seminars and conferences, national and international, all the time, somewhere or the other, which governments violating democratic rights, yet in search of legitimacy, are not afraid to sponsor, fund or join in... A new breed of human rights academics is on the way, just like the far too many we already have in areas become fashionable from time to time, opening up new, exciting possibilities far a career and for peer-group scholarship. The mundane interests of these academics apart, 'the empriricist method', 'specialisation' and 'functional rationality' rampant in the academy will, overcrowding notwithstanding, easily accommodate and sustain this 'new discipline' as they would describe it.

The *Economic and Political Weekly* comment, a few months back, remains relevant:

> Like tribal art and ethnic handicrafts, human rights appear to have become chic among members of the establishment. Delhi is hosting a World Human Rights Congress in December. The External Affairs Ministry is partly financing it and has put a senior Joint Secretary to officially represent it on the preparatory committee of the Congress which is going to be held in the five-star Maurya Sheraton hotel in the capital.
>
> The Capital's elite university, Jawaharlal Nehru University, has even started a Human Rights Teaching and Research Programme. The Director of this programme is in charge of organising the World Human Rights Congress. Curiously enough, this gentleman has never been known to have taken up any human rights issue, or sign his name to any petition or appeal protesting violation of civil liberties within India. Academic discourse on human rights at international fora is apparently not only a safer option, but also probably a convenient stepping stone to recognition in right circles.

Nothing can be more hypocritical than the government's

> patronage of the World Congress. New Delhi is yet to ratify the Optional Protocol to the International Convention on Civil and Political Rights, and the Convention against Torture. By refusing to ratify the Optional Protocol the government is denying private civil liberties groups in India the right to approach the UN Committee to investigate into such cases. The government is violating almost every day the major provisions of the International Convention which prohibits detention without trial, trial in camera, killing of citizens, torture in police custody, etc. One wonders how the official representatives of the government at the World Human Rights Congress will defend themselves if asked about the detention of thousands of people under NSA and TADA in Kashmir, Punjab and other parts of the country, or about custodial deaths, or about indiscriminate police firings upon peasants and workers fighting for their democratic rights. But will there be anyone in the Congress to ask such questions? Will the guests dare to offend the hosts?
>
> Under the existing laws, victims of police torture or next of kin of those killed in police custody, have no statutory right to compensation. Yet the government is spending several lakhs on preparations for this jamboree on 'human rights'...

Incidentally, the Government of India still refuses to allow Amnesty International and similar other civil liberties organisations to visit several parts of the country where the state's violation of democratic rights has become a routine affair.

It is the dominance of 'the metaphysical mode of thought' even with those on the Left who otherwise profess the Marxist, that is, the dialectical mode, which has over the years helped the ruling classes to define and pre-empt the terrain of Indian politics for their own purposes. They have posed the issues in this mode, asked the questions accordingly, and secured the answers they wanted to have. For example, this is how it has been in the recent crisis-ridden years: 'Are you for the Sikh/ Kashmiri/ULFA militants or the nation? For secessionism or the unity and integrity of India? For violence or democratic politics? For the Congress-I Government or that of the National Front? For communalism or secularism? For reservations or against them?' and so on. It is not difficult to see that in each case the choices are really foreclosed in the sense that whatever the answer it serves one or the other kind of ruling class politics.

The way the issues are posed consistently ignores the larger context and the deeper determinant interconnections, dissociates the issues form any consideration of socio-economic sturctures, class domination, or ruling class politics, and thus ensures that radical or revolutionary choices simply don't come up as answers, as real historical possibilities.

It is the same with the metaphysical mode's posing of the issues of terrorism, state terrorism and democratic rights. A certain sectarianism apart, it is the philosophical surrender here, and the consequent surrender to bourgeois politics, which has prevented the established Left as a whole from coming out actively in defence of democratic rights today, as their forbears, the united communist movement once did. During the British rule, defence of democratic rights was a major concern with the CPI, it was seen as a part of the Indian people's struggle for freedom and a better life.

Democratic rights have to be defended above all against their violation by the Indian state today. But for an effective defence these violations must not be seen, as the liberals generally do, as the result of some mistaken policies, unfortunate 'aberrations' or 'distortions', on the part of the Indian state. A Nehruvian vision of the post-colonial state has contributed much to cloud matters here. Nor is it enough to recognise this state, as activists, even 'theoreticians' of the civil liberties movement often do, only as a system of power, overgrown, much too-centralised and standing over and above the civil society, and therefore insensitive to the interests of citizens and intolerant of diversity and plurality, ever prone to abuse its power, to dominate and repress, to homogenise.

Such a view of the state has gained new endorsement these days because it is central to the argument of that most significant development in our social and political life, which has gone on to become an important, though somewhat problematic feature of contemporary social scientific concerns as well as social activism, namely, 'identitarianism', as I would like to describe it. I am not concerned with this development here except to point out that drawing our attention to the multiform oppressions prevalent in our society, as against the onventional focus on the economic oppression, it sees an overcentralised and powerful state, 'the at once homogenising and colonising juggernaut', as the enemy against which the rights and interests of our long oppressed and more disadvantaged social groups, 'identities' as they have come to be called—minor nationalities or ethnic groups, religious minorities, dalits, tribals, women, and so on—have to be fought for, won and defended.

In this perspective, even when they have crossed the traditional liberal threshold, studies have focussed on the state's obviously visible, politically repressive features but rarely gone deep enough to see its economic basis or class character. That remains a forbidden threshold, to be nodded at or flirted with occasionally, but never to be crossed. The state is studied as such but not as the organiser of society in the interests of the class (exploitative) structure as a whole, a function which decisively conditions its own structure and organisation. The state is seen in dissociation from this class structure, whose defence, of course with necessary modifications, is its defining characteristic. It is not seen that the Indian state does not merely *happen* to be violent or repressive, it is *inherently* so, by virtue of the society it presides over; it guards and keeps going, violently if necessary, an inherently violent society because it is a society of myriad economic, social and cultural oppressions. As a result, when it occurs, state violence is analysed in terms of violations of democratic rights but not as class violence, as an expression of class domination or policies, as a part of the ongoing open or hidden class struggle in society. A certain flirtation with the notion of class may be there, but there is no recognition that state power in India is also a form of class power and that this has its relevance for any effective struggle in defence of democratic rights of the Indian people against the Indian state.

It is this classlessness of their 'theorising' which primarily accounts for the fact that even with scholars who otherwise seek radical, even revolutionary changes in society, their discourse is strong only in its idealism or liberal rhetoric, that there is such a gap between the enormity of the oppressions they describe so well and the painful pettiness, the fragmentary and feeble nature of the political options which emerge from this description, that even as they speak of 'state against democracy', of a 'lecherous' or even 'a terrorist state', and warn other intellectuals against cooption, they themselves are quite comfortable with this state whenever the occasion arises, missing no opportunity to serve it as 'inside political advisers', pleading for the long lost 'Nehruvian consensus' or new 'social contracts' for 'nation-building', that the rhetoric of 'grassroots politics' and 'movements from below' is accompanied by yet other developmental solutions from above, offered in Planning Commissions and elsewhere. The critical intellectual, in spare time at least, gets reduced to an 'intellect worker' as Paul Baran once defined him. This is, in its own way, indeed tragic. For these scholars know better and mean well by the people. But then theory is a cruel mistress, like history. And like history, it has its tragedies too.

The need then is to move away from the metaphysical mode of thought, its 'specific narrow-mindedness' as Engels called it, and try to understand the issues of terrorism, state terrorism and democratic rights in a dialectical manner so that we don't miss the wood for the trees.' It is not my purpose to explore these essentially interrelated issues as they have emerged in different parts of the country. Here I can only again insist that we need to understand them in their 'whole vast interconnections' within the larger social reality of contemporary India. This will include, depending upon the particular issue, the more or less important interconnections in the areas of history, of caste, gender and ecology, religion, ideology and culture, ethnicity and nationality, and so on. But central to this understanding are the interconnections in the realm of economy and the ruling class politics spawned by it.

Even a cursory look, certainly one *from below,* will reveal that ours is a historically specific form of capitalist economy in which all the evils of a belated, somewhat lumpen or comprador capitalist development, semi-feudalism, bureaucratisation and bloated bourgeois politics daily enter into and reinforce each other. There is unequal and uneven development with its 'two nations' and the ever-widening gulf between the two, and an 'internal colonialism' at work in the more backward parts of the country, which together are turning all the divides and fissures of our society, such as class, caste, religion, language, region, ethnicity or nationality, etc. explosive and giving rise to strong disintegrative tendencies everywhere. An overcentralised and homogenising state, which is yet a weak state in its loss of legitimacy, only makes for more disintegration. Old organised structures of exploitation and oppression persist and myriad new oppressions, insecurities and alienations have emerged—'We suffer not only from the living but from the dead' also, as Marx once put it. The corrupt and criminalising mark of this socio-economic development is there on everything in our society, a society in deep economic, social and moral crisis today. We are indeed paying the 'terrible costs of not changing the existing order'—Nehru's words, uttered in an obviously more lucid Marxist moment. Unable to move forward in a revolutionary manner this society is steadily moving backwards, providing a continuing social material basis for all sorts of ideologically muddled protests around genuine grievances and any number of divisive or disruptive anti-people developments.

These protests and developments, ranging from 'terrorism' to communalism, have indeed materialised, above all as the consequences of a politics dominated by the ruling classes. As practised by their different political formations in recent years, in its utterly unscrupulous internecine competition for power and ineptitude of leadership, this politics has been producing one after another intractable problems for the ruling classes and tragedies for the people. A search for interconnections will show that within the larger socio-eonomic context of Indian society, it is the ruling class politics at the Centre and in the States which has, in each case, created and later sustained the political problems which have become or come to be perceived as 'the terrorist problem' in different parts of the country—an entirely indigenous creation which others, imperialism and its allies, are taking full advantage of. At the other end, bankrupt and increasingly bereft of legitimacy in facing the problems of its own generation, this politics, its powerlessness making it only more repressive all the time, has created and come to sustain 'a terrorist state', making the defence of democratic rights all the more necessary and urgent, though more risky also.

To advance these *general* propositions is not to deny the part of the *particular* in the emergence of terrorism, state terrorism and democratic rights as crucial issues at a given time or place in one part of the country or another. A recognition of their specific context and nature is in fact of decisive importance in each case, for this is how and where the state's violation of democratic rights occurs and where therefore the defence of democratic rights has to be undertaken. 'A concrete analysis of a concrete situation' is necessary, as always. But a dialectical as against a 'metaphysical' orientation in such analysis will give us a more adequate understanding of the specificities involved and make for a more effective struggle, here and now, in defence of democratic rights.

I don't need to pursue this subject any further. A slightly extended comment may be found in my *Of Marxism and Indian Politics. I* shall conclude with a somewhat different last point.

It is quite common for the critics or opponents of democratic rights organisations to question their protest against state terrorism and charge them with 'keeping silent' over terrorism of 'the terrorists.' They are constantly called upon to condemn all violence, to act in a 'responsible' manner and be at least equally condemnatory of 'terrorist violence'. The alleged silence is even interpreted and condemned as support for terrorism. This is nothing new. Civil liberties organisations the world over have regularly faced such charges, similar criticism and condemnation. This criticism or condemnation, however, is entirely misconceived. I am not here concerned to discuss the overall nature and scope of the work of democratic rights or civil liberties organisations. It only needs to be affirmed that it is quite legitimate for these organisations to make the distinction between terrorism of the state and terrorism resorted to by private individuals or groups. The reason is very simple. Whereas, in a law based state like India, there exists an elaborate code, an entire ensemble of laws, procedures, institutions and enforcement agencies to deal with private violence or lawlessness, there is nothing comparable, no genuine checks or controls, to take care of peaceful or violent lawlessness of the state, which is potentially, and often in actual practice, the most powerful violator of democratic rights in society.

It is this absence in our system of credible institutional safeguards against the illegal acts and terrorism committed or backed by the state and its functionaries that, more than anything else, makes the presence of democratic rights organisations necessary. These organisations locate their primary concern, *the* task as it were, precisely here—in the paramount need to protect the people's rights against their violation by the state or with its backing in one form or another. Such being the very *raison d'etre* of these organisations, to ask them to do anything else, least of all take care of private lawlessness and violence, or still worse, provide justification for the state's own violence or lawlessness is indeed misconceiving their role in our society. These organisations are not there to strike a balance between two kinds of violence or terrorism. By their very self-definition, their work lies elsewhere.

This is not to ignore or in any way underestimate the problem that private violence has come to be in our society today—its ever-growing level, scale and diversity are indeed frightening. More and more of the conflicts and tensions generated in this society, above all, by its economy and politics, are seeking to express themselves outside the constitutionally ordained institutional frameworks, including the electoral process which has witnessed a steady decline in popular interest or participation in recent years. If there is widespread socio-political turbulence in society, there is also the widespread, not unjustified, impression that peaceful ways seldom work and issues arrest political attention only through recourse to violence. But any adequate response to the problem of this spreading violence in our society demands, at the very least, the recognition that while any form of violence in due course acquires a certain autonomous dimension, it always arises on and is sustained by a given socio-material basis, and that its various forms, various because of differences of causation, context and conjuncture, need to be carefully distinguished from each other before we decide and act in the matter.

There is, for example, the ordinary personal-motivated violence of different kinds in our society; a most common occurrence, for so long as we have a money-and-profit dominated economy and society all forms of crime and violence which promise to pay will continue to be committed. Any effective response to this violence, obviously, must begin by questioning this domination. Or, again, given the fact that this society is full of glaring injustice and iniquities, oppression and exploitation, it will always have its victims, frustrated and desperate men and women, ready to avenge themselves or their fellow victims, violently or otherwise. The need here is not to pass moral judgements or condemn their motives and actions, but to do whatever we possibly can to change the conditions which make such frustration and desperation, and the accompanying violence, inevitable.

Yet again, along with this 'normal' violence, we have a great deal of specific anti-people violence do our society. There is the recurring violence among the people, on one issue or another, often generated, even actively promoted, by unscrupulous politics at the top. Communal or caste violence is an obvious example; its condemnation, or opposition to such violence does not pose any problems at all. But we need to take particular notice of a more pervasive kind of private anti-people violence, which has finally arrived. The crisis of our poor possessive-market society, its manifold conflicts, its lumpen rapacity and crumbling structures of authority, with the people desperately struggling to survive, has given rise to a great deal of private violence of the rich and powerful against the people below-landlord armies, armed gangs or vigilante groups of the dominant classes, a rich variety of mafias, all sorts of 'goon squads', often linked with the police, politicians and businessmen, and always available for hire, and so on.

This violence, which given its overall class character is generally backed, condoned or connived at by the state, deserves to be condemned without reservation. But this private violence, or for that matter lawless violence of the state itself, may provoke counter-violence on the part of the people. The people may be compelled to resist and even retaliate. They may find it necessary to turn to violence in sheer self-defence, or in defence of their democratic right to organise and struggle peacefully. They may need to resort to violence to defend the gains of their past struggles or to exercise the rights they still have, including the right to vote, and so on. Such private violence by or on behalf of the people is well justified; it certainly cannot be treated or condemned in the usual manner.

Our society has also given rise to certain specific forms of private violence, armed protests or struggles by individuals and groups, which are, despite their differences of causation, character and possible futures, generally lumped together as 'terrorism', country's foremost political problem today. It is not my concern to analyse this problem beyond the general observations I have already made. But one aspect of it does interest us here. We don't have to lump together the various historically specific expressions of this, private violence to recognise that even as this 'terrorism fights the Indian state, it is known to turn, to a greater to lesser degree, against the people too. And this calls for a brief comment.

In any armed protest, resistance or struggle, the quality of its politics, politics commanding the gun, is of decisive importance. If the quality of this politics is poor, the gun becomes increasingly more important, it tends to itself become politics, just as state terrorism tends to do at the other end. In other words, if an armed resistance or struggle lacks a coherent liberationist ideology and programme, the requisite revolutionary theory and practice, which may help it gain the willing support of the people and mobilise them in a popular movement, it will, sooner rather than later, seek to use force to gain this support—really the people's acquiescence or compliance through fear and terror-hardened sensibilities. The policies and actions of the 'terrorists' become increasingly self-defeating, harming the very people whose cause they otherwise claim to espouse in taking up arms against the state. Just as at the other end, seeking to gain their acquiescence or compliance the same way, state terrorism too harms the people, alienating them from 'India' it claims to be defending for them against the terrorists. In this situation, dependence on foreign aid, aids only the process of moral and political degeneration of the original armed protest or struggle. The consequences are the dead-end game of killing and getting killed, a vicious circle of competitive atrocities and reprisals, intermittent internecine warfare among the various groups and a brutalisation of everyday life of the common people, all of which provides an excellent cover to all sorts of anti-social elements, any and every kind of criminal activity. May be Punjab is very much on my mind, but the argument certainly has its general relevance.

Needless to add, terrorist violence against the people has no moral or political justification at all. It can only be condemned. Though, for obvious reasons, detailed knowledge and careful analysis is necessary before we pass judgement in each case. We need to know the truth and not its official version only.

In a society like ours which is *structurally* saturated with violence, with exploitation and oppression, injustice and inequality, there is always room for revolutionary violence. To reject such violence and, uphold non-violence on principle has no justification, rational, or moral, in the light of the historical experience of the struggles of the oppressed the world over. As the French philosopher Maurice Merleau-Ponty once put it, 'to teach non-violence is to strengthen established violence, that is to say, a system of production which makes misery and war inevitable.' Revolutionary violence aims at destroying this established violence and to create a new system of production and society in which 'misery and war' are no longer inevitable. It is a violence, as he put it, 'which transcends itself on the way to the human future'. Thus, for example, the problem that the 'Naxalites', as they are called, present our society is not one of private violence to be condemned, but of an exploitative and oppressive social order crying out for revolutionary change.

Revolutionary violence may indeed be criticised, even rejected, but not on abstract moral grounds. The grounds have to be specific such as a negative assessment about its 'appropriateness' in a given situation, a lack of 'proportionality' between means and ends, and so on. On the basis of historical experience, it is also possible to argue against the *general* efficacy and appropriateness of individual or group acts of revolutionary violence. Even when deemed necessary, one needs to be aware of the dangerous possibility of getting sidetracked or lost in a vicious circle of violence and counter-violence. It is thus absolutely imperative for those so involved to be constantly self-critical of their theory and practice in this regard, as elsewhere, in the interests of the revolutionary movement as a whole. It seems to me, however, that the real issue with revolutionary violence is not so much its rights or wrongs as the taking of sides in the ongoing class war between the people and their oppressors and exploiters.

Looming large over all these forms of private violence in our society is the violence that Indian state has come to represent today. The issue here is not its inherently violent nature *as a state*, or the violence implicit in the socio-economic structures this state normally defends, violently or otherwise. What needs to be noticed is its emergence as the single largest perpetrator of violence on the people today. Such is the explicit material expression of this violence in recent years that scholars and laymen alike have been compelled to speak of 'state terrorism' or 'the terrorist state' in contemporary India. There is the ever-growing draconian legislation and the ever-expanding apparatus of repression, and the ruthless use of both everywhere in this vast land of ours. The old, extended or new laws are there—ESMA. MISA, NSA. different Armed Forces Special Powers Acts, many kinds of Disturbances, Disturbed or Terrorist Affected Areas Acts, amendments to the Constitution and the Criminal Procedure Code, and, above all, the TADA, and so on —which provide for new structures of authority, new hierarchy of courts, new legal procedures, new ranges of offences, new and stiffer penalties, new detentions without trial and new and harsher powers for the police, paramilitary forces and the army. New restrictions have come to be imposed on the life and liberties of the people in violation of old and established constitutional safeguards and new authorisation provided for the lawlessness of the state, including extra-judicial kidnappings and killings known as 'encounters; and alongwith 'custodial deaths' even the phenomenon of 'missing', long associated with the dictatorial regimes of Latin America, has arrived.

To execute these laws and this lawlessness; alongwith the old we now have any number of new police and paramilitary formations, new security set-ups, armed wings, guards and protection groups and the rest, well-supported by the army on the one hand and the well-rewarded state or politician-sponsored terrorist or vigilante groups on the other. The much touted 'financial crunch' notwithstanding, financing all this has been no problem at all. In large 'terrorist affected' parts of the country, it is a situation of massive power, without any checks or accountability, but with an irresistible temptation to confuse every expression of popular protest, dissent or even recalcitrance with terrorism and therefore meant to be handled with ruthless brutality. Unchecked power has its own logic; corruption rampant in the system has taken care of the rest. Whatever its other problems, or problematic success in fighting 'terrorism', the state's terrorism has been remarkably successful in alienating the people and pushing them out of its own 'mainstream', leaving the 'national press' free to deceive itself and mislead the rest of 'the Indian nation'.

Only the nationalistically blind will fail to see that it is this mindless violence of the state, growing ever more mindless in its failure or impotence and the accompanying loss of legitimacy, which spawns anew and fuels the terrorist violence in the country. The two in fact regularly feed, justify and legitimise each other—all the while adding to the misery and suffering of the common people everywhere.

This digression on the subject of violence in our society, which is far from being exhaustive, should be sufficient to indicate the complexity of the issues involved which critics must show awareness of when they seek condemnation of violence qua violence, or make their more specific but simplistic demands on democratic rights organisations. It is simply not true that these organisations condone, approve or support private violence or terrorism against the people. Only they don't see its condemnation as a necessary part of *their* task. Nor is it that they don't take note of its excesses or violations of people's rights, or have not found it necessary at times to even publicly criticise or condemn these. They have indeed done so, or even otherwise intervened against them, not on abstract moral grounds or to oblige the critics, but for good reasons of their own which include defence of the larger interests of the people and securing greater effectiveness for the democratic rights movement itself. But by self-definition, they have not seen this as their *responsibility.* They are committed to use their limited resources, first and above all, to defend the democratic rights of the people against their violation by the state.

Besides, if they are rather wary and seemingly non-cooperative with their critics in this matter, there is a consideration which they simply cannot afford to ignore. They are well aware that concerning the state's current assault on democratic rights, we are in a situation where those who know will not speak and the vast majority of our people are simply kept ignorant about the violations, even crimes being committed by the state, often in their name and their supposed interests. Given the power and reach of the communication media, public and private, at the disposal of the state, given its extraordinary ability to project its own point of view and to manipulate public opinion by selective use of information, and given the fact that you cannot accuse the state, or the 'mainstream' private media, of fair or balanced reporting where the democratic rights movement or for that matter *any* popular democratic struggle is concerned, every concession made by the democratic rights organisations to their critics here is bound to be used, in the time-tested one-sided manner, to further condone, justify and legitimise state terrorism. This would mean, in effect, a denial of the very purpose for which these organisations have come to be constituted. Their work will lose its meaning, and so will the courage, dedication and sacrifice of their activists.

The democratic rights organisations and their activists have indeed reason to be wary. They have a right to their own democratic decision in this matter. You cannot blame them if they refuse to see the 'condemnation' demanded of them as an indispensable part of *their* concerns, a responsibility they must not evade. 'Law and Order' is not their business and they are not in the game to perform balancing acts, give evidence of their 'impartiality' or 'fairmindedness', or dish out evenhanded judgements on violence in our society. Nor are they in search of certificates of good conduct or 'patriotism' from their critics or the powers that be. They may in fact regard it ridiculous, even shameful to jump on their bandwagoon and join their chorus of righteous indignation against 'terrorism'.

They rafuse to join this chorus not because they love violence or have a twisted moral sense which can no longer distinguish between right and wrong, nor because they would condone actions which every decent person ought to condemn. Their work over the years in Andhra Pradesh and elsewhere should make it abundantly clear that they don't need to make any apologies for their moral sense. And they know what decent behaviour is as well as most, and certainly a lot better than their critics or other leaders of the anti-terrorist chorus—they owe no explanation to anyone here. They don't join this chorus simply because they are in the game, if not only, certainly primarily, to defend the democratic rights of the people against their violation by the state.

The way the critics continue with their criticism and condemnation and even betray a strong compulsion to misrepresent the motives and actions of the democratic rights organisations even when they are known to have condemned militant groups for their 'violation of human rights' or 'senseless killings', persuades me that there is more to the critics' umbrage, and one needs to look at *their* motives and compulsions, at their game. Maybe what is involved here, implicitly or otherwise, are the more basic issues of ideology and politics on either side.

For examplc, apropos 'terrorism' in Kashmir, one of India's top-ranking journalists, in a centrepage article in *The Times of India,* has written of the 'utterly one-sided pronouncements of do-gooder groups' and charged them with the view that 'mass kidnappings and killings of the innocent by terrorist and secessionist gangs are perfectly allright'. This, we all know, is simply false. No democratic rights organisation has ever subscribed to anything even remotely resembling this view. On the contrary, to give an example, with V.M. Tarkunde of the Coordination Committee on Kashmir and many others, they have, context permitting, more than once criticised and condemned such actions and urged the militants to stop them. Yet the critics persist with their charges—they are simply not satisfied. Obviously what really troubles them is not the lack of such criticism or condemnation. Obviously they are after something else or more. It seems to me that what they are really asking for, of course in 'the interests of the nation', is an acceptance and endorsement of the state's own terrorism in the Valley, the politics of this terrorism, in effect, the ruling class politics in Kashmir. I see no reason at all why the democratic rights organisations or their activists should be expected to so oblige these critics, in Kashmir or for that matter anywhere else in the country.

This is not to suggest that the democratic rights organisations are the vehicles of some other politics, as this term is commonly understood. If 'law and order' is not their business, 'politics' in this sense is not their business either. Racketeers abound in our country, they are everywhere. But there is no doubt that those genuinely attracted to the risky business of defence of democratic rights today are men and women of high moral sense and idealism, full of deep concern for the people. Many of them, if not most, may naturally tend to sympathise with the Left of one shade or the other, they may have their interest in radical or revolutionary politics. To this they are fully entitled. But the democratic rights organisations or those of their activists who have this other interest or activity well know that even though the abuse of state power, including the state's terrorism, ultimately grows out of the essential, structural compulsions of the prevalent economy and politics, *other* organisations, *other* struggles of the people, are needed for a change in this situation, and that it is going to be a long haul. They know that the democratic rights organisations are not the vehicles of this other struggle.

But then this other struggle is on in our society, between the people and those who oppress and exploit them—however weak or fragmented it may be, or beset with a thousand problems of theory and practice, politics and organisation. And no matter how the democratic rights organisations define or circumscribe their role, how scrupulously they stick to the self-imposed limits of their popular concerns, or how 'responsibly' they behave in pursuit of these concerns, their work yet remains a defence of the people's rights and places them firmly on the people's side of the barricades, if I may put it that way. It is and cannot but be also an entry, one among many, into this other struggle, and in this sense, more than only a defence of democratic rights. Even if the democratic rights activist somehow fails to see this, his critics, generally more perceptive and class conscious in these matters, see and understand this very clearly. So do the state and its functionaries. Hence the hostility and harassment, the persistent persecution. For the ruling classes, their representatives or spokespersons, democratic rights activity is, in the final analysis, a dangerously subversive activity. It has to be questioned, criticised and condemned and, as far as possible, suppressed.

The democratic rights organisations and their activists are, in their own way, standing by the struggling Indian people in these our troubled times, when so many others, from the intelligentsia and elsewhere, have deserted them—many of them deserting their people for 'the nation.' Such an understanding should make them rightfully more proud of their struggle in defence of democratic rights and, I am sure, it will also make this struggle more effective.

11

Marxists and the Sikh Extremist Movement in Punjab*

What I am saying below is part of a much broader analysis. A great deal is left unsaid and the several propositions I advance require sophisticated elaboration. But in this note, of necessity, I have to be brief. The purpose is to get the main point across. I hope this exercise of mine will be of some help towards clearer thinking in this area.

Before I directly confront the central issue raised in the debate, namely, what should be our attitude towards the Sikh extremist movement in Punjab, I would like to very briefly state how I understand the situation in Punjab today.

Early in 1984—much before Operation Bluestar and what followed—in an analysis of the developing situation in Punjab I had concluded: '*The* major political party of the Indian ruling classes, the Congress(I), and a minor political party of the same ruling classes, the Akali Dal, between them and with other political parties in tow, are heading for a tragedy for the Sikhs, for the Punjabis (including Hindus), and for the Indian people as a whole, in that inter-linked order'. The tragedy occurred, and in the period since it has only further deepened.

Punjab today, thus, is not merely a problem but a tragedy produced, above all, by the workings of the economy and

---

* Contribution to a debate among Marxists in Punjab, *Economic and Political Weekly* (1987).

politics of the Indian ruling classes. Visibly precipitated at the political level, the tragedy has its objective, economic structural basis in the prevalent mode of production, and a host of complex, historically produced factors have gone into its making. But the prime political responsibility for it lies, through acts of omission and commission, with the major political formation of the Indian ruling classes, the Congress(I), and its government at the centre. Punjab in fact is the best, and therefore also the worst, example, so far, of ruling class politics having become increasingly deadly for the Indian people in recent times.

This continuing and ever-deepening tragedy has led to a situation in Punjab which today is characterised by certain aspects or features, of which the following need to be especially taken note of:

(1) The most important aspect is the near-total alienation of the Sikh people in Punjab, more particularly of its youth, from the powers that be in this country. There is deep disillusionment, and disorientation, daily getting worse due to the still festering wrongs of the past, the current policies and pronouncements of Rajiv Gandhi and his government, the corrupt and partisan practices of the repressive organs of the state, the continuing hurt and humiliation in daily life, and the recurring 'backlash' outside Punjab, etc., etc. S. Mulgaokar has spoken of 'three years of sinning and injustice against the Sikhs'.

There have been, however, no communal riots, nor is there a separatist or 'Khalistan' movement of any significance whatsoever—so far.

(2) The second important aspect is the continuing fractured identity of the Punjabis as a nationality. Fed by the mutually reinforcing communalisms, and helped along by official policies and practices, and more especially by the terrorist design of communally selective killings, there exists today an ever-deepening communal divide between the Sikhs and the Hindus, with an overwhelming majority of the latter looking, even in this crisis, neither within nor towards the democratic or revolutionary movement in Punjab, but outside—looking, as always in the past, under cover of a spurious and self-defeating

communal nationalism, towards the larger Hindu constituency and state power in India, for protection and for the promotion of what they perceive to be their or 'national' interests.

(3) The third important aspect is the virtual collapse, at least for the time being, of conventional bourgeois politics—parties, elections, making and unmaking of ministries, etc. The traditionally important political actors are still on the scene but have lost their credibility. They are there, in Chandigarh or Delhi, in all sorts of committees and councils, even 'mass rallies', invariably under heavy armed protection and invariably exhorting the common man to show bravery in the fight against terrorism! Having produced the tragedy themselves, they now find themselves politically bankrupt and unable to cope with it.

(4) The fourth and the last important aspect to be noted in the current Punjab situation is that of terrorism. It is the most apparent or visible part of the problem, but only a part, as should be abundantly clear from the argument so far. It comprises the mutually reinforcing and justifying dimensions of extremist terrorism and state terrorism. The extremist terroism, initiated by Bhindranwale, got its major impetus from Operation Woodrose, carried out by the Indian army in the towns and villages of Punjab, following Operation Bluestar. Though diverse in its sources of inspiration and motivation—and this diversity needs to be noticed far any successful fight against it—this terrorism is increasingly an autonomous phenomenon with a logic of its own. We need to condemn and oppose its killing of innocents and political opponents, most unreservedly but from our own standpoint and not that of the state or ruling class politics. We need to condemn and oppose, equally unreservedly and again from our standpoint, terrorism indulged in by the state—its harassment, detention, torture and killing of innocent Sikh youth. The state in Punjab, while failing miserably in the discharge of its primary responsibility of protecting the life and property of its citizens, has in the name of fighting extremism, virtually extinguished all democratic rights of the people. Its past actions and current practices have long term negative consequences for both the Sikhs and the

Hindus in that they not only strengthen the forces of extremism and reactionary religious fundamentalism among the Sikhs, and not among them alone, but also, objectively, join with these forces in doing lasting damage to Punjab's social fabric, to the common life and culture of the Punjabi people as a whole.

I would add that it is this situation, essentially created by the Indian ruling classes, that the imperialists and their allies are, quite naturally, trying to take advantage of for their own purposes.

This being the situation, even if an exercise of the direct power of the state—which is indeed very powerful, and very indifferent to the sufferings of the people too—does succeed in finding some answer to 'the terrorist problem', as it well may, the basic situation in Punjab will remain unchanged. It will remain potentially explosive, and may even change for the worse, and thus continue to vitiate the situation in the rest of the country also. Consequently, the primary and most urgent need at the moment is to find, even within the limits of bourgeois politics, a political solution as against a police solution, to 'the Punjab problem'.

Insofar as the more basic problems in Punjab, as elsewhere in India, have a systemic, economic-structural basis, they can be resolved only through a revolationary, structural change in Indian society. If we still argue far an immediate 'political solution', it is not only because it will bring relief to the long-suffering people in Punjab, but even more because by ending a dangerous, messy situation, it will provide them with a less unfavourable environment for their own more basic struggles for the much-needed revolutionary change in our society. The present situation only favours the anti-people politics of the main contenders and those allied with them, politically or otherwise. Given the balance of forces as it obtains today in the Indian polity, it favours the powers that be in Delhi the most.

In the search for a political solution, a beginning can well be made by *forcing* the central government to regain some of its lost credibility with the Sikh people, and the Punjabis in general, by undoing some of the most obvious acts of gross injustice—

those relating to the November 1984 riots, the Jodhpur detenus, army 'deserters', etc.—and *then*, with due preparation, to call together, for the purpose of finding a solution, a broad-based, *open* conference of *all* the concerned parties and interests, in Punjab and outside. Needless to mention, 'the Punjab Accord', never worth much at any time, has now been dead, betrayed, for quite some tame.

Let me now come to the central issue in the debate, that of the general direction or thrust of our political intervention, as communist revolutionaries, in the Punjab situation; more specifically, the issue concerns our basic attitude towards the Sikh extremist movement in Punjab, insofar as it is a movement with a certain ideological-political dimension to it.

No doubt much of this movement, as it has come to be today, is the product, even a reactive outcome, of the politics of the ruling classes as it has been practised in Punjab in recent years. Nevertheless, it is correct, and not unfair, to assess the overall character of this movement to be socially reactionary, communal and divisive, anti-communist, even fascistic. Therefore our basic position has to be one of firm opposition to it, of uncompromising ideological-political struggle against it. We should however also note that insofar as it is a movement, like most socially significant phenomena, its complexity has diverse more or less important aspects, which would require differentiating tactical responses on our part, depending upon the concrete issues involved and the specific historical conjuncture in each case.

Given its *essential* character, we are in opposition to this movement. So are others—in other, different ways. And the differences here are the consequence of different understandings of the situation as it exists today, in Punjab and in India as a whole. At the present moment, in terms of their theoretical-political significance, there are three different lines or paths of this opposition:

(1) The first line or path of opposition may well be described as 'the Ribeiro-Girilal Jain-Bipan Chandra line'. *Via* different routes or analyses, and through frightening over-simplifications,

it comes to see the struggle primarily as a ruthless, uncompromising exercise of state power, as a 'war', which has to be 'fought out', and 'the perspective has to be of years and not months'. Any number of distinguished names, including intellectuals and academics, both of the right and the left, from 'the national mainstream', could be added to those above, though one must also take note of a significant dissenting minority which argues for a more sane approach. Here the important thing is not the subjective intentions, nor the theoretical frills of 'nationalism', 'secularism', 'democracy', 'all-out mass ideological campaign', or even 'Marxism', with which the argument is often adorned, but the practical-political prescription which flows from one's theoretical position. (Since the issue has been specifically raised in the debate, I would suggest that Bipan Chandra's overall theoretical position is better understood, not as Marxism, but as Left Nationalism, or to put it differently, as Nationalism influenced by or flirting with Marxism. Economic historiography or interpretation, opposition to imperialism or communalism, eclectic references to Marx or Lenin, etc., are not yet Marxism. It is certainly not Marxist to argue that 'it is communalism which has led to separatism and then terrorism', without any reference to the structural inter-connections of these phenomena, *via* mediations, with the historically specific but essentially capitalist development of India (including 'the Green Revolution' in Punjab), or, at another level, with the politics of the ruling classes—and so on. Even good bourgeois social analysis of the Punjab situation does not practise such barefoot empiricism these days. And it has to be emphasised, without being 'class—reductionist', that the basic concept for Marxism here still remains 'class'; it is not 'nation'.)

Needless to state, this line underlies the current policy of the Indian state, duly supported by the Congress (I), BJP, Bipan Chandra ('must give full support to the government') and others, with many pressing for going the whole distance, including the deployment of the army, etc. This policy is doomed to failure. And its success, such as it may be, will turn out to be even worse in its consequences than its failure.

(2) The second line or path of opposition may be said to be represented, above all, by the theory and practice of CPI, CPI (M), etc. Here there are inevitable ambiguities and confusions, conventional rhetoric about 'anti-imperialism, secularism, democracy' or 'the progressive foreign policy' and all that, a great deal of eclecticism and most pragmatic practice of politics (including praise for the CRPF, and exchange of compliments with Ribeiro!). But essentially they view the struggle against Sikh extremism/terrorism as a part of an overall struggle in defence of 'national unity and integrity', especially against 'destabilisation' by American imperialism and its allies, etc. We must recognise the valour and fortitude of the party cadre with many staking their very lives in pursuit of this line. But given the overall emphasis of this theoretical position, the practice that flows from it often obscures the professed dividing line between their politics and that of the parties of the ruling classes. An example is 'the united all-party rallies' in which the Congress (I), Akali Dal, BJP, etc., all partners in perpetrating the tragedy that is Punjab today, are neither self-critical nor are ever criticised by the communists, and together they all even preach 'secularism' to the people of Punjab! In general, this practice has a strong tendency, objectively, to subserve, in Punjab and elsewhere, the politics of the ruling classes, who not only speak the same language, and ever more loudly too, but are finding in 'nationalism' (increasingly defined in Hindu-chauvinist terms) a most useful ideological device to safeguard and legitimise their crisis-ridden class-rule.

Whatever success, real or imaginary, may come the way of this political line, it will again leave the objective situation essentially unchanged and therefore, as pointed out earlier, potentially explosive for all sorts of negative developments in future. Even otherwise, despite the sacrifices made at the altar of 'nationalism', the main beneficiary of this 'success' will be the ruling classes. It will not mean the advancement of the alternative politics of the people that revolutionary political formations in India are and should be striving for.

(3) The third line or path of opposition to the Sikh extremist movement in Punjab sees this struggle essentially as a part of

the broader all-India struggle against the ruling classes' economy, politics, culture, etc., a part of our revolutionary struggle against the present social order. It views the extremely important struggle against imperialism also as a part of this struggle, and not the other way round. For the imperialist intervention in our country today takes place, mainly though not entirely, by the grace of, and through the opportunities provided by, precisely the Indian ruling classes. And insofar as we today have a stake in the 'unity and integrity' of India, not as nationalists, but as communist revolutionaries, who, at the present historical juncture, view it as an important favourable condition for the advance of the Indian peoples' common struggle for socialism, this unity or integrity is also best fought for and preserved within this theoretical position and the political practice flowing from it, that is, as a part of the struggle against the Indian ruling classes, against their economy and politics. It is fashionable these days to speak of India as 'a nation in-the-making'. One might add that if you leave it to the ruling classes, India may well be on its way to be 'a nation-in-the-unmaking'.

This third.path is today the correct theoretical position for the pursuit and advancement of the alternative people's politics in Punjab and in India as a whole. As such it is also the only effective counter to the Sikh extremists' ideological-political practice—insofar as they have one-which, whatever immediate or continuing 'law and order' problems it may pose, constitutes no real threat to the ruling classes in India. On the contrary, it only serves their more basic political and ideological needs. The extremists with their muddled ideology and practice, and the dead-end game of killing and getting killed, advance no cause of theirs; they only play into the hands of the very enemy they claim to be fighting, namely, the *Dilli Sarkar*, 'the rulers at Delhi'. They are indeed helping this enemy in so many ways. They are helping *negatively* by diverting people from the real task of finding genuine answers to their problems, by dividing the people and derailing their discontent into dangerous channels, by weakening and undermining the democratic opposition in the country which would stand up for the rights of Punjab and of the Sikhs as a minority, by making increasingly more difficult the building up of united people's struggles which alone can be a real threat, a revolutionary as against a 'law and order' threat, to the powers that be, for they alone have the promise and capability of winning India for its people and building a free and just society, a genuinely socialist society, in this country. Needless to add, only such a society can guarantee a life of dignity and honour to all its citizens—and to all its minorities too (including the Sikhs in India and the Hindus in Punjab). And it is only such a society, and *the struggle for it today,* that can hold India together.

Negative help apart the extremists are helping 'the rulers at Delhi' *positively* too, both materially and ideologically, by providing them yet another pretext for the further strengthening of the repressive state apparatuses, and by making the ideological manipulation of the people easier through the use of not only the roused Hindu communalism—now increasingly sponsored by the state itself—but also the bogey of 'destablisation' or 'a threat to India's unity and integrity', etc. etc. This is grist to the mill of the Indian ruling classes, faced as they are with a worsening economic situation, mounting discontent, disruption and disorder in civil society, and their deepest ever crisis of legitimacy since independence —and increasingly seeking authoritarian, even fascist, answers to their problems.

In fact insofar as it is possible for us to reach out to the ideologically motivated Sikh youth in the extremist movement, we must help the saner elements among them understand the utterly anti-people and pro-*Dilli Sarkar* consequences of their ideological-political practice.

Before I leave off, let me acknowledge that the path or perspective of struggle I have argued for raises a whole lot of difficult tactical questions, made especially difficult by the specific character of the Indian social formation—what with its size and the complex, contradictions laden dimensions of history and social life, economy and ecology, class, caste and gender, thought and culture, religion and language, ethnicity and nationality, etc. etc. These questions will be sorted out and settled, above all, by the active revolutionaries themselves in the course of their political practice.*

* The original version of this note was published in the discussion columns of August 1987 issue of the Punjabi monthly *Samta*, edited by Gursharan Singh.

12

In Memory of Punjab Revolutionaries of 1914-15*

This festival in memory of the martyrs and heroes of the Ghadar movement and the uprising of 1914-15 is like a breath of fresh air in the frighteningly musty and polluted atmosphere of life and politics in Punjab or for that matter elsewhere in the country today. As a child I had heard of these men, they were spoken of with deep awe and respect in our home. And if Bhagat Singh's was soon a compelling presence for me, I also learnt that *his* hero was Kartar Singh Sarabha, the youthful leader of the uprising which failed; for Bhagat Singh, Kartar Singh Sarabha was indeed a model revolutionary. Later, after 1939, when I came into the Communist Party at Lahore, I had the opportunity to work with the legendary survivors of this uprising and its other successors in the Ghadar movement, who had in the meantime, almost naturally, moved on to Marxism and revolutionary socialism in their search for an answer to the problems of their country. Baba Bhagat Singh Bilga, our chairman at this session, was a senior comrade. A rare privilege for me was the savouring of life and politics of Baba Sohan Singh Bhakna and, somewhat later, of Baba Gurmukh Singh, my proposed work on whose biography was, like so much else, soon disrupted by the tragic partition of the country in 1947.

---

* English version of the address at *Babean da Mela,* a cultural-political festival in memory of the martyrs and heroes of the Ghadarite uprising of 1914-15, Jalandhar, Punjab, September 1992.

Out of these contacts, especially with the former, came a small fragment of writing: *The Ghadar Heroes—Forgotten Story of the Punjab Revolutionaries of 1914-15.* Published in 1945, it was, perhaps, the first such writing in the English language. It was soon translated into other major Indian languages.

For me, coming to participate in this festival is like a pilgrimage—the revolutionary ambience of the occasion restores its true meaning to this word, today much debased by the dominant ruling class politics and culture in our country. I see around me in this memorial building so many reminders of a movement whose revolutionary heroism, quality and sweep of martyrdom, and continuity of struggle and sacrifice can rival any other in the annals of the world revolutionary process. Among these reminders is .the magnificent gallery of portraits, the strong and proud faces of the insurgents, from all communities, even if mostly Sikhs, and from all part of India, even if mostly Punjabis—men who competed with each other to defy death and mount the gallows with a smile, spent long, very long years, the best years of their life, in prisons of India and the Andamans, in solitary confinement and iron cages, chained to walls and ever in handcuffs, bars and fetters, and subjected to every conceivable torture, men who yet never gave in—bleeding but dignified, they suffered but fought on. And once out of their prisons, unbroken and unbowed, they rejoined the battle and carried on the same way, openly or underground, in prisons again or outside, till 1947—and I must add, to the very end, after 1947 too, after India became free and passed into the hands of new, now Indian rulers! What vision these revolutionaries had, what giants of human beings they were in their life-long commitment to the cause of the Indian people. Contrast with the myopic pigmies who have today inherited this country is only too starkly obvious. And this does not preclude those on the Left who claim or are supposed to be their rightful heirs. This long-suffering land of ours, much too tired today, does not produce this breed of men any more. But our people need to remember and recover their revolutionary tradition and be worthy of it if they would reclaim this country for themselves, in Punjab or elsewhere.

I deem it an honour to be invited to address this session of the festival. I am no historian, nor any kind of scholar of the Ghadar movement. I shall be content therefore to make a couple of general observations and one specific *political* point which, I believe, is relevant for those on the Left who would recover the almost lost revolutionary tradition of the Ghadarites and continue their unfinished struggle for the liberation of the Indian people.

Earlier in the session there were efforts to 'analyse and sum up' the phenomenon that was the Ghadar movement. This is as it should be. I will however add that an excessive concern with 'summing up' may still be somewhat misplaced for this is best in order when a movement has either won or lost out finally. To me, while the Ghadar movement certainly has not won, it has not finally lost out either—its struggle is still very much on. A critical, historical look at the movement, a going over the past, needs to have as its main purpose, not 'a final summing up' but a recovery of necessary lessons, of its essential meaning and inspiration for a more effective prosecution of the struggle today.

Again, there were laudable, almost inevitable, exercises to recognise and emphasize 'Ghadar Party's contribution to India's freedom.' Inevitable, because in this its Golden Jubilee year, the 'Quit India' movement is supposed to have won freedom for India and a competitive chipping in of claims is on. Congressite sections of the Indian ruling classes, faced with increasing loss of their legitimacy and desperately looking for it anywhere and everywhere, from communalism to 'Quit India', have been busy building a mythology around the latter as *the* event that gave India its freedom. And this is simply not true. The 'Quit India' movement certainly undermined the British rule in India as did, and far more effectively, the earlier revolutionary movements including the Ghadar movement, and the later revolutionary developments on the eve of Indian independence, long after the few months old 'Quit India' movement had been well taken care of by the British rulers. In any case, in a long term perspective, there is no denying the historic contribution of the Ghadar movement to India's struggle for freedom. But today,

45 years later, perhaps there is need to take notice of, not what happened in 1947, but what did not happen and *its* consequences, namely, a revolutionary overthrow of the British rule in India that the Ghadarites had sought. The more important question today is that the freedom which came in 1947, through a compromise and settlement, with British Imperialism, was not the freedom that the Ghadarite revolutionaries had fought for. *That* freedom still remains to be won for the Indian people.

More interesting than these two issues is another which, though it came up only for a brief reference here, is commonly raised in academic discourses on the subject. A 'scholarly' or 'scientific' attitude apropos the Ghadarite revolutionaries and their attempted uprising often speaks, even if a trifle patronisingly, of such things as 'lack of theory' and 'unsound grasp of historical situation', of circumstances as 'unripe' and armed action as 'inappropriate', of a certain 'peasant-ness' and 'petty bourgeois romanticism' where, as against 'reason', 'emotions and sentiments' take over one's politics, etc., etc.

As I have already stated I am no scholar of the Ghadar movement, nor a historian of India around 1914-15. I will therefore concede that a such 'critiques' may have their validity. But this attitude towards revolutionary movements, especially when they are seen to be unsuccessful in their immediate aims, is quite widespread, and it is likely to grow among scholars now that the 'crisis of socialism' has added to the odds against such movements. This persuades me to make a slightly extended comment of a general nature, for the issue goes much beyond an assessment of the politics of revolutionary Ghadarites. It seems to me that in this matter scholars generally betray a singular inability to comprehend or appreciate what is central to revolutionary politics—the commitment and idealism of the revolutionaries. Conformity to the dominant mores of their society and an academic orientation with its empiricistic concern with the measurable and quantifiable, tends to make these scholars rather insensitive to the intangibles that define and govern the lucidity of life and action of the revolutionaries—a certain passion and moral fervour, absolute anger and hostility towards wrongs of society, its iniquities and injustices, and towards their perpetrators, the powerful moral and emotional charge of the 'dream' they cherish which makes the revolutionaries what they are and drives them to surpass themselves, to achieve, regardless of cost to themselves, in defeat as much as in victory, what is normally seen to be impossible. Scholars simply fail to recognise that 'wise men', men of 'reason' and 'calculations', loaded with 'soundness' and 'scientific theories', but without a dream, don't make revolution. It is those others, men and women of revolutionary idealism and with a dream, born of reality but dream nevertheless, 'Traum' as Marx called it, who do. It is this truly human and alive, death-defying realism that makes the revolutionaries attempt the impossible, that is make revolution. Finding it difficult to comprehend this, most scholars, with the wisdom of hindsight, are generally more comfortable with 'explanation' and 'interpretation', with mundane 'summings up' of revolutionary movements, supplementing their poverty of theory and lack of imagination with plodding research that passes for scholarship in our institutions of higher learning. Some among them, especially those with 'ex-communist's conscience', ever in search of self-justification, even seem to be happy with such movements' failures, 'explaining' and 'analysing' them, and profitably wrapping them up for their own Ph.D degrees and greater glory of others, 'the successful' of history, providing them with much needed assurance, with scholarly support and legitimacy in their search for hegemony. Recent research and writing on the revolutionary or communist Left in India provides quite a few examples. Nothing succeeds like success, in history and for a certain kind of scholar!

An additional point will not be out place for this gathering. Relevant here, maybe it needs to be made even otherwise. The Ghadarite revolutionaries even as they, in their continuing concern for the interests of the Indian people, made a transition to revolutionary socialism of Karl Marx, did so all the more naturally because they saw or sensed in him a kindred spirit, 'a fighter'. As Engels put it: 'Marx was before all else a revolutionist... Fighting was his element. And he fought with a passion, a tenacity, and a success such as few could rival'. It is only this fighter's commitment to socialist revolution that Marx made early in his life, and a moral passion that goes with it, which enables us to make sense of his life—a life full of all the trials and hazards of the life of a revolutionary, its political defeats, factional struggles and repeatedly dashed hopes as well as years of personal poverty and privations, 'the humiliations, torments and terrors', the *'petite miseres* (petty wretchednesses)' as Marx himself put it, of the struggle for sheer physical survival which did grave damage to his wife's health and his own and were a contributory cause of the death of a daughter and two sons, years when he had no money to pay rent or buy medicine or even coffin for a dead child, when his daughters were out of school because their winter shoes were with the pawn-broker, when for days the family fed on bread and potatoes and at times even these were not available... And all this while Marx refused those other easily available 'soft options'. This life is simply inexplicable in terms of conventional scholarship, of 'science' or 'reason' or any 'theory of historical development', of some 'pure logic'. It had an altogether different logic to it, one which underlay all of Marx's theoretical work and his life-long struggle, the logic of a revolutionary commitment, of the clear-eyed choice Marx had made in the fight between the people and those who oppress and exploit them. And he had chosen to stand by the people.

This choice was for Marx, as it has always been for revolutionaries, simply taking of sides in an on-going class war. It was not a matter of any scientific or historical analysis, knowledge of 'laws' or 'stages' or any other 'inevitabilites' of history, or 'predictions' about the future, etc. On the contrary, it entailed a seemingly 'romantic' but necessary boldness in pursuit of revolutionary possibilities. That is how, for example, even as Marx foresaw (in *Communist Manifesto)* the coming 'bourgeois revolution' in Germany, he also saw it as 'the prelude to an immediately following proletarian revolution'. And when this 'bourgeois revolution' indeed occurred, he proclaimed it 'our interest and our task' to seek 'to make the revolution permanent... until the proletariat has conquered state power'. Marx failed in Germany, but seventy years later, exactly as Marx had wanted, Lenin succeeded in Russia, though, I must add, to fail again, through unworthy successors, seventy years later. Such success or failure in struggle, in the epochal process of transition to socialism, however, is not my concern at the moment. The issue here is the commitment and conduct of Marx as a revolutionary, which for Marx also entailed contempt for the philistines who, as he wrote to an old friend 'consider people like you and me as immature fools who all this time have not been cured of their revolutionary fantasies'; told of a contemporary having 'mellowed with age', his response was a disdainful 'oh, has he?' 'To fight' was his 'idea of happiness' as he confessed to his daughter Laura, and to the very end Marx's sympathies always lay with fighters and revolutionaries whatever be the 'small print' of their creeds, as Shanin has put it. Marx had only scorn for the 'know all' types, the doctrinaire theorisers including Marxists, his own followers, when on scientific or theoretical grounds they questioned, criticised or rebuked revolutionary struggle.

We know that Marx had tried to persuade the workers of Paris, for good reasons, not to venture on a revolution. But once they did so he hailed them for 'storming heavens' and stood up magnificently in defence of the Paris Communards against their enemies and calumniators. Again, even as he persistently warned against utopianism and Blanquism in the movement, he was scornfully dismissive of socialists within his own party in Germany who 'keep themselves within the limits of the logically presumable and of the permissible by the police'. Yet again, when the issue was joined between on the one hand the revolutionaries of the People's Will—the indigenous revolutionary organisation of his times in Russia, remembered for its insurrectionary politics and heroic defiance of the Czarist state—who postulated an immediate Russian revolution and the possibility of 'revolutionary leaps' which may ensure Russia 'bypassing the stage' of capitalism on its way to a just society, and on the other Marx's own 'disciples' in Russia—Plekhanov and others—whose strictly evolutionist Marxism saw history as constituted by necessary stages and postulated the necessity of a capitalist stage in Russia's advance to socialism, and therefore criticised the populist revolutionaries in the name of Marxism and scientific socialism, Marx came down loud and clear on the side of the revolutionaries of the Peoples Will. He found these revolutionaries, on trial for life, not only right in the essentials of their stand but 'simple, objective, heroic'. Theirs was, Marx wrote, not tryrannicide as "theory" and "panacea" but a lesson to Europe in a "specifically" Russian historically inevitable mode of action; against which any moralising from a safe distance was offensive'. Marx always spoke admiringly of human qualities of these revolutionaries and to the end he and Engels consistently referred to them as 'our friends'. In contrast Marx spoke of the 'boring doctrines' of his evolutionist disciples and referred to them derisively as 'Russian capitalism admirers'—a political position which needs to be taken note of by our own 'Indian capitalism admirers', Marxist and other Leftist apologists for 'progressive', 'independent' or 'self-reliant' capitalism, who, additionally, so interpret historical processes in India as to go soft on the ruling classes to the point of rallying behind them in the name of Marxism or socialism. (Incidentally, later on, Lenin too seems to have shared Marx's 'deviation' on the Russian question. During and after 1905-07 revolution, he was accused of leaning towards populism, that is the Russian revolutionaries, by some of his associates and adversaries).

In a brief but brilliant exploration of the life and work of late Marx, drawing our attention to this particular aspect of Marx as a revolutionary and to a certain scientistic interpretation of Marxism, Teodor Shanin writes:

> It has been the way of many sophisticates of marxology to scoff at such utterances of Marx or to interpret them patronisingly as 'determined rather by... emotional motives' (an antonym, no doubt, of 'analytical', 'scientific' or 'sound'). To understand political action, especially the struggle for a socialist transformation of humanity, as an exercise in logic or as a programme of factory building only, is utterly to misconstrue it, as Marx knew well. Also, he shared with the Russian revolutionaries the belief in the purifying power of revolutionary

> action in transforming the very nature of those involved in it—the 'educating of the educators'. The Russian revolutionary populists' concern with moral issues found ready response in him. Moral emotions apart (and they were there and unashamedly expressed), revolutionary ethics were often as central as historiography to Marx's political judgement. So was Marx's distaste of those to whom the punchline of marxist analysis was the adoration or elaboration of irresistible laws of history, used as the license to do nothing.

Let me now turn to the substantive political issue that I wanted to raise.

Men of the Ghadar Party were revolutionaries par excellence. Secular and democratic to the core, patriotic in the best sense of the word, they were nationalists committed to insurrectionary politics, to a revolutionary overthrow of the British rule in India, which they saw as first step for India on its way to a just society. As expressed in the Ghadarite poetry and literature, they visualised this society as free from exploitation and oppression, a society of equality, fraternity and social justice for its citizens. It is this vision precisely which makes their later transition to Marx's revolutionary socialism an almost natural progress. Whatever the inadequacies of their theory and practice —and there were many as we now know them in the light of our experience with and knowledge of revolutionary movements since—the Ghadarites were remarkably perspicacious within the specific social and historical context of their times. In our own socio-historical context, in view particularly of the situation facing their heirs, the Communist Left in India today—in speaking of 'Communist Left', I shall be primarily referring to the mainstream communist movement represented by CPI(M) and CPI three closely interrelated aspects of the Ghadarite revolutionary politics deserve to be noticed.

In the first place, whatever the problems with their theory, organisation and tactics and these are always important, the Ghadarite revolutionaries had absolute clarity concerning the most important question, namely, their strategic aim. British imperialism in India was the main enemy and the Ghadarites sought its revolutionary overthrow. Their struggle was geared to this purpose, all activity subordinated to this strategic aim. In the second place, again, whatever the problems, theoretical and practical, with their politics of armed insurrection, they understood it as an independent and alternative politics which stood firmly demarcated from and opposed to the mainstream bourgeois nationalist politics of their time as represented by the Indian National Congress—be it 'constitutionalism' of the liberals or the emerging populist but reformist 'non-violence' of Gandhi. They had a genuine distrust of this politics, expressed most eloquently in their poetry. Even though their own insurrectionist politics failed, this distrust was well-justified; it stands vindicated by the manner in which freedom came to India, the compromise and settlement with British imperialism, the partition of the country with long term disastrous consequences for the common people on both sides of the borders, and the outcome of this freedom at the end of these forty-five years. In the third place, certainly sustained by the first two, is the last aspect to be noticed, the revolutionary elan and moral grandeur of the Ghadarite revolutionaries which expressed itself not only in their heroic defiance of the British rulers at the post-uprising trials, on the gallows and in the cells and cages of the Andamans, but even more in the life and conduct of those who survived and carried on their struggle to the end, even against the new rulers after India became free.

These three aspects are among the most vital prerequisites of any living and vibrant revolutionary movement anywhere. Today, one is compelled to note, the mainstream Communist movement, within which the survivors of the Ghadarite uprising and their successors worked for long years and which claims or is supposed to be heir to the Ghadarite tradition, is rather poor in all these three aspects. A clear strategic aim, an independent, alternative politics, and the moral elan of a revolutionary movement, all seem to have got lost somewhere along the way.

Central to this loss is an issue which was basic to the concerns of the Ghadarite revolutionaries also, the issue of nationalism. It seems to me that, to state it unambiguously, if in *their* historical context, a vibrant revolutionary nationalism was the source of the strength of Ghadarite revolutionaries because it grasped and sought to resolve the basic contradictions of Indian society of their times, in the changed historical context of *our* times, an ahistorical and almost unthinking nationalism has been a major source of the weakness of the Communist Left over these years, because it has served to prevent it from grasping the basic contradictions of Indian society *after 1947*; therefore the resolution of these contradictions never became central to its politics, contributing to its disorientation as a revolutionary opposition, an alternative, in our society.

It is true that we still do not have an adequate theory of nationalism, Marxist or any other—it remains 'an ambiguous identity'. However we do know that it is particular objective conditions or developments (economic, political, cultural and other) which combine to constitute and shape such or similar subjective identities as meaningful in society, making them terms for individual self-definition or identification, and diffusing them across population sufficiently to turn them into objective social components of society which read back to themselves affect social conditions or developments—the subjective identities coming to play an objective role, for better or worse, in social and historical processes. For the purpose of my argument, we need to recognise only this indisputable fact, namely, a most powerful social, political, and ideological force of our times, nationalism is yet a historical phenomenon, with class and society-specific character, potentialities and limitations, and uses, and thus capable of manifesting itself in a variety of forms. Located as we are in the Third World and with the still' alive though rapidly fading memories of the long struggle against imperialism, we in this country are conventionally inclined to see nationalism as a liberationist force or ideology. But we will do well to remember that during the same period ruling classes of the countries of imperialism were finding nationalism useful not only to consolidate their rule at home but also to defend and justify their aggression and domination abroad. More recently, we have witnessed several cases of similar political-ideological use of nationalism by ruling class politicians—among these by Margaret Thatcher in England with the Falklands War which routed the Labour Party as never before, or by Ronald Reagan in the US in his twice successful bid for the American presidency. Nearer home we saw Rajiv Gandhi romp home in the unprecedented electoral triumph of 1984 on a platform of nationalism, with strong Hindu chauvinist, even anti-Sikh, overtones—the emerging platform of Hinduised Indian nationalism, which has now been well and properly appropriated by another political formation of the Indian ruling classes, the Bharatiya Janata Party. And these days we hear of a desperate Yeltsin and quite a few of his equally desperate opponents turning to Russian national chauvinism as a diversionary device to retain or gain control over a deeply discontented and restive Russian people...Besides, we must not forget chat our times have witnessed nationalism of German, Japanese and Italian varieties which so obviously sacrificed the people to the 'nation'. With the ruling classes, in the normal pursuit of their interests or when faced with situations of crisis in the polity, nationalism has often taken all sorts of anti-people statist or racist or fascist or imperialist forms, providing ideological support or cover to the emergence of reactionary authoritarian regimes.

Thus understood, in historical terms, nationalism is not in itself progressive or reactionary, secular or communal, democratic or authoritarian, anything better or worse. It all depends upon its specific character, its programme and leadership, and 'above all, concrete historical context and conjuncture. Such are the factors which determine its precise nature and historical role. Nationalism in India before 1947 was indeed progressive; under a different, more advanced class leadership and programme, it could have been radical, even revolutionary. It was progressive because it aimed at resolving the basic structural contradictions of Indian society, congealed in imperialism, whose resolution, *against* imperialism, alone could clear the path for Indian people's continuing struggle for a better future. But nationalism need not be necessarily or entirely so in the post-1947 period. For the settlement of 1947 had its own harsh logic. It is customary in conventional scholarship or historiography to take a liberal, linear view of the historical process in India around and after 1947. In this view the Indian nation, or 'nation-in-the-making' if you prefer, is seen as winning *political* freedom for India in 1947, and then expectedly and almost unproblematically moving on to win *economic* freedom for the country—a movement which forty-five years hence is still on. The real historical process, however, has been quite different, essentially dialectical. The very manner in which the contradictions with imperialism were resolved, its 'transfer of power' involving no basic economic or social structural change, but putting new, now *Indian* ruling classes in control of the state power—this made the Indian people's struggle for economic freedom not only that much more complex and difficult but also primarily a matter of struggle against *these* classes. This is where, increasingly, the basic structural contradictions of Indian society now come to be located as the new rulers use their newly won state power to facilitate a historically specific form of capitalist development in the country, even as they continue to maintain, with due modifications, the old exploitative and oppressive socio-economic structures of Indian society. In fact, given the new configuration of classes, class interests and contradictions, even the Indian people's continuing struggle against imperialism or neo-colonialism is no longer simply a continuation of the old, pre-1947, anti-imperialist struggle. Henceforth it too can be effectively waged only as a part of the above-mentioned basic struggle *within* Indian society, for the imperialist intervention or domination, the neo-colonialist 'integration' into the global capitalist economy, now occurs, increasingly, by the grace of, through the opportunities provided by, or even at the invitation of precisely the new Indian ruling classes. (It should be obvious that Union Carbide once upon a time, and I.M.F. and World Bank more recently, don't just descend from the skies, they invariably arrive via New Delhi).

These considerations of systemic nature are of decisive importance for a revolutionary strategy; though I must hasten to add that within the same systemic context, it is always possible for the ruling classes to make good or bad choices and to pursue different, better or worse economic, political, cultural and other policies, and that this is a matter of great tactical significance for any revolutionary politics.

Social reality is invariably much too complex, above all in its interconnections and changeability, to be easily, much less fully understood or grasped by social theory. Marx's social theory recognised this. His achievement here was to provide what still remains, with all its problems and inadequacies, the best point of entry into understanding the systemic character of social formations by suggesting that a society be viewed as a *totality*, a historically specific, contradictions-laden, structured interdependence of parts, within which one part, the economy ('the basis', or more precisely, 'the economic structure') in an asymmetry of reciprocal influence, *decisively conditions* every other part or aspect of society, its politics, morality, culture, indeed the dynamics of its life as a whole. As Raymond Williams has more recently put it:' it is true that there are forms of material production which always and everywhere precede all other forms (in a society)... The enormous theoretical shift introduced by classical Marxism—in saying these are the primary productive activities—was of the most fundamental importance'. Again, if it was scientifically valid for Marx, in *Capital*, to posit a 'pure' or 'abstract' bourgeois mode of production for the purpose of analysing its basic 'law of motion', he knew that in history there are no 'pure' or 'normal' modes, capitalist or any other; they would be as hard to find as an 'average' man in real life.

Social formations thus remain a most complex affair. And Indian social formation is possibly the most complex in the world, with its continental dimensions and extraordinary diversities of economic and social life, long, relatively continuous history, colonial legacies, and all sorts of other material, cultural and ideological survivals from the past, etc. etc. For understanding the systemic character of this much too complex social formation, two passages from Marx, their different contexts notwithstanding, may still be helpful for their suggestiveness. He wrote:

> In all forms of society there is one specific kind of production which predominates over the rest, whose relations thus assign rank and influence to the others. It is the general illumination which bathes all the other colours and modifies their particularity. It is a particular ether which determines the specific gravity of every being which has materialised within it.

Again, elsewhere, he spoke of countries which

> suffer not only from the development of capitalist production but also from the incompleteness of that development. Alongside of modern evils, a whole series of inherited evils oppress us, arising from the passive survival of antequated modes of production with their inevitable train of social and political anachronisms. We suffer not only from the living but from the dead.

Thus in these forty-five post-colonial years, if capitalism has grown apace, and become increasingly pre-eminent in Indian economy as a whole, it has also been a specifically Indian form of belated capitalist development—'some strange kind of corrupted capitalist growth' in Romesh Thapar's words—with its particular propertied (exploitative) classes, big bourgeoisie and kulaks-cum-capitalist rich farmers, increasingly dominant in the industrial and agrarians sectors of Indian economy. And around them has grown a coalition of other main beneficiaries, among them the semi-feudal landlords and speculating businessmen, professionals in the public and private sectors including higher echelons of civil and military establishments, organized white collar workers and 'the political class' which, even as it serves as a varied broker in the system, has turned politics itself into an almost hereditary, a lumpen but very lucrative capital intensive business. Together they constitute, broadly speaking, the ruling power structure in the country as a whole.

Just as, before 1947, the structural logic of British imperialism meant the accumulation of wealth in England and poverty in India, the structural logic of Indian capitalism is most manifest today in the unequal and uneven development in the country over these forty-five years, in the emergence of the now universally admitted 'two nations'—the Indian 'twin nation' (K.N. Raj), 'socio-economic *dualism*' which is so very 'corrosive'

(Sukhamoy Chakravarty), 'this dualism in Indian society' which is threatening to become 'explosive' (V.K.R.V. Rao), the 'two Indias' of Rajni Kothari, V.P. Singh, R.K. Hegde *et al*, etc.—and a certain 'internal colonialism' in the more backward parts of the country. Its historical specificity has given it a strong comprador and lumpen character, presided over as it is by a bourgeoisie born old without ever having known youth, with none of the possible virtues of youth and all the vices of old age. Here all the exploitative and oppressive evils of belated capitalist development, semi-feudalism, bureaucratically-corrupt public sector and bloated bourgeois politics daily enter into and reinforce each other. All pervasive black money, flourishing as a parallel economy, only intensifies the structural biases of a white money of scams and swindles, even as it serves to sustain, with help from politicians, policemen and sundry state functionaries, an essentially illegal, secular or communal *mafiosi*-led parallel political polity, which has today come to acquire an almost legitimised coexistence with the formally legal state in large, especially urban, parts of the country. A long time ago, apropos the essentially *secondary* character of such capitalist development, Karl Marx had written: 'as is well-known, secondary diseases are more difficult to cure, and, at the same time, ravage the body more than original ones'...

The recent turn from a state-supported to an explicitly market-friendly capitalism only means that the predatory as well as comprador-lumpen nature of Indian capitalism will now manifest itself even more openly. Higher growth rates are promised, but if and when they do materialize it will only be a case of 'the economy is doing fine, the people are not', as a president of Brazil's military government once reported it in Washington. The Haward economist Robert Reich's phrase, 'the secession of the successful', well expresses the structural logic of capitalism as a market economy. The new economic policy means that 'the successful' of our 'national economy', 'a narrow section of Indian society' in V.K.R.V. Rao's words—the 'creamy layer' or 'privilegentsia' as it is also called these days—have decided, like their counterparts elsewhere in the capitalist world, to openly secede from the rest of their countrymen.

Almost everyone in our country these days, from the hack politician to the so-called intellectual, on the left as much as on the right, is busy urging almost everyone else to join some mythical 'national mainstream', mythical because nobody has so far told us what it is and where it flows. Accompanying this urging is deep anxiety and concern about 'national integration', there are desperate daily exhortations to promote and strengthen it. What is forgotten is that today every aspect of social life in India bears the signature of this historically specific Indian form of capitalist development—its mark is there on our morality, our culture, our politics, on everything, everywhere. Therefore if there is indeed a 'national mainstream' it is, bearing the impress of India's corrupt and corrupting, somewhat lumpen capitalist development, an increasingly dirty affair—corrupt, communal and criminalised, a repressively homogenising mainstream. Again, the fact to be deplored is not that we are not integrated but that we are integrated the *capitalist* way which, with its unequal and uneven development, its 'two nations', 'internal colonialism', and much else by way of exploitation and oppression of the people, carries within it strong disintegrative tendencies. Herein lies the basic reason why today all the divides and fissures of Indian society, around class, caste or religion, language, region, ethnicity or nationality, etc., have become sharpened and potentially explosive.

The Indian state, given the economic weakness and lack of legitimacy of the post-colonial bourgeoisie, has certainly acted as 'the executor of the economic necessities of the national situation', as Engels once phrased it, much in the manner of the state in France with Louis Bonaparte, or in Germany with Bismarck, or the Czarist state in Russia. It has facilitated, as V.K.R.V. Rao pointed out, ' a type of capitalist development in the interests of a narrow section of Indian society'. But contrary to the nationalist hopes and liberal expectations, it has failed to serve as an agent of equity and distributive justice for the Indian people. If, nevertheless, something has got done for them in response to the demands of 'democratic politics', or to gain legitimacy, it has not to any significant degree curbed the structurally inherent predatory logic of India's capitalist development. In fact even of the funds directly allocated for poverty alleviation, only 'the leakage', a bare fifteen per cent, is supported to have reached the people, as Rajiv Gandhi told us, and he, if any one, certainly knew. While there has been an increasing use of 'state as private property', and any kind of power within the state as a means of 'rapid private accumulation', now, with the turn to a 'free' market capitalism even the paltry effort aimed at equity or distributive justice, indeed the very pretence of 'growth with justice', is being abandoned. And the Indian state has all along served, and continues to serve, as an instrument of coercion and repression against the common Indian people.

Here I would like to suggest that it is not adequate to describe the state, as the Communist Left traditionally does, primarily in terms of 'an instrument' or 'an organ' —this, at best; grasps only one, albeit an important, aspect of the modern state. We need to recognise the obviously *non-monolithic nature,* on the one hand, of class domination where, almost invariably, what we have is an alliance or a coalition of ruling classes with real, even if non-antagonistic, internal conflict of interests, and on the other, of the material and ideological structures of the modern state that are today far too many and massively diverse and scattered all over vertically and horizontally—which, incidentally, makes the state itself a possible 'arena of class struggle'. The metaphor of 'instrument' or 'organ', being very partial, can be quite misleading. It fails, for example, to make sense of the role of a Louis Bonaparte, or Bismarck, or the Czarist state as mentioned above, and it certainly obscures the important possibility of state's relative autonomy from any given ruling class or classes, which the state often, if not always, needs to have precisely in order to manage and promote *the common interests* of the ruling classes *as a whole.* The state, however, is never autonomous from the socio-economic structure of a class-divided society which it essentially serves.

This is not to deny that different structures of the state, its institutions and apparatuses, at a particular point of time may be in the hands of a particular fragment of ruling class or classes, who may use them to promote particular interests or even settle intra or inter-class quarrels or conflicts. But a proper Marxist view of the state must see it as the organiser of society in the interests of the class-exploitative structure taken as a whole—and this includes, as Gramsci put it, 'the entire complex of practical and theoretical activities with which the ruling class not only justifies and maintains its dominance, but manages to win the active consent of those over whom it rules'. This is indeed how the Indian state has functioned over these forty-five years; it is above all in this sense that it has been and continues to be a class-state. It is thus that if India's 'national economy' has been anti-people over these forty-five years, so has been India's 'national state'. The state in India, far from being a part of the solution is itself a part of the problem.

All those who seek a genuine radical or revolutionary transformation of Indian society, including the best of those involved in 'grassroots' activism, or 'new social movements' as they are called, will do well to recognise this harsh fact—the class nature and power of the Indian state. Those who would leave the state alone, as a certain kind of radicalism suggests, need to know that the state will not leave *them* alone. The question of political power, the people's power in the state, the struggle for 'political supremacy' or 'state power' of the exploited and the oppressed, is central to any struggle for a better life for the common Indian people.

Of course, dangerous aberrations or departures notwithstanding, we have had democracy and democratic politics so far. And democracy in India is, whatever its limitations and however weak or fragile, a hardwon achievement of the Indian people, and they certainly need it, more than the ruling classes do. It has certainly served to somewhat curb the authoritarian political logic of the Indian economic system, and brought benefits, however marginal these may have been, even to the common Indian people. They certainly need to struggle to defend it, to preserve and expand it. And they *have* so struggled all these years, as best as they could—the threats to democracy having invariably emanated from one or the other political formation of the ruling classes, often from their internecine struggle for power in the state. Yet, as Bagehot observed, with obvious satisfaction, in an earlier, more honest age: 'democracy is the way to give the people the greatest illusion of power while allowing them the smallest amount in reality'. And this is indeed how it has worked in India.

Obvioulsy, democracy has not meant effective political power for the Indian people. Within almost two decades of Indian freedom and democracy, even so sympathetic a scholar as Gunnar Myrdal, a personal friend of Nehru, wrote of 'the new government's role as the successor to the British raj', of 'the gulf between rulers and ruled', and the life-style and conduct of the new rulers which 'encouraged the view that political independence had done little more that displace a foreign with a native privileged group'. Pointing out that 'India is ruled by a select group of upper class citizens who use their political power to secure their privileged positions' and that 'the power struggle has mainly remained one between individuals and groups in the upper class in the broader sense', he concluded : 'Democracy has not enabled the majority of poor people to grasp, and organise themselves for utilising, political power to advance their own interests'. In 1973, V.K.R.V. Rao spoke of 'a political alliance of the intermediate classes with the upper classes, resorting to socialist ideology only to win mass support but using all levers of power to facilitate a type of capitalist development in the interest of a narrow section of Indian society'; and fifteen years later he most emphatically stated that so far as 'the poor and deprived sections of the people' are concerned, 'parliamentary democracy has not been able to meet the challenge'.

How, despite democracy, 'reality' of power has remained with the ruling classes, not only in India but elsewhere too, how 'the taming of democracy' as it may be called, occurs, is not my concern just now. Suffice it to state here that this 'happening', the wide gulf between people and political power that democracy has come to mean, is not only universally recognised in contemporay capitalist-democratic systems, it has been defended and actually celebrated in bourgeois social science as 'democracy' itself. With a slight exaggeration—but then all science and art is an exaggeration one could even argue that the most important if not the sole discovery of modern political science, its ultimate wisdom on the subject is: if you want to have democracy, or to save it, keep the people away from it! Though, in fairness to Aristotle I must add that he had discovered and said as much, far more honestly and intelligently, more than two thousand years ago. Be that as it may, the relevant point I want to make is that where the people have failed, the rulers everywhere have succeeded eminently, they have been able to use democracy 'to advance their own interests'. This has happened because, putting it most briefly, democracy is particularly useful to the ruling classes in two ways: it helps ensure their hegemony in society, legitimising their class domination as never before, for now they exploit the people and rule over them with their own consent; and it provides the ruling classes with an impersonal, non-arbitrary device for articulting and resolving their inevitabe internal conflict of interests, even as the democratic state promotes these interests as a whole.

This two-fold usefulness of democracy to the ruling classes has been central to India's 'democratic politics' since independence. In the earlier Nehru era, the golden age of the post-colonial state, this politics was conducted by their political formations, the dominant Congress (I) and the rest, more or less as a 'Hindu Undivided Family', on the basis of a working 'consensus', a 'balance' of power and interests among them, the beneficiaries of the system as a whole. But after the economic crisis of the mid-sixties, and subject to the continuing constraints of the economic situation since then, the 'family' has badly divided up, the earlier 'consensus' or 'balance' has been lost and the beneficiaries have been engaged in an utterly unscrupulous, on-holds-barred infighting for power and pelf in the state, where it is truly the end justifying the means, literally any means: It is thus that the inept and myopic rulers, violating every rule of their own game inside the state institutions and outside, making bad choices and pursuing worse policies, have been producing intractable problems for themselves and one tragedy after another for the people, as in Punjab, each of which soon comes to acquire autonomous logic and dimensions of its own. Perhaps the rulers can indulge in this reckless and fratricidal 'politicians' politics' *(la politique politicienne,* Malraux's phrase), which has much undermined the legitimacy of both their politics and the political system as a whole, because they face, as yet, no significant threat of a 'peoples' politics' from below.

If India's 'national economy' has been generating any number of potentially explosive issues, the 'national politics' pursued by the ruling classes in recent years has been regularly turning these issues into problems, problems into running sores, and these sores into tragedies for the Indian people. Disastrous in its consequences for the people as it is, this politics has today become the most potent threat to the rulers' own much touted 'unity and integrity' of India. Years ago, apropos Punjab, I had advanced a proposition which, more than vindicated by the developments since, still holds. I had written:

> It is fashionable these days to speak of India as 'a nation-in-the-making'. One might add that if you leave it to the ruling classes, India may well be on its way to be 'a nation-in-the-unmaking'.

Such being the situation, nationalism or a nationalist perspective today—with its wide array of supportive concepts like 'national economy' or 'national development', 'nation-building' or 'state-building', 'national mainstream', 'national integration' or 'unity and integrity of the nation', etc. conceals the essential character of Indian social reality as it has come to be as a result of an India specific capitalist development. Nationalism not only serves to cover up, or provide alibis for, the historic default of the post-colonial ruling classes in India, it increasingly turns into a legitimising ideology for these classes in need of defending and safeguarding their eonomic and political domination. By obscuring the most basic division in our society, between *we* (the people) and *they* (who exploit and oppress them), nationalism permits the latter even to get away with plain lies to justify and gather support for their policies and politics.

Witness, for example, the lie that was the well-orchestrated national chorus to launch the recent class-interests dictated surrender to global capitalism: 'the country has been living beyond its means'. For a good majority of our people have simply no means at all to live, and most others nothing much to indulge any 'living beyond'. The nationalist lie provides a cover for those who have indeed been living beyond this country's poor means for long and are now set on continuing to do so via the 'free' market, those whom the Latin Americans have learnt to call 'anti-nation within the nation'.

Nationalism is certainly being used by the ruling classes and their diverse political formations today to manipulate the common people ideologically in support or defence of their crisis-ridden class-politics and class-rule. More the crisis deepens, discontents mount, disruption or disorder spreads, and the ruling class legitimacy gets undermined, louder become the exhortations in the name of nationalism or patriotism. And as these exhortations are increasingly recognised as so many cliches, as nationalism continues to wane and patriotism grows flabby, they are sought to be flogged into some semblance of life, through the media controlled by the state, through editorials and advertisements in the press, through wayside hoardings and interminable singing and running for the country on the television and elsewhere, through the rhetoric of politicians and the laboured theorising of in-house scholars and through extravaganzas, *utsavs* and centenaries of all sorts...All of which reminds one of what Marx once spoke of as 'opium of patriotic feelings', which the ruling classes often find useful for their purposes, especially in troubled times.

It is my argument that a simplistic and unthinking, essentially ahistorical nationalism, an internalizing of a nationalist as against a Marxist perspective for its theory and pratice in the post-independence period, has contributed much to Communist Left's loss of a revolutionary, that is, genuinely *socialist* strategic aim, which could only be formulated on the basis of a sophisticated class analysis—if I may still argue for that much-maligned and misused concept—of the new, post-1947 Indian situation. This has naturally led to a failure to develop an independent, alternative politics in the country which can only be a class-based people's politics geared to a revolutionary transformation of Indian society. These two defaults have almost inevitably resulted in a steady erosion of revolutionary clan in the mainstream Communist Left in India, for this clan is simply impossible in the absence of an independent revolutionary strategy and politics.

Nationalism has virtually disarmed the Communist Left ideologically, depriving it of the 'independent political position' that Marx always emphasised and Lenin repeatedly endorsed as absolutely necessary for revolutionary politics. Joining in the competitive nationalism of the dominant bourgeois politics, speaking the same language and loud-mouthing the same slogans of 'national development', 'national integration', 'national mainstream', 'unity and integrity of India', and sharing the same fears of 'destabilisation' etc.etc., has led this Left again and again to an 'appealing' or 'deploring', more or less active, tailist alignment with one or the other ruling class political formation, often helplessly advising those in power with 'wise' and 'sensible' solutions to problems of their own creation, which 'solutions' are invariably ignored by the latter as they go on to create new problems and further mess up the old ones. Such 'nationalist' blurring of the distinction between bourgeois and communist politics has, in it own way, reinforced parallel, reformist tendencies in the mainstream communist movement, reducing its theory and practice—jousting inside the Parliament, bandhs, rallies, marches outside, and radical rhetoric everywhere notwithstanding—to one of seeking only a more rational working of the present socio-economic system, in the interests of the system itself, rather than its revolutionary transformation that a communist politics must work for. In the absence of an independent Left politics, all 'joint actions', or 'united fronts' end up only serving the needs of the politics of ruling classes. But the bogey of 'sectarianism', 'adventurism', even 'political immaturity' is raised to deny the demand for such an alternative politics, and to justify or condone any and every kind of pragmatic, even opportunist practice on the terrain of bourgeois politics.

In fact socialism itself has come to be seen as an adjunct of national aspirations. Put simply, Left criticism or argument here is that it is not through capitalism but socialism that national development can be realised. And this leaves socialism very much an utopian affair. In a Marxist understanding, socialism is born of the irrationality and contradictions of capitalism, it is not just another 'vision' of a good society. In its essential character, socialism is a *negation* of capitalism. (This, incidentally, should also make it clear that so long as capitalism lasts, socialism necessarily remains on the agenda of the future progress of humankind.) There is thus always the need to analyse the irrationality and contradictions of capitalism which generate the conditions and forces for socialist politics. A nationalist perspective which obscures this need, which is unwilling or unable to concretely analyse the contradictions of India's historically specific form of capitalism, to locate the main victims of its irrationality, its inadequacy, injustice and inhumanity, who, having gained the requisite revolutionary consciousness, that is, having 'won the theoretical awarenesss of their loss', as Marx put it, shall be the driving social forces of a socialism-oriented struggle, and to develop appropriate programme, politics and organisation for this purpose, such a perspective cannot provide for socialism as a historically viable project to struggle for. It only reduces socialism to 'a vision', much in the manner of Nehru once upon a time, and many well-meaning intellectuals on the Left these days, 'reluctant socialists' and others who somewhat sad and lost after the Soviet collapse, are busy 'exploring' and 'filling in' 'visions' of socialism, proclaiming their faith, and frailty of theory as, well, with such propositions as: 'socialism as a vision is, of course, immortal'...

It needs to be clearly understood that the struggle for socialism in India or, in more precise historical and theoretical terms, for *a society in transition to socialism,* is a process of class-struggle in the proper Marxian sense, which eschews its narrow economistic or reductionist interpretations. No doubt a great deal of tactical resilience is necessary in relating it, theoretically as well as practically, to the obviously important issue of nationalism. But even if this struggle is viewed as a *national* struggle of the Indian people, it can be nothing else but fighting the 'anti-nation within the nation', or 'rescuing the nation' from its ruling classes, and thus remains in its essential content, a class struggle; it is not a collective national struggle of *all* Indians for a socialist society. The national task, recovering India for its people, yet remains a class-task. This task certainly involves a stake in the unity and integrity of India because at the present historical juncture this is an important favourable condition for the advance of Indian people's struggle for socialism: But insofar as capitalist economy and ruling class politics are the major sources of the present threat to the unity and integrity of India, its defence too is a part of the class-task mentioned above, a matter of class struggle. Neither Indian people's interests nor unity and integrity of India are today possible of defence or promotion in any other way. And this struggle requires no 'opium of patriotic feelings', only a *socialist* commitment to the cause of the Indian people.

Such has to be the strategic thrust of an independent Left politics in India today.

The absence of an independent Left politics in our country has meant that a festering economic, social and moral crisis in society which has sharpened all the conflicts and contradictions within, has come to be combined with a political system which, however well it may have functioned once, today, in its mafia-like degeneration from top to bottom, can only go on creating problems but is unable to find any effective solutions; the deceptive motions of electoral politics, almost exhausted of constructive possibilities, only hides the reality of a political gridlock which is pushing our society into ever deeper crises. The political costs of solutions seem to be more difficult to bear for the rulers than those of the problems. They are even beginning to find these problems, at least some of them, ideologically and politically useful; more specific mundane benefits apart, they certainly help divert attention from the more basic and bothersome isssues of poverty, hunger and disease, unemployment and illiteracy etc., and also provide pretexts for further strengthening of the repressive apparatuses of the state and for better ideological manipulation of the people by rousing and playing upon their fears for country's 'unity and integrity' etc.—the rulers are therefore quite content to live with these problems. Indeed, when the very existence of a problem serves the purpose, why seek a solution?....

It is the people, left entirely at the mercy of the politics of the ruling classes, who suffer—they are the victims and it is they who are paying the real costs. Ideologically disarmed and disoriented, they daily breathe in and internalise the ruling class ideology which, it is well to remember, is seldom, if ever, all of one piece, but is generally constituted by all sorts of competing and even contradictory ideas and doctrines which yet supplement each other, above all, in their practical implications, and hold together to serve the same ruling class interests. Subject to popular awareness as well as corruption of popular consciousness that electoral politicisation and communication revolution entail, used and manipulated by the rulers in so many different ways, the people struggle as best as they can. Their discontent is finding expression in all sorts of ideologically muddled protests around genuine grievances and in any number of divisive and disruptive developments all over the country. Unable to fight the right battles, they fight the wrong ones—for this is what the hegemony of a bankrupt ruling class politics means. Unable to move forward in a revolutionary manner, the people are inevitably moving backwards, as is happening in other parts of the world too. Politics, I believe, is where answers to the problems facing our people are to be found. This is indeed the arena of struggle for India's future. Therefore the present political logjam created by ruling class politics has to be broken, space has to be won and expanded for an alternative politics of the people. The failure of the Communist Left here is its real tragedy, part of the larger tragedy of the Indian people.

A nationalist perspective on politics, as against a Marxist, class perspective, is not the only reason for Communist Left's surrender to bourgeois politics and its failure to develop an independent, alternative politics for the Indian people. There are several other reasons too. For example, participation in parliamentary politics, which poses so many still unresolved, almost intractable, problems for those seeking a revolutionary transformation of Indian society. If as a general principle, such, participation is absolutely necessary at the present historical juncture, in fact whenever and wherever possible, not only are exceptions to it admissible, but it always needs to be subordinated to extra-parliamentary class and mass politics, whose rich and complex array has to include what I would describe as a communist variant of Gandhi's 'constructive programme'—something never easy to achieve, yet most imperative for any success in the struggle for hegemony in society. People's power grows only out of their own activity, organisation and struggles and the revolutionary consciousness these come to be suffused with. This apart, parliamentary politics, even as it corrupts in so many ways, exercises a most 'civilizing' influence on revolutionaries as Laski was fond of pointing out. It is significant, perhaps also symbolic of the tragedy of the Communist Left that, when looking for 'the most outstanding parliamentarians', models of 'parliamentary rectitude', 'ornaments' of Lok or Rajya Sabha, or even 'statesmen' of Indian politics, for their awards and honours, the custodians of bourgeois politics and their media have increasingly come to discover them among the communist leaders. And even as these leaders are happy garnering their awards and accolades, their followers are moving away from 'the Party' and the Indian people from parliamentary politics itself! When the bourgeoisie begins to find the communist leaders adorable, perhaps it is time for them to stop and take another look at themselves and their politics. But problems of parliamentary politics or the other reasons contributing to the stagnation or loss of initiative of the mainstream Communist Left is not the subject I want to pursue here...

I would, however, like to deal with one reason which is in a way linked to and supplements the surrender to bourgeois politics on the question of nationalism. I am referring to the philosophical surrender on the part of the Communist Left to the dominant bourgeois mode of thinking, which Engels chose to describe as the 'metaphysical mode of thought'. Writing on the subject in *Anti-Duhring,* Engels noticed that 'at first sight (the metaphysical) mode of thought seems to us extremely plausible because it is the mode of thought of common sense'. But he found it to be 'one-sided, limited, abstract' because it studies things ' in their isolation, detached from the whole vast interconnection of things; and therefore not in their motion, but in their repose; not in their life, but in their death'. He added: 'in considering individual things it loses sight of their connections; in contemplating their existence it forgets their coming into being and passing away; in looking at them at rest it leaves their motion out of account;... it cannot see the woods for the trees'. This is the mode of thought which has come to govern the theory and practice of the Communist Left. And this philosophical surrender has inevitably led to a political surrender, a surrender to bourgeois politics.

It is a mark of the dominance of the ruling class politics in India over these forty-five years, after an early, much confused, communist protest and the surrender and suppression of the great Telengana struggle, that it has always succeeded in effectively defining and pre-empting the terrain of Indian politics, setting the parameters of intellectual discourse and political action, imposing its own issues and choices, concepts, language codes and forms of politics on others—in the process appropriating, marginalising, and suppressing whenever necessary, those of any kind of alternative radical or revolutionary politics, which has thus survived only at the fringes of Indian polity. What I want to suggest is that it is the dominance of 'the metaphysical mode of thought' even with those on the Left who otherwise profess the Marxist, that is, the dialectical mode, which has over the years helped the ruling classes to thus define and preempt the terrain of Indian politics for their own purposes. They have posed the issues in this mode, asked the questions accordingly, and secured the answers they wanted to have. For example, this is how it has been in the recent crisis-ridden years: 'Are you for the Sikh/Kashmiri/ULFA militants or the nation? for violence or democratic politics? for Congress (I) government or that of the Janata Party or National Front? for communalism or secularism? for reservations or against them?' and so on. It is not difficult to see that in each case the choices are really foreclosed in the sense that whatever the answer, it serves one or the other kind of ruling class politics. The way the issues are posed consistently ignores the larger socio-historical context and deeper determinant interconnections, dissociates the issues from any consideration of socio-economic structures, class domination, or ruling class politics, and thus ensures that radical or revolutionary choices simply do not come up as answers, as real historical possibilities. Given the 'specific narrow-mindedness' (Engels) of the essentially ahistorical 'metaphysical mode of thought', a revolutionary strategic aim and political practice geared to it is impossible. The Left has simply failed to develop an independent, alternative politics of its own.

The failure to see Indian social reality in its 'whole vast interconnections', to recognise its issues, processes and problems in their *real* relationships with the 'economic basis' and with each other and 'the whole', 'the structured interdependence of parts' that is Indian society, which recognition is basic for a revolutionary strategy—this failure is obscured by essentially *imaginary* or *ambiguous* substitute relationships of 'a national whole' which a nationalist perspective postulates for Indian society. Once, during the Nehru era, the era of post-independence possibilities, this postulation was most apparent and very successful too. Working with concepts of 'national freedom', 'national development', 'national consensus' and so on, the 'nationalist discourse' even appropriated the concepts of 'socialism' and 'social transformation', obscured the class character of the compromise and settlement of 1947 and the consequent reality of a state-supported, India-specific capitalist development, and marginalised all radical or revolutionary thought and action. In more recent years, when the memory of 'national freedom' has almost faded away, 'national development' is seen to be not what it was supposed to be, 'national consensus' survives only as an yearning and the loudness of the 'nationalist discourse' both hides and betrays a real and rapid waning of nationalism, it is the metaphysical mode of thought that effectively supplements the nationalist obscuring of *real* relationships of social reality in India to ensure continued definition and pre-emption of the terrain of Indian politics for the ruling classes. Postulation of *imaginary*, certainly *ambiguous* relations of nationalism, of whatever variety, is today meaningful primarily as an ideological device in the service of the Indian ruling classes. For the people it can be meaningful only if the postulation is in terms of a struggle against 'anti-nation within the nation' or 'rescuing the nation' from its ruling classes or, as Marx would put it, the people 'establishing itself as the nation'. But this, as already suggested, is no longer a national but a class perspective, a perspective of revolutionary class struggle.

The Communist Left needs to move away from its simplistic, ahistorical nationalism and the metaphysical mode of thought, and return to Marxism, in order to recover its essential character as a revolutionary movement. Let it not remain content with operating on the terrain of bourgeois politics only, responding to the issues it presents, accepting the choices it offers, and succumbing to the corruption of consciousness all this involves, in the process not only getting marginalised again and again but also losing the revolutionary commitment and elan that defines it as Left. It is time the Communist Left sought to establish and function on its own terrain, the terrain of independent class-based people's politics which, even as it confronts bourgeois politics on the latter's terrain, knows how to pose its *own issues, its own way*, before the people, present them with genuine choices, and, most important, organise them to fight around these issues, in defence of their own choices, for not some phoney electoral gains but real political advance.

The constituency of active struggle for socialism, or, more precisely, for a society in transition to socialism, is still very large in this country, and it will grow as the new economic policy of the ruling classes gets underway: major communist parties, CPI(M) and CPI, needing to break out of the quarantine that parliamentary politics has become for them; smaller communist formations like People's War Group, somewhat differently quarantined by violence of the state and own politics; but searching and struggling to reach beyond their limited strongholds; growing movements like Indian People's Front, successfully making space for their refreshinghly more adequate revolutionary politics; minor Left parties with their committed cadre and own areas of influence; socialists who are still not irretrievably lost to anti-communism or bourgeois politics; the best of activist groups, 'new social movements' including those around ecology, and others from among the long disadvantaged but now awakening sections of our people—minor nationalities, dalits, tribals, women, religious and ethnic minorities, and so on—who will out of their own experience come to recognise the need to articulate their struggles with a class-based people's politics; Shankar Guha Niyogis and A.K. Roys, scattered all over this country, carrying on against the heaviest of odds; militant sections from among the workers and peasants, youth and intelligentsia, looking for a more positive and hopeful politics; and many more... The need is for the Communist Left to regain clarity about its strategic aim, develop its own alternative terrain of people's politics and thus recover the moral elan of a revolutionary movement actively struggling for the interests of the common Indian people. This is a difficult task but not impossible. This is what the situation demands as does the heroic revolutionary tradition of the Ghadarites whose heir the Communist Left claims to be and, I would add, which it today needs to be worthy of.

While in the Party I always had the feeling that, with its rather scientistic view of Marxism, it was somewhat wanting in its treatment of revolutionaries and the revolutionary traditions it inherited, in imbibing the revolutionary morals and culture that the Ghadarites, Bhagat Singh's comrades and different streams of 'revolutionary terrorism' brought to the movement. And the feeling has persisted. These traditions were used instrumentally to gain prestige, and what little was imbibed seems to have been lost somewhere along the way in the movement's progress on the reformist path. While the young

Ghadarites grew into *Babas* and simultaneously into giants of human beings in their revolutionary commitment, their heirs seem to have dwindled into pigmies lost on the terrain of bourgeois politics. This, like so much else in today's communist movement may yet change. One always hopes.

Possibilities of a change for the better are far more open today than ever before. The new turn in ruling class policies and the world-wide crisis of the communist movement together provide not only an occasion for the movement to undertake a serious self-critical review of its theory and practice but also an opportunity to break away from the past and recover itself as a genuine revolutionary movement.

The Indian ruling classes have decided, notwithstanding their internal conflict of interests which is always there, through the state power currently operated by their major political formation, the Congress (I), to shift from a government-supported to a more explicitly market-friendly capitalism. Product of a dead-end crisis caused by previous development, especially the policies pursued in recent years, the shift, an almost natural progress for Indian capitalism, has been facilitated by the defeat of Soviet Union in the cold war and its eventual disintegration. The Indian ruling classes have lost the manoeuvrability that contention between two super powers once provided them, leaving them more vulnerable to the pressure and demands of the dominant global capitalism. Given the strong comprador and lumpen strain inherent in their character, they have succumped and opted for what may well turn out to be junior partnership within the global capitalist system. Giving in to the dictates of International Monetary Fund and World Bank, the Indian ruling classes have decided, as we have already noticed, to openly 'secede' from the Indian people.

But this 'secession of the successful' has at least one advantage for the common Indian people, 'the unsuccessful' of Indian society. To the extent the new policies get implemented, they will clarify as nothing else could, the real issues of Indian economy and politics. In the new dispensation, even as a 'free' market will lead to greater disproportionalities within the Indian economy, sharpening and revealing its basic contradictions as never before, the turning away of the state even from its 'socialist' rhetoric and symbolic concern for equity and distributive justice will further undermine such, legitimacy as the system still has. The globalisation of India's economy and therefore its politics; culture and much else besides, may in its ultimate outcome well confront the Indian people with the choice : socialism or peripheralisation within the global capitalist system. In such a situation the class issues will stand out more clearly, making for more, normal class struggles in Indian society. A class-based people's politics will not only become more necessary but also more possible.

The collapse of Soviet Union is certainly a setback for popular struggles everywhere. Its 'actually existing socialism', a deeply deformed version of socialism as it is visualised in classical Marxism, was yet the symbol of a possibility, the possibility of escape from that essentially predatory system, capitalism. Also, while Soviet Union had long lost interest in any world revolutionary process, for compulsion of its own history and ideological legitimacy, national interest or *real politik* or plain super-power politics, it did give some sort of aid or help to radical or revolutionary movements abroad, and provided a certain degree of support and protection when these movements emerged as revolutionary regimes. But the collapse of Soviet Union has its advantages too for the revolutionary socialist movements everywhere, including India. They no more need to carry the burden of a deformed and degenerated 'socialism', no longer are they answerable for its ugliness and cruelties—though the burden of a genuine, Marxist explanation of this collapse has still to be carried. But most importantly, there is no so-called 'Party of Lenin' now, with its Ulyanovskies and the rest, to mislead them or subordinate the communist movements abroad to the requirements of the 'national interests' or *raison d'etat* of Soviet Union. No longer for us those parodies of Marxism—the non-capitalist path of development, India's 'progressive' foreign policy and 'reactionary' domestic policy, large-scale radical renovation of India's national movement and its dominant leadership, or apologetics for the statecraft of it new rulers, with certificates of anti-imperialism for them merely because their foreign policy interests for the moment coincided with those of the Soviet state, etc.etc.—parodies and the accompanying pseudo internationalism which, even as they disoriented the movement, provided a whole generation of Party-allied intellectuals and others avenues (together with those provided by peace, friendship, solidarity and sundry such organisations) for racketeering in Left politics and making the best of both worlds. Certainly, Communists no longer need to—of course if they really don't want to—associate with any and every crook or adventurer from bourgeois politics willing to travel Moscow-wards at Moscow's expense and be certified as 'a progressive', taking away with him some of the progressiveness of the Communist movement itself!...

Our people today face an unprecedented situation, one fraught with most dangerous possibilities. For Communists who would lead their struggles, the road ahead is indeed an uncharted territory, there are no easy solutions or ready made answers, not any more. But the situation also leaves them free, after a long time, for a better, revolutionary practice of Marxism, for a bold and confident, truly innovative and non-sectarian Left politics in the tradition of revolutionary Marxism. The alternative is a total loss of their identity as a revolutionary movement. They must seize this opportunity. This is what they owe to their revolutionary inheritance, to the memory of countless martyrs of their movement, including the heroic Ghadarites. Difficult, near impossible perhaps, yet not impossible as I said earlier, and, again, one always hopes.

Or, perhaps, it is now for others to carry forward the tradition of Ghadarite revolutionaries.

13

'Visions for the Future': One View*

Many years ago, a scholar, Hayakawa, in his *Language in Action*, noticing the inevitably value-laden nature of human language which, presumably true of the language of the social sciences also, points to the entire 'fact-value controversy' being a wasteful exercise—made a distinction in political speech of 'purr' words and 'snarl' words. 'Vision', now, is pre-eminently, though not invariably, a 'purr' word, suggestive of optimistic possibilities, of a future full of promise and achievement. Even otherwise, it is an optimistic view of India's present and future that has been endorsed at this seminar, most of the time—even if a trifle cautiously, *via* the conventional 'on the one hand, on the other hand', 'balance-sheet' approach, typical of the academic and the scholar these days. This optimism, however, seems to me to be misplaced in view of the existing or emerging social and political reality in our country. When not a consensus of the arrived and the complacent, this optimism is only an expression of nationalist faith or habit, of a patriotism which has grown tired and flabby over the years and which is nowadays daily sought to be flogged into some semblance of life or movement by the powers that be—through the media controlled by the state, through editorials and advertisements in the press, through wayside hoardings and interminable singing and running for the country, on the television and elsewhere,

* A Marxist view of 'India since Independence' presented at a seminar, *Economic and Political Weekly* (1989).

through the rhetoric of politicians and the laboured theorising of scholars, and through extravaganzas and *utsavs* and centenaries of all sorts....

These goings-on, desperate daily exhortations, not only betoken a certain waning of Indian nationalism in recent times, but, given the deepening crisis in our society and politics, they also remind us of what Marx once spoke of as 'opium of patriotic feelings', which the ruling classes often find useful for their purposes, especially in troubled times. Lest I be misunderstood —though I do carry 'a certificate of patriotism', having spent nearly a year in prison during the freedom struggle in 'those ancient days'—let me repeat what I have already stated elsewhere, namely, love for the Indian people, for India's glorious heritage through the ages, including those magnificent expressions of our people's creativity in the then inevitable religious Idiom, or a *socialist* commitment to the unity and interests of the Indian people and an abiding faith in their future—all this certainly does not require this opiate, which in fact carries within it the possibility of sacrificing the people to 'the nation', as has happened before, elsewhere, and is almost beginning to happen, in its own way, in this country too. To borrow an analogy from Tom Paine's famous rejoinder to Burke, admiration for 'the plumage' of India's development over these forty years should not make us forget 'the dying bird'. The world indeed looks very different from below, when the poor and the oppressed of 'our nation' look at it. I agree that we need to cultivate optimism, today more than ever before, but it needs to be made of sterner stuff....

I am aware of the problems besetting the making of meaningful, that is, reasonably valid, generalisations in social sciences. Yet generalisations have to be made if we would move from information to knowledge, which necessarily relative, partial and incomplete, is nevertheless, for us, valid knowledge. And this has to be done even when the social reality being considered is the complex, contradictions-ridden continental social formation, India. I am also aware that in making these generalisations it is necessary to provide empirical evidence, notice the historical specificities, and, almost always, qualify them to secure better validity for them. But given the constraint of time it is impossible to do this. I will, therefore, proceed to offer a few generalisations only, very briefly but with clarity and firmness, which is rather risky and which scholarly sophistication, with its 'now black, now white' style of argument, generally tends to avoid, oblivious of Bacon's aphorism that 'truth emerges more easily from error than from confusion'. Confusion, laced with ambiguity and jargon has in fact increasingly become the art of the scholar, and the teacher, in this dishonest and hypocritically verbose age...

Central to my argument is an understanding of social reality as a historical process. Thus: the character of our national movement determined the nature of its outcome, *the* independence, which, in turn, became the basis for the development of India in the next forty years and more, providing us with the present for our future to grow equally 'naturally' out of it—unless, of course, a *revolutionary* break occurs, sometime, somewhere...

Hence the heed, for the sake of our future, to take a close look at the present that is ours.

In every historical process there is continuity and there are breaks, at times even revolutionary breaks which involve a change in *the economic basis*, the economic-structural relations of a society. In India, in our times, no revolutionary break has occurred, neither at independence, nor afterwards. The balance of social forces and ideals in the national movement resulted in the settlement of 1947—its 'transfer of power' involving no basic economic or social structural change, but putting new, now Indian ruling classes in control of the state power in India. (Nearly two decades later, Gunnar Myrdal was to write of 'the new government's role as the successor to the British raj', of 'the gulf between rulers and ruled' and the life-style and conduct of the new rulers which 'encouraged the view that political independence had done little more than displace a foreign with a native privileged group'.) And these new rulers, subject to the necessities of the objective situation, soon set about using their newly-won state power to facilitate the growth of a government-supported capitalism, even as they maintained, with due modifications, the class (exploitative) structure of the Indian society as a whole. The logic of this structure, the new and the old in it well articulating with each other, is today writ large in the emergence of the now universally admitted 'two nations' in our country in the post-independence period.

In these matters, the *subjective* concerns of political leaders, of rulers or their political representatives, matter—but only marginally. In the absence of revolutionary politics which changes the economic-structural basis of society, not only does the logic of this basis assert itself in the economy, it also decisively conditions developments in other areas of social life, in politics, morals, culture, ideology, etc.—all changes, no matter how important otherwise, yet remain essentially super structural. Thus, for example, we know of Gandhi's love and concern for the Indian people which to him meant, above all, the impoverished peasantry of India— 'the semi-starved masses...slowly sinking to lifelessness as he once put it—a love and concern, rather paternal in nature, which was possibly the most distinguishing feature of Gandhi's social philosophy. Metaphorically speaking, he wanted the peasant to inherit this country. Yet it is not Gandhi's peasant but a Birla who inherited India in 1947, alongwith, of course, communal violence, the partition, and all that. And of decisive importance here is the fact that, besides other limitations, Gandhi's political theory and practice (non-violence, trusteeship, satyagraha, etc.) had no room at all for any genuine economic-structural change, not even for land reforms, a necessary though not sufficient condition for any improvement in the life of the vast masses of Indian peasantry. Inevitably he failed, here as also elsewhere in most of his declared purposes. Seeking to ensure 'the rights alike of prince and pauper', Gandhism, in effect, only served as a petty-bourgeois ideology in the service of the big bourgeoisie, in the Indian historical process. It is a mark of the greatness of Gandhi, a truly magnificent Human being with all his faults, frailties and foibles, that in sharp contrast to the pettiness of his many followers, he recognised his failure when it finally occurred, and confessed it—'I do not understand how all these terrible things are happening in our country... What mistakes have we made, for we must have made mistakes? Otherwise how could all these things happen?'—and died, as he had lived, fighting for his people, a fulfilled yet disillusioned and disconsolate man.

Or, again, we know of Nehru's concern to build socialism in India. He not only argued that 'the only key to the solution of... India's problems lies in socialism', but had also insisted: 'and when I use this word I do so not in a vague, humanitarian way, but in a scientific, economic sense'. Aware of the need for 'vast and revolutionary changes', he most perceptively spoke of 'terrible costs of not changing the existing order'. Yet, once in power, Nehru shied away from the costs of even genuine land reforms— 'they will present numerous practical problems involving basic social conflicts (and may) give rise to organised forces of disruption', the *Draft Outline* of the First Five-Year Plan warned. What is more, he simply abandoned socialism 'in a scientific, economic sense', that is, as a basic economic-structural change. Apart from the insistence on the state playing 'a vital part in planning and development', the focus is increasingly on the need to ensure 'rapid economic development with continually rising levels of production', 'to exploit natural resources', 'to take sufficient advantage of the advance in science and technology', etc. In fact, in a subtle, perhaps unconscious but politically most convenient shift, he now sought 'the key' not in socialism but in the development of 'science and technology'— 'the temples of new India' and all that. He increasingly opted for what I would describe as 'fetishism of science', that is, investing science with powers it does not in itself have, expecting it to do the job of a social revolution, which it simply cannot. Inevitably, once again, the logic of the economic structure asserts itself: what has got built in India is not socialism but capitalism, a state-supported capitalism. Even the noisy advocates of 'the non-capitalist path of development', in India and elsewhere, now recognise this. Rhetoric of socialism, now redefined as 'a socialistic pattern of society', whatever that means, has served only to deceive and win mass support. And Nehru, even as he gave India the much lauded 'vision of socialism', in effect, helped reduce it to only 'a vision' in India.

History is indeed a very cruel mistress.

It is not possible here to explore the historical specificity of Indian capitalism except to state that, presided over by a bourgeoisie born old without ever having known youth, with none of the possible virtues of youth and all the vices of old age, it has been described as 'some strange kind of corrupted capitalist growth' (Romesh Thapar), where, in the words of Marx, 'We suffer not only from the living but from the dead' also. But we do need to notice its essential logic as a *capitalist* economic system. Just as, before 1947, the structural logic of British imperialism meant the accumulation of wealth in England and of poverty in India, the structural logic of Indian capitalism is most manifest today, as already mentioned, in the creation of 'two nations' in this country in only 'forty years of freedom'. And this structural logic should not be allowed to be obscured by a narrow economistic concern with growth rates. It is well to remember what a president of Brazil's military government once said. On a visit to the United States in the late sixties, and asked about the situation back home, he replied: 'The economy is doing fine. The people are not.' Indian economic development, with its structural logic of inequality and unevenness, has produced not only 'two Indias' and an ever widening gulf between the two, with all its disintegrative consequences, but also, together with poverty and hunger and heart breaking inhuman conditions of life for the vast masses of our people, a society of myriad old and new oppressions, insecurities and alienations, with no jobs or ideals for its youth or vision and values for the people, a society in deep social and moral crisis indeed; which has, incidentally, provided a continuing social-material basis for the production and reproduction, sustenance and reinforcement of all sorts of religiosity or *dharmikta*, revivalism, fundamentalism and obscurantism, and also ideologies and practices like communalism—all of which, especially the Hindu variety, is now being actively sponsored and utilised by the state in India, with Congress (I) in power, to secure a newer basis for the increasingly undermined hegemony of the Indian ruling classes.

Today every aspect of social life in India bears the signature of this historically specific Indian form of capitalist development —its mark is there on our morality, our culture, our politics, on everything, everywhere. It is there, for example, on, our 'national integration', or the so-called 'mainstream'. The fact to be deplored is not that we are not integrated but that we are integrated the *capitalist* way, which carries within it, strong disintegrative tendencies. It is not without reason that today, especially in the absence of class-based people's politics, all the identities, all the divides and fissures of Indian society, are simultaneously becoming significant and *explosive.* In this connection I recall my visit to Imphal some years ago. At the end of my talk a Naga student argued and then asserted: 'We refuse to be integrated'. I politely inquired if they had any corruption there, in Manipur or in Nagaland. He immediately answered and with great anger: 'Of course, it is there, all over the place, heaps of it.' I then told him: 'In that case you are already integrated, you are very much in the mainstream'. More seriously, I went on to explain that having been drawn into India's developing market economy and, therefore, into its morality, and culture, and politics, they, the Nagas and others, are already in the 'national mainstream'. Only, since it bears the impress of India's corrupt and corrupting, somewhat lumpen capitalist development, it is increasingly a dirty mainstream—corrupt, communal and criminalised, a repressively homogenising mainstream. I added that their *only option now*—for, given the power of Indian economy and the Indian state; other options are closed—is to join with the struggling Indian people and together build a clean and healthy, many splendoured, *socialist* mainstream.

Incidentally, with us on the plane to Imphal travelled a Delhi-based forest contractor. He spoke of freedom and its new opportunities, of patriotism, profits and entrepreneurship, and economic development of the north-east, and then, peering through the early morning mist at the barely visible vegetation below, casually informed us: 'We have cleared the forests on this side and now we are going to clear them on that side too.' Some 'national development' this—plain, profit-powered plunder of local resources for the benefit of others, a few, eleswhere! This apart, it should not be difficult to understand that given the logic of an essentially capitalist development, all effort at saving our natural heritage or environment is only a labour of Sisyphus.

This is the Nehru centenary year. A flourishing business is on, 'the Nehru business', for politicians and others, and for scholars as well, ostensibly to honour the memory of one who was undoubtedly a most remarkable man of our times. There is widespread yearning for 'the age of Nehru'—indeed the golden age of the post-colonial state in India, which seems to have passed away all too soon. There is widespread lamentation too, for the 'distortion' that is supposed to have occurred in the Indian political system since Nehru's days. But if my argument so far has any meaning, it is this: it is not that the system has got 'distorted'; rather, *distortion is the system* that Nehru built and presided over, only its dormant contradictions are now surfacing with explosive force. That is why so many of those yearning and lamenting these days, politicians as well as scholars, especially the more innocent ones who remember 'the deeper historical forces' only when criticising Maulana Azad but forget them when assessing Nehru, appear to me to be as many orphans from 'the Nehru era'.

I have so far dealt with the Indian economy and its structural, exploitative logic, today manifest in the Indian society as a whole. But what of the state, the Indian democratic state? I shall be content to make only a very brief comment.

After 1947, the state in India—as in other old or newly independent capitalist countries of the third world, suffering from endemic economic backwardness and poverty, above all as a result of colonial domination, old and new—was the focus of two seemingly interrelated hopes or expectations. In the first place, given the economic weakness and lack of legitimacy of the Indian bourgeoisie as a whole, the state was expected to intervene, help, and actively participate in the process of economic development of the country. In the second place, it was expected to be an agent of equity in social life, of distributive justice for the people, which economic development by itself may not be able to ensure. It is obvious that, subject to the historical constraints, external as well as internal, the state in India, acting, in Engels' words, as 'the executor of the economic necessities of the national situation', has fulfilled the first expectation reasonably well; it has facilitated the development of a state-supported capitalism in India. But it has sadly belied the second hope or expectation. The policies and practices of the Indian state have failed to secure equity or distributive justice, 'growth with justice' as the cliche goes, for the vast masses of Indian people. On the contrary, even as it has continued to serve as an instrument of coercion against them, significantly enough, even of the funds directly allocated for poverty alleviation—to gain legitimacy or in response to the demands of 'democratic politics'—only the 'leakages' have reached the poor, the 'flood' has gone elsewhere. This apart, the state in India, over these forty years, has certainly not been wanting in carrying out what has been the basic function of the state in all class-divided societies, namely, to serve as the organiser of society in the interests of the class-exploitative structure take as a whole.

Of course, dangerous aberrations or departures notwithstanding, we have had 'democratic, politics', so far. And democracy in India, whatever its limitations and however weak or fragile, is a hard-won achievement of the Indian people, and they certainly need it, more than the ruling classes do. It has certainly served to curb the authoritarian political logic of the Indian economic system, and brought benefits, however marginal these may have been, even to the common Indian people. They certainly need to struggle to defend it, to preserve and expand it. And they *have* so struggled all these years, as best as they could. Yet, as Bagehot observed, with obvious satisfaction, in an earlier, more honest age: 'democracy is the way to give the people the greatest illusion of power while allowing them the smallest amount in reality'. Here, I might mention that over the years I have asked my students the question: ' Who rules India?' Invariably, having learnt their 'political science' well, they have answered without the slightest hesitation: 'The people rule India'. I have then asked: 'Who is starving in India?' Now they would hesitate, hum and haw, shift uncomfortably and then rather unwillingly concede: 'The people are starving'. So the rulers of India are starving! No wonder Marx had insisted: 'all science would be superfluous, if the appearance, the form, and the nature of things were wholly identical'. Obviously, democracy has not meant effective political power for the Indian people. Even so sympathetic a scholar as Gunnar Myrdal has pointed out: 'Democracy has not enabled the majority of poor people to grasp, and organise themselves for utilising, political power to advance their own interests. V.K.R.V. Rao too has noticed that so far as 'the poor and deprived sections of the people' are concerned, 'parliamentary democracy has not been able to meet the challenge'. He has spoken of 'a political alliance of the intermediate classes with the upper classes, resorting to socialist ideology only to win mass support but using all levers of power to facilitate a type of capitalist development in the interest of a narrow section of Indian society'. In other words, if India's 'national economy' has been anti-poor over these forty years, so has been India's 'democratic state'. It has been and continues to be a class-state. The state in India, far from being a part of the solution, is itself a part of the problem.

One final point and I conclude. And this concerns contemporary Indian politics, the arena of decisive struggles for India's future. Following independence, throughout the Nehru era, what dominated the scene was politics of the ruling classes as conducted by their political formations, the dominant Congress (I) and the rest, more or less as a 'Hindu Undivided Family', on the basis of a working consensus, a balance of power and interests among them, the beneficiaries of the system as a whole. But after the economic crisis of the mid-sixties, and subject to the continuing constraints of the economy situation since then, this 'consensus' or 'balance' has been lost, the beneficiaries, ever more greedy and grasping, have been violating the rules of their own political game, inside the parliament or legislatures and outside—and 'democratic politics', insofar as it also provides a basis for the hegemony of the ruling classes and serves as an impersonal, non arbitrary device for resolving their internal conflict of interests while articulating and promoting these interests as a whole, has been seriously undermined. Ruling class politics, led by the Congress (I), has in fact increasingly acquired a no-holds-barred quality, and with its corruption, criminality, communalisation and lumpenism, its philandering populism and utter unscruplousness, today become a potent threat to Indian democracy as we have known it, and a deadly exercise for our people, producing one tragedy after another for them. Punjab is the worst example—so far. Faced with popular discontent, disruption and disorder in civil society, and an everdeepening crisis of their legitimacy, the ruling classes, above all through their dominant political formation, the Congress (I), are increasingly seeking authoritarian, even fascist, answers to their problems.

But there is another reality too in Indian politics, the struggles of our common people, which are emerging on the material basis of an economy which has meant not only exploitation and oppression of the people but also unequal and uneven development in the country as a whole; and these struggles today include those of our more disadvantaged nationalities and ethnic groups, and various oppressed and discriminated-against minorities or identities, religious and other, women, dalits, tribals—whose struggles, however, need to be infused with *socialist* concerns and articulated with a class-based people's politics, if they are not to divide the oppressed even more, distort or corrupt their consciousness still further, disrupt their actual or potential common struggles, and end up serving only the exploiting elements and vested interests within, who would he content to find a place for themselves in India's underdeveloped capitalism and overdeveloped bourgeois politics. I am aware, in fact painfully aware, of the weak and fragmented condition of these struggles, of the extraordinarily complex and difficult issues of theory and practice, politics and organisation, facing them. Yet, outside and beyond the present day bourgeois politics, it is here, in the emerging struggles of our common people, that hope for India's future lies...

At the outset, I had mentioned the need to cultivate

optimism, optimism of a sterner sort. In today's India, this optimism is possible *a la* Romain Rolland's maxim only, a maxim that Gramsci, sick and slowly dying in Mussolini's prison, endorsed: 'Pessimism of the intelligence, optimism of the will'. Gramsci had also insisted: 'It is necessary to direct one's attention *violently* towards the present as it is, if one wishes to transform it' (emphasis added). Obviously, this is addressed to the revolutionaries. And we here are no revolutionaries. But as scholars we should certainly be aware that India's future will be determined by the larger historical forces which revolutionaries in India represent, and that it is possible for us to recognise and help these forces wherever we are. And we must so recognise and help, as best as we can; this alone is everybody's guarantee of honour in other people's thoughts. It may be that this will not add up to much. I am in fact convinced that what goes on at these seminars, or, for that matter, in our universities and social science research institutes, is only of marginal relevance to the problems and prospects of the Indian people's struggle for a better future. But then this is where we work. And we make our efforts where we work, or we shall make no effort at all.*

---

* This is a written version of the oral presentation made in the Panel Discussion on 'Visions for the Future' at the seminar on 'India Since Independence', organised by the Indian Council of Social Science Research in New Delhi, December 26-30, 1988.

Index